MW00991289

OFFENHAUSER

Gordon Eliot White with the assistance of Kenneth Walton

Motorbooks International
Publishers & Wholesalers ®

First published in 1996 by Motorbooks International Publishers & Wholesalers, 729 Prospect Avenue, PO Box 1, Osceola, WI 54020-0001 USA

Library of Congress Cataloging-in-Publication Data

White, Gordon Eliot.
Offenhauser / Gordon Eliot White
p. cm.
Includes bibliographical references and index.
ISBN 0-87938-883-8 (alk. paper)
1. Offenhauser engines--History. I. Title.
TL210.W44 1996
629.228--dc20 96-9402

On the front cover: This Jim Bruni artwork depicts Andy Dunlop and Pete Salemi at work on the 252-cubic-inch Offy in the *Central Excavating Special* #82, an upright Kuzma chassis. Chuck Weyant drove the car to 14th place in 1957.

On the frontispiece: Offenhauser inspects a blueprint of an early 255. *Gloria Madsen collection*

On the title page: Offy-powered roadsters in action at Indianapolis in 1962. Jim McElreath #15 leads Eddie Sachs #2. Sachs would finish third that year while McElreath came in sixth, both behind 252-cubic-inch Offenhauser-engined cars. *Bruce Craig collection*

On the back cover: Offenhauser was *the* American race engine for more than 60 years. Its dominance was exhibited by a wide variety of racing equipment including midgets, sprint cars, Indy racers, sports cars, even race boats.

Top right: Briggs S. Cunningham powers the Offy-engined C-6R around Le Mans in 1955. *Collier Historic Motor Cars*

Top left: Two Offy midgets battle it out at Williams Grove, Pennsylvania, in 1962. Bob Harkey is in the rear in the Hespell #8 while it's Ralph Ligouri in front along the rail. *Venlo Wolfsohn collection*

Bottom: 1972 Indy winner Mark Donohue at speed in his turbo Offy-powered Penske McLaren. *Indianapolis Motor Speedway*

Printed in Hong Kong

CONTENTS

Dedication

To Bill Schindler
1908–1952

Who, despite giving a leg to the sport in 1936, became an honored champion in midgets, big cars, and at Indianapolis, and who taught me much about life, racing, and the Offenhauser engine.

Bill Schindler at his garage in Freeport, NY in 1950, working on his Offenhauser- powered Kurtis midget. As a 16-year-old fan I wrote Bill asking his advice on a three-quarter midget I was building. He responded, writing on stationary headed by a photo of the Caruso #3, beginning an all too brief friendship that ended at Allentown, Pennsylvania, in 1952. *Author*

Foreword

"The sound of an Offenhauser and the smell of burning castor oil will live in my memory forever."

For Mike Heffron, general manager of the Minnesota State Fair, who uttered those words, and for those who remember what auto racing in the United States was like when it resumed following the end of World War II, the race track was their church and the unique exhaust note of Offenhauser engines their own special choir. The Offenhauser was for many, and remains for some, a near-religion.

Those who worshipped at the altar of the Offenhauser did so for many reasons, not the least of which was its astronomical cost (for the day), superb quality, invincibility, and exalted reputation. An Offenhauser was unlike all other racing engines of the time. Its surfaces were smooth and polished, not coarse and black. The Offy was a smorgasbord of brightmetal, sanitary in appearance. It was a sparkling diamond amid a sea of gravel. But the converted loved the Offenhauser for its sound, a low, deep-throated four-cylinder growl—unlike the high-pitched soprano scream of today's high-revving, multicylinder engines. The roar of the Offy was likened by many to that of the lion in the forest, and in its heyday the Offy was the king of the racing jungle.

The magic of the Offenhauser name was evident when the dormant motorsports scene resumed after the war-induced three-year hiatus. Beyond its all-powerful aura, the name carried with it a mystique marked with descriptions such as superiority, grandeur, and above all, skill and daring, for the Offenhauser was a beast which it took a full measure of both to master.

A pasteboard example of the Offy's special place in racing history once confronted Corn Belt and Plains states fans whose racing was done on dusty fairground ovals. It was a poster widely seen on billboards, telephone poles, and in shop windows from the Rockies to the Mississippi, Ontario to Louisiana. Below a head-on view of a broadsliding car throwing up a huge roostertail of dirt was the message:

Auto Races
Starring Emory Collins
and his
$10,000
Offenhauser
Special

These words appeared above a white space in which the town, track, and date were printed. You had to go! Regardless of the type of machine to which it was fitted—midget, big (sprint) car, or championship vehicle—the Offy commanded attention and respect.

Its eventual departure from the entry lists of American racing was in no way due to its outperformance by superior handiwork, but rather by the surreptitious waving of wands held by mercurial rulesmakers. Its disappearance from the midget ranks where it had dominated for so many years was brought on by the appearance of the stock-block Sesco, which was granted far more cubic inches of displacement than the Offy (155 versus 110) by officials aware of the Sesco's pushrod shortcomings alongside the twin overhead cam Offy. It was the same in sprint cars, where the small-block Chevy was at first allowed 350 cubic inches to the Offy's 220, with a resulting disparity in power.

At Indy the reduction of turbocharger boost pressure to half of what it had been, allowed the then-fragile Formula One Cosworth Ford to outstrip the Offy. Had boost pressures remained unregulated, the Cosworth would never have finished a race, let alone become dominant.

Though gone from today's professional arenas of speed and excitement, the Offy is certainly not forgotten. Indeed, the jewel of racing in America still retains an emotional grip on many who have heard its unmistakable sound, smelled its pungent exhaust and seen it in fast and furious action.

As antique auto racing grows in popularity, the Offy is once more the centerpiece of the faithful, commanding respectful attention from its loyal subjects. Indeed, some events at today's old-time race meets are reserved exclusively for cars using Fred Offenhauser's long-lived thoroughbred.

When a driver of one of these legendary four-cylinder powerplants lets out the clutch and drops the rope from the tow truck, a cloud of smoke and a strong smell of castor oil is followed by the Offy's throaty rumble reverberating across the ages—a sound sweeter than the strains of Gabriel's horn to those from the Offy's era.

As you read the pages of this book which detail the painstaking development of the Offenhauser engine by some of motorsport's brightest minds over 40 long years, let the sounds described here wander through your mind. Imagine what it must have been like to hear a full field of Offenhausers ready to strip the paint off the walls and bombard the paying fans with a hail of dirt. It was a heady period in American racing, and for some a far more religious experience than anything else heard on a Sunday afternoon.

—Chris Economaki, editor, *National Speed Sport News*

Preface

The Offy, the old growler, was an engine that powered American auto racing for three decades and became a legend. With a flat crankshaft and no heavy flywheel to smooth out the power strokes of its four cylinders, the Offy was notoriously rough, yet it pumped out torque that would make a car jump off the corners of a race track. The straight-cut timing gears in the cam towers were noisy and its vibration would rattle small parts off the chassis. Despite all that, its power swept everything before it from Wilbur Shaw's day in the 1930s to A.J. Foyt's in the 1960s.

The first Offenhauser-powered racing cars I saw were lined up outside the Freeport Municipal Stadium on a warm and sunny Labor Day afternoon in 1945. I was not quite 12 years old. The midgets became my youthful passion, and the Offys were the best of them. They were beautiful, sleek creations, their drivers the embodiment of skill and daring. Any Offy-powered car was like the New York Yankees of the time: unbeatable. Those cars were to me the most wonderful mechanical creatures I had ever seen, their paint and chrome shining and polished, ready for the resumption of racing after World War II which had ended just three weeks before.

I followed the midgets at Freeport and other tracks in New York, New Jersey, Pennsylvania, and New England for much of the next seven years including a stint at Sorranno Park in Morristown, New Jersey, where I got onto the track briefly myself. I was not cut out to be a race driver, it seemed, but I wrote occasionally for the now long-gone *Illustrated Speedway News* and reported for racing broadcaster Ted Webbe.

A career as a political and investigative reporter took me away from racing for 30 years, but after college, marriage, three children, and a career in Washington, I stumbled across a USAC sprint car race in Reading, Pennsylvania, felt the dirt in my face, smelled the castor oil, and was hooked once more.

In 1978, I was too involved in my newspaper career to either drive or own a contemporary race car, but I managed to buy a much-raced, often victorious Kurtis-Kraft midget chassis for $200. Stock-block engines had nearly driven the Offenhausers off the tracks in both midgets and sprints, though the Offy was still competitive at Indianapolis, thus I was able to find an engine to put in my midget to run in "vintage" events: those friendly, tire-kicking, storytelling gatherings of old race drivers, mechanics, and fans.

My Offy went to a score of antique auto shows and after much research, paint, polish, and chrome, won the Antique Automobile Club of America Grand National First Prize in the race car class. Through all those shows I was repeatedly asked the inevitable question: "How fast will it go?" Through research I knew that my childhood hero, Rex Mays, had driven an Offy midget to a U.S. record of 147.095 miles per hour on the Bonneville Salt Flats on September 19, 1949. I had no idea how fast I could go in my own Offy, but I was determined to find out. To answer that I had to go to Bonneville, and yes, the old Offy can still go fast.

The story of that effort is told in this book's Epilogue—a small footnote in homage to the brave efforts of the drivers who risked far more for so many years behind Offenhauser engines. In the process I learned a great deal about those engines, thanks in part to that great Offy mechanic, Ken Hickey, of Ambler, Pennsylvania.

Of course, the Offenhauser engine is really a Miller, designed by Harry A. Miller and Leo Goossen, back in the high-flying decade of the 1920s, but it was Fred Offenhauser who machined the engines for Harry and who kept the flame alive, gave it his name, and propelled it into lasting fame after Miller's bankruptcy. Without Fred Offenhauser there would not have been such an incomparable racing engine.

After going to the Smithsonian Institution as auto racing advisor and collecting, with great pride, an Offenhauser precursor—Bob Rubin's #18 1929 Miller front-drive Indianapolis car—I felt a need to tell the Offenhauser story. I had long wanted to write a history of American auto racing and have considered many of its parts, including racing at Freeport, the Gilmore of the East. It was not until Motorbooks International offered me the opportunity to write this history of Fred Offenhauser and his engines, however that the wish became a reality. I hope this volume has done Fred and his engines justice.

Fred Offenhauser's contribution to the engine that bore his name began in Harry A. Miller's shop in 1913, before the creation of the first Miller engine. It continued through Miller's best years and in Offenhauser's greatest act in this long-running story: his rescue of the Miller four-cylinder engine upon Miller's bankruptcy in 1933. Ever-practical Fred and mild Leo Goossen built the four-cylinder Offy into the most formidable racing engine of the mid-20th century and passed the torch to Louie Meyer and Dale Drake, who gave it its greatest years until age, racing politics, and quixotic fuel economy rules ended the Offy's reign in 1980.

This volume attempts to go further in the history of Fred Offenhauser and his engines than Borgeson and Dees felt necessary in their Miller books, and to record in more detail the Miller developments that led to Offenhauser's success, including the bankruptcies of Miller-Schofield and Harry A. Miller Inc. I have tried to analyze Offenhauser's success in the debris of Miller's failure and to spell out where and how the Offy won.

ACKNOWLEDGMENTS

THIS BOOK ON FRED OFFENHAUSER, THE ENGINES THAT BORE HIS NAME, AND the men who built, developed, drove and worked on them should have been written a quarter-century ago when most of the principals were still alive to tell their tales. The written record is almost always incomplete, and the stories handed down by word of mouth often conflict. When the research for this book was done, of the major players in the events described, only the redoubtable Louie Meyer, three-time Indianapolis winner and partner in Meyer & Drake, survived. His gracious personal help was vital, but Louie lived only a part of the Offenhauser story.

There is much that is new in this book, particularly many photographs which to my knowledge have not been previously published, and some that last saw print in the 1930s. There is new evidence about the Schofield and Miller bankruptcies and observations from participants in the struggle between Drake Engineering and the Ford Motor Company. That said, however, such a book could not be written today without the dedicated spadework of those who have gone this way before to tell the stories of Harry A. Miller and the marvelous Miller and Offenhauser engines. It was historians Griff Borgeson and Mark Dees, two friends who labored in the Southern California vineyards of speed, who have made this Offenhauser history possible.

Griff Borgeson rediscovered Miller when he had been all but forgotten. Mark Dees built greatly upon Griff's work and made it marvelous in *The Miller Dynasty*. I am incredibly indebted to them. Griff's *Miller, The Golden Age of the American Racing Car*, and *The Classic Twin-Cam Engine*, among other of his writings, educated me in the genre. Mark's book brought all of the known Miller material together and is the beautifully written definitive history of Harry A. Miller. In addition, Mark was most gracious and helpful in providing me with photographs, drawings, and leads to Offenhauser information. Nevertheless, most of the material in this volume has been corroborated by more than just a single source, no matter how authoritative. I have relied where possible on the oral record left on tape by Walter Sobraske and Leo Goossen, though even there the material has been checked with other sources (including my own archive of racing publications and AAA documents 1908–1956), since memories of even the most reliable participants fade.

I am especially indebted to Emil Andres, George Bignotti, John Drake, Chris Economaki, Ken Hickey, Karl Ludvigsen, Gloria Madsen, Sonny Meyer, Herb Porter, Jim Toensing, Buster Warke, A. J. Watson, Paul Weirick, and particularly, Chuck Davis and Joseph Freeman. Each of them read all or portions of the manuscript and offered numerous suggestions and corrections, but any errors in fact or judgment that may appear in this book are entirely my own. Finally, I must thank my editor at Motorbooks International, Zack Miller, whose patience with me was great and whose professionalism and sensitivity to the Offenhauser story was remarkable.

This is not a shop manual on the construction and care of every Offy model. For that we must look forward to my colleague, Ken Walton's, forthcoming book. Ken's assistance and participation in this effort were highly important. He provided much research and several photographs and drawings. Thanks go also to Angela Tyler, who prepared the charts and graphs on engine production and the Offenhauser records at Indianapolis and the championship Trail.

I owe my 50-year Offy education to many others. Some taught me about racing, about engines, and about life as it was for those who built and raced the Offys; some provided information, assistance, photographs not seen before, copies of Leo Goossen's marvelous drawings, and insights to the people who surrounded the Offy. I have undoubtedly overlooked some who helped, but in addition to those already mentioned, the following individuals deserve recognition for what they did to make this book possible:

Bill Akin; Bob Anderson; Don Anderson; Jim Ash; Jack Balch; Jewel Barlow; Francis Barrineau; Eddie Baue; Ellen Bireley; Gary Brey; Allan Brown; Jim Bruni; John Burgess; Dean Butler; Michael Caruso, Jr.; Tommy Caruso; Andrew Casale; Bill Chapin; Miles Collier; Briggs Cunningham; Bob DeBisschop; William A. Digney; Bill Doty and Clair Malervy at the National Archives Pacific Southwest Region office in Laguna Nigel, California; J. Neal East; Steve Earle; Don Edmunds; Randy Ema; Neil Freeman; Richard Freshman; Andy Furci; Joe Gemsa; Brad Gray; Roy Hagedorn; Philip Harms; Jerry Helck; Bob Higman; Tommy Hinnershitz; Ron Hoettels; Jim Hoggatt; Ernie Holden; Roscoe "Pappy" Hough; Ed Iskenderian; Bruce Johnston; Grant King; John Klann; Tom Konop; Jim Lattin; John Laux; Jack Layton; Joe Lencki; Chris Leydon; Kent Liffick; Stan Lobitz; Don Lockwood; Edward MacFarlane; Richard Maloumian; Jon Mauk; Bob McConnell; Bob McGee; Phil Merrill and the Washingtonian Racing Team; Gene Meyer; Louis Meyer, Sr.; Dale Miller; David Miller; Bill Milliken; Tommy Milton III; Bill Montgomery; Jim Mortimer and the *Deseret Racing News* Team; John Nance; Duke Nalon; Bob Nowicki; Edna Offenhauser; Fred C. Offenhauser; Jim O'Keefe; Don Orosco; Fran Parsons; Lynn Paxton; Ralph Prueitt; Roy Query; Ed Raschansky; Joe D. Rice; Fred Roe; Robert M. Rubin; John Russell; Tom Saal; Tom Schmeh; Lou Senter; Bill Smith; Bill Spoerle; Bill St. George; Dick Simonek; Steve Stapp; Robert Sutherland; Bob Swarms; David Uihlein; Stuart Van Dyne II; Mark Wilke; Ralph Wilke; Crocky Wright; Brock Yates; and Smokey Yunick.

I am also indebted to a number of magazines and newspapers, some of them no longer published: *Speed Age, The Automobile, Automotive Industries, Motor Age, Motor Trend, Hot Rod, Car & Driver, Sports Cars Illustrated, Road & Track*, the *Bergen Herald, National Speed Sport News, Illustrated Speedway News, Coastal Racing News, Speedway, and National Speedway Weekly*, among others.

Photo Credits

More than two dozen individuals, institutions, and corporations provided photographs, blueprints, drawings, charts, maps, and other documents that aided in the preparation of this book. To organizations stretching from the Federal Archives Center in Laguna Nigel, California, to the Library of Congress in Washington, D.C., and all of the many individuals, I am grateful. Ron McQueeney and Pat Jones of Indy 500 Photos graciously assisted with a number of Indy photos, and all those identified as *Indianapolis Motor Speedway* are published under the copyright of the Indianapolis Motor Speedway Corporation.

Others who provided photos or other material are as follows: Gloria Madsen, Buck Boudeman, Marvin Jenkins, John Drake, Mark Dees, Gordon and Carmen Schroeder, Bruce Craig, Sotheby's Inc., Robert Binyon, Rolla Vollstedt, George Parker, the Library of Congress, Carl Sweigart, The Huntington Collection, Don McReynolds, Venlo Wolfsohn, NASCAR, Larry Jendras, Smithsonian Institution, Frank Guidatis, Collier Historic Motors, Vic Yerardi, Johnny Pawl, *Car & Driver*, Preston Lerner via Mrs. Dean Batchelor, Lou Ensworth, Jim Etter, Marty Himes, Jim Toensing, Ralph and Mark Wilke, Frank Kurtis, and the U.S. Patent Office.

The Offy in its glory days. Five champ cars bear down on the photographer as they battle into a corner on the dirt at Williams Grove, Pennsylvania, in 1958. In the #48 is Len Sutton, Don Branson is in the #10, Earl Motter in #25, A. J. Foyt in #29, and Buzz Barton in #86. Offenhauser engines, 255s, with their distinctive growl, powered men such as these to fame, fortune, and occasionally, violent death. *Venlo Wolfsohn collection*

INTRODUCTION

FOR NEARLY A HALF-CENTURY, WHEREVER AMERICANS POWERED THEIR WAY to automobile glory, whether on the two-and-a-half-mile Speedway at Indianapolis, the short quarter-mile midget tracks or the dusty half-mile fairgrounds where sprint cars plied their fearsome trade, the name Offenhauser long meant the most dominant engine to power a racing car. Even today, long after the 1980 Indianapolis 500-Mile race when an Offenhauser-powered racing car last ran in the world's most prestigious motor competition, Offenhauser, or "Offy", is still recognizable. There were only a handful of Offenhauser racing *cars*. Fred Offenhauser built perhaps 150 racing engines, but his shop turned out few complete vehicles such as Paul Pold's 1940 midget and one or two junior midgets. He generally hired out chassis and body building to men like Myron Stevens, Curly Wetteroth, and Frank Kurtis. What Offenhauser built was engines.

Leo Goossen, late in life, with a 270 Offy, the engine he nursed from its origins in the 1920s to its days of glory in the 1950s and, finally, its soaring power with turbocharging. *Gordon Schroeder collection*

Offenhauser engines, and their predecessor Miller, dominated, indeed sometimes reigned, as sole competitors for two-thirds of the entire history of auto racing in this country. Yet when Fred Offenhauser died in Los Angeles in 1973, the local California newspapers ran only the briefest of obituaries. The leading racing paper, *National Speed Sport News*, ran four short paragraphs. *Illustrated Speedway News* took no notice of his death at all, nor did *Road & Track* mention his passing.

In a brief three-paragraph Associated Press story, the *New York Times* remarked that Fred Offenhauser took over the production of Miller racing engines when Harry A. Miller Incorporated went bankrupt in 1933 and that he continued to build them under his own name until 1946 when he sold the concern to Louis Meyer and Dale Drake. With those few words was closed a remarkable chapter in racing and automotive history; a history worthy of closer examination. In 1922 Harry A. Miller, "an unknown from out in California," as Leo Goosen described him in a 1974 interview, designed and built a 181-cubic-inch, twin-cam engine that Jimmy Murphy put into his Duesenberg chassis and with it won the Indianapolis 500-mile race. Miller's shop in the 1920s went on to build the greatest racing engines and automobiles the world had yet seen. Not only were they blindingly fast, they were works of art.

Lovingly built and exquisitely finished, they represented a high point in the history of competitive machines; indeed in Miller's shop even the internal portions of a car's crankcase were scraped and burnished by his workmen. The 91-cubic-inch, supercharged, front-wheel drive 1929 Miller car of Leon Duray was a good example of Miller's automotive artistry. Its polished axles, steering, and other hardware were finely shaped, and its long, low hood expressed the beauty of speed and inspired a generation of designers of high-powered road cars.

While it is true that Offenhauser carried on the production of Miller engines after his employer went broke in the Depression, that is but a fraction of the Offy story. Fred Offenhauser was more than a successor to Harry Miller. He started out with Miller in his machine shop in 1913, just six months after Miller began to manufacture "Master" carburetors of a new and unique design. Throughout Miller's reign, Offenhauser's Germanic thoroughness and practicality as a toolmaker and shop foreman were necessary foils to the leader's equally Teutonic romanticism.

Fred Offenhauser and draftsman Leo Goossen not only gave Miller's automotive visions practical expression in steel and aluminum, they brought ideas to Miller and studied other engineer's advances in racing engine design, copying those features they found useful. But Fred Offenhauser's greatest contribution to auto racing was in continuing to build the Miller engines and in adapting them to the real world of racing in the 1930s after Miller's bankruptcy. He saved the Miller engine from extinction and, under his name, kept it on its nearly 60-year course, updating.it whenever necessary.

Offenhauser was a reticent but practical man, without Miller's tendency toward flights of automotive fancy. Though he passed from the world with little notice, he was an essential part of the history of the most long-lived engine to ever power racing cars down the long and dangerous course of speed.

Offenhauser retired after World War II and Louie Meyer and Dale Drake picked up the Offy mantle. With Leo Goossen still at his drawing board, Meyer & Drake's Offenhauser engines continued to dominate American racing in midgets, sprint cars, and at Indianapolis. From 1950 through 1962, 424 of 429 cars that qualified at Indianapolis were powered by a Meyer & Drake Offenhauser engine or by a Novi, an engine designed by Leo Goossen and initially built in the Offenhauser shop.

Nowhere in the history of the automobile can one find an engine that lasted so long or ran so successfully as the Offy. Neither the fabled Model T Ford, nor the Ford V-8 flathead, nor even the later overhead-valve Chevrolet V-8 matches the magnificent four-cylinder Offy in longevity and prowess.

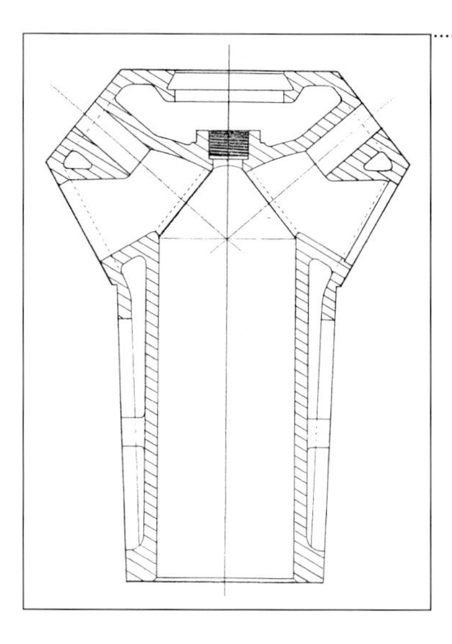

The block for the 122 Miller. The basic architecture for all of the Miller and Offenhauser engines to come was established here by Leo Goossen—the clean, short intake and exhaust passages, the center-mounted spark plug, the symmetrical valve layout. *Buck Boudeman collection*

Early Racing and the Rise of Harry Miller

Auto racing began in America in 1895 with a race sponsored by the *Chicago Times-Herald*. That early contest was run on a snowy November day on the streets north of Chicago by cars that were more buggy than automobile. It was won by a tiny American-built Duryea at a speed of 10 miles per hour in what was a test of endurance, not speed. Though auto racing was at first a contest between individuals to see who had the faster car, as hot-rodders have done for a century, major events soon pitted factory-entered cars against all comers in the struggle for recognition and publicity in the early auto industry.

Ten years after the *Times Herald* race a young man named Harry Miller was hired to manage the Oldsmobile team's entry in the 1906 Vanderbilt Cup races. Miller was a mechanic, driver, and inventor who had grown up in Wisconsin but sought his fortune in California. He left Oldsmobile in 1907 and set up shop in Los Angeles to manufacture carburetors of his own innovative design.

While Miller honed the practical skills that would support his budding genius, four Frenchmen at the Peuguot company, drivers Paolo Zuccarelli, Georges Boillot and Jules Goux, with the aid of draftsman Ernest Henry, were developing the world's first twin-cam racing engine. They were tinkerers with big ideas, not engineers, and the Peugeot factory's university-trained staff were so appalled at the effrontery that they labeled the four "Les Charlatans." But in 1912 the Charlatans brought to the world the engine layout that would lead to the Miller, the Offenhauser, and most other high-performance engines built since. Similarly the Offy engine, from first to last, owed its continued existence for half a century not to factory engineers, but to a constantly renewed group of brilliant drivers, dedicated mechanics, persistent car owners, and others in racing who willed its success.

The Peugeot racing cars crossed the Atlantic and were as successful in American racing as they had been in Europe. A Peugeot won the Indianapolis 500 in 1913, and top drivers such as Eddie Rickenbacker raced in them. In early 1915, Rickenbacker blew the engine in his Peugeot; it was sold to Harry Miller, who tore it apart to see what gave the French car its winning ways. With a flair for improving an already good design, Miller rebuilt the Rickenbacker Peugeot and another for Bob Burman, beginning an enormously successful series of engines that came out of Miller's shops for the next 15 years.

Miller, more of an artist than a businessman, reached the pinnacle of his success in 1928, and shortly thereafter sold out to the Schofield Company. When Schofield failed in the Depression, Miller returned to Los Angeles and attempted to revive his business, only to fall into bankruptcy himself in 1933. From that wreckage, Fred Offenhauser, Miller's machine shop foreman, pulled together enough fragments to keep the Miller legacy alive. An ever-adaptable Offenhauser rebuilt the business and added to it the diminutive midget engine that was the first "Offy." Together, Offenhauser and Leo Goossen developed the former Miller 255 engine into the powerhouse that was to rule Indianapolis and the Championship Trail for so many years under Dale Drake and Louie Meyer.

What Was the Offy?

For those who may have never considered the technical design of the Offy, just what was it and what gave the Miller-Offenhauser-Meyer-Drake engine its power, and its importance?

From 1920 until 1979, every Miller, Offenhauser, and Drake engine followed the basic layout of an integral head and block with double overhead cams on a separate barrel-type aluminum crankcase. All of the Offy and Drake engines were fours and, with a few exceptions, the large engines had four valves per cylinder in a pent-roof configuration. The midgets and a few special engines were built with two valves per cylinder in hemispheric combustion chambers.

Harry Miller, Fred Offenhauser, and Leo Goossen assimilated the best engine design ideas from around the world. The basic double-overhead-cam (DOHC) architecture of the engines was, as far as we know, first tried in 1905 by Delahaye in France. As noted, it was brought to maturity in 1912 by "Les Charlatans."[1] Today, late in the 20th century, the double-overhead-cam engine is common in everyday cars and offers more power per cubic inch and better mileage than either the flathead engines built through 1949, or the rocker-arm overhead-valve engines that were built in the 1950s and endure in larger cars to this day. One feature modern auto builders have abandoned that Miller and all of his followers adhered to was the integral cylinder head and block. The block on all Millers and Offys is, however, separate from the crankcase. It can

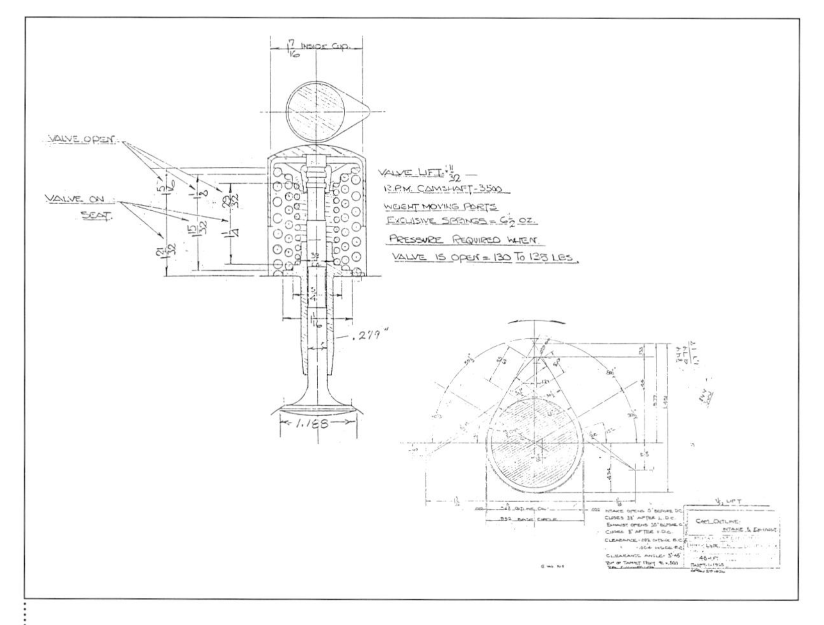

Leo Goossen's drawing, dated September 1, 1925, of the valve assembly for the 91-cubic-inch Miller engine. As with the 122 Miller block, this arrangement set many of the parameters for all future Miller and Offenhauser engines. Note how "pointy" the cam lobes are. Miller's engines also had much less overlap than would become common later. Wilbur Shaw and many other drivers and mechanics had their own cams ground to hot up Miller's conservative valve timing. *Mark Dees collection*

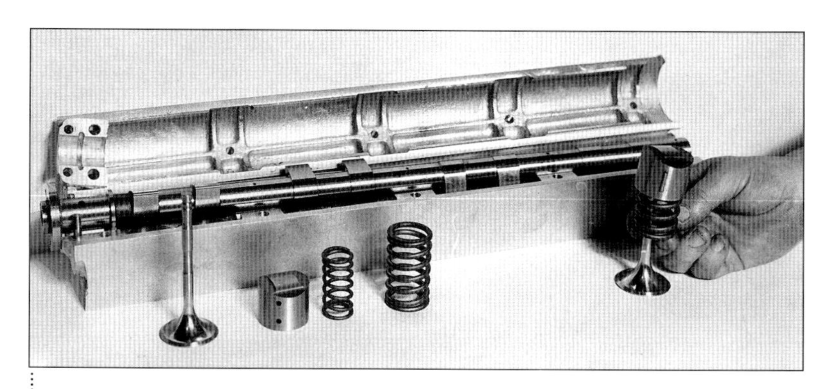

Offenhauser cam and valve gear. The cam lobe rides on the rounded top of the cup, which absorbs the lateral thrust and does not transmit it to the valve stem. *Gloria Madsen collection*

be lifted off to service the engine's upper end. The cam housings are also separate pieces, as is the gear tower. That unpremeditated modular construction offered the great advantage to the racing mechanic of allowing him to replace broken parts for far less than the price of an entire new engine.

The one-piece block and head design eliminated head gasket failure as no head gasket was required. The one-piece design also eliminated the distortion that tightening head studs introduce into a cylinder.

From its inception the overhead-cam design has proven the most efficient possible layout of the four- stroke, internal-combustion engine. All other valve arrangements involve either inefficient combustion chamber shapes or pushrods and rocker-arms between the camshafts and the valves. Pushrod systems are inherently heavier and add inertia to the valvetrain. They are also more inclined to flex and cause troubles than direct-acting valve mechanisms.

Time having proven that the basic DOHC layout is the ultimate internal combustion engine architecture, improvements since 1912 have been incremental: more efficient combustion chamber shapes, smoother intake ports, larger valves, subtle cam timing changes, better lubrication, different connecting rod lengths and bore/stroke ratios, crank-trigger ignition, electronic black boxes, and the like.

A four-cylinder engine like the Offy generally has a longer stroke than a six–eight–or more-cylindered engine of the same displacement, and thus produces more torque. This torque, which provides the power to accelerate off a corner, was always the Offy's greatest strength. For that reason Offy mechanics clung to the engine's long stroke and were reluctant to shorten it to gain rpm.

However, in spite of the punch of its mighty torque, two theoretical advantages of six-or eight-cylinder engines always lurked over the Offy four: (1) more valve and piston area per unit volume of displacement, and (2) a shorter piston stroke allowing more revolutions per minute.

Any twin-cam crossflow engine such as the Offenhauser can have very short intake and exhaust gas ducts. Shorter passages contribute to better "volumetric efficiency," the most complete filling of the cylinder with its fuel-air mixture. Since the hot exhaust gas is in contact with the cylinder block for only an inch or so, it transfers the minimum amount of heat into the engine. (By comparison, the well-known Ford "flathead" V-8 of 1932–1952 had long exhaust gas passages in the block and was notorious for overheating.)

A DOHC design also makes possible good thermodynamic efficiency through the use of a two-valve-per-cylinder "hemispheric" shaped combustion chamber with the least internal surface area for its volume and thus the minimum loss of heat from the cylinder itself to the engine block. Engine buffs will recall the mighty Chrysler "Hemi" engine of the 1960s muscle car era. This design lives on in current drag racing and Bonneville straightaway cars. Most Offys, except for the midget, however, were built with four valves per cylinder for greater intake efficiency.

Miller and his team of draftsmen also designed supercharged engines to produce awesome amounts of power for their time. In the 1920s, they were locked in competition with Fred and Augie Duesenberg, a contest that drove racing science to heights not seen for another 40 years. In 1920, the Duesenbergs added supercharging to their already formidable engines, and by 1924 the science was well enough developed to allow Joe Boyer to win the Indianapolis 500 with a blown Duesey. Miller took up the idea and quickly perfected it. His blown engines reached their highest development in 1928 when Leon Duray qualified a 91.5-cubic-inch Miller straight eight at Indianapolis at 122.391 miles per hour, a record that stood for nine years. Forty years later Dale Drake was to revive the aging Miller/Offy engine with another type of supercharging, the turbo.

It was in taking such a variety of practical and theoretical design ideas and making them succeed in racing, that Miller, Offenhauser, Goossen, and Meyer & Drake excelled. Those ideas kept the basic Offy engine design current for more than half a century and made it always the engine to beat, if you could.

For many of those years the Offenhauser engine reigned absolutely. In the 1950s and 1960s entire 33-car fields at Indianapolis were powered by Offenhauser engines. On the Championship Trail, 100-mile contests run chiefly on one-mile dirt tracks, 270 and 255 Offys won every race but two for the 17 years between October 1946 and August 1963. (The exceptions were the Pikes Peak Hill Climb in 1947 and 1955, where specialized chassis were involved.) Offenhauser-powered midgets swept their class of racing from 1934 through the 1970s, and the 220 Offy was the most successful engine on the fairground circuits for at least as long.

In the 1930s, while Harry Miller, the genius of engine design, continued to pursue his dreams, Fred Offenhauser, the disciple, carried on the basic, solid Miller designs with pragmatic determination. This then is the story of the engine that Offenhauser saved, strengthened, and sent into battle on a thousand race tracks from Hinchcliffe Stadium in Paterson, New Jersey, to Western Springs, Australia, Monza in Italy and at Indianapolis, Indiana.

The timing gears from the front of an Offenhauser engine. The small gear with the large hole was mounted on the nose of the crank. The gear below it drove the water and oil pumps. Above that is the large "half-time" gear that reduces the crank speed by half. Next is an idler that also drives the magneto shaft via bevel gears, then another idler and the gears that drive the intake and exhaust cams. Note the ten mounting holes in the cam gears. These are spaced such that by rotating the gear on each cam the valve timing may be varied by a few degrees. When Smokey Yunick had a reverse-rotation Offy built, the gear train had to be redesigned to rotate the water and oil pumps and the magneto in the correct direction. *Kenneth Walton collection*

Harry Miller (fifth from left), Fred Offenhauser (fourth from left), Frank Adamson (hand resting on block), and some of the Miller staff pose proudly with the block for Bob Burman's reconstructed Peugeot engine in 1915, apparently aware that something historic has taken place. This engine, with its single-carburetor manifold, resembles the original Peugeot but is clearly not of Peugeot manufacture. The two cam housings attach to the surface where the dog is standing. Several of the staff are unidentifiable here but were among those who worked for Miller for another 18 years and then for Offenhauser.
Gloria Madsen collection

CHAPTER ONE

THE MEN WHO BUILT THE OFFY

THE ENGINES THAT BECAME THE OFFENHAUSER WERE BORN ORIGINALLY IN the fertile mind of Harry Miller, their design polished, refined, and committed to drafting cloth by Leo Goossen, and turned into objects of steel, bronze, and aluminum by skilled machinists like Walt Sobraske and Fred Offenhauser himself. While it has been said that Offenhauser carried on the Miller engines, in truth Offenhauser was present at the creation of the Miller engines and provided Harry Miller with much of the information from the race track, and other builders, which gave those engines the distinction that marked their 60-year span of life as the best engines in racing.

Harry A. Miller

Harry Arminius Miller had no formal engineering education. Like three of the four Charlatans, his knowledge was won through experience, and his science was a combination of inspiration and experiment. Tracing their ancestry to the 1912 Peugeots of Rickenbacher and Burman, the Miller engines were the result of a little copying and much brilliant improvisation, an American trait that was always sneered at in Europe. Leo Goossen had, like Ernest Henry, enough technical training to make Miller's genius work, and Offenhauser had the practical skills to turn it into aluminum and steel.

As the philospher Hegel had said, "The idea of an epoch always finds its appropriate and adequate form," and improvisation would do quite well for Miller, Offenhauser, and later Meyer & Drake. In the beginning of the 1920s, the board speedways were at the peak of their popularity, and Miller's finely built cars were eminently suited to them.

Miller 183-cubic-inch engines and Miller cars won Indianapolis in 1922, and Miller 122s won again in 1923 against competition chiefly from Duesenberg. Miller and the Duesenberg brothers fought back and forth throughout the 1920s. Fred and Augie's cars won at Indianapolis in 1924 and 1925 on the strength of supercharging, done with the help of Dr. Sanford Moss of the General Electric Company Miller consulted with his own experts, James Allison at Allison Engineering in Indianapolis and ex-driver Guy Ball who had driven a Great Western at Indy in 1914

Memorial to Harry Miller at the Indianapolis Motor Speedway, 1991. Shown is one of Miller's wonderful supercharged straight-eight 91s and three Miller racing cars. *Author*

Harry Miller with his masterpiece, the supercharged Miller 91-cubic-inch engine, the highest expression of his art and the most successful of his and Goossen's creations. *Bruce Craig collection*

Frank Lockhart, the most talented of all the drivers of Miller cars in the Roaring Twenties. Frank won the 1926 Indianapolis 500 in this beautiful single-seat, rear-drive Miller 91. He was killed in 1928 trying to set a new land speed record at Ormond Beach, Florida. *Gloria Madsen collection/Indianapolis Motor Speedway*

(but failed to qualify) and worked with the WWI Liberty aircraft engine[2] at Chanute Field. Goossen said years later that they got their first ideas of blower speeds "from the grapevine" and built their first impeller with steel blades. With Goossen's technical aid, Miller designed his own aluminum centrifugal blowers which produced boost pressures as high as 30 to 35 psi.

Under the new 91-cubic-inch formula, blown Millers dominated the 1926 Indianapolis field with 18 cars to Duesenberg's two and won the 500. In 1927, there were 28 Millers in the 33-car field against five Duesenbergs. Though a Duesenberg won, Miller 91s took 10 of the top 12 finishing positions. In 1928, there were 24 Miller 91s in the 29-car Indy field. Lou Meyer drove a Miller to first, and Harry's creations took nine of the first 10 finishing places.

Miller cars and engines were even more dominant on the board tracks. It was a heady time for the master of the shop on Long Beach Avenue in Los Angeles. By the end of the 1920s, Harry Miller's cars were all-conquering on the race tracks.

Fred Offenhauser

When Fred Offenhauser was born on February 11, 1888, Los Angeles was a little town of 40,000, but one growing rapidly as surrounding subdivisions began to replace the orange orchards, vineyards, and ostrich ranches. The city was a rail terminus; the tracks of the Southern Pacific and the Santa Fe framed downtown like a giant T, and horse-drawn trolleys ran as far as the port at San Pedro, 20 miles south. At the time, Los Angeles had less than a mile of paved roads, but it would shortly become the American City of the Automobile.

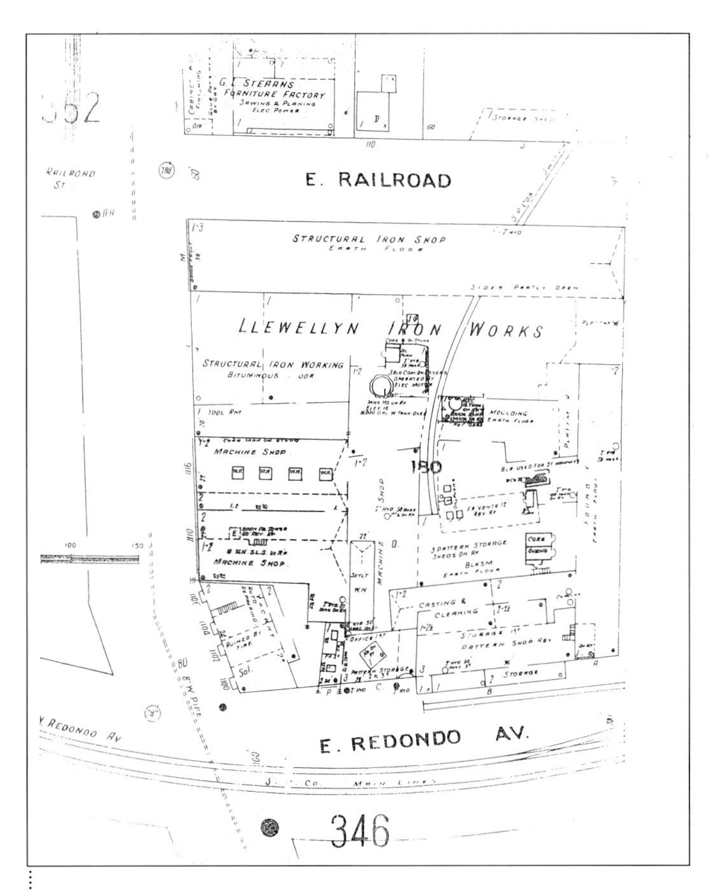

In 1900, when he was in the seventh grade, young Fred Offenhauser would run after school to watch the heavy machines of the Llewellyn Iron Works at East Railroad Street and Redondo Avenue (now Roundout Street). Fred got his first job there and there he began his lifelong love of machinery. *Library of Congress*

Where irrigation ditches watered thousands of acres of farm land, and wineries and distilleries dotted the map, would soon grow gas stations and truck depots. Its distance from deposits of coal, limestone, iron, and Eastern financiers as well as its location far from the center of the nation, prevented it from becoming a center of auto manufacture, but Los Angeles was to become mesmerized by the new invention and its spreading suburbs were fertile soil for the car culture of the emerging 20th century. Shortly it became a center of automotive sport and within a radius of a dozen miles of Los Angeles City Hall there sprang up a crop of speedways unmatched anywhere in the nation. The world's first board track for autos was constructed on the Pacific at Playa del Rey in 1910 and the original Ascot, a former horse track at Slauson Avenue between Avalon Boulevard and Central Avenue, became in 1912, the site of championship racing for the likes of Ralph De Palma, Eddie Rickenbacker, and Barney Oldfield. During Fred Offenhauser's career, at least 15 major speedways existed virtually in his back yard along with another dozen or more of lesser rank. For a man who loved to build fine machines, Los Angeles was to become the place to work.

By the time Fred was 12, Los Angeles had burgeoned into a small metropolis of 270,000 people, served by 150 miles of interurban lines. Downtown, though smaller than New York or Chicago, boasted blocks of large buildings. Heavy industry lined the railroad tracks. The roaring forges and whirring machines of Western Machinery & Milling, Hanke Gustave's boiler works, Fulton Engine, Keystone Iron & Brass, and the Pacific Boiler Company were a fascinating attraction for the young Offenhauser. He later said that after school he would run six blocks down to the Llewellyn Brothers' Columbia Foundry at Redondo and Main to watch the machines.

Frederick H. Offenhauser, Jr., (he soon dropped the "H." and ignored the "Jr.") was, like Harry Miller, a son of German immigrants. Frederich Offenhauser, Sr., was born in Berlin in 1844—a time of turmoil in Europe. Hegel had, since the Napoleonic wars, been preaching a "powerful doctrine of self-realization and the supremacy of reason" to a generation of ardent young liberals hemmed in by an autocratic Prussian regime. Frederich became an officer in the West Bavarian army. Influenced by the tenor of thought such as Hegel's, he developed so much pride that after a minor military disagreement he broke a sword over his knee and threw it in the face of his captain—a serious offense in Germany. He fled to America on a sailing vessel and arrived in New York in 1861. He set out across the United States, working as a barber and a wigmaker, eventually arriving in Los Angeles. In 1886, at the age of 41, he married Martha Muller, a 29-year-old German immigrant from Saxony. He worked as a court interpreter and as a barber, providing enough income for the Offenhausers to own their own home at 810 Mateo Street near Atlantic. Two years later when little Frederick was born, the second of what would be nine children, he was called simply Fred to distinguish him from his father.

In succeeding years the family grew as Charlie was born in August 1889, Margarette

Second and Spring Streets in Los Angeles about 1910. The city had grown from 40,000 in 1888, when Fred Offenhauser was born, to more than 300,000 in 22 years. Despite the rapid spread of the Red Trolley Cars of the Pacific Electric Railway they could not keep up, and the sprawling metropolis became addicted to that new contraption, the automobile. *Huntington collection*

in May 1891, Paul (nicknamed Mike) in August 1892, Martha in 1895, Otto in 1898, Francis in February 1900, and the baby, Agnes, in 1905.

Papa Offenhauser was an artist as well as a barber. He would disappear into the hills east of Los Angeles for days at a time to paint. When he was at home he was both strict and formal—he wore a Prince Albert coat—and difficult to get along with. He raised the children with an autocracy much like that he had fled in Germany, imposing harsh discipline in the family when he was at home. Despite that he and Martha, who was also a barber, were good providers. The Mateo Street house burned in 1895 when a stove exploded, but the Offenhausers rebuilt it to house their growing family. Until Fred went to school he spoke only German but then Papa issued a dictum: "No more German will be spoken in this home. The children must learn to speak English."

Fred related that when he was in the seventh grade at the Seventh Street School he rebelled, quit his classes in the middle of the day, went to the iron works and got his first job. He was just 12 years old, but machinery held his interest better than books. "Working there," he said later, "was like being in heaven." The Llewellyn Company had foundry, structural iron, and machine shops that made elevators and other metal products, a fair training ground for the career Offenhauser would follow.

The surviving record suggests that his father did not allow his son to quit school at 12. Frederich Offenhauser appears to have spoken to John and Reese Llewellyn and arranged for Fred to work at the foundry for a time after school. The senior Offenhauser preferred that Fred follow his own footsteps as a barber, and indeed in 1906 Fred and his father operated a barber shop together at 1758 East Ninth Street in Los Angeles.

Life as a barber with his alternately stern and mystical father was not what Fred wanted. In 1903, he became an apprentice machinist in the Pacific Electric Railway shops at East Sixth and Central, just across the Southern Pacific tracks from Mateo Street. By the time he was 21 he was a journeyman

The Offenhauser family, five of the children, and two playmates at their home at 810 Mateo Street in Los Angeles about 1894. Fred is perched on his mother's shoulder. This house later burned when the stove exploded, but they rebuilt the house. *Gloria Madsen collection*

A young Fred Offenhauser was photographed at a big LeBlond-Bay City lathe in the Pacific Electric Railway shops at Sixth and Central streets in Los Angeles about 1910 when he was 22 years old. *Gloria Madsen collection*

Fred and Ethel Offenhauser enjoying a watermelon party with some of Fred's brothers and sisters, about 1909. *Gloria Madsen collection*

Offenhauser was a new machinist when this photograph was taken in the Miller carburetor plant at 922 Los Angeles Street, between Ninth and Olympic, about 1914. Miller is on the far left and Fred is in the far rear, sixth from left. On the bench in the foreground is an early flow-measuring apparatus. *Gloria Madsen collection*

machinist. There, at Pacific Electric, with discipline and thoroughness, he rose to the machine shop's version of stardom, a toolmaker—the man who makes, installs, and cares for the tools and machines in the shop. Fred did not simply run the machinery that maintained the railroad equipment, he built it.

In 1909, Ethel Lowery of Elwood, Indiana, and her brother, Arthur, visited California with their father, a blacksmith. Ethel and Fred met at a seaside pavilion. Fred fancied himself quite a dancer and the two hit it off at once and were soon married and living at 2836 Boulder Street in Boyle Heights, a mile east of the heavy industrial section of south-central Los Angeles. Dancing remained an attraction, and for years afterward they would swing each other around the dance floor, regularly winning waltz contests.

Offenhauser worked on the Pacific Electric Red Cars for eight years and was always proud of being a railway man, learning his trade in what was then the best of schools. Technical schools taught theory; their students visited shops to find how those theories were applied. Fred was learning the science of setting up lathes, milling machines and presses, the arts of cutting metal, pattern-making

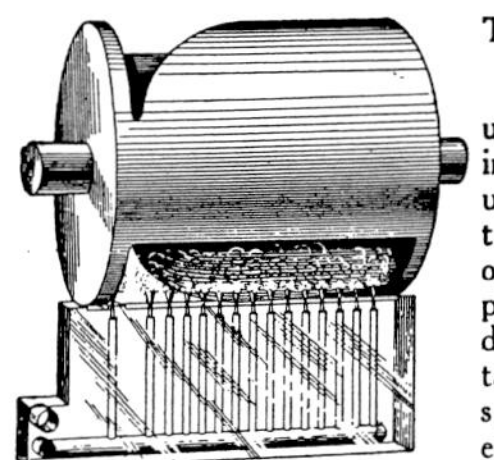

The ROTARY THROTTLE uncovers the holes in the Fuel Distributer in proportion to the Throttle opening, aiding in producing the wonderful results obtained in power, speed and fuel economy.

Write Dept. B. for MASTER Booklet

Master Carbureter Corporation
Woodward and Hancock
DETROIT, MICH.

Pacific Coast States should address
MASTER CARBURETOR COMPANY, INC.
922-24 So. Los Angeles St. LOS ANGELES, CAL.

Advertisement for Harry Miller's *Master* carburetors. It was his carburetor inventions that made Miller enough money to develop successful racing engines. He sold the carburetor business to entrepreneurs in both Indianapolis and Detroit. *Mark Dees collection*

and foundry work, watching the draftsmen at work, learning to read a blueprint and to tell when the draftsman had drawn a line that did not match the measurements given. In later years he would hire a machinist from a railroad shop whenever he could find one. He also spoke admiringly of the boss of the Pacific Railway shops, Edward Strang, who insisted his workers keep their lathes and milling machines clean and well-oiled. Later Fred would assign a man in his own shop to spend an hour a day just in caring for the machines.

Los Angeles, the City Made for the Automobile

By 1913 the population of the city had grown to nearly 500,000. The interurban Pacific Electric Red Cars tied together the growing southern California cities, but the automobile was about to sweep away both farms and trolleys. Fred, sensing a better opportunity, applied for work at a company building carburetors to a new design developed by 38-year-old Harry A. Miller.

When Offenhauser arrived at Miller's door the carburetor company was located at 922 Los Angeles Street. Harry Miller was neither a graduate engineer nor a machinist, but he was experienced in foundry techniques and, as the world was about to discover, was gifted as a designer at an empirical level. (Miller worked empirically, choosing what worked and looked good to his eye—a typically American approach to invention and markedly different from the more cerebral European scientific method. Americans eventually learned to combine mathematics with the "feel" and "eyeball" method, but Miller was unable to make that leap.) He had developed a series of carburetors of which one, the "Master," he sold to a group of Indianapolis and Detroit investors. His carburetor designs attempted, as did others in the field, to deal with the problem of controlling fuel-to-air ratios over a range of throttle openings, a continual challenge to designers of automobile engines that require quite rapid throttle changes. The light Miller carburetors were built of aluminum rather than bronze and for that reason they were taken up by aircraft builders. In fact in 1910, Glenn Curtiss used a Miller carburetor on one of his aircraft engines. Miller carburetors were based on a then-new design with a rotary barrel and multiple jets that turned out to be unusually efficient on racing engines.

Over the decades after 1910 Los Angeles would see built such auto racing tracks as the Playa del Rey, Beverly Hills and Culver City board speedways, Legion Ascot, Gilmore Stadium, and the Coliseum. The mild climate allowed auto racing to continue almost year–round. After Playa del Rey burned in 1913 old Ascot opened and there was shortly Vanderbilt Cup racing at Corona. Whether or not there was racing, when winter shut the tracks in the rest of the nation, racing drivers preferred to spend the cold months in southern California where they rebuilt their machines for the coming season. They and their mechanics soon flocked to Miller's plant and not only bought carburetors but asked him to repair and improve their engines.

Although the 25-year-old Offenhauser was a junior man in a staff of more than 60 workers, Fred proved uniquely able to take Miller's verbal suggestions and rough sketches and turn them into finished parts. Within two years[3] Miller put Offenhauser in charge of designing special tools and production fixtures. Photos at the time show Fred as a slim young man with a shock of black hair parted in the center. Before he was 30 he would fill out in the middle and thin out on top.

In 1914, racer Eddie Rickenbacker acquired a Peugeot, then one of the fastest cars in the world. Unfortunately, the French car did not hold up well. After a race late in 1914 at Corona where the transmission failed and another on January 9, 1915, at Point Loma in San Diego in which the Peugeot broke a rod on lap 23 while leading, Rickenbacker in his words "unloaded it on . . . Harry Miller."

The exterior of Miller's plant, 1914.
Mark Dees collection

"That," Rickenbacker later said, "was the major mistake of my racing career, because he made a tremendous car out of it." Miller, eager to see the world-famous Peugeot engine, had Offenhauser tear it down and search out the reasons for its fabulous power. The Peugeot was the most advanced racing engine in the world at that time, consisting of four cylinders in a separate block mounted on a barrel-type crankcase using dual overhead camshafts to drive the valves. The crankshaft bearings were held in removable bulkheads known as webs. Each cylinder had two intake and two exhaust valves in a "pent-roof" arrangement. The valve gear used L-shaped, spring-assisted lifters. The cams were driven off the crankshaft by a train of gears. In photos the engine looks much like the 270 Offy.

Earlier in 1914, Bob Burman, with the sponsorship of W. A. Thompson, of Battle Creek, Michigan, had built a pair of cars for Indianapolis he called "Centipedes," powered with the Wisconsin Company's version of the French Delage four-cylinder, 16-valve twin-cam pushrod engine. Both cars were disappointing, Burman's breaking a rod on lap 47 and the other, driven by Louis Disbrow, suffering the same fate on lap 128. Rene Thomas, in the Delage they had copied, won. Angry at the Wisconsin (or Case, as it was sometimes described) engine, Burman, like Rickenbacker, bought a 5.65-liter (344-cubic-inch) Peugeot.

Eddie Rickenbacker in his 1913 Peugeot, after he left the Maxwell team. The French car, though very fast, broke down so often Rickenbacker unloaded it on Harry Miller. *Author collection*

Burman's new Peugeot also broke a rod and the crank at the 1915 Point Loma race in San Diego and a third Peugeot, driven by a mechanic named Fred McCarthy, burned a rod bearing. By then France was involved in World War I and replacement parts were not available from the factory. Burman went to Miller for repairs and at the same time asked him to reduce the displacement to meet the new Indianapolis rules for the 1915 race which limited engines to 5.0 liters (305 cubic inches).

Late in January Miller, with the Rickenbacker Peugeot already in hand and the McCarthy Peugeot in for repairs, consulted with Offenhauser who recommended they take the Burman job at a price reported in different accounts to have been $2,000 or $4,000 (about $60,000 in 1996 dollars), a great deal of money in 1915. Burman, Miller, Offenhauser, and draftsman John Edwards worked out improvements which made the Puegeot more reliable. They replaced the iron pistons with a lighter aluminum alloy ("Alloyanum" was Miller's name for the alloy he used[4]) and installed tubular connecting rods. The Peugeot's splash lubrication was replaced by a pressure oiling system. The chassis was rebuilt with a savings of 200 pounds. A new crankshaft was made to replace the broken Peugeot piece.

Offenhauser did most of the machine work himself and the project brought Fred close enough to Miller to gain an understanding of how his mind worked and what were proper features of a successful racing engine. It was the beginning of an association that was to be vitally important to both men. For Miller's success only one more thing was needed, an engineer with the technical training both he and Fred lacked.

Burman took his new engine out to Ascot on April 4 and defeated Disbrow and Earl Cooper by more than a lap. According to contemporary reports, Bob kept the original Peugeot block and had Miller cast him a second of 293-cubic-inch displacement. He used the big 344-cubic-inch block in the match race at Ascot and in Oklahoma City where the new 5-liter (305-cubic-inch) formula was not yet in effect.

During 1915 Burman drove cars carrying seven different numbers, but whether these were different cars is unknown. He did try to qualify two Peugeots at Indianapolis. With Peugeots he won four races and placed second three times. He finished sixth at Indianapolis with his 293-cubic-inch engine in 1915 after spending time in the pits repairing a fractured copper oil line, and he won races at Narragansett Park, in Providence, Rhode Island; Burlington, Iowa; and at Oklahoma City, Oklahoma. At the end of the season he brought the engine back to Miller for new rings and bearings, then in 1916 he again raced it successfully, winning at the San Diego Exposition and taking a second at Ascot. In April Burman entered it in the Corona, California, road race. While fighting Ed O'Donnell for the lead, a tire blew. In the ensuing crash both Burman and Eric Schroeder, his riding mechanic, were killed. The car was rebuilt and apparently was raced with indifferent success by other drivers until the racing rules eliminated 5-liter engines at the end of 1919.

Barney Oldfield, driving a Delage, threw a rod in a race in the fall of 1915 and he, too, turned to Miller's shop for repairs. The Delage used

These drawings illustrate imagined race engine valve arrangements of the 1912 period. Two were spurious versions that were not corrected for half a century. At lower right is a cross-section of the French Peugeot engine, designed by *les Charlatans,* as contemporary journalists supposed it to be built. At center is one drawing of the French Delage which had semi-desmodromic valve action with a spring to help the valve close. On the left is a detail of the supposed Peugeot. At top center is a layout of the actual Peugeot top end. This drawing was made from the Grand Prix Peugeot by Jim Toensing, a volunteer curator at Briggs Cunningham's auto museum in Orange, California. Toensing persuaded Cunningham to open up the car and make an accurate drawing of the valve arrangement which had been a mystery for so many years. *Library of Congress/Jim Toensing*

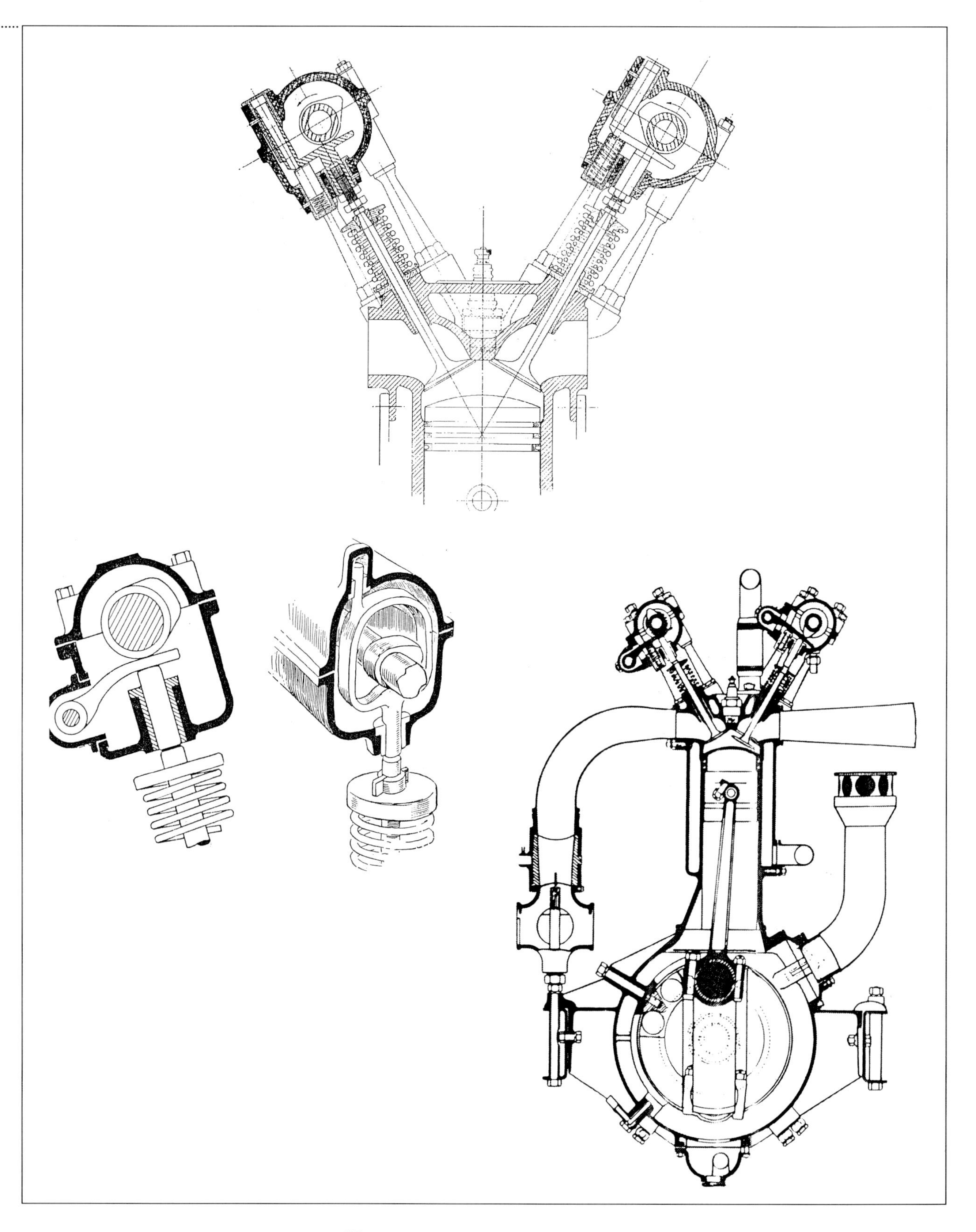

Mechanic Eddie Arnet and Fred Offenhauser sitting in Bob Burman's Peugeot equipped with the first engine built by Miller, 1915. *Gloria Madsen collection*

tubular rods, which may have been the source of Miller's inspiration for the rod design that was to mark his and Fred's engines for the next 40 years.

In 1916, after the success of the Burman engine, Miller began to make Alloyanum pistons for other Indianapolis drivers. The Peugeot factory in fact adopted them for the team cars. Miller jumped into the business of building engines. He won a contract to build the Christofferson aircraft engine, whose cylinders bore a marked resemblance to those of later Millers and Offenhausers. Fred Offenhauser was made head of Miller's engine shop with the power to hire and fire workmen, though, as Myron Stevens later wryly remarked, that authority did not extend to the body and chassis shop. With the raise that came with the promotion, he bought Ethel a new 1915 Studebaker touring car.

That same year Oldfield, the archetypical American racer, asked Miller to build the car that became known as the "Golden Submarine," an enclosed and, for its day, a fantastically advanced aerodynamic vehicle. For the Sub Miller made an entirely new single-overhead-cam engine. The use of only a single cam may have been due to considerations of weight, simplicity, and cost, or to experience with the engine he had built for the Christoffersons. Its other features resembled in large part, the Peugeot design.

The Golden Submarine may have been Oldfield's idea, or Miller's or, originally possibly even Bob Burman's. It was radical and impressive.

Barney Oldfield in the Golden Submarine in a match race against Ralph DePalma and Louis Chevrolet at Sheepshead Bay , New York, in 1917. The Sub's four-cylinder, single overhead-cam engine was the first racing powerplant Miller built to his own design. *Smithsonian Institution*

Fred and Ethel Offenhauser, left, at their first home, 2836 Boulder Street, Brooklyn Heights, in Los Angeles. *Gloria Madsen collection*

In that regard it matched the reputation of the flamboyant, cigar-chomping Oldfield, the Babe Ruth of American racing. (For those too young to remember, Oldfield set a great number of speed records. Some of them may have been a bit fraudulent, but he did legitimately turn the first 100-mile-per-hour lap at Indianapolis. So well-known were Barney's exploits that well into the 1950s it was a cliché that when stopping a driver for speeding, a policeman would often ask, "Who do you think you are, Barney Oldfield?")

By this time, Offenhauser had developed a reputation as a master machinist. He had short, stubby fingers, but that did not hinder him at work at the shop's lathes and milling machines. He had a sense of humor that rested just under the surface—some who did not know him well in later years would call him dour, but to family and colleagues he was warm and friendly. He had a high voice, and he sang tenor with some gusto.

Offenhauser was never a racer himself. When Barney tested the Golden Submarine at Ascot in 1917 he gave Fred a ride back to Miller's shop, bouncing over open fields, and Fred vowed never again to get into a race car. He did, once more, when testing Miller's TNT car at Beverly Hills in 1919, but it was his last ride. In 1946 Offenhauser said, "I once rode around the track as a mechanic and that was enough for me."

World War I Intervenes

The Miller shop was just getting into stride as a builder of racing engines and cars when United States involvement in World War I put a damper on auto racing—a sport that was already staggering. The deaths of Spencer Wishart, Harry Grant, and others had thrown a pall over racing and as a result manufacturers Maxwell, Mercer, and Mason had withdrawn from competition. Then in the early fall of 1918, a shortage of gasoline led the federal Fuel Administration to require "gasless Sundays" when only emergency vehicles could be driven. The ban severely cut into race attendance. Finally, in early October, the Fuel Administration banned auto racing entirely until the war was over (which, as it turned out, was only about a month).

When the United States declared war on Germany Miller and Offenhauser shifted to defense work full-time. In May 1918, Fred left the Boulder Street house and moved with Miller to a four-story brownstone at 109 West 64th Street in New York City (now the site of the Metropolitan Opera House). In New York, they set up a plant to manufacture carburetors, fuel pumps, and other engine accessories for the Duesenberg brothers who were building a 16-cylinder Bugatti-designed French aero engine. It was predicted to be for combat planes what the famed Liberty was to training aircraft. The Duesenberg Company, already tooling up to build Liberty engines, was diverted to the Bugatti design. An entire system of manufacturers was assigned to the project, including Miller, the American Fiat works in Schenectady, New York, Herschell-Spillman Company, of North Tonawanda, New York, and others. But as Benedict Crowell, assistant secretary of war, reported, there were numerous problems in adapting the French design to American manufacturing methods. Ultimately, the Bugatti U-16 was a dismal failure. By the time of the Armistice in November, 1918 only 11 engines had been delivered and none passed the 50-hour tests required by the Joint Army and Navy Technical Board.

Fred and Ethel Offenhauser photographed in New York City in 1918, when Offenhauser was working with Miller to make carburetors and fuel pumps for the Duesenbergs and other defense contractors. *Gloria Madsen collection*

Return to Los Angeles

The brief wartime emergency brought tragedy to the Offenhauser family as Fred's father succumbed to the 1918 influenza epidemic, and the family doubled up in the Boulder Street house while Ethel joined her husband in New York. With the Armistice, the wartime contracts were canceled, and the following February Miller and Offenhauser wound up their wartime affairs in New York, dismantled their machinery, and shipped it to Los Angeles, setting up shop again at 1630 South Los Angeles Avenue. Fred and Ethel moved into a rented home at 327B East 33rd Street.

Within another year Miller moved his operation to the plant where he would have his greatest years, a substantial brick building at 2652 Long Beach Avenue. The new plant featured brass and aluminum foundries, offices, and

The notorious failure: the Bugatti U-16 aero engine of World War I. Offenhauser and Miller set up a plant in New York City in 1918 to manufacture carburetors, fuel pumps, and other engine accessories for the war effort and particularly for the Duesenberg brothers who were attempting to build a U-form (two eight-cylinder engines geared together within a single crankcase) 16-cylinder Bugatti-designed French aero engine at the American Can Company factory in Elizabeth, New Jersey. Miller's distinctive carburetors are clearly shown on this Army photo. The War Department ordered 2,000 of the Bugatti engines, but despite the millions spent, only a handful were built and none were ever used. *War Department*

assembly areas for engines and complete racing cars. In 1922 Fred and Ethel moved again, this time to a duplex at 319 East Washington Boulevard, not far from the Miller plant. Offenhauser was a thrifty man with a dollar, and as Miller flourished, he was able to buy a comfortable home at 1159 Huntington Avenue in South Pasadena in 1925. Before the end of the 1920s, he was able to put money down on a beach-front lot on Bay Street in Hermosa Beach and build a small cottage where he and Ethel could escape the summer heat. He was also driving a new $1,495 8-90 Auburn boat-tailed Speedster, a car that Miller acquired from E.L. Cord.

On Long Beach Avenue, Miller's new building had an excellent drafting loft, and Harry and Fred were soon to meet the draftsman who would occupy that room and supply just the technical expertise they lacked: Leo Goossen.

Goosen Comes to the Table

Leo Goossen was born in Kalamazoo, Michigan, 140 miles west of Detroit, in 1892. His immigrant parents moved to Flint, 60 miles north of the Motor City in time for Leo to go to high school. When he was 16 years old the family's fortunes forced him to go to work, and he started at $4.00 a week in the blueprint room of the Buick Motor Division of the General Motors Corporation, a major employer in Flint. Goossen thought the date was around 1908.

Leo was a good student. He went to night school and studied mathematics and mechanical engineering subjects. Within months he was given a raise by Buick and made the head clerk in the file room for engineering drawings. He was an excellent draftsman and his work came to the attention of E. A. de Waters, head of Buick engineering, and Walter L. Marr, Buick's engine designer.

Marr assigned him the task of making tracings of parts for the Buick *Bug*, a semi-streamlined racing car built for the 1909 season. Eventually, Goossen related, Marr asked him to draft the layout of a 138-cubic-inch engine for a Marr cyclecar.

Marr retired from day-to-day work at Buick in 1917 but kept his hand in as a consultant from his home in Chattanooga, Tennessee. He took Goossen along to do his drafting work and as liaison with the Buick factory.

When the United States entered World War I on April 6, 1917, the enthusiasm for fighting the Hun caught up the 26-year-old Goossen and he volunteered for military service. The enlistment physical found a spot on one lung, and a more extensive examination at the Michigan State Sanatorium at Howell confirmed a diagnosis of tuberculosis. Goossen remained in the sanatorium for several months, hoping to recover well enough to serve in the military.[5] He found it very quiet. "The most exciting thing done to date," he wrote in a letter in August 1918, "is swiping apples from the farmer's orchards." He gained several pounds and seemed to be improving, but his doctor recommended Goossen move to a drier climate.[6]

Buick continued to pay his salary while he was in the sanatorium, but what he described in one letter as his "pension" came to an end when he left Michigan. Goossen arrived in Silver City, New Mexico, in the winter of 1918–1919 and although a more quiet, gentle cowboy can hardly be imagined, he took to the outdoor life with gusto.

"Am getting along very nicely out here in the West," he wrote. "Living on a ranch, a cowboy of the wildest variety, punching cattle for a livelihood and obtaining experiences I'll never forget."

His tuberculosis cleared up by summer 1919, and Goossen moved on to California. He took a student room at a Young Men's Christian Association (YMCA) in Los Angeles and looked for work. In July, he got a recommendation from the YMCA's secretary to Kimball Motor Truck Company as "an experienced draftsman." The truck company did not have a place for him, but he walked into the Miller plant just as Miller was re-establishing himself after the wartime work in the East. On the strength of a letter of recommendation from Walter Chrysler (whom Leo had met while at Buick), Miller hired him at $30 a week, a fairly handsome salary for the time.

Goossen had more technical knowledge and experience with stresses, bearings, fasteners, and the engineering details of engines and chassis than did Miller or anyone else in his plant. Miller was fond of imagining a project, giving it a general, indeed often quite brilliant, outline, then leaving it to others to execute.

It was an arrangement supremely suited to both men. In his eight years in Flint and later with Marr, Goossen had learned to turn a mentor's ideas into workable, buildable drawings. The visionary Miller, though a decent if self-taught design engineer, needed the discipline of a draftsman with the kind of experience and training Goossen had gained at Buick. He arrived at the brink of Miller's greatest successes and helped make them possible. Leo considered it an act of providence.

Goossen's original job with Miller, as he wrote to his brother, Abe, was on the chassis of the TNT racing car. The most striking feature of the TNT

Bull of the Woods

Written by an anonymous worker at the Miller shop, circa 1928 (somewhat abridged)

Ohio State University Libraries

There's a shop at East Adams and Long Beach Avenue,
where they make Miller race cars and boat engines, too.

Offenhauser is boss, he's the "Bull of the Woods,"
He's not much for looks but delivers the goods.
If his brains were as scarce as his hair seems to be,
He wouldn't last long in this factory.

There is Ray Perkins on the Browne & Sharpe Mill,
Time is one thing he surely can kill.
He makes superchargers, that's why he was hired,
If he don't get them out he's gonna get fired.

Old Eastman the preacher has the mind of a fish,
Belching religion is surely his dish.
He makes little pistons and washers and screws,
Half what he makes they're not able to use.

That's Wenger on the lathe where the cam rods pile up,
He's worked on that job since heck was a pup.
He jazzes up work in a marvelous way,
It keeps two men busy carting his scraps away.

Walter Sobraske is sheik of the works,
He always works steady, yes steady in jerks.
He will not buy tools, he borrows you see,
How he holds his job is a deep mystery.

John Anderson wrestles with a big engine block,
On the Milwaukee mill in the back of the shop.
He never spoils anything, at least that's his claim,
If something goes wrong the machine gets the blame.

Hamilton works the gear shaper there,
He is the guy with the strawberry hair.
There's a queer-looking bimbo, he's Spengler by name,
Who mills off the crankshafts, no two are the same.

There's a guy on the Lucas we all know as Mac,
The clothes that he wears fit just like a sack.
He bores out the crankcases there on his machine,
If he's made any right they've never been seen.

The next is Ott Sandau, a wobbly young cuss,
He makes all the crankshafts and argues with us.
The babbitting's done by Bolshevik Fritz,
The way that he moves, the foreman throws fits.

Out there in the foundry, half buried in sand,
Are a couple dumb clucks that ought to be canned.
They croak like two bullfrogs down in a deep well,
The short one is Harper, the tall one Coryell.
They pour in the soup, their molds fall apart,
Each blames the other for such a bum start.

Heinie works over in chassis room there,
If he had to leave, there's no one would care.
He's a sawed off short Dutchman with a gut like a tank,
Just a misfit, a bum and a sap-headed crank.

Marble-top Leonard is such a lame brain,
He lacks enough sense to get out of the rain.
He works on the grinder, and drill press and such,
He's worth all he gets if he don't get too much.

Of the engine room gang I'll speak with disgust,
Everything in there is covered with rust.
What parts they have there are all over the floor,
But nevertheless they all holler for more.
They wrangle and jangle and debate on the weather,
When they ought to be putting the engines together.

Ed Sobraske is first on the bench,
Tightening nuts with a big Stilson wrench.
He builds up the blowers with the gears in the back,
But they all fly apart when they get to the track.

Shorty Barnes is just loafing nearby,
The goof with a faraway look in his eye.
He puts in the valves and some other parts,
It's no dog-gone wonder they're all hard to start.

Oh heave a big sigh, yes shed a big tear,
For Leugers is back, our brave engineer.
He scrapes in the con rods and sets on the blocks,
Every engine he's worked on is full of loud knocks.

The drafting department sure is the bunk,
No wonder the work that we turn out is junk.
Orsatti and Goossen are both quite a wheeze,
They'd blow off their heads if they happened to sneeze.

One bird drives up in a big Auburn Eight,
He and his dog never get here 'til late
He makes a trip east in the spring of each year,
To rake up some work for the bunch of scrubs here.
He sports a small mustache that comes to a point,
It's none other than Miller, Big Boss of the joint.

The machinist who wrote this must be a queer guy,
Writing bum poetry, he's sure flying high.
The meter's all wrong, but I'm bound to admit,
That the descriptions he gives no doubt are a fit.

was the body, made of cast aluminum like the 1914 Pierce-Arrow passenger cars. The engine was designed by Miller to have been completely enclosed, forming the hood in a cast envelope, though the car as it was actually built had only a cast tail and a normal sheet-metal hood. Many of the features in the patent drawing were very advanced for its day and foreshadowed, as Borgeson points out in *Miller*, use of the engine as a stressed chassis member and the cast-aluminum wheels that Bugatti built four years later. (Miller filed a patent application for the chassis design in September 1919, only a

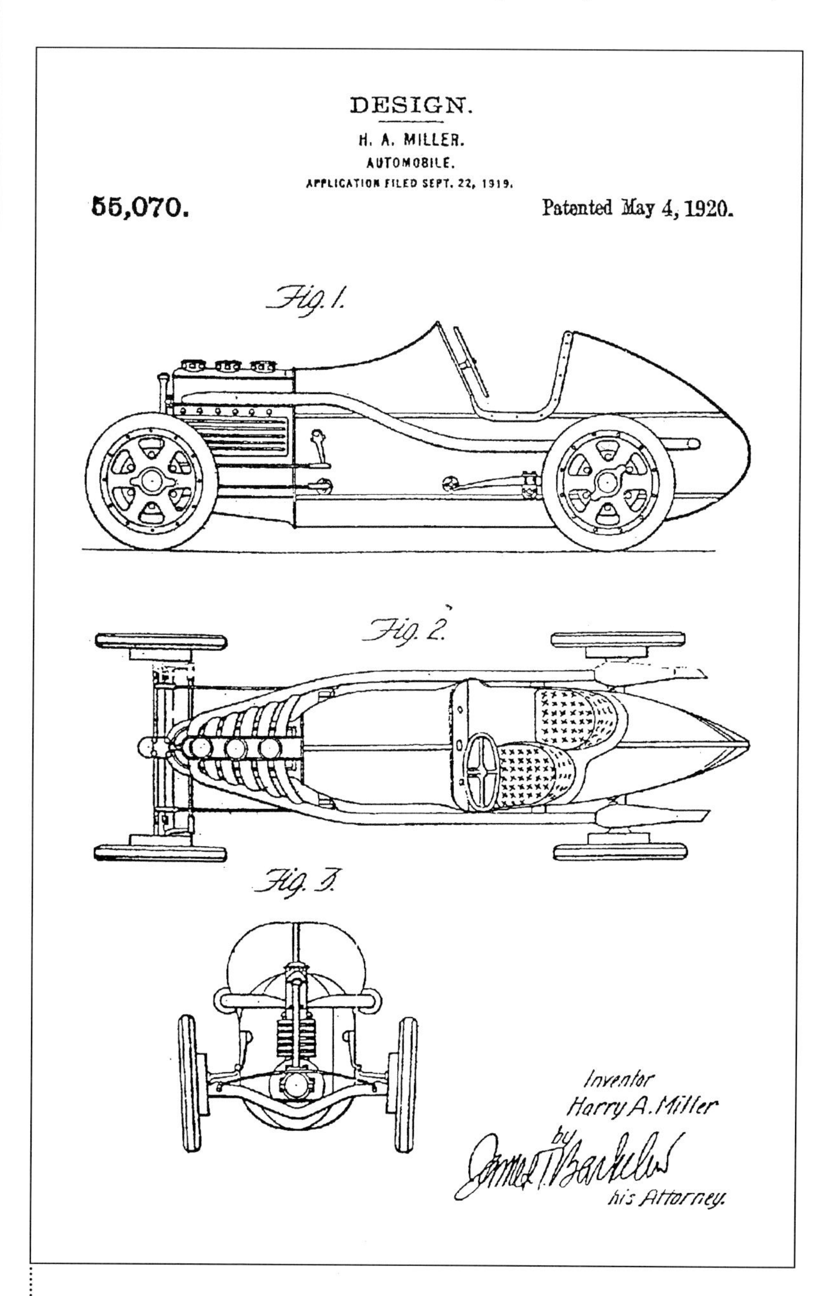

U.S. Patent # 55070 for the Miller TNT racing car which was designed to have an all cast-aluminum body. As actually built the tail and radiator shell were castings, but the engine hood was conventional sheet metal. *U.S. Patent Office*

Ralph De Palma in his Ballot at the Beverly Hills board track in 1921. While practicing for the February 28, 1920, race he blew the engine. When he asked Miller to repair it, Fred Offenhauser discovered the unique cup-type valve tappets that were quickly adopted by Miller and used thereafter on all the Miller and Offy engines. *Author collection*

month after Goossen was hired, so it is unlikely Leo did more than merely execute the drawings.)

Historian Mark Dees has recorded that in February 1920 Ralph De Palma asked Fred Offenhauser to repair his French Ballot after it broke a crank in practice at the Beverly Hills board track. Offenhauser noticed its innovative cup-type tappets—patented by French engineer Albert Morin in 1916—and immediately realized their significance. They were an elegant and important advance in the twin-cam racing engine, and in racing, patents were ignored.

The cups were important because they provided a simple, lightweight solution to the problem of transferring the rotary thrust of a cam to the up and down motion of a valve stem (without a tappet the cam would exert unacceptable side pressure on the valve stem). Ballot's original cups were flat, but Goossen, to deal with valve spring breakage, designed cups with a radiused top that mimicked a roller-type tappet. Radiused cup-type valve tappets became standard on all Miller and Offenhauser engines while the Ballot Company abandoned racing altogether. (Cup-type lifters would return to European engine designers in 1929, copied from a Miller racing car Leon Duray sold to Ettore Bugatti.)[7]

Next Goossen was handed the job of drawing up plans for a four-cylinder engine for the TNT racing car. This engine, in many ways, set the stage for the later four-cylinder Offy. The T-4 engine for the TNT was the first Miller-designed engine to move from a single overhead cam to the more efficient twin-cam configuration. It used cup-type tappets in the valve gear and the cams were chain-driven. Apparently, the T-4 engine's final design was not decided upon until late winter 1920, when the surviving Goossen drawing is dated. It

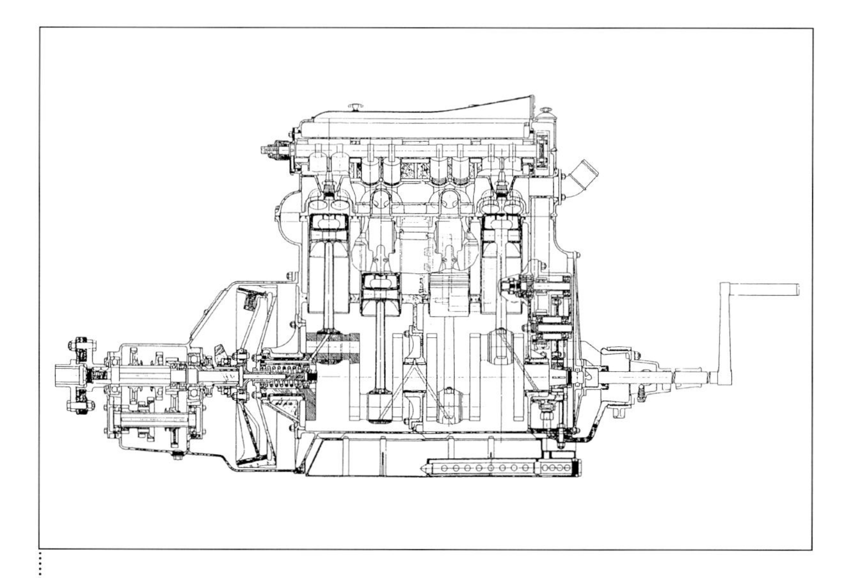

Leo Goossen's drawing of the Miller T-4 engine, 1920. The design incorporated the cup-type valve tappets that Offenhauser took from the De Palma Ballot, the barrel-type crankcase, and four valves per cylinder—all features that became part of the Miller and Offy engines built over the next 60 years. *Mark Dees collection*

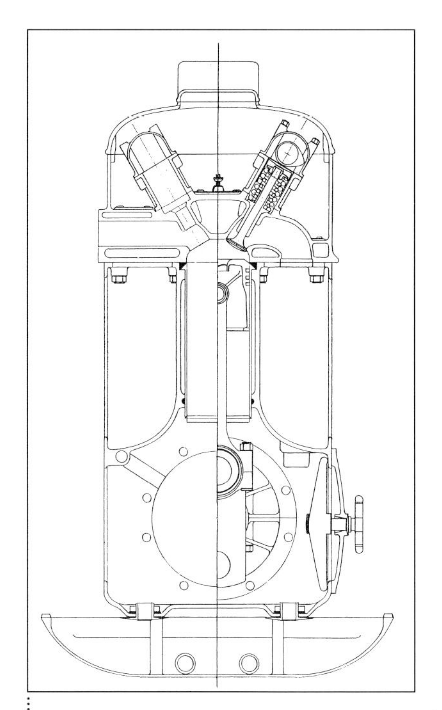

Cross-section drawing of the 1919 Miller TNT engine, which was enclosed in a cast-aluminum housing. Leo Goossen went to work for Miller after the TNT was designed, but apparently drew some of the tracings for the final product. *Kenneth Walton collection*

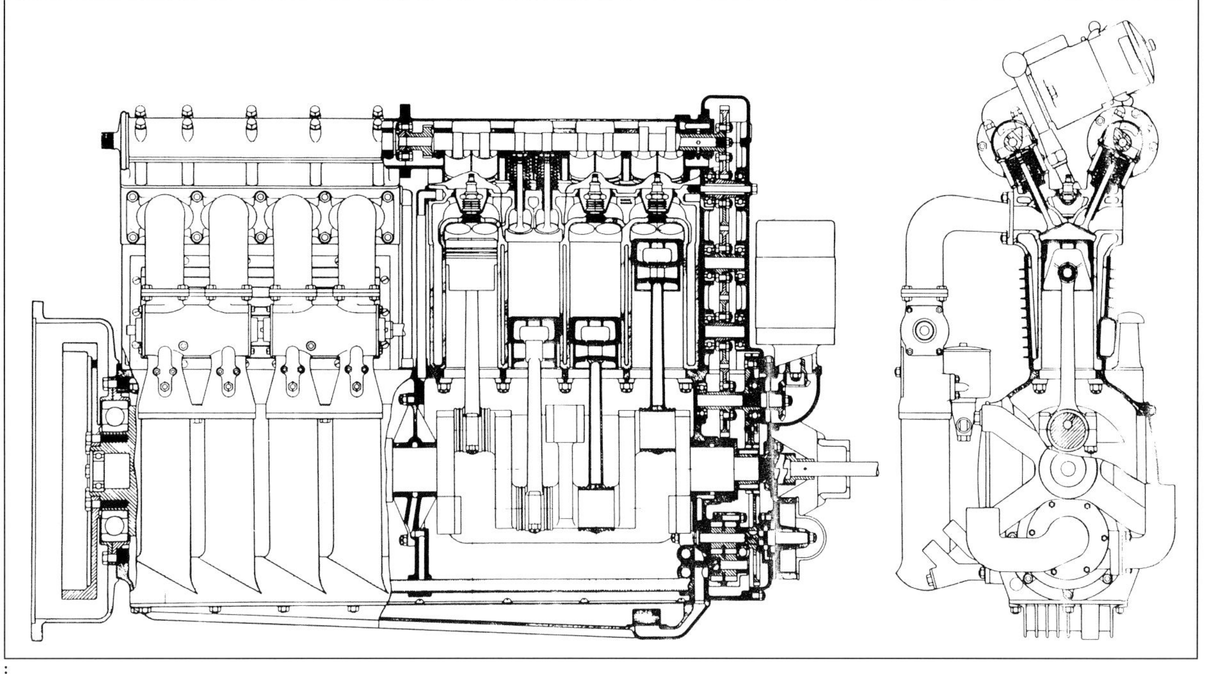

The 183-cubic-inch Miller straight-eight of 1920 was clearly of the same lineage as the 1913 Peugeot and the 1919 T-4. It seems to show Leo Goossen's touch here with cooling fins and the somewhat more elegant and compact styling that became a Miller hallmark. *Mark Dees collection*

displaced something under 180 cubic inches (accounts of it vary), and had four valves per cylinder. The TNT design was never developed, apparently because the sponsor, Eddie Maier, either lost interest or ran out of money. Two models were entered at Indianapolis in 1920, but did not arrive at the Speedway.

Miller then had Goossen design a 16-valve twin-cam head to go on the Ford Model T block. The conversion was most successfully used at Ascot in 1922 on Harry Hooker's #99 dirt-track racer. Shortly afterward Goossen, his talents and technical expertise recognized, was made head of the Miller drafting and design room.

The next step in Miller's path to greatness was the 183-cubic-inch straight-eight. Driver Tommy Milton credits Leo with the engineering skills that made that engine durable and unbeatable in the early 1920s. The 183 combined a spare elegance of form and beauty that set it aside from earlier Miller designs, and without a doubt it showed Goossen's influence. The 183 contained all of the mechanical features—twin cams, barrel crankcase, one-piece head and block—that continued to make Miller, Offenhauser, and Drake engines so successful for the next 60 years. Leo was to go on to become the only American to make his living designing racing engines or chassis for the next half-century. In Europe, only Dr. Ferdinand Porsche was in Goossen's class and in England, briefly, Reid Railton. For 30 years, Leo was the man most racing people turned to to draw up an engine or chassis and the designer who updated the Miller-Offenhauser-Drake engines until he died in 1974.

The mid-1920s were good years for Goossen. He was making his mark designing world-class racing engines and cars that won at Indianapolis and on the glamorous high-banked board tracks. By 1922 he was doing well enough with Miller that he and his first wife, Vera, were able to buy a comfortable house at 1328 Linwood Avenue, near Westlake Park. His pay from Miller in October 1923, when he was 31, was good enough that he could buy four building lots in Palos Verdes Estates. Goossen, in his usual self-effacing way did not press Miller for a raise, but Harry gave him one, to $1 an hour in 1924. By 1928, the last full year Leo worked for Miller, he was paid $3,447.08. Goossen, who was willing to work for such wages, was stoically philosophical, an attitude he expressed upon hearing of his brother Lester's death by drowning. "Life is uncertain and death always near. . . . One feels so helpless." In such fashion throughout his life Goossen would allow his talent to be exploited by Harry Miller and a succession of would-be engine designers of which only Offenhauser and Meyer & Drake would be successful.

Leo Goossen at the home on Linwood Terrace that he bought while working for Harry Miller. Leo and Vera lost this house in 1933 when Harry A. Miller Inc. went bankrupt. *Mark Dees collection*

Golden Submarine just after completion, ready for its golden paint job. Note the sign on the house in the background: "Gilding." *Author collection*

Walter Sobraske

Walter Sobraske was a machinist in the Miller plant, one of the group of about 20 remarkable workmen who turned Miller's ideas and Goossen's drawings into masterpieces.

Sobraske was born in West Virginia January 2, 1901, and as a young man apprenticed in the Baltimore and Ohio Railroad shops. When he moved west in 1921 he found work in the machine shop of the Los Angeles Shipyard. He was living at the time at 203 West 42nd Street, and it was a long ride on the Red Cars down to San Pedro. The shipyard's straw boss wasn't to Sobraske's liking. When the foreman insisted that Sobraske hurry up machining some hardened boiler studs that hadn't been annealed, Sobraske quit.

Looking for work closer to home, he found the Miller plant on 17th and Los Angeles Streets. Offenhauser told Sobraske they weren't hiring, but as Walter started to leave, Fred asked him where he had been working. Told that he had gotten most of his experience in the railroad shops, Fred said to him, "Come back on Monday. I think we can use you."[8]

Walt Sobraske at work machining a crankshaft on the big Kempsmith mill in Miller's shop. Sobraske went to work for Miller in 1921 and subsequently worked for Schofield, Harry A. Miller Inc., and Offenhauser, becoming shop foreman for Meyer & Drake in the 1960s. *Gloria Madsen collection*

Miller: Dominant . . . but Boring

By 1929, Miller had become so successful with his high-priced racing machinery (a rear-drive 91 went for $10,000, a front-drive for $15,000 in a day when a Ford automobile sold for less than $500) that the Detroit auto manufacturers seemed unlikely to return to competition. Rickenbacker, by then President of the Indianapolis Motor Speedway Corporation and a power in the American Automobile Association whose Contest Board controlled the top rungs of American racing, decided to change things. Early in 1929, five months before the Wall Street crash that ushered in the Great Depression, the AAA decreed that in 1930, racing engines could no longer be supercharged and that "stock" or semistock passenger car engines of 366-cubic-inch piston displacement would be allowed to compete, an effort in part to entice the major motor manufacturers back into racing.

A change in formulas can be good for an engine builder, since it outmodes older engines and requires new ones, but Miller had his eye on ever more-exotic and costly machinery. When it appeared early in 1929 that such engines were going to be outlawed by the AAA and replaced by what was truly a "junk" formula, Miller sold his business to a group of investors headed by George Schofield. A Miller won at Indianapolis in 1929, and there was a 27-car Miller phalanx arrayed in the starting field, but no longer would Miller himself dominate the Speedway. Harry Hartz' one-off 182 did win at Indy in 1932, but never again would Miller's own products dominate the entry lists at the 500.

To Eddie Rickenbacker the changes of 1930 brought "remarkable . . . results" and a "more successful and interesting event."[9] To Harry Miller they were a disaster. Overnight, his beautiful and sophisticated supercharged engines were made obsolete, not by technology, but by racing's rulesmakers. In 1931, as Schofield sank into bankruptcy, Miller returned to building racing engines of ever more exotic designs, but in the depths of the Depression there was not enough money in racing to support those ideas.

Goossen in Miller's drafting room in the Long Beach Avenue shop. *Bruce Craig collection*

Shorty Cantlon and Lou Miller, his riding mechanic, in Bill White's Schofield-built car that finished second at Indianapolis in 1930. It was equipped with a 183-cubic-inch Miller-Schofield four-cylinder engine, one of five in the race. It was the first four to finish in the top 10 since 1923, and its success paved the way for the Offy. Fours, which were cheaper, simpler, and had greater torque than the eights, were better adapted to racing on relatively flat tracks like Indianapolis and the dirt tracks of the 1930s. Fours based on the same design would compete at the Speedway for the next 53 years.
Indianapolis Motor Speedway

CHAPTER TWO

MILLER BANKRUPTCY

HARRY MILLER'S HIGHLY REFINED SUPERCHARGED ENGINES AND FINELY finished racing cars made up what was then an astounding 83 percent of the fields at Indianapolis between 1922 and 1928 with Miller cars winning the 500 in 1923, 1926, 1928, and 1929. The racing world eagerly awaited the arrival each year of Father Miller's latest creation. The winning Duesenbergs in 1924, 1925, and 1927 were also costly, high-technology racing cars, but after 1927 the Duesenberg brothers were on the ropes. Their cars continued to compete but would not win another 500. On the board tracks the Millers were even more dominant than at Indianapolis, winning with repetitive regularity.

Success spoiled Harry Miller's business. The Miller monopoly was becoming an expensive bore to fans and officials alike. As early as 1928 members of the racing press were agitating to break Miller's stranglehold, much as people chanted "break up the Yankees" when the New Yorkers dominated baseball. The argument went that racing should attract back into the sport the major auto manufacturers who had retired from direct participation by 1913 when the "specials" began to outclass the factory cars on the track. There was also strong feeling that racing had become too expensive, a cry that has been heard again and again over the years.

The rulers of auto racing were also concerned about the "excessive" speeds at Indianapolis and on the boards. The top qualification speed at Indy was 88 miles per hour in 1914. Engine sizes were cut from 5.5 to 5.0 liters and the pole speed climbed to 98 miles per hour. For 1920 the engines size was again reduced, this time to 3.0 liters (183 cubic inches), but the pole speed crept up to 99 miles per hour. In 1922 Jimmy Murphy took the pole at 100 miles per hour and engines were reduced to 2.0 liters (122.047 cubic inches). By 1925 the top speed at Indy was 113 miles per hour and engines were cut yet again, to 1.5 liters (91.5 cubic inches). The result, in 1928, was a record speed of 122.903 by Leon Duray in his long, low black supercharged Miller front-drive.

Secure in his success, Harry Miller had a comfortable home in Los Angeles where he lived the life of a well-known, if mildly eccentric, motor tycoon. In 1923 he built a ranch in the Santa Monica Mountains where he kept so many animals it was licensed as a zoo. A natty dresser with a small waxed mustache, he rubbed elbows with the stars of nearby Hollywood and kept a girlfriend on the side for a time.

Miller was typical of the Roaring Twenties, when the nation was at a peak of celebrity-worship. Athletics had blossomed as never before. Knute Rockne's Notre Dame team in football, the Yankees in baseball, Susanne Lenglen and Big Bill Tilden in tennis, Bobby Jones in golf, De Palma, Milton, Lockhart in racing—all had become superstars in a golden new era of sports heros. Little did any of them know the precipice upon which they stood. It had been "a binge of distraction, self-involvement, heedlessness,

INDIANAPOLIS MOTOR SPEEDWAY CORPORATION

MAINTAINING THE GREATEST RACE COURSE IN THE WORLD

INDIANAPOLIS, INDIANA

April 20, 1933

Lt. Commander H. S. Kendall
Navy Building
Washington, D. C.

My dear Commander:

May I remind you that you are expected as my guest during the annual Five Hundred Mile race on May 30 with headquarters on the fourth floor of the Judges' Stand. The necessary credentials are in the hands of Mr. T. E. Myers at Indianapolis awaiting your advice.

The remarkable results and tremendous increase in speeds which were evidenced by the breaking of the international record last year by almost four miles per hour is indicative of what we may expect in the way of additional speed and performance this year.

Further changes in the rules and specifications have been made for this year's event, the outstanding one being the limiting of the gas tank capacity to a maximum of fifteen gallons per car, and the maximum oil capacity to six gallons per car.

This will require at least three stops for fuel at the pits during the Five Hundred Mile race which will mean constant changing of positions and great pit activity, and further will force engineers to develop motors and carburetion systems with maximum efficiency.

There will be all types, sizes and shapes of cars participating in this event, plus the fact that for the first time in many years several of the large manufacturers have decided to enter teams of cars under their own name and with their whole-hearted support.

Will you please advise Mr. Myers if possible for you to attend and whether any further accommodations can be arranged.

Sincerely,

Eddie Rickenbacker

President.

Letter, 1933, from Eddie Rickenbacker, president of the Indianapolis Motor Speedway to an aide to the Marine Corps Commandant inviting him to the 1933 500 and commenting on the apparent success of the new rules. While the junk formula made the racing more interesting—absolute speed was slower than in the late 1920s but the variety of machinery was greater—it posed problems for Miller that he was unable to overcome. *Smithsonian Institution*

Workmen at the Miller plant, about 1925. The forest of overhead shafts and belt-drives to the machines was a relic of the days when machine shops were powered by waterwheels or stationary gas or steam engines. The big Monarch crankshaft lathe in the foreground had been converted to an electric motor drive. The tired machinery was thoroughly obsolete, and four years later Miller unloaded it upon the Schofield Corporation. *Gordon Schroeder collection*

even hedonism."[10] Harry A. Miller was wealthy and popular among Hollywood society leaders. He seemingly had everything a man could want, but as for many on Wall Street and Main Street, a sudden wind was to blow it all away.

From that pinnacle Miller began a slide into disaster. What happened to change success into ultimate failure? The answer reveals as much about Harry Miller's character as about the times in which he lived. So successful were his beautiful 91s that he thought he could afford to branch out and indulge other motor fantasies. In pursuing those dreams he seemed inattentive, even cavalier, about bringing in the cash the business needed. In quick succession he suggested Goossen design and Offenhauser and the shop crew build, 8-, 4-, 12-, 16-, even 24-cylinder speedboat engines; an outboard motor; a flat-eight aircraft engine; and a V-8 and a V-16 front-drive passenger car. He promised a few customers even more exotic machinery. Later, Fred's niece Gloria Tinley said, there was a small airplane in the Gramercy Place shop, being fitted with a Miller 91 engine. This was probably the *Buchanan Zipper*, which was entered in the National Air Races in Los Angeles during the 1936 Olympics but which, according to Mark Dees, never got off the ground.

Miller grew ever more careless about the business. Once they were under construction, the successful cars and boats appeared to bore him. Even before the rules were changed to make his supercharged engines obsolete,

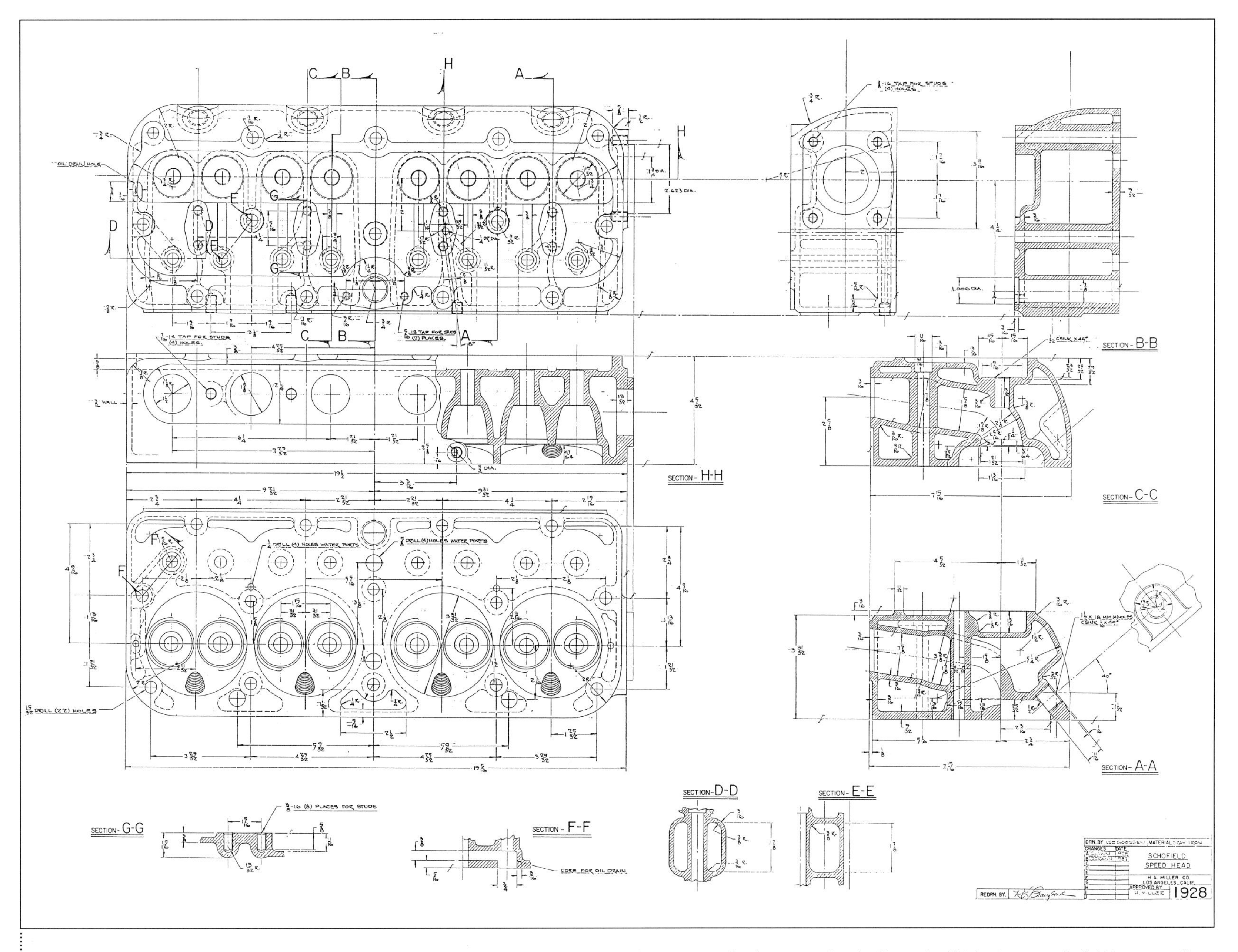

Leo Goossen's drawing for the aftermarket head for the then-new Ford Model A. If the 1928 date is correct, the drawing predated Miller's sale of his business to Schofield in 1929. Miller had earlier produced a DOHC head for the Hooker # 99, a Ford Model T, and he had Walter Steele draw up an F-head which he peddled to the Vosburg Brothers in 1931. Most of the Miller Model A heads were built by Schofield. After Miller-Schofield collapsed, Craney Gartz bought the residue and sold the heads as Cragars. In addition there were F-head and twin-cam Cragars, most of which were produced in later years by George Wight's Bell Auto Parts after Cragar itself went out of business. *Kenneth Walton collection*

Miller had begun to stray. Spoiled by the ability of Goossen and Offenhauser to turn his designs into metal, Harry left more and more decisions up to the shop staff. He maintained his fanatic attention to fit and polish, but his balance sheet was deteriorating.

More and more Miller would say to Goossen and Offenhauser, "There, that's about what I want. Now you make it work," and head off to his ranch, in search of another "deal" or a special new kind of car. Other days he would visit the apartment where he kept his mistress.

Goossen said years later that when, in the summer of 1925, Miller had laid out the basic dimensions of the awesome Miller 91 engine "he left it up to me to decide the size of the crankshaft, the mains, the length of the rods, the bore and stroke, and other things"—bearing dimensions, oil pump capacity, cooling passages, and the like. "I figured the velocity [of the intake mixture and the exhaust] going through the valves to determine their size. And of course I drew up the front drive transmission layout. Miller looked at the drawings but he left it largely up to me."[11]

Leo's drawings for the 91 went straight to the pattern makers and the machine shop where a group of six engines were made. In a 1974 interview Goossen said, "No one else looked the drawings over." Most Goossen drawings that survive have no entry in the "checked by" block.

That 1926 91.5-cubic-inch engine was the pinnacle of Miller's greatness. Goossen said it produced an amazing 154 horsepower on a gasoline-benzine fuel mix, nearly 1.7 horsepower per cubic inch. Fortunately for Miller and his customers Leo Goossen was a brilliant engineer and an accurate draftsman. Unfortunately for Miller and his business, racing officials and writers were ever more bored with parades of Miller racing cars.

The ax fell in 1929. The AAA ruled the finely constructed, aerodynamic, one-man Miller chassis off the tracks. When the change came it was the end of two decades of triumph for Harry Miller. At first he took the junk formula as a signal that it was time to retire. He was only 54, but he had been hard at work for nearly 40 years and the world was changing. He was quoted as being uninterested in building cars for the new formula of unsupercharged engines with minimum weight rules. Miller thought it was time to get out if he could sell his about-to-be-obsolete 91-cubic-inch racing business to somebody for a good price. At the time he was paying himself a salary of $7,500.00 a year and had begun receiving $1,000 a month in royalties from Errett Lobban Cord of the Auburn Automobile Company for the right to use the Goossen-designed front-wheel drive transmission for the L29 Cord.[12] Miller's company, according to tax records, had a nice operating profit of $39,469.37, (not including his salary) in its last full year of operation.

Schofield Inc. was set up to build aircraft, boats, and cars. Its organizers were well-known investors, but they were not technically sophisticated. They expected to get Miller, the brilliant automotive engineer, to handle that side of the business.

Miller Hi-Speed "single-stick" overhead valve conversion for the four-cylinder Model A Ford. An F-head design, this was not successful because the intake passages in the Ford block were not designed to be used for exhaust and, having too little cooling water around them, tended to crack. Miller also peddled the Hi-Speed head to the Vosburg Brothers. *Bruce Craig collection*

On February 7, 1929, Miller signed a contract to sell the plant on Long Beach Avenue and its contents to the Schofield Corporation. Schofield formed a subsidiary known as "Miller Production Corporation Limited." The new company, styling itself "Miller-Schofield," got the machinery, drawings, patterns, Goossen's design for an aftermarket "Hi-Speed" overhead-valve setup for the Model A Ford, the other physical assets of the Miller plant, and the considerable human assets of Goossen and most of the Miller staff. Goossen got a raise in salary to $100 a week, "pretty good pay for the time," he said half a century later.

Offenhauser did not go to Schofield. As the money grew tighter he and Ethel put their place in South Pasadena up for rent and moved for a time into a little house over a three-car garage on Bay Street in Hermosa Beach where he and Goossen worked to finish an ill-fated $30,000, Miller-designed, front-drive, supercharged sports car for Phillip Chancellor. Then, Offenhauser said later, he took a vacation. Eventually he set up a little shop of his own on West 62nd Street.

Miller received $122,000 in cash from Schofield (he contracted to receive $130,000, but a customer refund for a never-completed, horizontally opposed aircraft engine may account for the difference). He was also to have been paid $1,500 a month, a percentage of Schofield's profits, and a block of stock with a face value of $400,000. He agreed not to compete with Schofield under the Miller name as long as he received his salary and royalties. The contract he signed provided that he was to continue to operate the plant in Los Angeles and to work full time for the new company for at least five years.

So much for contracts. Once it was signed Miller collected his cash and departed. He took off for the East on an extended vacation and did little or nothing to earn his Schofield salary. Just over a month later, on March 5, more than 300 new cars, including a new Miller completed in the Schofield plant, were destroyed when fire whipped through the tent roof of the annual Los Angeles Auto Show. It was a portent of things to come. Goossen and most of the ex-Miller employees were turning out Miller products such as the 151 Marine engine, spare racing parts, and a few four-cylinder engines for the dirt tracks and Indianapolis. Schofield also sold a number of Goossen-designed aftermarket heads for Ford Model As and at least two complete cars for Indianapolis.

Miller's old staff contrived to produce most of the salable Miller-Schofield hardware in 1929 and 1930, but without Harry there to conjure up new racing engines there was not enough business to keep the company afloat. Schofield had a large tri-motor aircraft and other expensive hardware, but its seeming affluence was a facade. When the stock market crashed in October 1929, Schofield, like a good many thinly capitalized companies, was exposed as a house of cards.

Meanwhile in March 1930, 10 months before Schofield went under, Miller took $79,000 of his money from the Schofield deal and went back into the engine business. He first set up shop at 1348 Venice Boulevard (using Walter Steele as his draftsman since Goossen was then still laboring at Schofield). He used the name RELLIMAH briefly before Schofield's collapse made a legal disguise unnecessary. Offenhauser went back to work for Miller. Since the South Pasadena house was under lease Fred and Ethel moved into temporary quarters in a duplex a block away from the plant.

At Schofield three factors conspired to do the company in: first, it was conceived at a time when everything seemed possible. For example, they

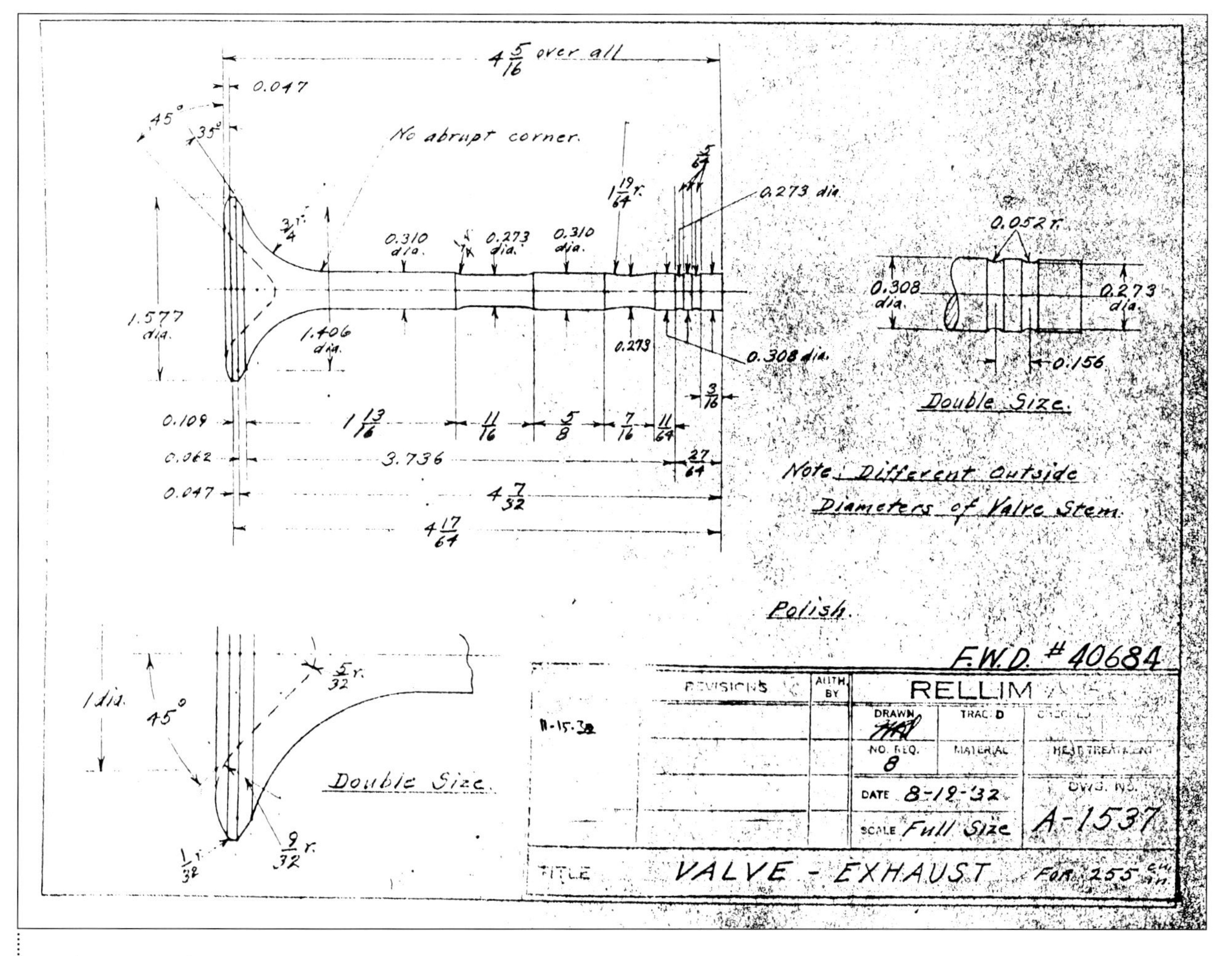

Exhaust valve for 255 drawn by Goossen on RELLIMAH tracing cloth. *Buck Boudeman collection*

Maude Yagle's Miller driven by Frank Farmer. With a 91-cubic-inch engine bored out to 101 inches, it was hopelessly outclassed at Indy in 1930 and finished 21st. It did not qualify in 1931. Dickie Smith was chief wrench for the car. It is seen here at Woodbridge, New Jersey, later that year. Larry Beals later drove the car and Farmer was killed in it at Woodbridge on August 28, 1932. *Dixon Singiser collection*

bought the big—and aptly named—Albatross plane to develop and promote the sale of aircraft equipment, which apparently was never accomplished. Second, the changed formula in racing meant there would be no more sales of existing Miller 91.5-cubic-inch eight-cylinder engines, and third, the stock market crash of October 1929 ended the possibility of raising new capital. Within another year Schofield was finished.

The final stroke in the disaster was the revelation that Schofield Director Gilbert Beesemyer had stolen millions from Guarantee Savings & Loan Association of Hollywood, of which he was president. Beesemyer had put almost $30,000—possibly fleeced from Guarantee Savings' depositors—into Miller-Schofield, but he would finance the company no longer. Before the end of 1930, he was a resident of San Quentin Prison. Schofield filed a petition for voluntary bankruptcy on December 29, 1930 and the Miller Production Company Limited, which held the assets of Schofield, filed for bankruptcy the same day.

The bankruptcy trustee, V. W. Erickson, attempted to keep the plant running in order to get what income he could out of work-in-progress. Several racing people pleaded with him to finish engines on which they had made deposits. Speed Gardner had paid $1,200.00 to have blocks and pistons made to repair the engine of his Miller 91 (converted to 151 cubic inches) for the 1931 Indianapolis race and begged successfully for the unmachined castings and Goossen's drawings so he could have them completed elsewhere. Ira Vail claimed three boxes containing disassembled Miller engines.

The list of claims by employees of Schofield does not include Goossen, or Walt Sobraske. They and some of the other ex-Miller men had bailed out before the end, a few, in desperation, to go back to Miller. Goossen did freelance drafting and followed Miller around on his excursions to the East. Draftsman Everett Stevenson and machinists John Anderson, Herman Kuhn, Otto Sandau, and Herman Vogel stayed until the end. When the Schofield bankruptcy proceedings were wound up they received the back pay they were owed. They would not fare so well when Miller himself went bankrupt, two and a half years later.

There were half a dozen well-known racing people who owed Schofield money at the end, including Peter De Paolo: $638.57, Ralph De Palma: $6.00, Dick Loynes: $417.51, Art Sparks: $30.00, Bill White: $40.55, and Paul Whittier: $450.78.

The Schofield collapse was unpleasant but not disastrous for Miller. The shop equipment he had sold was old and obsolete, driven mostly by a forest of belts from overhead shafts, many of the lathes and milling machines left over from the days before individual electrically motor-driven machinery; indeed, he probably got more for it than it was worth.

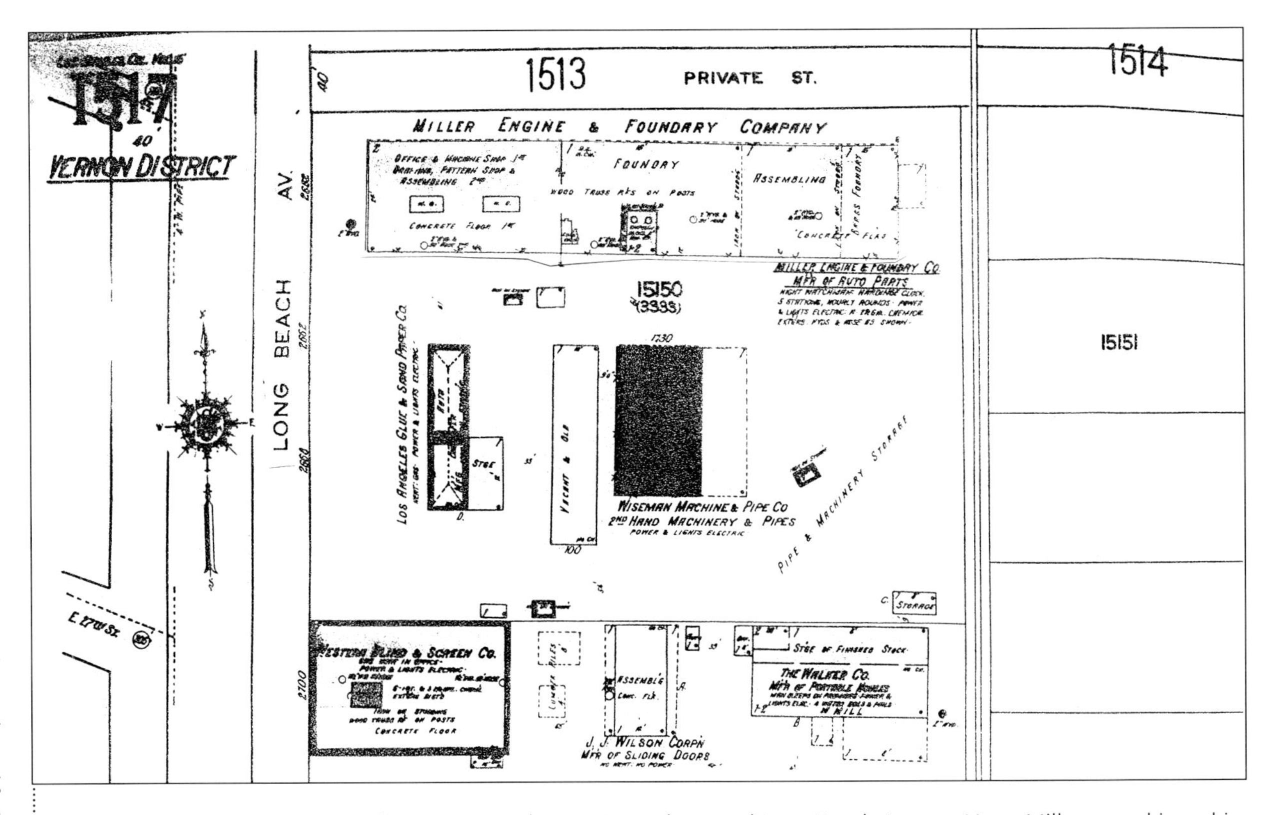

Plat of the Miller Engine & Foundry Company. plant at East Adams and Long Beach Avenue. Harry Miller moved into this building in 1920 and sold it to Schofield in 1929. This shop was witness to the glory days of the 122 and the 91. It had machine and pattern shops, aluminum and brass foundries, a chassis and body area, Miller's office, and the drafting loft where Leo Goossen worked. *Library of Congress*

Interestingly, papers from the debacle[13] suggest that Beesemyer did not plunder Schofield. In fact, he was listed as a creditor who lost $27,890.00. The trustee, who appears to have been assiduous in eliminating questionable claims including more than $80,000 by Harry Miller, accepted the Beesemyer figure. When creditors were paid about 15 cents on the dollar Beesemyer was sent a check for $4,183.50, care of San Quentin. Miller's claims were trimmed to $24,269.45 for which he received $3,640.42.

Miller sought to wring one more payoff out of the debacle. By early 1931, there was no more hope of money from Schofield. In need of cash, he peddled the design for the "Hi-Speed" F-head for the Model A Ford to a group of investors known as the Vosburg Brothers, who planned to produce 750 of the heads a month. On April 16, 1931, Miller and Vosburg signed a contract for the drawings and patterns, the exclusive use of Miller's name, and a commitment by the Miller shop to make carburetors and manifolds. He took $1,500 in up-front money, but neither the carburetors nor the manifolds were delivered, nor did Miller do much more on the deal. In fact, he left shortly for another trip, first to Indianapolis, then on to Detroit.

The Vosburgs soon discovered that Cragar had bought the same F-head design with Miller's name on it at the Schofield bankruptcy sale. They filed suit in Los Angeles Superior Court on December 10, 1931, asking $11,185 for what they paid Miller, the cost of patterns and fixtures, and their other start-up costs. They later added $50,000 in claims for lost profits, but by that time the Depression had well and truly hit and no one would have been likely to sell 9,000 special Ford heads a year anyway. The Vosburg demand, which totaled $61,185.00, was the largest claim in the bankruptcy of Harry A. Miller Inc. 18 months later.

By mid-1931 Miller had moved his operations from Venice Boulevard to a larger building at 6233 South Gramercy Place. Some of the workers drifted away, but most were rehired by Miller. Walt Sobraske was typical. He left Schofield and went to work in May 1931, for a company making matchbook machinery. He worked there for two months before Offenhauser called him back to Harry A. Miller Inc. to work on a V-16 speedboat engine.

Between 1931 and 1933 Miller conceived exotic designs for boats and cars. At the insistence of Fred Offenhauser, Miller allowed Goossen to draw blueprints for a mundane four-cylinder, 255-cubic-inch racing engine to take the place of the 220. The racers had been asking for larger blocks for the 220, an arrangement that Miller thought was not going to be reliable. Tough, powerful, and affordable, the 255 was to be the key to the Offenhauser story at Indianapolis but the engine did not much interest Harry, who was mesmerized by the race track success of his highly-strung supercharged, front-drive designs.

For much of 1931, Miller was away from home, chasing elusive deals that might put Harry A. Miller, Inc. into the black again. There was considerable resentment among the workers at the plant on Gramercy Place as it became apparent that Miller was not bringing in enough paying business to keep the plant going. A skeptical Fred Offenhauser, already operating his own shop at 1935 62nd Street, was taking liens on certain machinery in lieu of salary. Miller did not have enough money to hire Goossen full time, so Leo worked for him

The key members of Harry Miller's staff at the Gramercy Place plant in 1932. Left to right are Miller, Business Manager Bill Jenkins, Fred Offenhauser, Draftsman Walter Steele, Leo Goossen, Assistant Draftsman R. E. Stevenson, Ted Miller, and Office Secretary Ted A. Heinhold. Jenkins departed within a year, leaving the thankless task of managing Miller's affairs to Heinhold. *Bruce Craig collection*

Cam diagram, with typically conservative Miller timing. This particular drawing is for the 308-cubic-inch V-8 for the four-wheel-drive Indianapolis car, a costly exercise at a time when his creditors were already complaining about Miller's late, or nonexistent, payments. A two-valve-per-cylinder design, it was Miller's first racing V-8. Author Mark Dees collection says these cars "cinched his bankruptcy." *Robert Binyon collection*

as a consultant. Indeed, in 1931 few of the regular employees were being paid.

With the onset of the Depression, racing sponsorship money had dried up. Purses at Indianapolis were reduced. The smooth, high-banked board tracks for which the fine Miller 122 and 91.5-cubic-inch eights were supremely suited had all but disappeared, replaced by flat dirt tracks where the hard accelerating fours fared better. By 1931 they were all gone except for Altoona—Akron, Bridgeville, and Woodbridge victims of weather, fire, and the end of the easy money that had financed such marvelous white elephants. What championship racing there was aside from Indianapolis was done at Altoona and on the dirt tracks at Syracuse and Detroit. Still, Miller went to Indianapolis in May of that year. There he met Gar Wood, the speedboat racer, who was desperately seeking engines powerful enough to hold off a challenge from the British, who had new Rolls-Royce Schneider Cup aero engines in their hydroplane hulls. In only two months' time Leo and Fred designed and built a 1,113-cubic-inch V-16, using some parts designs from the 310 Marine engines. The engine was supercharged with Roots blowers hastily bought from the Louis Schwitzer Company in Indianapolis. (Roots superchargers were originally conceived by Philander H. and Francis M. Roots of Connersville, Indiana.) Later, Wood used the V-16 for a 117-mile-per-hour record run in Michigan.

After Indianapolis, Harry Miller and Harry Hartz took a nostalgic trip through Wisconsin in Miller's L-29 Cord and stopped at the FWD Company in Clintonville. Harry had the germ of an idea, of course, and he broached it to Walter Olen, president of FWD. In a follow-up letter of July 3, 1931, Miller proposed building two four-wheel-drive racing cars that would be ideal promotional tools for the FWD company. Miller so badly wanted to build the cars that he offered them to the company at the impossibly low price of $15,000 for a V-8 engine model or $10,000 for one equipped with a four. (Two Four Wheel Drive cars were eventually sponsored by the FWD corporation in 1932. Mauri Rose used one of them to win the 1936 AAA Championship. The car ran at Indianapolis as late as 1938. After World War II it was driven by Bill Milliken in hill climbs.)

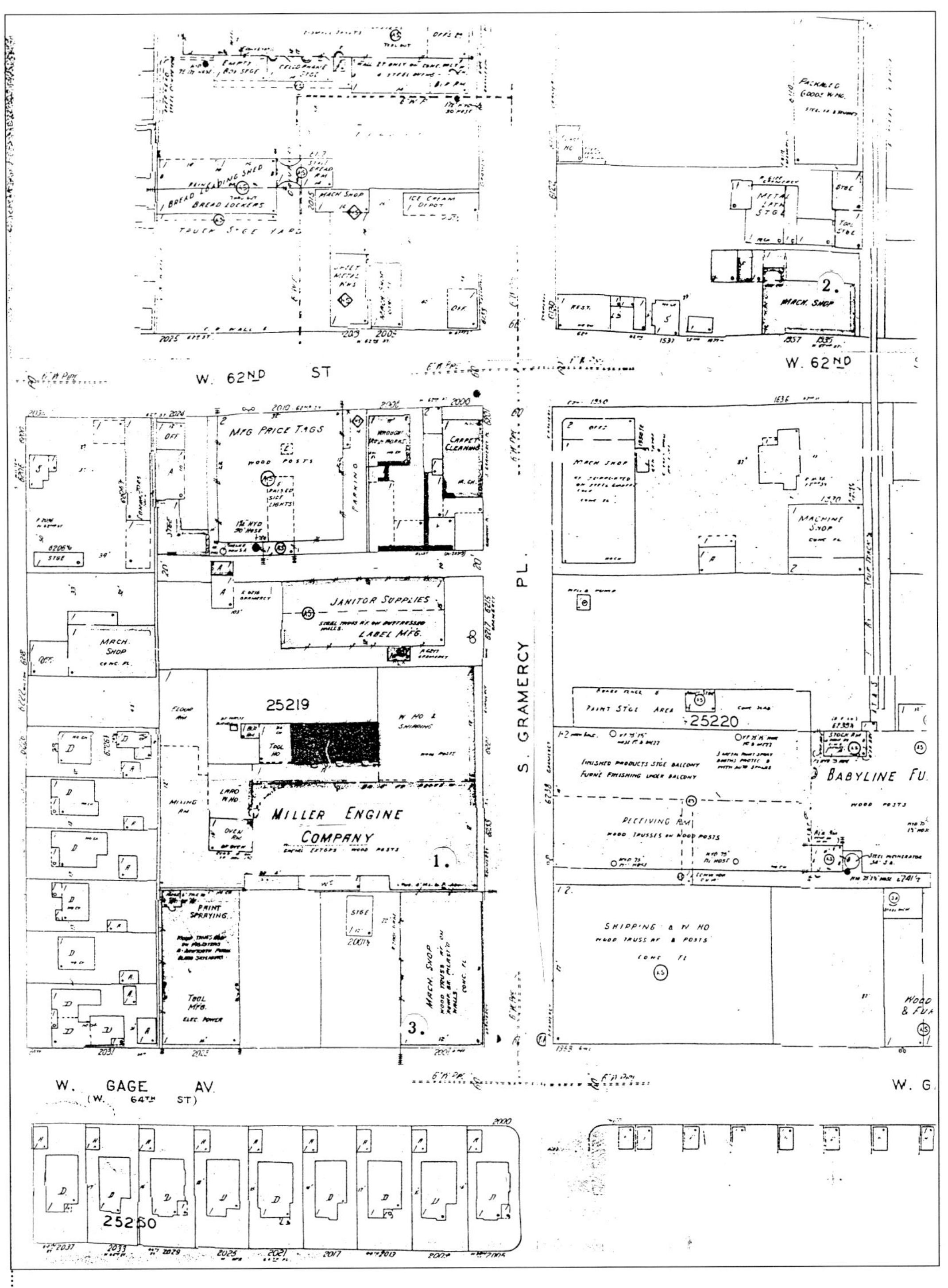

Plat of the Gramercy Street plant (1) where Miller moved in 1931 from temporary quarters on Venice Boulevard. A former laundry, it had no foundry for aluminum and brass casting work, an omission that contributed to the downfall of Harry A. Miller Inc. two years later. Meanwhile, Fred Offenhauser set up his own little shop (2) at 1935 West 62nd Street, a block away. In 1941 when he needed to expand for defense work, Offenhauser put up a building (3) on the corner of West Gage and Gramercy, next door to the old Miller plant which by then had been converted to a bakery. *Library of Congress*

In August Miller departed for the Harmsworth Trophy hydroplane races in Detroit, to be joined later by Goossen to help him attempt to sort out the V-16 engine. Goossen's daily letters home tell of following Miller around the northeast United States, living in YMCAs and eating for 50 cents a day while Miller hobnobbed with the wealthy in search of sponsors for his ideas.

The only real success for the new Miller shop came in 1932 when, working with money from ex-driver Harry Hartz, Goossen and Offenhauser managed in about a six-week span to build a 181.8-inch straight-eight (known as the "183") to Hartz' specifications. Fred Frame drove it to victory, the last Indianapolis-winning car to come out of Miller's shop, but after that Miller's business unraveled. He contracted to make exotic road cars for two wealthy eastern businessmen, Victor Emmanuel and William Burden, and poured money into the four-wheel-drive Indianapolis machines, one of which he said he planned to race in South America. The last L-29 Cord had been built and the Auburn Company was no longer paying Miller front-drive royalties. Mark Dees suggests that the four-wheel drive designs were the last nail in Miller's financial coffin. He had bounced from impossible deal to impossible deal without bringing in the cash needed to keep his shop afloat. By October, only a little over a year after he had set up shop again, Miller filed his first financial reorganization. The next month his creditors established a committee to watch over their interests, which seemed best-served by allowing Miller to try to recoup by completing his several automotive projects. The committee, overseen by the Board of Trade, continued for eight months to hope that with extensions of time to meet his obligations Miller might recover, but it was not to be. His ever more-exotic, unrealized developments eventually exhausted his funds and his creditors' patience.

Thus, on July 8, 1933, Wismar Brothers Pattern Works, Goerz Pattern Shop, and the Pacific Casting Company filed a petition of involuntary bankruptcy against Harry A. Miller Inc. Miller owed them a total of $3,142.98, and they had discovered that he was allowing Offenhauser to take away equipment in lieu of salary to the detriment, they said, of other creditors. They alleged that Miller gave Offenhauser three pieces of machinery and that Offenhauser had moved the equipment to his own shop.

That was the end for Harry A. Miller Inc. The federal bankruptcy court moved swiftly to padlock the plant and attempted to prevent removal of any more machinery. Sadly, Miller had not paid his staff, including Goossen, for more than six months and Fred Offenhauser for two years. They had struggled to hold on for the occasional payment of expenses when Miller closed one of his deals. The company's suppliers were less forgiving.

When the bankruptcy court took over Miller's affairs his creditors claimed debts of about $165,000 including unpaid wages. While Offenhauser had taken machinery and other items in trade for his pay, Leo Goossen had $1,943 coming and would get none of it. Goossen and his wife were forced to move from their comfortable Linwood Avenue home to a smaller place out at 6641 West Fifth Street in the new subdivision of West Hollywood. The bankruptcy trustee agreed to accept a payment of $500.00 and the waiver of Offenhauser's salary claims—reduced by then to $2,009.17—for three pieces of machinery he had removed (a Springfield lathe, a #20 Van Norman milling machine, and a 14 x 8-inch Rockford lathe, together with all of their tooling and equipment).

According to Goossen, when it was clear that everything was lost Miller went into the drafting room and stood and looked for a long moment at the cabinets that held Goossen's drawings of every Miller engine and Miller car built over the years since 1920. He took out copies of the blueprints, rolled them up, stuck them under his arm and left, never to return.

Between July 8 and the end of 1933 when the Miller plant was finally emptied and rerented, the trustee reported having to travel out to Gramercy Place six times to repair damage to broken locks and doors and to try to "recover assets removed from factory by employee[13]."

The sale of the residue at the plant was held on October 11, 1933. Though the physical assets were appraised at $23,175, at auction, everything in the Miller shop brought only $5,375. Other receipts brought the total realized for the creditors to $6,087.72. Miller's unsold four-wheel drive, 308-cubic-inch V-8 Indy car went to Frank E. Scully for $1,600, a fraction of the $15,000 the trustee had valued it at on the inventory.[14] The factory's remaining equipment was knocked down to a dealer for $3,750. Of the total assets, $2,150.29 went for administration and the attorneys' fees, $600.00, to company secretary Ted Heinhold on a prior claim, and the balance of $3,337.43 to the Internal Revenue Service on a $9,000 tax lien against Miller's income from the 1929 Schofield sale.

Although speedboat racer and marine industrial supplier Dick Loynes bought the 255 and many of the other Miller patterns and drawings for $25.00, he got only well-used prints and the patterns that had been recovered from the Macaulay Foundry in Berkeley and the Supreme Foundry in Los Angeles. Later correspondence involving Offenhauser suggests that Loynes' windfall was incomplete. (His purchase receipt from the bankruptcy sale supposedly excluded patterns and drawings in the Miller plant.) The 220 patterns and many drawings, along with special tools and jigs, ended up at Offenhauser's shop. What was left was sold to equipment dealer Michael Weisz with the rest of the fixtures. Interestingly, although the patterns and drawings were inventoried by the trustee at a value of $6,208.80, what could be found brought only Loynes' $25.00 bid.

Harry Hartz rented the Miller building until the end of the year, and then it was sold to Pacific Cracker Company which converted it into a bakery. Dick Loynes bought the engine patterns primarily for their utility in making parts for his racing boats. He soon disposed of the chassis patterns for lack of storage space. He told the FWD Company 16 years later that he still had the V-8 engine patterns if FWD was interested, and noted in a letter dated August 31, 1949, that as recently as a few months earlier he had supplied a casting for a four-cylinder Miller block to a customer in Pasadena. (Loynes offered to send FWD a full list of the Miller engine patterns he had. Unfortunately for historians, G. J. Fabian, FWD's senior design engineer, replied negatively on September 23, 1949, writing, "In the event we need anything we will contact you.")

Offenhauser had his little shop around the corner where he took in what machine work he could get, chiefly on truck engines. Only the ever-practical Fred thought there was any chance of keeping the tottering Miller legacy alive.

In the shambles of Miller's fortunes there was at least a certain amount of rancor among his ex-employees. Miller had not only shuffled his loyal staff to Schofield in 1929, reaping a tidy sum for himself while they ended up on the street, but when Miller's new shop closed in 1933 they lost more than $17,000 in wages. They knew Harry's misfortunes were due partly to circumstance, but also that he had failed himself and them. Despite their respect for Miller, the shop's workers knew he had frittered away his chances to survive. Miller virtually ignored the four-cylinder engines that were to be eminently successful for 40 years, clinging to more sophisticated designs that were obsolete once the board tracks disappeared. Goossen lost wages he could ill-afford, and even mild Leo was bitter over the debacle. Though Goossen seemed resigned to let fate take him where it would, four years later, when Miller asked him to join him in Detroit to design cars for Ira Vail (later the first Gulf-Millers), he refused.

Fred Offenhauser was able to adapt to reality, then dominated by the Depression. Miller was not. Offenhauser was a thrifty man who put money aside, never bought on credit, and owned his home free and clear. He had seen to it that as long as possible the men were paid enough to eat, even if he got no salary.

When Miller went bankrupt, his employees encompassed 30 of the finest racing car craftsmen of the 20th century. The list of his creditors included most of the suppliers to the racing industry of the 1930s, many of which remain in business in the 1990s.

The list of those who owed money to Harry Miller is much shorter, but includes interesting names: Leon Duray: $170.05, Fred Frame: $33.31, Shorty Cantlon: $72.25, Ralph Hepburn: $440.16, W. A. M. Burden: $23.35, Harry Hartz: $22.00, Ralph De Palma: $89.75, Art Sparks: $19.83, Danny De Paolo: $46.00, Harvey Ward: $69.53, Peter De Paolo: $85.75, and Bill White: $1.10.

Of these, Hepburn paid the trustee $75.16, Hartz paid the $22.00 he owed and $25.00 in rent for the month he used the building. One might suppose that the others slipped Harry the money they owed him later on, perhaps at the Speedway. Under the disgrace of bankruptcy he fled for a final time to Detroit to escape his friends and ex-employees.

Miller ran into Walt Sobraske at the Speedway years later, threw his arms around him and promised that some day he would pay the boys at the shop what he owed them. Sobraske, who was then working for Offenhauser, recalled in 1980, "I never saw Mr. Miller again."

Although Harry Miller designed the Miller-Ford Indianapolis cars in 1935 and built more exotic racing vehicles for the Gulf Oil Company in the late 1930s, none won races and he was never again a principal in the fortunes of his best legacy, the four-cylinder racing engine. Fred Offenhauser had one final recorded contact with him. In 1938, when Miller was working on the Gulf cars in Harmarville, Pennsylvania, he arranged for Offenhauser to buy the failed and by then derelict V-16 road car from William Burden for $400.00 in order to put the engine into an Indianapolis car. Fred made the deal, taking a $200.00 profit for his trouble.

On May 3, 1943, Harry Miller died, alone and in poverty, in Detroit, severing the last tie to the shop at East Adams and Long Beach where he, Fred Offenhauser, Leo Goossen, and the gang had created the 122s and 91s that defined racing in America in those long ago golden 1920s.

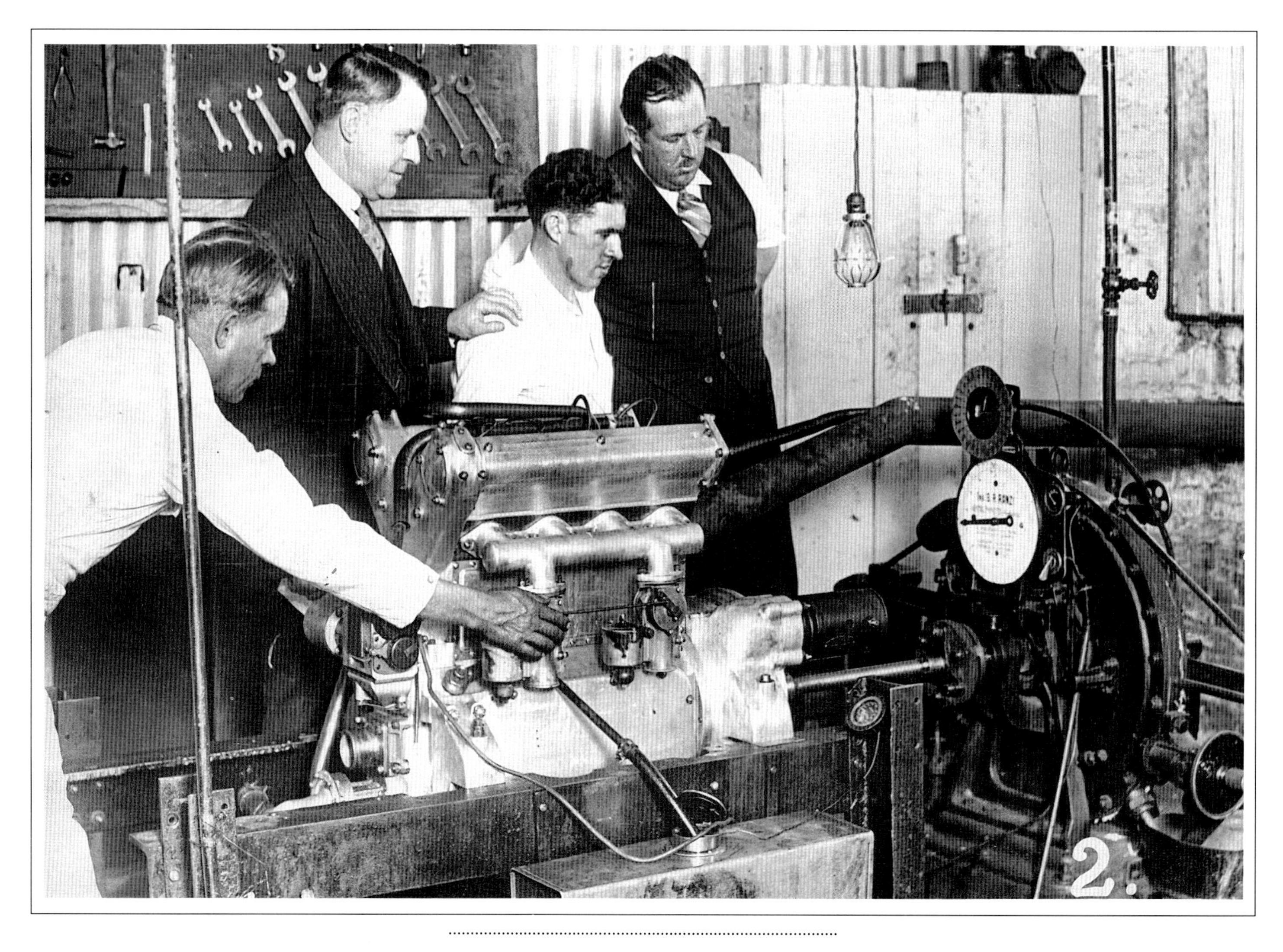

A Miller Marine engine on Miller's E. R. Ranzi dynamometer about 1929. With Ernie Olson at the throttle linkage of the two Miller carburetors, Ed Wintergust, Shorty Cantlon, and Bill White watch the rpm and the torque readings. This engine has the rigid mountings for a boat installation, but it also has a snout under the magneto to permit a three-point attachment that allowed the car's frame to twist without transferring the stresses directly to the aluminum crankcase.
Jim Etter collection

CHAPTER THREE

The Miller Marine—Forerunner of All the Offys

Let us stand aside for a moment from Miller's tribulations and look at the marine engine that was the forerunner of all the Offy engines to come, an engine that grew up while Harry was preoccupied with more exotic designs. The Miller Marine engine led to the 220 and 255 Millers and from them to the 270 Offy. In a sense it was the ancestor of the Offy, though as Leo Goossen who designed both engines made clear, "It was no copy whatsoever. The only thing that was the same about the Marine and the 220 was that both were fours." And both had the basic twin-cam architecture. Nonetheless, the Miller Marine set the stage for the Offys that followed over the next half-century.

Speedboat racing, like many other sports, bloomed in the roaring twenties, and few engines roared more impressively on the water than those Harry Miller built for hydroplane competition. There were larger engines, notably those from Packard, particularly the World War I torpedo boat engines that found their way into Gar Wood's speedboats and a certain number of rum runners during prohibition, but in their own displacement classes, Miller engines were supreme.

As had auto racing folk, top speedboat builders asked Miller to produce new engines that could beat their competition. John L. Hacker, a builder of high-speed racing boats in Detroit, was one of those who approached Miller looking for more speed—in this case for Junior Gold Cup boats. In 1925, Miller built Hacker a 310-cubic-inch straight-eight to compete in the American Power Boat Association's (APBA) class for engines of that size. The 310 was fairly successful, powering Hacker's displacement hydroplane, J-32 (*Lady Helen II*), to victories in Detroit and Washington, D.C., in 1926. About a half-dozen 310s were built in the mid-1920s. They were large engines, with little of the usual

A 151-cubic-inch Miller Marine engine, built in 1926 for use in racing hydroplanes. Note the squared-off cam housings, the marine type water pump, the starting crank, and the mounts to install it on the bed stringers of a boat. The curved carburetor horns have screens on them, a U.S. Coast Guard requirement to reduce the danger of a backfire setting fire to fuel that might have dribbled into the bilges. *Gordon Schroeder collection*

Miller Marine 151 (left) and 255 Offy in the Indianapolis Speedway Museum. This example of the Marine engine has the automotive-style water pump on the front of the engine. The photo shows clearly the differences in the two engines' crankcase and cam housings, as well as the ancestry of the Miller as seen in the Offy. *Author*

Miller concern for weight, and none, so far as is known, ever found their way into cars.

However, the APBA looked dimly on such custom, high-priced hardware, and imposed dollar as well as displacement limits on some classes. There was also at the time a speedboat class for 151-cubic-inch, unsupercharged engines, using Hacker hulls with restrictions on the cost of the engines. It occurred to Miller, or perhaps California speedboat racer Dick Loynes, that the front four cylinders of the 310 would make a nice package for the 151 class without the expense of completely new drawings and patterns. Thus was born, almost unnoticed, a kind of modular engine design in which nearly identical four-cylinder blocks could be used in a variety of 4-, 8-, and 16-cylinder engines at great savings in time and cost.

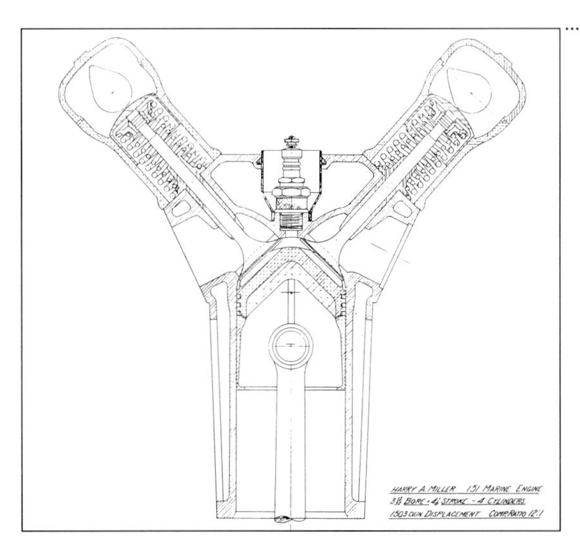

Cross-section of the top end of a Miller 151-cubic-inch marine engine as drawn by Leo Goossen. Actual displacement was 150.3 cubic inches. The valve-included angle was 86 degrees but all of the other characteristics—the spark plug cups, the valve cups, the one-piece head and block—were identical on future Miller and Offenhauser engines. *Mark Dees collection*

The resulting Miller Marine engine was a fine boat powerplant and turned out to be a most economical racing engine for automobiles as well. It was a twin-cam four with a bore and stroke of 3.406x4.125 inches. There were only two valves per cylinder with a valve angle of 86 degrees. The magneto was mounted crossways in front of the engine on the left side. The relatively heavy 151 was a little less than perfect for racing cars on the shorter dirt tracks where acceleration was important. However, properly geared, the marine engine put out 125 horsepower, and its heavy crankshaft and pistons were not too much of a problem on longer courses. On the water its torque gave a wonderful jump off tight one-buoy turns, at least for speedboat pilots used to previous marine powerplants.

Miller ran the first 151 in his own boat, *Angeles I*, and after it set new class records at San Diego in 1927, the boat racers quickly ordered copies. There was a story that Loynes paid for the project and had exclusive use of the 151 design for a year during which his boat, *Miss California*, beat all comers in his class. Other evidence from contemporary press reports suggest that Loynes actually bought Miller's first engine after Miller sold *Angeles I*. Chris Rip ran a 151 in his *Miss Daytona*. Loynes is supposed to have bought a supercharger for his engine, which allowed him to race in both blown or unblown categories. These boats were running at speeds of nearly 60 miles per hour—fairly fast on the water, as anyone who has done it can attest.

Francis Quinn at Ascot in 1931 in his second car to use the Miller Marine engine. *Bruce Craig collection*

Sea to Land Conversion

The 151 engine was attractive to auto racers almost at once, in part because of its high horsepower-to-dollar ratio. It was also much more reliable than its Fronty-Ford Model T-based competition. The first example known to have been used in a racing car is believed to have been run at Ascot Speedway in Los Angeles in 1927 in Francis Quinn's *Dayton Thorobred Tire Spl.*[15] By 1929 Hollywood promoter Bill White put a Miller Marine into his rear-drive Miller chassis used at Ascot, and with Fred Offenhauser's help developed a land-going package for the boat engine.

The most convincing early use of a 151 Miller Marine engine on land was by Wilbur Shaw in his *Whippet Spl.* Shaw was running at Daytona Beach for Floyd Smith of Detroit for a world's four-cylinder speed record in 1928, using a Frontenac conversion of a Model T Ford engine. The fragile Fronty caught fire and Shaw ran it into the surf. The engine, which was still turning over, sucked water into the cylinders and bent the rods and crank. Shaw had another opportunity to run at Daytona later that year, but needed a new engine. He had seen a Miller 151 Marine engine in a boat in Florida, and thought it might be exactly what he needed. Miller agreed to sell him one converted (to designs drawn by Goossen) for auto use for $3,800.00.

The Miller 151 repeatedly blew pistons and finally cracked its block, and Shaw had to wire Miller to ship a replacement to Florida.

Shaw's Miller, still only a slightly modified version of the boat engine, could only get up to 134.831 miles per hour, too slow to beat Bob Burman's record of 141.732 miles per hour set with the *Blitzen Benz* in 1911. The 151 gave him continual piston problems and swallowed a good many valves. Later, in 1929, two broken valve springs knocked him out of a 100-mile race in Detroit. Typical of the way drivers and mechanics helped to improve the Millers, Shaw went to the

Wilbur Shaw pilots his *Whippet Spl* down Daytona Beach in 1928 in a vain attempt to take Bob Burman's 141-mile-per-hour record. After his Fronty-Ford conversion blew up, Shaw bought a 151-cubic-inch Miller Marine engine that took him to 135 miles per hour—still not quite fast enough. *NASCAR*

Another 220 Miller is seen here in Chuck Davis' hydroplane *Angeles I,* a reconstruction of Harry Miller's own racing boat, which at one time carried a blown 151. These later engines were built for use in racing cars, but were installed in boats as well, leaving a certain ambiguity as to whether they are properly Miller *marine* engines. *Author*

NATIONAL EDITION — SCHRADERTOWN NEWS — NATIONAL EDITION

Circulation 150,000 | Circulation 150,000

VOL. II — APRIL, 1930 — No.

NEW RACER BUILT TO SMASH TWENTY-ONE-YEAR OLD RECORD

4-Cylinder Car with Estimated Speed of 160 M. P. H. Out to Break Long-Standing Record

Los Angeles.—Since 1911, nobody has been able to break the world's speed record for 4-cylinder cars. Now, at last, somebody is going to make a try at breaking it. And the motor with which it is hoped to accomplish this feat is less than a third as large as the record-holder in cubic inch displacement!

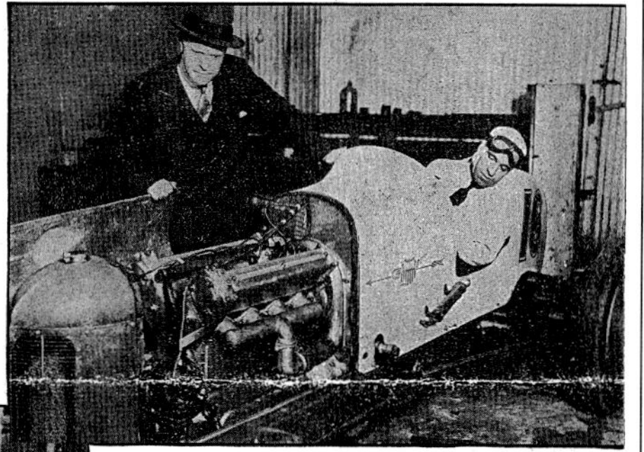

Photos Courtesy P. & A. Photos

The Schofield Special, pictured at the top of this page, weighs 300 pounds, has a displacement of 183 cubic inches and develops 198 horsepower. It is intended to travel at 160 miles an hour over the hard-packed sand of Muroc Dry Lake in the Mojave Desert. Bill White, famous race car owner, had it built in the attempt to snatch Bob Burman's title, which was made twenty-one years ago, with a 200 horsepower motor having a cubic inch displacement of 600.

The photograph at the left demonstrates how light this motor is. Its 300 pounds are easily carried by one man. The driver shown in both pictures is "Shorty" Cantlon, who will drive the car in its test run, as well as at Indianapolis, where it will be entered in the May races.

If the record is finally to fall, there will be no doubt about it. For this new car's test run will be held under the supervision of the N.A.A. and any record established will be clearly authentic. The motoring and racing public alike are much interested in the event, which promises to revive interest in 4-cylinder cars.

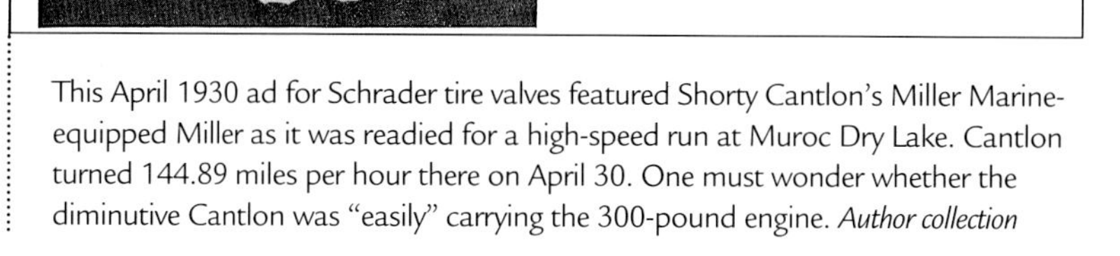

This April 1930 ad for Schrader tire valves featured Shorty Cantlon's Miller Marine-equipped Miller as it was readied for a high-speed run at Muroc Dry Lake. Cantlon turned 144.89 miles per hour there on April 30. One must wonder whether the diminutive Cantlon was "easily" carrying the 300-pound engine. *Author collection*

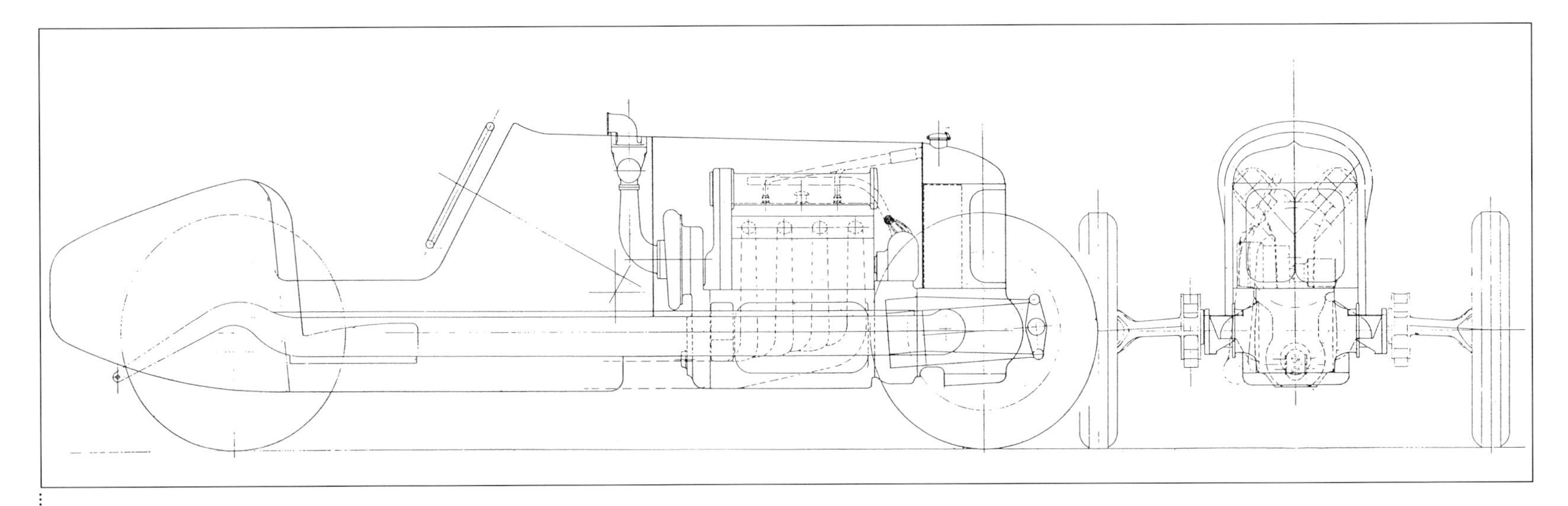

In 1928, when Wilbur Shaw asked Miller to adapt one of the 151-cubic-inch speedboat engines to his Whippet Special, Goossen sketched this installation of a 151 Marine Miller in a single-seat racing car. Mark Dees believes no complete Miller 151 chassis was built to this drawing, but it shows how the heavy boat engine might have been mounted. *Robert Binyon collection*

J. A. Young Company for valve springs with better heat-treating. He then roared on to wins at Bridgeville, Toledo, and Syracuse.

Shaw also had better camshafts made for his Miller. Harry Miller was very conservative with cam design, and the original cams were "pointy" with very little intake and exhaust valve opening overlap. The cams had nowhere near the overlap now considered necessary to get the best power out of a racing engine. As 1928 was fairly late for Miller to be still experimenting with cam profiles, they may have been made for what Miller thought would be relatively low-revving marine use. Shaw had cams ground with blunt shapes that left the valves open much longer. They were undoubtedly rough at low speeds, but much better at high revs. Tommy Milton later claimed that he "stole" the Duesenberg cam profiles from E. H. Hall for the Miller 122 engine. Eventually Ed Winfield, a former Miller employee, became the ranking expert in racing cams. Winfield or Winfield-derived cams of various types were used in almost all Offy engines right to the end in the 1970s.

By the time Miller left Los Angeles, Schofield was producing a hopped-up version of the 151, bored out to 183 cubic inches. Bill White put one of them in a car for Shorty Cantlon to drive at Ascot around 1929. Cantlon ran it for straightaway records at Muroc Dry Lake in April 1930, setting international class D records of 144.89 miles per hour, supercharged, and 141.75 miles per hour, unblown. Shaw's successes in 1929, and Francis Quinn's West Coast AAA championship in a 151 in 1930 established it as a hot engine, by then fairly well-tested and developed, if not perfected, for auto use. One recurring problem was crankcase cracking. Part of the problem was the boat engine's rigid mounts, designed to be set on fairly heavy timbers. The racing cars of the day had only sadly flexible rails made of sheet metal hammered over forms. If an engine with such a rigid mount was installed in

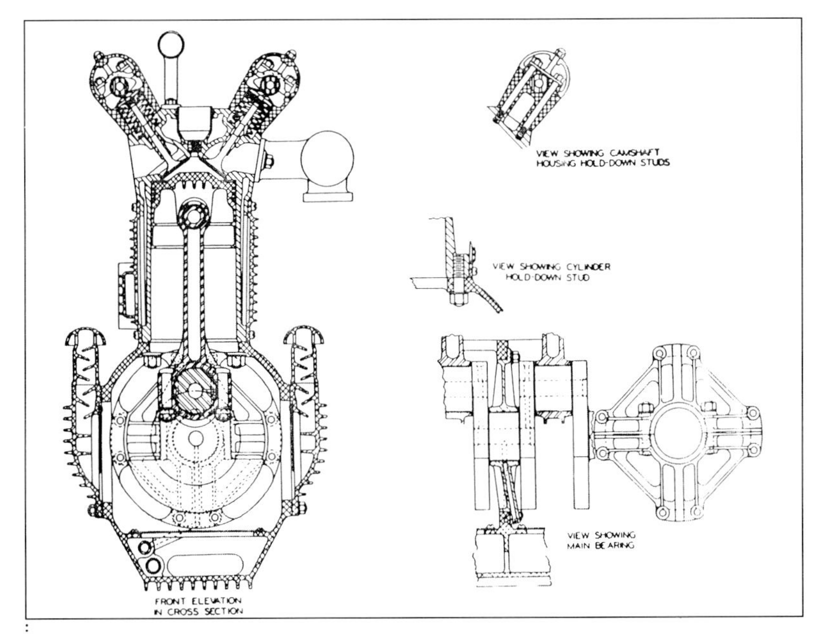

A 220 Offy drawing by Goossen at the time Fred Offenhauser was beginning to produce them under his own name. *Buck Boudeman collection*

a racing car, flexing of the frame would transfer stresses to the crankcase. The Miller Marine 151 was not designed to be a stressed part of the chassis, but drawings of Shaw's engine installation and photos of Bill White's 151 on the Miller dyno show the marine engine mounted that way (noted Miller restorer Chuck Davis believes that most if not all, Miller Marine engines that went in racing cars had three-point mounts). Since his earliest 183 in 1921, Miller had used a yoke or trunnion mount at the front of his engines (at least when used in rear-drive chassis) that gave a three-point mounting, allowing the chassis to twist a good deal without overly stressing the engine's aluminum crankcase. One of the improvements in the next generation of the Miller Marine was to reinstall that type mount.

ed Miller in late 1930 to have to counter the Ford T conver- cubic inches. The bore, stroke, e not the same on the 200 and valve, while the 200 had four on. The 200 was designed for ore quickly. A half-dozen or so each. They were a little small- and there were a host of other tened to improve acceleration from 440 pounds to 325; the 72 degrees, the main bearings slightly to allow future bore become the nearly immortal

with little cash, managed to T at Ascot and later a Miller etitive engine. Sparks did not id haughty toward customers a technical inspector at Ascot nade racing equipment.

. He received Sparks in his htly larger model of the 200, White came along and paid the second engine. This did Miller, and the two seldom

pleted engine, instead taking nself. Paul Weirick,[16] Sparks' partner, was an ice deliveryman, and he carted the parts from Miller's shop in his wagon. Sparks and Weirick bought their own cams from Ed Winfield, and also their own pistons and valve springs. Sparks and Weirick added balance weights to the Miller crank and beefed up the clutch. They had considerable trouble with the center main bearing, then made from poured babbitt metal. Car owner and racer Joe Gemsa said years later that Sparks replaced the babbitt main bearings in his 220 with Dodge truck inserts. Sparks' eight-valve 220 engine and chassis was the first of a series of his cars to be labeled *Poison Lil*, and poison they were for his dirt track competition.

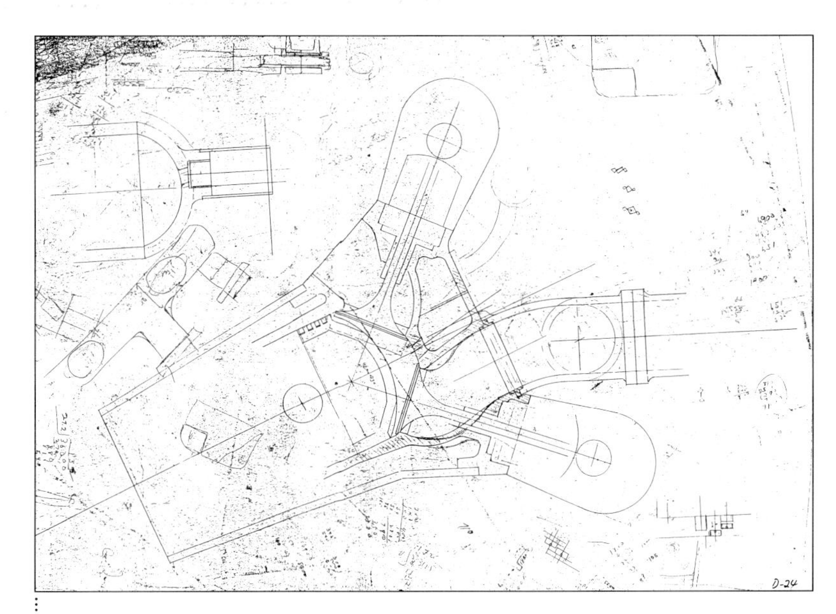

Goossen's rough drawing of the downdraft ports on the 200 cubic inch variant of the Miller Marine. Art Sparks found, as was predictable, that having two cylinders share a single intake port led to interactions in the flow of the fuel-air mixture that robbed the engine's power. *George Parker collection*

Some of the early 200s were built with the magneto driven off a simple, inexpensive spur gear arrangement that put the magneto under the carburetors on the engine's left side. That was fine when the intake ports were on top of the engine, but it restricted the options for manifolds on the side-port versions and eventually it was found that dribbles from the carburetors could get into the magneto and cause fires. The magneto drive was then changed to a slightly more expensive bevel gear drive that put the magneto in front of the engine on the right side.

That redesigned Miller four-cylinder engine was visibly different from the marine engine and had downdraft intake ports on top of the engine, an idea attributed to Riley Brett. The new engine was used in several cars and at least one boat. The displacement of the 220 was shortly increased by stroking it to 247 cubic inches, and Spark and Weirick built both 247 and bored-out 269-inch versions.

At the Miller shop the crankcase was beefed up to deal with the problem of cracking in the web supports. In addition, Bill White ordered at least a few with cases having no notches in the interior bulkheads where the webs bolted. The notches allowed the "ears" on the webs to be maneuvered through the case when installing the crankshaft. Eliminating them added strength to the case itself. Even so, mechanics objected to the circular, "notchless" bulkheads because they added hours to the assembly process. In the 1940s, Tommy Hinnershitz drove and maintained the former Haskell Miller for Ted Horn, which had a 220 Miller with an early-1930s Bill White notchless case.

"It took hours longer to put a crank into that case," Tommy recalled. "You had to put the crank in and slide the webs in through the sides of the case. It was just a whole lot more work." By the time the engines were produced in quantity, the mechanics' complaints had been addressed, and from 1931 until the exigencies of the 1,000-horsepower turbo Offys in the mid-1960s, the notches remained. To survive under the power the turbos unleashed, the solid bulkheads were reinstated, and damn the time it took to put them together.

Miller-Schofield built Goossen's twin-cam head for the Ford Model A block, a conversion that looked a lot like the top end of the Miller Marine and was occasionally confused with that Miller engine. The patterns were sold to Cragar in 1931, and those engines were thereafter known as D. O. Cragars.

Bill White's 220 won the Pacific Coast championship for Ernie Triplett in 1931. Sparks and Weirick developed their 247 to meet its challenge. Sparks had some flow-bench work done and discovered, not surprisingly, that the first 200/220s with two downdraft intake ports on top of the engine led to interactions in the flow that hurt power. He had some blocks made that put four intake ports on the side, as had been previous Miller practice, and opened the ports up to an oval shape. Sparks found that his porting arrangement made a great difference in the engine's power, and Miller apparently agreed as all subsequent large Miller and Offy engines were built that way for the next fifty years. (The midgets and

The 205 engine in the *Haskell Miller Spl*. Note the downdraft intake manifold feeding through ports on top of the engine but fed by a single updraft as required by the Ascot rules at the time. Also note the equalizing tube on the side of the block where the intake manifold would be installed on later versions of this popular engine. With the sidewinder magneto seen here, drips from the carburetors were a fire hazard, and the magneto mount was soon returned to the front of the engine. *Bruce Craig collection*

a few other special eight-valve engines had *round* side ports.) Sparks said that Goossen and Offenhauser helped him develop his engine, but he never gave Miller much credit.

(The very earliest 200/220 Miller engines are easily dated by the fact that they *do* have the carburetors sitting on top of the block. The first of the 220 line, displacing 151 cubic inches and carrying an inboard-outboard drive, went into a boat and may thus be identified as a "Miller Marine." Paul Weirick recalled that very few of the top-intake, 3.875-inch-bore 200s were built for auto racing.)

White took two 183-cubic-inch Miller-Schofields to Indianapolis in May 1930, and Cantlon surprised everyone by qualifying second-fastest at 109.810 miles per hour and finishing second in the race. Al Karnatz failed to qualify the car in 1931, but as the *Lion Head Special* with Howdy Wilcox driving, it finished second again in 1932 with a newer version of the Miller engine, this one a 220-cubic-inch 16-valve. The car, under a variety of sponsors, went on to run at Indy for 12 years before being retired.

In 1933, when Offenhauser urged Miller to enlarge the 220, the new engine followed the lines of Sparks' developments. The resulting 255-cubic-inch engine was just slightly larger overall than the 220, and the same valve layout was used (valve-included angle of 72 degrees) The 255 was influenced somewhat by the 1,113-cubic-inch, four-valve V-16s that Miller built for Gar Wood in 1931. The valve gear and dimensions of the 255 were identical to the V-16 block. The unfortunate downdraft intake of the early 220 was originally transferred to the 1,113, but before the engines were built the oval side ports of the 220/255/270 had re-emerged. As Mark Dees noted in *The Miller Dynasty*, the 1,113 was in a sense the father of the 255 and the 270.

With Miller staggering toward disaster, the 255 was a last grasp for solvency among the litter of exotic, over-ambitious, unpaid-for projects. The first one went to Joe Marks for a car to be driven by Bob Carey who was killed in it at Ascot on April 16, 1933. Three others went to Gus Schrader (always on the lookout for a bigger engine to take to the International Motor Contest Association's "outlaw" wars), Harry Hartz, and Billy Winn or Frank Brisko. A fifth was not finished in the Miller collapse, and the parts were assembled by Bunny Phillips for the Maley & Scully Foreman Axle Special. Lou Moore drove it to third place at Indianapolis in 1933. The sixth was built by Lou Meyer after Miller's collapse during the winter of 1933–1934, and a seventh was machined and assembled by Frank Brisko at the FWD Company. After the Brisko and Meyer 255s, Offenhauser built most of the engines, first as "Millers" and then, in 1934, under his own name.

The 255 engine was responsible for an outburst of complaints from owners of lesser powerplants to which the AAA responded by reducing dirt track, less than championship, engine sizes to 220 cubic inches.

Up until 1933 "outlaw" dirt track racing had been a largely "run what ya brung" affair. There were giant engines made from the World War I-era Hispano-Suiza aircraft V-8 and the like. In AAA racing, the cutthroat competition for prize money killed so many drivers in the first three years of the 1930s that the contest Board decided to trim back the power a bit. They first set a limit of 366 cubic inches for championship dirt cars, similar to the limit

After he retired from racing, Frank Elliott went to work for the Ethyl Corporation, which was developing tetraethyl lead as an antiknock compound for gasoline. In those long-ago more carefree days, the lead (which was a blood-red color) was administered by the drop into a racer's gasoline. Elliott would ask the mechanic what compression ratio he was using and then calculate the dosage and administer it with his beaker. Leon Duray, believing if a little is good a lot is better, used so much in his fuel he left a trail of red fumes from his tailpipe. Few were aware that lead would foul spark plugs and for a time, few knew how deadly the potion was. Elliott at least wore heavy gloves. *Indianapolis Motor Speedway*

at Indianapolis, and 220 cubic inches for non-championship cars, eliminating the Hissos. Then in April 1934, they cut engine sizes back to 205 cubic inches, approximately the size of a stock Ford or Chevy conversion. That left the 255 to run only in full AAA championship events: Indianapolis and the 100-mile contests on mile dirt tracks.

It was not until after World War II that 220 inches became the AAA standard for nonchampionship overhead-cam engines, a dimension that lasted until the Chevy V-8 came to rule the sprint car tracks in the late 1950s.

At some tracks in the early 1930s any valve arrangement was allowed. At a few, like Altoona, only two-valve-per-cylinder designs were permitted. Officials could tell the difference by the engine's sound. There was even a one-carburetor-only rule by AAA at Ascot until the end of the 1933 season.[17]

The 255 was enlarged to 270 cubic inches in 1937, and it ran at that size until 1957 when the displacement limit at Indianapolis was downsized in another attempt to control racing speeds. It was the engine that was to write racing history for nearly half a century.

The Miller-Marine engine established the architecture of all Miller and Offy four-cylinder engines to come. The basic four-cylinder engine remained in the long-lived Miller idiom of twin overhead cams, valves operated through cup-type lifters, separate iron block, and one-piece barrel-type aluminum crankcase with removable webs for the main bearings. Connecting rods were tubular, machined from forgings. Access to the lower end of the engine was via crankcase side plates. The dual-stage oil pump for the dry-sump lubrication system was mounted in the bottom of the front of the engine below the gear tower, and the water pump was driven directly off the gear train. Ignition was magneto, usually Bosch. Fuel was normally delivered by a hand air pump that pressurized the tank, rather than by a mechanical pump.

There was never a shop manual for the engines, though there was a table of recommended clearances and torque wrench values. Cam timing was varied by rotating the drive gear on the end of the cam itself in a kind of vernier arrangement. Valve clearances were set by grinding the tip of the valve stem. The 18 mm spark plugs were mounted in receptacles pressed into the top of the block and sealed by rubber O-rings. They fired in "cartridge" type recesses at the top of the combustion chambers.

Cams were ordinarily a Winfield grind—# 4s show up in engine build sheets into the 1950s. The most astute early mechanics had different grinds to change engine torque curve characteristics for different tracks, especially since there were few quick-change gear boxes before World War II and it was difficult to swap ring and pinion gears rapidly.

Valves started out as 1.5 inch on the intake side and 1.375 inch exhaust. Engine lubricant was usually a 50-weight oil. Oilzum, a castor-oil based product made by White & Bagley Company of Worcester, Massachusetts, was preferred, sometimes even when another oil company was the car's sponsor.

The original 220s produced about 190 horsepower at 5000 rpm on pump gas, though many owners boosted the octane with benzol, naphtha, and even tetraethyl lead (administered by eyedropper). Retired driver Frank Elliott worked for the Ethyl Corporation, and if a mechanic told him what compression ratio he was running, Elliott would calculate the proper amount of lead to mix in the fuel. Lead was highly toxic and was eventually abandoned for personal administration in favor of 100-octane aviation fuel and other professionally produced mixtures.

Initially, carburetors were Miller updraft or downdraft types, but after Offenhauser took over production of the fours—and Miller carburetors were no longer made—most owners used Winfields. After World War II, Riley carbs were favored until Hilborn developed direct fuel-injection in 1950.

The crankshaft was in most cases (with "notched" bulkheads) assembled to the webs that carried the bearings. The crankcase was stood on end and the crank and web assembly lowered as a unit into it. Because the "webs" were an interference fit, the case had to be warmed—usually by an acetylene torch using a rosebud tip—so that as the aluminum expanded the webs could be set into place and then bolted.

After the webs were secured and safety-wired the rod and piston assemblies would be placed in the cylinders. The block would then be fitted down on the crankcase and the rods bolted to the crank. With the block in place, the cams would be mounted and timed and accessories such as the water pump, magneto, and fuel pump bolted on.

The 220 set the stage for the Miller/Offenhauser engine to become the standard for what were then beginning to be called "big cars" to differentiate them from midgets and Indianapolis, or championship, cars. These racers are now known as sprint cars, alluding to the fact that they run chiefly on half-mile tracks and distances shorter than the 100-mile minimum championship distance.

In the days of the Pacific Coast Championship, awarded while Ascot ran under AAA sanction from 1929 to 1935, Miller, Miller-Schofield, Cragar, and Sparks (a modified Miller 220) won nearly 200 races.

The 220 Miller, soon to be known as an Offy, and some 255 and 270 Offys ran against a wide range of four-cylinder competition, most of it based on Ford A and B blocks. There were a few special-built engines like the HAL and the Dreyer, and later GMC in-line sixes and flathead Ford and Mercury V-8s were used to effect on the dirt, but the Offy was always the engine to beat on the half-mile bullrings.

Miller and Miller-Derived Engines Pacific Coast Championship Victories 1929–1936

Engine	Wins
Miller Marine	27
Miller-Schofield	17
Miller	102
Sparks	26
Cragar	21

Pacific Coast Circuit victories (Ascot), 1929–1936, won with Miller and Offenhauser engines. Millers and Offys (often indistinguishable after 1934, since Fred Offenhauser was building them all) dominated the California tracks in the 1930s. The Sparks engine was an improved version of the 220 and the Cragars were either Fords with Goossen-designed heads or a Cragar adaptation of the Miller-Schofield engine. The Pacific Coast AAA racing could well have been called the Miller-Offy circuit, as indeed USAC midget racing in the 1960s was the "110 Offy circuit." *Author, Jim O'Keefe*

Fred Offenhauser going over one of Leo Goossen's blueprints for a two-speed transmission in his shop at 1935 West 62nd Street in 1934, a year after he took over the engine business from Harry Miller.
Gloria Madsen collection

CHAPTER FOUR

OFFENHAUSER TAKES COMMAND

IN THE LATE SUMMER OF 1933 AFTER MILLER'S BANKRUPTCY, ONLY THE practical Fred Offenhauser could keep life in the dynasty Miller had begun. Fred had his little shop on 62nd Street around the corner from Miller's padlocked plant where he took in what work he could find, at first rebuilding truck engines and making a few racing parts. As he had done in 1929 with an unfinished Miller passenger car for wealthy young Philip Chancellor at the time of the Schofield sale, Offenhauser took over the incomplete supercharged Miller V-16 road car. He charged the buyer, William Burden, $15,000 to have Eddie Offut finish it; money that financed the first three months of the Offenhauser Engineering Company's existence.

If Offenhauser was going to build racing engines, the 220 was winning lots of races at Ascot, and at the time, was potentially the best money-maker. He had emerged from Miller's bankruptcy with the patterns for that engine. It is inconceivable that he would have passed up anything really useful that was in Miller's shop at the time of the bankruptcy. He could get drawings at any time from Goossen, then freelancing, who had copies of most of them dating back to 1920. The 183, 122, and 91 patterns floated around Los Angeles for years and many passed from Loynes to author Mark Dees and to Bonneville racer George Parker.

Whether Offenhauser surreptitiously moved much of the Miller equipment to his own place and slipped tools, patterns, and drawings out of the shop after it was closed will never be known with certainty. Miller himself moved material from his old East Adams and Long Beach plant to 1348 Venice Boulevard after Schofield went bankrupt, and it is certainly possible that the arrangement with Offenhauser over the three machines was made with something similar in mind. As noted earlier, Goossen recalled seeing Miller go to the drafting room at Gramercy Place and take away an armload of engine drawings.

It is probable that Offenhauser saw where Miller's folly was leading well before the final collapse. He had done what he could to prepare for it. Offenhauser lost much more in backpay than the three machines he got were worth. (Miller had bought the machines in 1931. The Van Norman #20 universal mill was still in use when Drake Engineering ceased Offy production 56 years later.) He said he paid $800 for everything he got from Miller's bankrupt plant. The court records document that he paid $500 in cash to be allowed to keep the machinery he had spirited away. Offenhauser's other $300 probably covered a deal with Weisz or Loynes for whatever else he needed.

The key to staying in business was the special tooling, jigs, and fixtures, all of which Offenhauser got with the machines. The 255 engine was in transition at the time Harry A. Miller Inc. collapsed with the patterns and

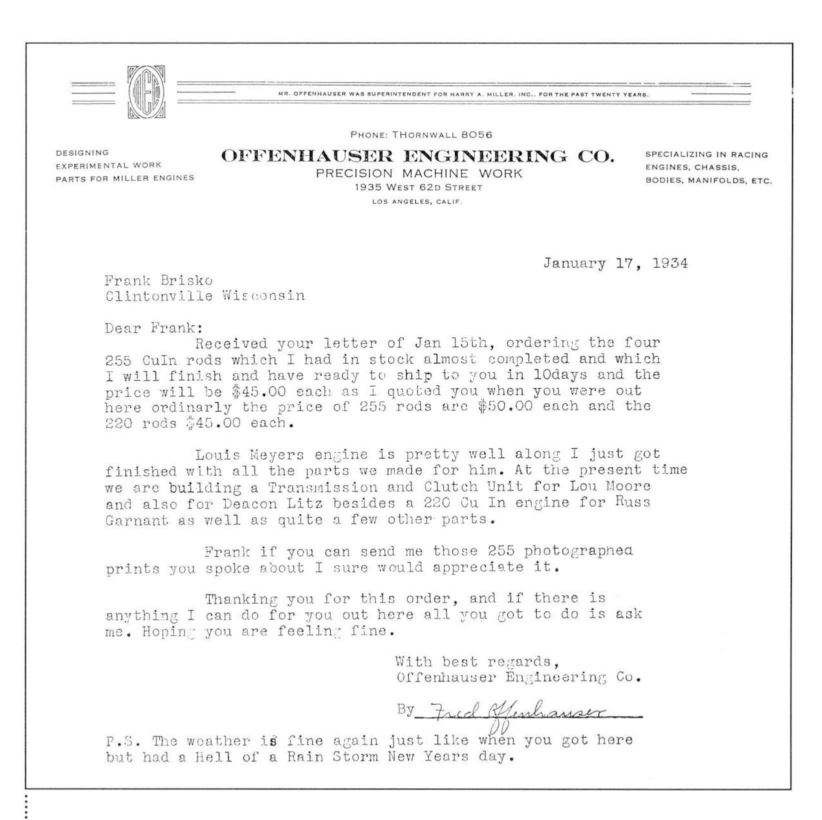

MR. OFFENHAUSER WAS SUPERINTENDENT FOR HARRY A. MILLER, INC., FOR THE PAST TWENTY YEARS.

PHONE: THORNWALL 8056

DESIGNING
EXPERIMENTAL WORK
PARTS FOR MILLER ENGINES

OFFENHAUSER ENGINEERING CO.
PRECISION MACHINE WORK
1935 WEST 62D STREET
LOS ANGELES, CALIF.

SPECIALIZING IN RACING
ENGINES, CHASSIS,
BODIES, MANIFOLDS, ETC.

January 17, 1934

Frank Brisko
Clintonville Wisconsin

Dear Frank:

Received your letter of Jan 15th, ordering the four 255 CuIn rods which I had in stock almost completed and which I will finish and have ready to ship to you in 10days and the price will be $45.00 each as I quoted you when you were out here ordinarly the price of 255 rods are $50.00 each and the 220 rods $45.00 each.

Louis Meyers engine is pretty well along I just got finished with all the parts we made for him. At the present time we are building a Transmission and Clutch Unit for Lou Moore and also for Deacon Litz besides a 220 Cu In engine for Russ Garnant as well as quite a few other parts.

Frank if you can send me those 255 photographed prints you spoke about I sure would appreciate it.

Thanking you for this order, and if there is anything I can do for you out here all you got to do is ask me. Hoping you are feeling fine.

With best regards,
Offenhauser Engineering Co.

By Fred Offenhauser

P.S. The weather is fine again just like when you got here but had a Hell of a Rain Storm New Years day.

In this letter, dated January 17, 1934, Fred Offenhauser lists some of the jobs he is working on: rods for the Brisko 255, several parts for Lou Meyer's 255, a 200 for Russ Garnant, and drive line components for Lou Moore and Deacon Litz. *Robert Rubin collection*

drawings for the latest engine not yet complete. Frank Brisko and Lou Meyer rented the patterns from Loynes, and when Goossen finished the drawings, Offenhauser soon had both drawings and patterns and could produce complete engines himself.

Without the cost of servicing the Miller company's debts, and with the meager wage and material costs common in the depths of the Depression, Offenhauser struggled along through the end of 1933. At first he had only Offut with him in the shop, but shortly he brought three more of Miller's old staff back to their machines. Soon he had seven men helping him, including

Offenhauser Engineering Company ad, Fred was producing the 220- and 254- cubic-inch engines as Millers. *Author collection*

Walt Sobraske. Sobraske would eventually do almost every job in the shop from running the South Bend lathes and the milling machines to foundry work and engine assembly.

By Christmastime, Offenhauser had a logo and a letterhead as the "Offenhauser Engineering Company, capable of Precision Machine Work." He began to advertise in the racing papers that Offenhauser Engineering was "the builder of the famous Miller 220 and 255 cubic inch 4-cyl engines." By January 1934, the shop was producing parts for the 255, as Fred wrote to Frank Brisko, then working in Clintonville, Wisconsin, for the FWD Company producer of four-wheel drive trucks.

Indianapolis had tightened the rules on fuel and oil consumption to a degree that the Miller 308 V-8 in the FWD Company's Indianapolis car could not hope to meet them. The engine was of dubious reliability anyway, so the car needed a better, smaller engine. Brisko, with some help from the Marchese brothers in Milwaukee, built up a 255 using castings, forgings, and what drawings he could get from Dick Loynes. From their correspondence it is clear that both Brisko and Offenhauser had some of the 255 blueprints and they exchanged the copies each needed. Machining the rough castings into an engine without the shop fixtures was tricky, and Brisko took a touch too much off either the top of the case or the bottom of the block and had to make a shim to maintain the proper timing gear alignment. Brisko had rough forgings but found the machining too difficult and ordered 255 rods, a crank, timing gears, and cams from Fred along with oil pumps and the cam towers.

Lou Meyer, had Brisko machine some of 255 castings in Clintonville. There exist Goossen drawings for both engines, some labeled "Meyer engine," with FWD drawing numbers superimposed on the old RELLIMAH tracing blanks Leo was still using. Meyer called his engine a Miller, but Offenhauser's shop did much of the work. A 220 for Russ Garnant as well as quite a few other parts were being made at Fred's shop at the time. Soon Goossen drew a slightly improved version of the 255, identifiable by the oil sump pickup tubes offset to the right rather than being located in the center of the pan.

Miller's name was part of the bankrupt property and therefore disposable for whatever it would bring at the September 1933 auction. Similarly, Louis Chevrolet lost the right to use his name on automobiles when he was forced out of General Motors (he called his products "Frontenacs"). Fred could have bought the Harry A. Miller Inc. trademark, but he did not bother. He simply called his 220s and 255s "Millers" until he began building his own midget engines under the name "Offenhauser." From comments Offenhauser made later, however, it is clear that he felt that he had a right to put his name on engines he had helped build since the beginning of Miller's business. He had contributed to their practical design and construction and had provided ideas and expertise that helped make them successful. He told people he had built 75 engines for Miller. As Mark Dees related, Offenhauser "certainly nurtured the birth of the 255 and it is fitting that later examples of the engine bore his name into automotive legend." Brisko described his 255 as a "Miller/Offenhauser" on a dyno chart done at the FWD Company. The midget engine was the first "true" Offy, of course, and the dividing point between Miller and Offenhauser falls somewhere in mid-1934 when Fred put his nameplate on the larger engines. Fred turned out a nice engine, almost as nice looking as a Miller, and he charged as near to Miller prices as the Depression years would permit.

The shop turned out half a dozen fours by May 1934. Bill Cummings won that year's 500 in a 200 that mechanic Cotton Hennings had bored out to 220 cubic inches. The engine had a Miller Marine crankcase with a big bore block made by Frank Brisko that "worked real well," Emil Andres recalls. It ran a 10:1 compression ratio, all that the pump gasoline then required at Indianapolis would allow.

Leo Goossen, Freelance Designer

Leo Goossen had been a freelance designer and draftsman since leaving Schofield in 1930. He worked for several clients and Miller had paid him $300 for designing the 1932 Hartz Indianapolis engine. After Miller's bankruptcy, Goossen continued to do work from his West Hollywood home for Offenhauser and others in racing. He said years later that Miller's failure in 1933 to pay him for six month's work forced his first wife, Vera, who was in fragile health, to go to work teaching school in Beverly Hills. It may, he said sadly, have hastened her death in 1935. Goossen would occasionally go on Offenhauser's payroll—Fred paid him 75 cents an hour to design the midget Offy in July 1934 and paid him a $25 royalty on the first two engines. Later when Lew Welch started work on the Novis, Lew financed them through Fred who paid Goossen an hourly salary for the work.

Some, including Goossen, had great admiration for Offenhauser's abilities as a machinist and manager but did not see his talent as a self-taught engineer doing the production engineering of the powerplants Goossen designed. As gentle a man as he was, Goossen tended to sell Offenhauser short.[18] Goossen never let anyone forget that it was Miller who designed the basic engine. "Fred was a

Frank Adamson precision grinding a shaft on Offenhauser's Brown & Sharpe mill. The small motor at the center of the picture is driving the workpiece via a small belt which absorbs the pulses of the 60-cycle alternating current that would otherwise cause fine lines to be left on the bearing journal. *Gloria Madsen collection*

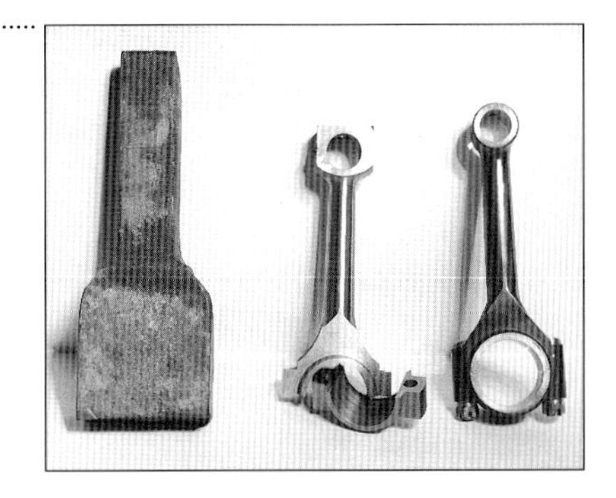

Three steps in manufacturing an Offy connecting rod. On the left is the forged blank. In the center is the semi-finished rod after being partly machined, and on the right is the completed part with its poured-babbitt bearing. *Gloria Madsen collection*

Semifinished castings for 220 and 255 Offy engines. From left to right: 255 and 220 blocks, a 220 case with mount for the sidewinder magneto, and a slightly longer 255 crankcase with notched bulkheads, partly machined. *Gloria Madsen collection*

nice guy, but he was not an engineer," Goossen insisted to interviewers. "He was more interested in making chips [a compliment to a hard-working machinist] than he was in designing. He was the world's greatest machinist, especially when he was getting along with a very few tools."

Offenhauser was more than merely an unimaginative machinist who had some business sense but no ability as an engineer. He had enough skill to put together a plant capable of building successful racing engines at a profit with only the most ordinary lathes and milling machines and none of the sophisticated tools such as centerless grinders that manufacturers of common road vehicles considered necessary in their plants. Although Goossen was available to draw designs for new engines, he was not on Offenhauser's staff until World War II. Anyone familiar with the technical demands of making even such a seemingly simple piece as a piston must realize that Fred had absorbed a significant amount of engineering knowledge. The high-strung Millers were not built in a backyard. To master them and to continue to build the engines at the highest level of competition was not the work of a mere machine operator. For example, the job of setting up a crankcase to be machined on Offenhauser's basic machinery was demanding. Where does the machinist take the first cut on a rough casting to establish a flat area square and at the proper distance—within 0.001 inch—of the axis of the crankshaft? At that point the machinist's skills merge with those of an engineer.

Goossen gave Offenhauser credit only for the midget engine. "He set the sizes for that one, he paid for it, and he built it. That was the only true Offenhauser," Goossen contended. "Still," Leo conceded, " the whole [business] would have gone down the drain but for him."

The 255 Engine

As Offenhauser had thought, the 220-cubic-inch four and its variants sold well and had great success at Indy and other venues. Lou

Moore and Wilbur Shaw placed second and third at Indianapolis with 220 Millers in 1933.

After the 220, the next most readily salable product was the 255. And it was the 255 that was about to make the Offenhauser name famous. In 1932, Offenhauser had persuaded Miller to build from scratch an engine to succeed the bored-out 220s that were beginning to show up. Five were made before mid-1933, for Joe Marks, Gus Schrader, Harry Hartz, Billy Winn, and Al Scully (Bunny Phillips had to do most of the finish machine work for Scully's, as Harry A. Miller Inc. had by then sunk into bankruptcy).

For a time, the 255 was just a little large and consumed a bit too much fuel. The AAA rules allowed 366 cubic inches in Championship competition—and even at times on half-mile dirt tracks—but the fuel consumption limits at Indianapolis discouraged using all of that displacement. In addition there was a rule that required seven pounds more chassis weight per cubic inch of engine size over 200.

The 255 used a slightly larger block and case than the 220 but the same 72-degree valve angle. Early 220 and 255 engines are difficult to tell apart without a tape measure. The 255 block was originally 10.6 inches tall, compared to 10.0 inches for the 220. Standard versions of both used four valves per cylinder. Offenhauser and early Meyer & Drake 255/270 engines can be identified by the somewhat rounded three-eared covers on the front of the cam housings.

Once Offenhauser had his own shop he ran it sternly, and his employees grumbled about their pay, which Fred admitted was barely a living wage. Grumbling was not an uncommon thing around a machine shop in the Depression, but Offenhauser was driving a LaSalle, one step below a Cadillac, which didn't help matters. Still, Offenhauser could be a generous man. When his brother, Charlie, couldn't make a go of his ranch in the 1930s Fred put him on the payroll. He also hired his nephew, Fred C. Offenhauser, for a time, but the two Freds didn't get along well. They argued about everything from shop work to politics. The younger Offenhauser later quit to found a speed parts business now known as Offenhauser Sales Corporation. For years Fred and Fred C. sparred over the use of the family name in the racing business, a fight that at one time led Fred to call in his attorney.

Some of the customers continued to identify as "Miller" 220 and 255 engines that were produced in the Offenhauser shop. On the other hand, in his autobiography Wilbur Shaw identified as an "Offenhauser" the engine in Leon Duray's 1932 dirt track car. By the time Offenhauser sold the business after World War II, his name was an honored one and so firmly associated with the engines that Lou Meyer and Dale Drake did not put their own names on the engines when they took over the operation.

Offenhauser built modified parts for the old Miller Marine, as Buster Warke related to the author, making a stronger crankcase for the surviving marine fours. Ralph Morgan had one of the beefed-up marine engines for Jimmy Wilburn to drive in IMCA competition in the 1930s. Morgan later sold it to Joie Chitwood who took it to Langhorne in 1941 for an AAA race, but the crank threw off one of the welded-on counterweights, damaging the engine too badly to be quickly repaired. Chitwood sold the car as-was to Ted Horn, then putting together a four-car team to run with Ralph Hankinson.

Offenhauser Engineering Company, about 1941. Seen on the bench are two completed midget engines, a block for a third, and to the left, an unidentified centrifugal supercharger that does not resemble either that for Lew Welch's 1937 Indianapolis car or Stanley Dollar's speedboat engine. As can be seen, the early midget engines had the oil pickup tubes in the sump mounted in the center of the crankcase. Later they would be relocated to the right side of the sump where oil gathered due to centrifugal force from all-left turns on oval tracks. *Gloria Madsen collection*

The engines produced by Offenhauser continued their success on the track. While Miller pursued exotic new designs, Offenhauser was cranking out his stout, simple update of the four-cylinder. The design was virtually unchanged from the Miller, but Offenhauser claimed he was using better materials. His blocks were "cast of virgin iron ore specially imported from the Far East." He cited better heat treating of valves, crankshafts, and other steel parts and nitriding done, he said, by heating the steel to 1,200 degrees in an atmosphere of pressurized ammonia.

Many of the earliest Offenhausers were almost custom-built and all were hand-fitted—parts from different engines do not always interchange easily. Pistons, rods, and gears may be made precisely according to the drawings, but holes for the studs holding the cam covers to the gear towers may not line up from one engine to another. Some engines were sold "semifinished" for the skilled buyer to complete for himself.

The Midgets Appear

In 1934, a new kind of racing burst on the scene that was destined to put Offenhauser Engineering Company on firm footing indeed: midgets. As will be detailed in chapter six, the midgets sprang up in 1933 as cheap but exciting racing. Promoters spread midget racing across the country and midgets were running indoors in New York and Chicago and getting coverage in the *New York Times* by the end of the year.

Earl B. Gilmore promoted the first track built specifically for midgets in Los Angeles. The collection of converted and cut-up passenger car, boat, and motorcycle engines that ran at his stadium were unreliable and made it difficult to run a show. His patience exhausted, Gilmore sent his manager, David Koetzla, to see Fred Offenhauser about building a real racing engine for the little cars.

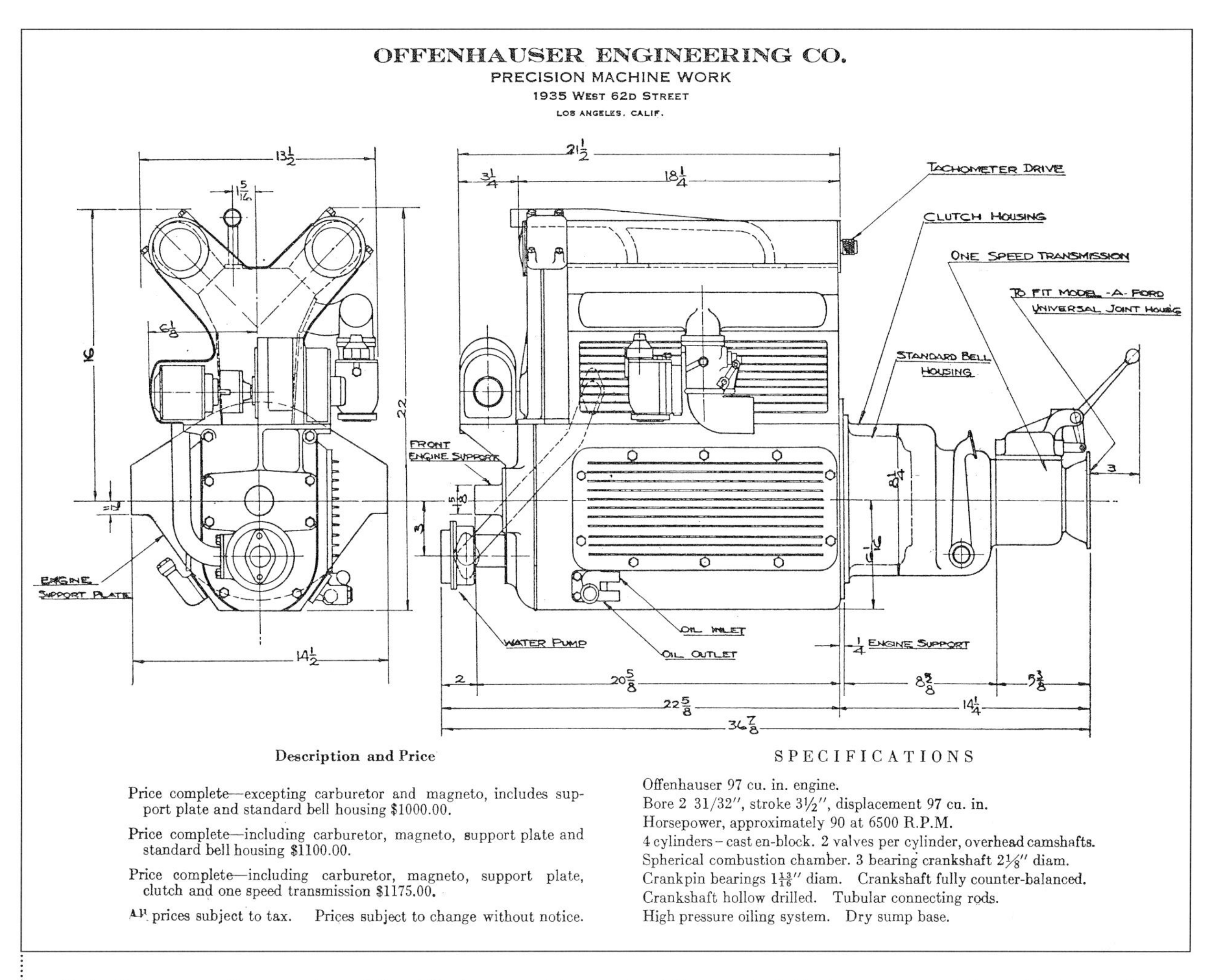

Early Goossen outline drawing of the Offenhauser midget engine. The nominal displacement was 96.9 cubic inches, but most engines were slightly larger. It was the popularity of the midget engine that gave Offenhauser enough income in the depths of the Depression to stay in business. *Mark Dees collection*

Leo Goossen quickly drew up a 97-cubic-inch engine based on half of the 181.8-cubic-inch straight-eight of Harry Hartz's 1932 Indy winner. Since that engine consisted of two four-cylinder, cast-iron blocks set end-to-end on a single aluminum crankcase, it was an easy job, which suited Koetzla who wanted to make the end result as quickly and as cheaply as possible. Because Offenhauser was cutting the eight-cylinder crankcase in half, the resulting four-cylinder engine ended up with only three main bearings. Conventional practice would have probably given it five, as Goossen did with the subsequent Sampson midget engine. Aside from possible special blocks for Lou Moore and Wilbur Shaw, the midget was the only Offy to be made with two valves per cylinder. The eight-cylinder1932 Indy engine that gave birth to the midget had its magneto mounted on the left front, opposite to the 220/255/270 versions. The midget cam drive gears used fine pitch teeth also taken from the Hartz Indy engine. The first ones used a single updraft Winfield 1 1/2-inch Model S carburetor, and early versions were equipped with small multiple-disc clutches, similar to those on 1928 Model A Fords. A few had two-speed transmissions, though the low ratio was useful only for getting out of the pits.

Offenhauser sold five midget engines in 1934, and they kept him in business. He sold a basic engine for $1,000, or $1,175 with carburetor, magneto, clutch, and one-speed transmission. Some buyers did the final assembly on their engines right at the Offenhauser plant. Fred had a healthy profit margin on them, and with the help of those midget sales, the firm cleared $18,000 for the year.

Soon the midgets were running almost every night of the week, and with admission at 50 cents, packing in the fans. Promoters began paying appearance money of $100 or more to top drivers. With a more reliable and powerful car than most of the competition, an Offy owner, pulling down 60 percent of a car's winnings, could pay for an engine reasonably fast. Hence the little Offys sold, if not quite like hotcakes, at least like the hot engines they were.

Offenhauser was a member of the racing establishment and served on the Board of Control of the National Midget Association which sanctioned midget racing at Gilmore, Emeryville, Oakland, Seals Stadium in San Francisco, and Navy Field in San Diego. His vision was wider than simply

Curly Mills in the first "Mighty Midget," August 1934. The body of the Curly Wetteroth chassis was still unpainted at the time. Note the single, updraft Winfield carburetor and the rod for the mechanical brake. *Bruce Craig collection*

Fred Offenhauser liked to award prizes at the races at Gilmore. Unlike some sponsors, the ever-practical Fred gave checks, not trophies. Here Roy Russing holds Fred's check and the trophies for winning both the 1940 Thanksgiving Grand Prix and the Pacific Circuit AAA Midget Championship. His car's owner, Rex Mays, also holds a check from Offenhauser. At left is Pat Cunningham in the third place car. To Fred's right is Ed Haddad, who finished second in the Grand Prix, Ed Wallace, Gilmore Manager Dave Koetzla, and Paul Weirick. The Mapelli Offy at the far right is the original Gilmore Mighty Midget under different ownership. *Gloria Madsen collection*

oval track racing: In 1935, he suggested building an engine with which to reclaim the unlimited speed record for the United States. "We can raise Campbell's speed by fifty miles per hour," he said, but no one turned up to finance the project and the idea withered.

Offenhauser was kept busy by the many racers in Los Angeles having cars repaired or updated. He spent most of his time at the shop. Ethel stayed at home and sewed her needlepoint. On slow days Offenhauser would go home for lunch, then take her grocery shopping before he went back to work. During World War II, he worked far longer hours, and Ethel, he said, covered the house in stitchwork. As the couple had no children of their own, at Christmas Fred would dress up in a red suit and play a German Kris Kringle for his nieces and nephews, making merry for the children of his eight sisters and brothers. Gloria Tinley, who came to be the keeper of Offenhauser's

Wilbur Shaw's 1935 220 Offy. A special crankcase was built for Shaw's front-drive Pirrung. The magneto was driven by the exhaust cam. This was one of the first Indianapolis engines to carry Fred's name; it has an OFFENHAUSER identification plate on the right cam housing. The intake manifold was specially built by Pirrung; note the end caps attached with machine screws. Note also the eight-cylinder Bosch magneto with four plug leads grounded to a special fixture. These magnetos, from 1920s Miller eights, were the best going at the time but in order to use them on a four, the unused leads had to be grounded to prevent internal arcing in the magneto. *Indianapolis Motor Speedway*

Offy's First Indianapolis Win

In the Offy's first year at the Speedway, its engines powered two cars; both qualified and they finished one-two in the race. That was success of a kind likely to make car owners notice.

Kelly Petillo was a driver at Ascot for Art Sparks and Paul Weirick, in 1934. The next year he took his life savings and borrowed money from his family to build his own Indianapolis car. His father, Michelli, mortgaged the family store on South Compton Avenue in Los Angeles for $600 and other Petillo relatives kicked in $50 and $100. Arrigio Balboni, who ran an aircraft salvage yard, gave his countryman instruments and other parts from wrecked airplanes. Curly Wetteroth built the body, and Petillo, scrounging what he could, made the rest of the car in his own shop. The front axle came from a wrecked Plymouth, the transmission from a Studebaker. Offenhauser related in 1937 that Petillo came to him for an engine but couldn't afford the $3,500 price. Fred agreed to provide him one credit in order to prove that he could make equipment that was competitive at Indianapolis. Petillo was to pay if he made money at the Speedway. It was the only engine Offenhauser ever built on speculation, though he would occasionally let a driver he knew have parts on credit.

In his first qualifying attempt in May 1935, Petillo turned in a 121-mile-per-hour performance that would have been good enough to earn the pole. However, in those days of fuel limits, AAA officials determined he had burned more than the allowable quantity of gasoline. Offenhauser, who was in the pits to advise the Petillo crew, adjusted the carburetors, and on his second qualification run Petillo burned up the track again, but broke a connecting rod on his third lap.

Petillo, accompanied by his wife and child, was down to $18. His engine was crippled, and he had no money to fix it. Offenhauser wired Los Angeles and had parts shipped to the Speedway by air. Karl Kizer, then running an engine shop in Indianapolis, rebabbitted the bearings and welded the block on credit, charging Petillo $800. A week later, on his third attempt, Kelly made the race.

To control fuel consumption as closely as possible, Offenhauser rigged up a linkage that allowed Jimmy Dunham, Petillo's riding mechanic, to shut down the idle jets while the car was on the track, then to open them when Petillo pulled into the pits (this would become a standard feature on Offenhauser-prepared cars during the days of the 37 1/2-gallon fuel limits).

As the race developed, Rex Mays, driving a 220 Miller built by Offenhauser, led the race until a suspension part broke. Shaw found himself in second place, chasing Petillo. His strategy was to conserve his car and his fuel in the expectation that Petillo would break down or run out of gas before the race's end. However, light rain began falling and the last 23 laps were run under caution forcing everyone to hold their positions. Petillo beat Shaw by 40 seconds. He won

Kelly Petillo, winner at Indianapolis in 1935 and his riding mechanic, Jimmy Dunham, with the first big engine to be entered at Indianapolis under the Offenhauser name. Petillo and Curly Wetteroth built the chassis, with its typical heart-shaped grille, in Wetteroth's Figueroa Street shop in Los Angeles, and Fred Offenhauser himself helped tune the 260-cubic-inch engine. *Indianapolis Motor Speedway*

$35,000, paid Offenhauser and Kizer, and the Offy engine had acquired a reputation.

Petillo went on to win AAA 100-mile championship races at Langhorne, Pennsylvania, and St. Paul, Minnesota, and to take the 1935 national AAA title.

With Petillo and Shaw's one-two finish at Indianapolis, Offenhauser Engineering prospered. In 1935 they built 11 complete engines for midgets and half-mile dirt track cars, grossing $30,000. Fred hired four more men, including two of his nephews who had lost their jobs. (Fred was always good for a shop job for his brothers and their children when the Depression left them unemployed.)

The Depression was still ravaging the nation in 1935, but in two years Fred Offenhauser had put his shop on a strong footing on the race track and at his bank, setting the stage for an Offenhauser dynasty that was to rule for another 41 years.

memory and papers, lived in the Offenhauser home as a member of the family for more than a year.

Offenhauser produced 101 midget engines before his production shifted over entirely to defense work in 1941. Turning out about a dozen engines a year does not seem like much, but spare parts brought in additional income and in the Depression, the income from the Mighty Midget engine was the backbone of Offenhauser's business.

The 255 Becomes an Offy

Offenhauser continued to update the four-cylinder engine throughout the midget frenzy. Its design was in direct contrast to the longtime Miller philosophy of more but smaller-displacement cylinders. Although there is a theoretical advantage to more cylinders per cubic inch of total displacement, the four generally produces more torque. It was the great torque of the long-stroke Offy, as well as its proven reliability, that maintained its lead in racing despite theoretical drawbacks.

During the early-1930s the competition at Indianapolis was chiefly among old Miller eights, Miller/Offenhauser fours, and the converted passenger car engines allowed under the junk formula. While Studebaker and Ford mounted factory teams, individuals entered converted Buicks, Hudsons, even, in 1934, a Graham. Frank Brisko, Joe Lencki, and others tried their own designs.

To handle new business in 1935 Offenhauser increased his staff to 16, and with Myron Stevens' help, the first complete race car was built in the shop. Wilbur Shaw got sponsorship from wealthy Yale-educated engineer Gil Pirrung, and the pair asked Goossen to design a car for Indianapolis according to Shaw's particular ideas. It was a front-drive, though more stout and simple than the Miller FDs. Stevens, who was one of racing's premier aluminum-shapers and an ex-Miller workman, did the body work and rode in the 500 as Shaw's mechanic. Offenhauser did part of the fabrication of the chassis and also built Shaw a special eight-valve 220 engine. It was one of two he built as part of his first effort at Indianapolis with engines carrying his own name. The other was a 255 for Kelly Petillo (actually displacing 262 cubic inches) that went into a Wetteroth chassis. That engine had a "low" block, measuring 10.625 inches to distinguish it from a later "high" block that was 0.46875 inches taller from the crankcase to the top of the block, not including the camshaft housings.

Standard 255's in 1934 had a bore and stroke of 4.25x4.50, five main crankshaft bearings, four valves per cylinder, and a pair of 1 3/4-inch Winfield carburetors. They weighed 345 pounds and, Offenhauser said, took 1,500 hours of labor to produce, The factory recommended that the engines be redlined at 5,200 rpm. The standard compression ratio was 13:1. Offenhauser made his 255 bearing journals 1/8 inch larger than the Miller 255.

Offenhauser 1936–46

As he had hoped, the success at Indianapolis in 1935 brought Offenhauser new business. Driver Emil Andres recalled that several car owners went to Offenhauser and asked him to build them 255s beefed up as Offenhauser had done for Petillo. To cover the costs of making new, updated patterns, Offenhauser stipulated that they buy six engines. Those first engines went to Joe Lencki, Lou Moore, Cotton Hennings for a Boyle car, George Lyons for Freddie Winnai's Midwest Racing Team car, Red Shafer, and Ralph Hepburn. By May 1936 he had orders for three more 255 engines from Wilbur Shaw, Gil Pirrung, and Chet Gardner.

Shaw decided in 1936 that he did not wish to share his winnings with a car owner any longer. He got oil company owner Earl Gilmore to sponsor a new vehicle he dubbed *Pay Car*, which was presumably going to pay Wilbur a lot of Eddie Rickenbacker's Indy prize money. Myron Stevens built the car in Offenhauser's shop. It was modeled somewhat along the aerodynamic lines of the Sparks-Weirick *Catfish*, and indeed Sparks offered to let Stevens borrow the Catfish plans, but the drawings got lost and Stevens worked from photos. It was extremely smooth aerodynamically for its time. Andres, who later drove both Shaw's car and the *Catfish* said the *Pay Car* was a magnificent machine, by far the better of the two. (Strictly speaking, according to Goossen, Offenhauser built no complete chassis, but workers such as Stevens, Curly Wetteroth, Emil Deidt, and others, working with Offenhauser, put several complete cars together.)

In 1936, Offenhauser's shop built nine engines for Indianapolis. A total of 10 Offys entered that year, and all of them qualified. Many of the 15 four-cylinder engines that were entered as Millers had also come out of the Offenhauser plant. Altogether, the Miller/Offenhauser contingent made up 68 percent of the field.

The 1936 Indianapolis race marked the realization that stock-block engines in cut-down Detroit chassis were not going to be winners. In fact, only one stock-block made the 1936 Indy field: Zeke Meyer's *Boyle Special*, a Studebaker in an ex-Cooper front-drive. Lou Meyer won the race in his own car, powered by an Offenhauser-built 255 that Meyer

KELLY PETILLO

CAVINO MICHELLE "KELLY" PETILLO WAS AN ITALIAN-AMERICAN, BORN IN Pittsburgh, Pennsylvania, in 1902. In 1921 his family moved to Huntington Park, California, just east of Los Angeles. As a young adult, Petillo made a name for himself making speedy runs in his produce truck over the ridge of the San Gabriel Mountains delivering fruit from Fresno in California's Central Valley to his family's market in Los Angeles. Not surprisingly, racing attracted him and he combined truck driving with a few turns on the class B dirt tracks in Southern California. By 1928 he had wrangled a practice ride at Indianapolis, but he crashed Henry Kohlert's car in the attempt. He began racing at Ascot in 1929 and rode as a mechanic at Indianapolis in 1930 to get a little seasoning. He got a ride at Ascot in the former Francis Quinn car, and subsequently drove for Sparks and Weirick in *Poison L'il*.

Petillo was a voluble, argumentative, quick-tempered little man—a leadfoot in a race and hard on equipment. He qualified on the pole for Indianapolis in 1934 in Joe Marks' Miller 255 but finished 11th. He won $3,500, first-place money in the December 23, 1934, Mines Field race for Sparks-Weirick, finishing in a pea-soup fog. His Mines Field winnings helped finance his 1935 Indy-winning car. With Fred Offenhauser at his side, 1935 was his best year. He retired during World War II and died in 1970.

WILBUR SHAW

WILBUR SHAW WAS BORN IN SHELBYVILLE, INDIANA, IN 1902, 21 MILES FROM the Indianapolis Speedway. He built himself a race car out of junk in 1921, but it was so bad the AAA starter at the Hoosier Speedway track, Roscoe Dunning, refused to let Shaw race. Dunning took Shaw under his wing and helped him build a Fronty-Ford-powered car known as RED for Dunning's initials. Shaw drove the RED Special to many dirt track victories in the Midwest and picked up enough experience to try for Indianapolis in 1927. He was as much a leadfoot as Petillo but smarter and much more polished. He crashed cars many times on his way to the top but was lucky enough to survive them all.

Shaw won the 500 in 1937 in the streamlined Gilmore Special and twice more in Mike Boyle's 8CTF Maserati in 1939 and 1940.

After World War II, Shaw persuaded Tony Hulman to rescue the decrepit Speedway, and he became its president. Shaw was killed in a plane crash in 1954.

Offenhauser, Myron Stevens, and Wilbur Shaw look over the smooth nose on Shaw's 1936 *Gilmore Spl*, also known as the "Pay Car." The hood came loose in the 1936 race and a 17-minute pit stop to fix it cost Wilbur the race. *Gloria Madsen collection*

Wilbur Shaw in the *Gilmore Special*, 1936, with riding mechanic Myron Stevens, who built the chassis and body. *Indianapolis Motor Speedway* helped assemble. Meyer considered the engine a Miller and indeed felt that way until the end of his life, never becoming nostalgic about Fred Offenhauser's role in its history. The engine had nitrided wet-sleeves which turned out to expand at a different rate than the block, causing the engine to blow three times during practice and qualifying. Fred dispatched replacement blocks by air, and Lou got the engine back together by race day. Shaw was leading Meyer when the *Pay Car*'s hood came adrift and he lost so much time in the pits securing it that he could only manage seventh place. Shaw subsequently blamed Stevens for failing to rivet the hood straps properly, but Stevens maintained that he had warned Wilbur that air flow under the hood would cause trouble unless there were exit louvers to allow it to vent.

In 1937 Fred's 15 employees produced 16 255, 270, and 318 engines. He was selling his big Offy engines for $2,500 at the time, and the midgets for $1,175 (including one midget to German stunt flyer Gerd Achelis).

The Offenhauser plant was at the center of racing activity in the winter of 1937. Garages all over Los Angeles were building or rebuilding race cars. Joe Marks' 255 Miller was being rebuilt at Carl Ryder's, and at the Altadena Garage, Kenny Jacobsen was working on the *Atlas Chrome* big car. Joe Zottareli was building a new *Hal*, and Joe and Sam Pintarelli in their own garage were furiously at work on an F-head of Joe's design for a Ford B-block to race at El Centro (Ascot had finally been shut down). Ted Horn was rebuilding his Miller at Ray McDowell's machine shop, and the Fromme-Taylor shop was getting the Petillo Offy ready for Floyd Roberts to drive at Indianapolis. At Offenhauser's shop, Lou Meyer was having a new crank and bearings installed in his Indianapolis car, and Fred was tuning up engines in two of Red Shafer's cars.

While Gus Schrader was at Curly Wetteroth's shop on Figueroa Street having a chassis built for his new 255 Offy, he had to double as a fireman. Wetteroth, though a fine metal worker and chassis builder, was accident-prone. In 1935, he cut his hand so badly he was unable to work for three weeks, and in 1936 he tripped over a car frame and broke an elbow. While building the Schrader car in 1937, the shop's kerosene heater overflowed spreading flaming oil across the floor. Wetteroth tried to extinguish it with a shop coat, but Schrader, with a heavy piece of canvas, was able to smother the flames before they reached his own new car and Henry Topping's Maserati.

Meanwhile, Fred's crew worked from November through May on larger engines and during the summer on midgets. He had taken in commercial work after Miller's bankruptcy in 1933 and continued to do machine work on truck engines if there was slack time in the fall. He told one interviewer he was experimenting with marine diesel engine designs in the off-season and his records show orders for experimental diesel engines, one a single-cylinder model, of which few details survive.

When the stringent fuel consumption rules at Indianapolis were eased for the 1937 race, Offenhauser put together an engine for Lou

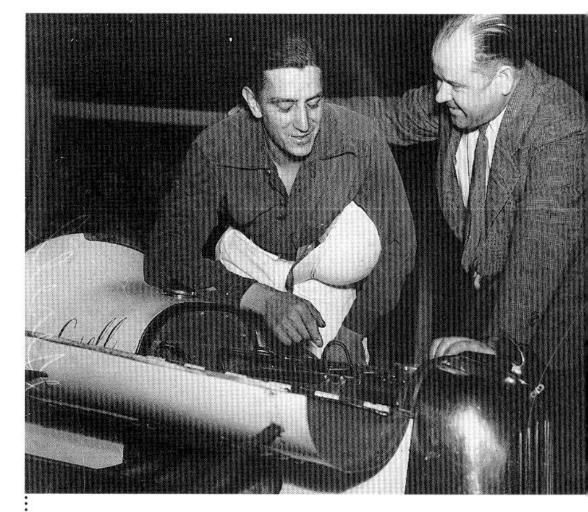

Fred Offenhauser, like any good salesman, seems to be telling Ernie Gesell, "You"ll love the power this baby has." Gesell, an East Coast driver, was one of several brought to Los Angeles in 1936 by Gilmore Speedway manager Dave Koetzla to run with his Owners and Drivers Association when the National Midget Association went on strike (and eventually disappeared) over the success of the Offy-powered cars which were at that time only a minority in the group. Offenhauser had been an officer in NMA, but was more interested in selling engines. Gesell returned to the East and in 1939 found himself on the other side of the anti-AAA strike that resulted in the formation of the Eastern group, the American Racing Drivers Club, which is still going strong in 1996. *Gloria Madsen collection*

Offenhauser Engineering Company financial results, 1934–1942. Offenhauser struggled in 1933 after Miller's bankruptcy, but he reported $18,000 in sales in 1934 when the Offy midget engine was first produced, and by 1936 he had a profit of more than $2,000 and was taking home a salary of about $70 a week. By 1942, with war work keeping the shop running around the clock, Fred paid himself $230 a week and cleared nearly $100,000 for the year. Taxes, however, were as high as 91 percent during the war, and for corporations there were contract renegotiation and excess profit taxes that took some of that income away. *Gloria Madsen*

Financial Statements, Offenhauser Engineering Co. 1934–1942

Year	Gross Receipts	Shop Labor	Managing Salary (Offenhauser)	Rent/repairs/ misc expense	Material Costs	Profit
1934	$18,000.00	unknown	unknown	unknown	unknown	unknown
1935	$30,000.00	unknown	unknown	unknown	unknown	unknown
1936	$35,531.71	$13,457.07	$3,600.00	$1,743.90	$14,213.27	$2,517.47
1937	$40,584.99	$16,219.64	$3,600.00	$2,526.31	$16,300.25	$1,938.79
1938	$46,315.58	$18,655.52	$3,600.00	$2,271.14	$14,705.84	$7,053.08
1939	$68,498.36	$26,502.72	$6,000.00	$2,019.49	$29,972.61	$4,003.54
1940	$72,532.57	$28,721.86	$6,000.00	$1,182.38	$24,830.08	$12,798.25
1941	$130,577.26	$47,650.79	$12,000.00	$2,958.98	$33,691.57	$34,275.02
1942	$203,629.96	$68,893.55	$12,000.00	$2,976.43	$19,858.32	$99,901.66

Fred Offenhauser's shop and some of the staff, 1937. The six-cylinder engine at center is Joe Lencki's special. From left to right are Frank Adamson, Ernie Weil, Ben Derks, Claude French, Fred C. Offenhauser (Fred's nephew), Heinie Kramer, Ray Rogers, Walter Sobraske, Herman Kuhn, Ed Kramer, Roy Smith, Frank Smith, John Anderson, and Fred Offenhauser. Others, not shown, included Otto Sandau, Ray Perkins, Ed Sobraske, Shorty Barnes, Harry Coryell, Ted Heinhold, Ed Kramer, Casper Olepiewicz, and, among others, Herman Vogel. Leo Goossen did not go on the payroll until 1944. Arrayed on tables are a 97-cubic-inch midget engine, a tall-block 270, the Lencki six, a 255 case, and a completed 255. This was the point where the 255 crankcase was redesigned to become the 270. *Bruce Craig, Jim Etter*

Moore with a bore and stroke of 4.3125x4.625 inches which works out to 270.2 cubic inches, a size that became virtually the standard Championship Offy displacement. Once again, Offenhauser's record at Indianapolis was excellent. There were 10 Offenhauser-powered entries and nine qualified. Shaw, in the *Pay Car*, took command of the race early and held on to defeat Ralph Hepburn by 2.1 seconds in the closest 500 to that time.

In 1937, there arose a demand for an even bigger Offy. Goossen drew plans for what became the 318: a 4.5x5.0-inch bore and stroke, big-bore version of the 270. A half-dozen or so of the engines were built. They were run chiefly on the International Motor Contest Association (IMCA) "outlaw" circuit, though Petillo had one at Indianapolis in 1937 that pumped out its oil by lap 109. Don Lee put what may have been the first 318 built into a street roadster and ran it at Muroc Dry Lake. Machinist Al Long said years later that the 318s had the heaviest blocks he ever finished on the shop's Van Norman mill in all his years at Offenhauser and Meyer & Drake. As related elsewhere, Emory Collins was in Los Angeles at the time and ordered a 318 with which to challenge Gus Schrader in the IMCA wars.

Some of the engines were still being sold on a partially finished basis, and even complete ones were usually torn down by the buyer for the special "secret" touches each mechanic considered his own, a process known now as "blueprinting." Even the best of Fred's engines were not an off-the-shelf item. Sometime in 1937 a new customer asked Offenhauser about the guarantee on an Offy engine. Fred pondered the life of a highly stressed race engine for a moment and then replied, "Well, we guarantee that all the parts are there." In another context Fred said he expected the engines to be pushed to their limits. "I build my engines to win, not to keep as pets," he said.

Floyd Roberts and Bud Winfield look over the Winfield carburetor-equipped 270 Offenhauser engine in Joe Lencki's 1936 car. *Indianapolis Motor Speedway*

National Championships Won with Offenhauser Engines 1935–1946

Year	Driver	Car	Engine
1935	Kelly Petillo	Gilmore Speedway Spl	Offy (260)
1936	Mauri Rose	F.W.D. Spl	Miller (255)
1937	Wilbur Shaw	Gilmore Special	Offy (255)
1938	Floyd Roberts	Burd Piston Ring Spl	Offy (270)
1939	Wilbur Shaw	Boyle Maserati	Maserati
1940	Rex Mays	Bowes Seal-Fast Spl	Winfield (partly Offenhauser built)
1941	Rex Mays	Bowes Seal-Fast Spl	Winfield
1942–45 no racing			
1946	Ted Horn	Peters	Offy (270)

National AAA Championships, Offenhauser Engines, 1935–1946. Kelly Petillo and his 260-cubic-inch Offy ran away with the 1935 AAA Championship after his Indy win. Mauri Rose took the crown in 1936 in the Miller 254-powered FWD car, but Wilbur Shaw and Floyd Roberts won with Offys in 1936 and 1937. Mays won in 1940 and 1941 with the Bowes engine, but since it was largely built by Offenhauser, that only enhanced Fred's reputation. Ted Horn gave a solid performance in 1946 with a 270 Offy in Fred's last year. *Author*

In early 1937, the plant produced a dozen more midgets, bringing the total number of the little engines built to 21. Offenhauser grossed $40,584.99 for the year and he paid himself the same salary of $3,600.00 he had taken in 1936, according to statements Offenhauser Engineering Company filed with the Air Corps during World War II.[19]

The Offenhausers had moved out of their rented apartment in 1932, returning to the house in South Pasadena. For a time they lived over a three-car garage Fred built in Hermosa Beach, nearer the shop. In 1938, he paid $7,000 cash for a comfortable Spanish-style bungalow at 3211 W. 78th Street, close enough to go home from the shop for lunch most days.

In addition to building his own engines, Fred was also doing a fair amount of custom work. He and Goossen were the only freelance high-performance engine builders in the United States, and they had the priceless experience of 20 years with Harry Miller. American racing people—drivers, owners, and mechanics—had been raised with Miller products as the standard for high-performance engines. When they had their own ideas for new engines they would naturally build on what Miller, Goossen, and Offenhauser had done. It was far easier to use Goossen's designs for gears, connecting rods, camshafts, crankshafts, oil pumps, and the other proven details to go with their ideas for numbers of cylinders, valve angles, supercharger drives, and the like.

Another 10 Offenhauser engines were entered at Indianapolis in 1938, and five of the first six finishers were "Miller" or Offy fours. Floyd Roberts won with a 270-cubic-inch four that, while entered as a Miller, could only have been Offenhauser-built. The 270 configuration was about to become the standard Offy displacement under a new AAA formula that permitted a maximum of 274 cubic inches. In order to allow either a longer (8.25-inch) rod or a higher piston dome, 270 blocks were produced that were 11.09375-inches tall. The FWD Company asked the price of a new 270 to replace the Frank Brisko 255, and Offenhauser quoted a figure of $2,850.

Offenhauser thought of himself as a forward-looking machine shop owner, but his readiness to adopt new methods applied only if they didn't cost him too much money. Until the war came, he said he never borrowed money and only bought new equipment when he could pay for it with cash. Except for details, there was really no need to tamper with the Offy's proven DOHC, 16-valve design, except for incremental improvements drivers and mechanics might suggest.

The Europeans Challenge

In the 1939 starting field at Indianapolis, 14 Offys were among the most diverse group of cars in years to face the green flag. Entries included two Alfa Romeos, three Sparks, a Brisko, a Studebaker, a Duray, and a Lencki six. Offys powered about a third of all the entries.

Undoubtedly the most impressive car in 1939 and 1940, though, was Mike Boyle's 8CTF Maserati Grand Prix car. In fact, Boyle's Maser would become the first European entry to beat the American engines at Indianapolis since 1919. The Indianapolis formula gave the supercharged Maserati a 100-horsepower edge on the Offy, though with its 5-inch stroke it, like the 318, was not reliable at more than 5,000 rpm. Cotton Hennings, a master mechanic, had adapted the Maserati, with its twin Roots blowers, to oval-track racing, and it carried Wilbur Shaw into Victory Lane both years. He would have won in 1941, too, but a wheel collapsed and Shaw crashed.

A Technical Look at the Offy

THE 220, 255, AND 270 OFFYS LOOKED MUCH ALIKE, AND AS MANY OF THE parts would interchange, many rebuilt engines contained a variety of parts. The 220 and the midget engines had flat side plates, while the early 255 cases needed more clearance for the rods and their side plates were curved outward. Sometime later, the cases were widened and 270 and late 255 and 252 side plates were flattened.

Offenhauser took pains with heat treating, which in Miller's shop had not always been done carefully. As Offenhauser described the process of relieving casting stresses and annealing engine parts: "The block is heated to 1,250 degrees, a glowing, cherry red, and allowed to cool slowly for about twelve hours." Offy valves, generally bought from Jadsons, were also heat-treated. They were tulip-shaped, he said, to improve the flow of the incoming fuel mixture. Dual concentric springs prevented "fluttering." He used Jadson piston rings, later Perfect Circle, unless a buyer specified another brand for sponsorship reasons. Recommended Offy engine clearances at the time were considerably greater than those of passenger cars in the days before the development of modern bearings and lubricants, and before strict limits were imposed on oil consumption at Indianapolis. Piston-skirt-to-cylinder-wall clearance was 0.0120 inch, compared to .001 inch on Ford V-8 engines of the day. Offy rods were fitted to 0.003 inch compared to 0.0025 inch in the Ford. Those specifications were made quite a bit closer after World War II when Clevite inserts were used instead of poured babbitt bearings. Thirty years later Meyer & Drake recommended piston skirt clearance of 0.008 inch and rod bearings fitted to 0.002 inch.

The Wilke Agency

By the late 1930s, Offenhauser's success, particularly with the midget, had given the company something it had not had before: a nascent dealer network. Bob Wilke was the first to handle more than an occasional sale.

Wilke was born in Waukeegan, Illinois, on December 31, 1908. By the time he was 30, he was living in Milwaukee where the family owned Leader Cards Incorporated, a large producer of envelopes and business stationery. He bought his first midget, powered by a cut-in-half Miller eight, from the Marchese brothers in 1938. Though the Marcheses did well with their Millers, Wilke found that the Offenhauser engine was the ticket to winning midget races.

In 1940, he bought his first Offy and soon ordered four more, making a deal with Fred Offenhauser to handle the engines as his Midwest dealer. According to Offenhauser Engineering Company. records, the first Offy Wilke bought was a 95-cubic-inch engine, serial number 70.

The Wilke Agency represented Meyer & Drake until 1949, the longest-running dealership for the Offenhauser engine in the company's 50-year history.

Ralph Wilke collection

The Maseratis had a reputation in Europe as fast but not reliable, but Hennings worked his magic well enough that Shaw's mount went 500 miles—twice—at more than 114 miles per hour. Shaw's success attracted four more Maserati entries at the Speedway in 1940, but none of their mechanics had Hennings' touch. Maseratis continued to race at Indy, but with indifferent results well into the 1950s.

Defense Work

In May 1940, Franklin Roosevelt announced the buildup of a 40,000-plane Air Corps and that summer Lockheed Aircraft Corporation came to Offenhauser to do some of its machine work. Counting defense contracts, Offenhauser Engineering shipped $73,532.57 in parts and engines before the end of the last full peacetime year.

While increasing his aircraft work in 1940, Offenhauser continued to supply the racers. Of the 17 Offys entered at Indianapolis that year, 15 qualified but only two of the top 11 finishers were his. Rex Mays' *Bowes-Winfield* that finished second had been designed by Goossen and largely built in the Offenhauser plant, as had Ted Horn's fourth-place Miller, so Fred's team was not unhappy with the results.

By the 1940s, the Offenhauser shop was acquiring a reputation almost as impressive as Miller's in the 1920s. Not only racing people but other celebrities stopped in to see the source of the famous Offy engines. Gary Cooper, Amelia Earhart, Clark Gable, and foreign athletes and fliers clamored to see the little plant on West 62nd Street. In 1941, the last Indianapolis race before World War II, there were 16 Offys entered, 39 percent of the cars that qualified were Offenhausers, and Floyd Davis and Mauri Rose shared the victory in Lou Moore's 270 Offy.

Offenhauser's workload and income soared as the company picked up more and more work from the aircraft industry. Business was good and Offenhauser bought a new Cadillac—with cash—to carry him through the coming conflict. In early 1941, to handle ever greater defense contract demands, Offenhauser rented out his little 4,540-square-foot shop to Corliss Machine Company and moved his plant and 28 machinists to a 7,800-square-foot brick plant at 2001 West Gage Avenue next door to the building on Gramercy Place where Harry A. Miller Inc. had had his last Los Angeles shop. On January 4, 1941, before moving the machinery in, Fred and 400 guests celebrated the opening of his new shop with a gala party complete with potted palms and a five-piece band.

Offy Goes to War

Soon after the 1941 Indianapolis race, the shop all but ceased race engine production. The last engine, a midget, serial number 101, was shipped on July 17, 1941. That year the company grossed $130,577.26, seven times what Fred had made in his first year after Miller's bankruptcy. Offenhauser took home a salary of $12,000.00. The company went into debt in 1941 for the first time, borrowing $10,000 to buy new machinery. During the war Fred worked from 7:30 AM to 9:00 PM five days a week and 7:30 AM to 4:00 PM Saturdays, Sundays, and holidays. He went two years with only one Sunday off. Working

Mike Caruso, one of the top Eastern car owners, seen here at the Freeport, New York, Municipal Stadium in 1940. Caruso was born in San Pedro, Italy, March 4, 1899, and came to America as an infant. He operated a salvage yard in Hicksville, Long Island, and got into racing big cars in 1926. In 1935, when the midgets appeared in the East, Caruso built one powered by a four-cylinder engine out of a Bugatti Brescia. Later Caruso either cut an eight-cylinder Bugatti in half or used a somewhat larger Type 40 (two-liter) engine. Although Caruso bought an Offy in 1936, the Bugatti was so successful that Ernie Gesell was able to beat Ronney Householder's Offy when Householder came east in 1937. A visitor to the Bugatti plant recalled that Ettore Bugatti kept a photo of the Caruso Bugatti midget on his desk. When Caruso bought other Offys, Fred Offenhauser gave him a 15 percent discount off the $1,200 price because of the influence Caruso had as a showman. Mike Nazaruk, Ted Tappet, and Bill Schindler were three other noted Mike Caruso midget drivers. After the midgets began to fade, Mike stretched the #3 Kurtis into a sprint car and installed a Roots blower on the midget engine. Caruso died in 1982. David Uihlein bought the Bugatti Brescia chassis in 1960, retrieved the engine from Caruso, and restored both to running condition. *Bruce Craig collection*

those long hours, Offenhauser Engineering turned out $203,629.96 worth of defense work during the first full year of the war.

By the time World War II stopped race engine production, Offenhauser-powered cars had won seven out of the 15 100-mile championship dirt track races run between 1935 and 1941. Three national AAA champions—Kelly Petillo in 1935, Wilbur Shaw in 1937, and Floyd Roberts in 1938—had won their laurels behind Offy engines. Seventy- six Offenhauser-powered cars had been entered at Indianapolis and 69, an enviable 94 percent, had qualified. Offys had won the race four times[20] in seven years and a Miller engine Offenhauser's shop had built won another 500. It was a record to savor for the steady businessman machinist with no pretensions to genius.

After Pearl Harbor was attacked on December 7, 1941, Offenhauser's plant went to work 24 hours a day, seven days a week helping Lockheed develop and produce hydraulic booster control valves for the twin- engine P-38 Lightning fighter and the model 49 Constellation four-engine transport. In 1944 Goossen returned to the Offenhauser shop as a full-time employee where he was to remain as staff draftsman and engineer for 30 more years, guardian of the Miller designs to the end of his life.

George Mather of Pasadena watches as Fred Offenhauser points out the one-cylinder "Offy" engine in son Dickie's Junior Midget in 1941. The car was a replica of Sam Hanks' famous #5 *Black Beauty* midget which had been built by Roy Richter. Contemporary reports credit Offenhauser with building these Junior Midget cars, but it is more likely he had Richter or Myron Stevens make the bodies and frames while he supplied the modified Lauson engines, made originally for a washing machine or a lawnmower. Offenhauser built a special piston, rod, and head. The little cars had four fake exhaust pipes on the right side added to resemble the Offy midgets. In 1941, the popularity of the midgets bred these as an early form of 3/4 midgets (TQs). "Little rich kids" drove the miniature race cars on weekends at a 1/10-mile track Johnny McDowell operated for Lou Fageol. Offenhauser employees Al Long and Hal Minyard ran the shows for McDowell in exchange for play time themselves in the little cars. Fageol's son and those of Willie Tupman and Sports Briggs' son were among dozens of youngsters under 14 who raced these little cars. Long recalled years later that girls were allowed to drive until one incident in which a girl lost control, drove off the track, and froze on the gas until she hit a wire that nearly decapitated her. After that girls were demoted to trophy queen duty. Dickie Mather won the 1941 championship and Yvonne "Sissy" Johnson awarded the trophy to him at a ceremony at Gilmore early in the 1942 season, according to *National Auto Racing News* for April 2, 1942. Frank Kurtis and the Lucas Auto Co. also built pre-war junior midgets. Several of these cars survive and are run as vintage TQs. *Gloria Madsen collection*

Lew Welsch, Bud Winfield, and Cliff Bergere with the two Novi cars behind Winfield's place in LaCanada, California, in 1946. *Gordon Schroeder*

CHAPTER FIVE

Oval Track Engines, Large and Small

While Offenhauser was building and improving his own four-cylinder engines in the 1930s and 1940s, others were experimenting with their own ideas for racing powerplants. Floyd Dreyer, Hal Hosterman, and others built four-cylinder engines for the dirt half-miles, but Championship engines required a higher level of expertise, though Charley Voelker and Skinny Clemons tried their hands at Indy engine-building. There were few men capable of doing the sophisticated design work of sizing ports and bearings, selecting valve angles and other such necessary details for Championship-level competition. The major auto manufacturers did not have the racing experience, and the backyard mechanics lacked the money, the sophistication, and the equipment to turn such ideas into successful Indianapolis engines. Almost all of the "new" engines raced on American tracks between 1930 and 1963 were really variations on Miller/Offenhauser designs.

Offenhauser and Goossen were capable of building almost anything that the state-of-the-art engine required, and were glad to do it for anyone willing to pay the cost. For a half century the Miller, Offenhauser, and subsequently Meyer & Drake plants were where most Indianapolis-class racing engines were built in the United States. They could handle the design details, the casting and the machining. As Miller's shop was the place where Bob Burman went to have his Peugeot repaired and updated, so the tradition continued.

Of course auto manufacturers in Europe devoted a great deal of effort to high-performance engines, too, but the Europeans were not generally successful on American-type oval tracks. The Boyle 8CTF Maserati was the only foreign car to win at Indianapolis in the 45 years between 1920 and 1964. The foreigners *did* invade Long Island for the Vanderbilt Cup revival in 1936 and 1937 and whipped the Americans on a specially built road course at Roosevelt Raceway, but that simply proved what everyone already knew: American cars were designed for ovals, and foreign race cars were designed for twisty road tracks.

After Fred Frame bought the Sparks-Weirick "Catfish" in 1932 he campaigned it around the country and entered it at Indianapolis in 1934 with Johnny Seymour driving. Later he sold it to Charles Worley. In 1937, Frank Brisko entered it at Indianapolis as the *Elgin Piston Pin Spl*. By 1938 it had been rebuilt with a conventional one-man body, and Emil Andres drove it at Indianapolis. Andres said it was "a monstrosity" that nearly killed him when a wheel collapsed on the 45th lap. According to Andres, the car was totalled in another race and scrapped. It is seen here at Union Speedway in New Jersey in 1932. *Dixon Singiser collection*

If you wanted to develop a successful new engine for championship racing in the United States between 1925 and 1964 you went to one place: the Miller and then the Offenhauser shops in Los Angeles.

A Score of Custom-Built Engines

Fred and Leo built some 20 special engines over the 13 years, 1933–1946, the exact number depending upon how one describes some of the variations. In addition there were a few relatively minor modifications of standard Offenhauser engines for racing on either water or land, or for street use.

Sparks and Weirick Specials

The first of the four-cylinder specials was the Sparks 220 of 1931, described in chapter three. The 220 antedated the Offenhauser shop, but illustrates the process.

Art Sparks and Paul Weirick raced at Oakland in the early 1930s and one of the fans who hung around their pit was a noted academic aerodynamicist from Stanford, Dr. Elliott Gray Reid. Reid offered to work with the air flow characteristics of the 200\220 and found that, not surprisingly, siamesed ports led to interference between adjacent cylinders. Sparks' solution was to use four oval-shaped intake ports on the side of the block, a fix adopted thereafter by Offenhauser for all his subsequent engines except the Offy midget, which had round ports for its single intake and exhaust valve per cylinder. Bill White took a hand in upgrading the 220, paying for engines built with notchless crankcases (an idea some attribute originally to Sparks) in which the bearing webs had to be inserted from the side, a laborious process.

Sparks and Weirick, who had collaborated on the 220, were looking for an edge over their Ascot rivals by improving the usual Miller/Offy iron. Indeed, Sparks thought he knew more about engine design than Miller himself.

The mighty Novi engine being assembled in Bud Winfield's garage in La Canada, California, in early 1946. Contrast the rough, unfinished garage—woodworking tools hung on its walls—with modern engine shops! This photo shows clearly that the Novi was not simply a pair of Offy midget blocks hung on a V-8 crankcase. From left to right: Pete Clark, Tony Morosco, Winfield, Marvin Jenkins, and Lewis Welch. *Marvin Jenkins collection*

Reid and Stanford engineering instructor Ulysses A. Patchett told Sparks and Weirick that they could design an aerodynamic body that would have far less wind resistance than contemporary race cars. The Stanford professors made the design a graduate class project and Clyde Adams built the car. The underlying racing chassis of the day was a three-spring design with a cross spring in the rear and parallel semi-elliptics in the front. Shaping the sheet metal to cover the front springs gave the aerodynamic bodies of the Sparks and Weirick car a strange shovel-nosed appearance. (When chassis builders adopted the two-spring or later torsion bar suspension, body shapes became more attractive.) Tested at Muroc Dry Lake, the car ran 147.355 miles per hour on methanol fuel for a new class C international record.

Quickly dubbed the *Catfish* because of its shape, it could only manage 13th at Indianapolis in 1932, and Sparks and Weirick sold it for $8,500 [21] to Fred Frame. Frame used its odd shape as a drawing card to boost his appearance money at tracks around the country. He and Harry Hartz later used the car, powered by a 255 Offy, to set Class C straightaway records of up to 152 miles per hour, a mark Offenhauser used widely in his advertising. The chassis ran at Indianapolis in 1934, and for six more years, carrying a Cragar and then a Brisko engine. It was one of Duke Nalon's early rides in 1937, but in 1938 it crashed on the 45th lap, nearly killing driver Emil Andres who called it "a monstrosity."

Sparks put the money from the Catfish into a pair of 220 engines stroked to 247 cubic inches that Offenhauser built in Miller's struggling shop. As previously discussed, the first of the two single-seaters known as *Poison Lil* proved to be a hot ticket at Ascot and other tracks around the country. Sparks had Goossen draw up plans for a 220 stroked to 239 cubic inches to run at Indianapolis in 1934. Goossen, at Art's suggestion, gave the engine a two-valve hemispherical shape offering the smallest possible combustion chamber surface area per cubic inch of capacity to squeeze the most energy out of each charge. At Indianapolis, driver Al Gordon qualified the Sparks car at 116.273 miles per hour, which would have put him on the outside of the front row if he had made the run on the first day. As it was, the Sparks car was late in making its trial and had to start 17th. Gordon crashed on the 66th lap.

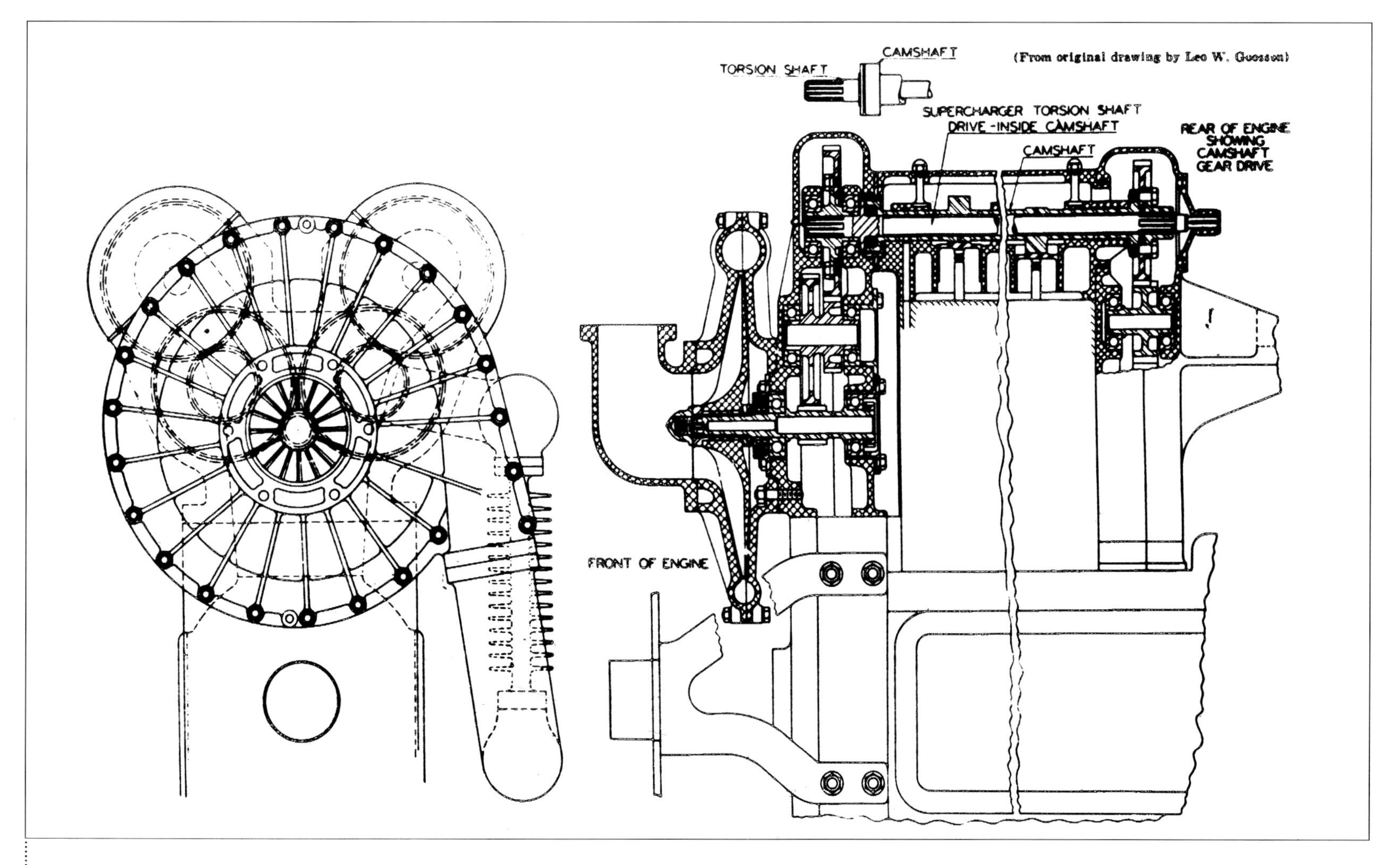

Details of the supercharger drive of the Winfield straight-eight, as drawn by Leo Goossen. Note the drive shafts to the supercharger ran through hollow camshafts and were long enough to twist slightly and absorb some of the shock of acceleration and deceleration. *Mark Dees collection*

THORNE ENGINEERING: PROMISE UNFULFILLED

JOEL W. THORNE, JR., WAS BORN IN NEW YORK IN 1914. WHEN HIS FATHER died 10 years later, Thorne inherited a fortune, albeit one tied up in trust funds that doled out money to him on a monthly basis. He went to Rutgers and the University of London, majoring in motorcycles, fast women, and faster boats. He sponsored a car, unsuccessfully, at Indianapolis in 1934. His own first auto race was the 1935 Automobile Racing Club of America (ARCA) "Grand Prix of America," run on country roads in Briarcliff, New York, near the estates of its wealthy members. Joel, driving a Ford roadster that had been prepared for the Elgin Road Race, was leading until a late race pit stop. He showed his sportsmanship by storming off after protesting that he should have won.

In 1936, he took two cars to Indy, but could not pass the drivers' test. The other car failed to qualify. The next year he bought Art Sparks' Big Six and after it showed promise, made Sparks an offer Art could not refuse. Joel was competent enough behind the wheel to finish fifth at Indianapolis in 1940, but he continued to behave like the spoiled brat he was, crashing cars and motorcycles. Thorne Engineering and Sparks parted ways in 1943.

After World War II, Thorne pulled the cars out of storage and persuaded Sparks to help prepare them for Indianapolis. Rudi Caraccolia was given one of them, but crashed it in practice.

Thorne Engineering could have been real competition for Offenhauser. Joel Thorne had the money to create a top-notch race engine and chassis company. The original capitalization was $300,000. Compare that figure to the $75,000 value Offenhauser placed on his shop in 1946. Art Sparks had proven he had good ideas. He was able to apply scientific solutions to engineering problems, and he had access to Leo Goossen's talents. Two talented metal workers, Clyde Adams and Frank

Kurtis, helped build the next generation of Sparks' racing cars. If all of them had been able to work together, the combination could have become a top race car and engine builder that might have eclipsed Offenhauser.

Sparks hired several ex-Miller employees, including such well-known names as Joe Petrali, Red Garnant, and Eddie Offutt. Bill France was part of the Thorne pit crew at Indianapolis in 1938. But Thorne was a dilettante who began to use the company's capital as his personal slush fund when the allowance from his trusts ran short. Thorne Engineering never fulfilled its promise.

Indy and the AAA rewrote the rules for 1938, and allowed only 183 cubic inches for supercharged engines. To meet the change Sparks had Stevenson draw up a 179-cubic-inch six, most of which, aside from connecting rods that Offenhauser made, was built in Thorne Engineering's own new machine shop. Much of the Little Six engine was made of magnesium which is subject to damaging corrosion when exposed to methanol, the alcohol normally used as racing fuel. To overcome the problem Sparks had to burn ethanol, or grain alcohol, which is less corrosive and gives slightly better mileage than methanol. As grain alcohol is raw whisky, it is taxed by the Treasury, and Sparks had to take out a federal license to buy it in racing quantities.

Thorne Engineering built three of the Little Sixes for Indianapolis in 1938 and during May had several inquiries from prospective purchasers. If the engines had performed to expectations they might have been off and running, and a six might have conquered Indianapolis instead of the Offy four. As it was, valve spring failure put them out of the race again. Nonetheless, orders came in for 11 of the engines. Thorne, however, refused to allow Sparks to sell them to competitors.

Two workers move the Sparks Little Six engine of 1938 off a mill in the Thorne shop. This engine powered George Robson's *Thorne Engineering Special* to win the 500 in 1946. In many ways the Sparks engines followed tried-and-true Miller/Offenhauser engine architecture, while foreshadowing the Drake-Goossen-Sparks turbo-Offy of the 1970s. This was the first asymmetrical Miller/Offy/Goossen block and the first one with a manifold to direct extra water to the exhaust valve area until the turbo Offys of the 1960s required more exhaust-side cooling. *Gordon Schroeder collection*

In 1935 Sparks and Weirick had Offenhauser build a larger "220" with a bore of 4.25 inches, displacing 269.4 cubic inches. Rex Mays put the car on the pole at Indy at 120.736 miles per hour but fell out of the race with a broken suspension on lap 123 while leading. In 1936, the car ran out of fuel, eight laps from the end.

The Big Six

In 1937, in order to attract foreign cars and drivers, the new Indianapolis rules lifted the blown engine limit to 366 cubic inches and did away with fuel restrictions. Looking at that as an opportunity for a world-beating supercharged engine, Sparks decided to build a blown six-cylinder. At the time neither Miller nor Offenhauser had ever built a six. (Miller was to build them later for Gulf Oil.) The design does offer some advantage in smoothness and relatively more valve area per cubic inch though with potentially less torque than a four. The resulting 337-cubic-inch engine came to be known as the "Big Six."

Art rented a shop near Goossen's office on Florence Avenue in Los Angeles so he and Leo could work closely on the engine. (Offenhauser did not have enough drafting work to keep Leo on the payroll, and Goossen was working as a part-time freelancer for Harry Miller, Offenhauser, the aircraft plants, and anyone else who needed a top-notch draftsman and designer.) Goossen drew up an engine that had a bore and stroke of 3.875x 4.750 inches. It sported only two valves per cylinder but, of course, was supercharged. The engine looked much like a stretched-out 220 but had quite a few special Sparks-requested features. For example, it used a blower impeller that Dr. Reid had based on the superchargers then used on Curtis aircraft engines in which diffuser vanes were abandoned and an advanced "spiral volute" or snail-shell-shaped housing focused the compressed air-fuel mixture into the manifold.

The Big Six was built by Offenhauser's plant to Goossen's designs, though Sparks' own crew of Takeo Hirashima and Otto Wolfer probably did the final assembly.

The supercharged eight-cylinder Winfield engine in Mays' *Bowes Seal-Fast Special*. Designed originally for Lou Meyer, it was a forerunner of the Winfield-designed Novi of 1941. *Marvin Jenkins collection*

The Big Six set a qualifying speed record of 125.287 miles per hour for the 1937 Indy race, but because it missed the first day of qualifications it started 19th in the field. Driver Jimmy Snyder easily took the lead on lap five, but too little time had been spent on testing and on the 20th lap the engine's Buick valve springs began to fail, one by one. Immediately after the race, the Cummins Diesel Company offered to buy the six and hire Sparks at $5,000 a year as a consultant—a lot of money in 1937. Before Sparks could make up his mind wealthy playboy Joel Thorne appeared and offered him $12,000 for the car and a lifetime contract at $100 a week to set up a race shop to be known as Thorne Engineering Company.[22]

The Bowes Winfield Eight

In 1938, with sponsorship money from Robert Bowes of the Bowes Seal-Fast tire patch company, Lou Meyer decided to create his own blown 183-cubic-inch engine. He turned to Offenhauser, Goossen, and Bud Winfield to design and build an engine which would be the last of the line of Miller/Offy straight eights. The first blower they used was an English vane type, which was not satisfactory, nor was the next, a Roots supercharger. In April, in desperation, almost as the car was being readied to go to Indianapolis, Goossen drew up a tried-and-true Miller-style centrifugal blower. The result was, in effect, a slightly larger Miller 122 with an improved supercharger drive arrangement using long torsion bars inside the camshafts to absorb acceleration-deceleration shocks to the blower. The engine closely resembled the 1932 Hartz and the 1934 midget in bore and stroke and in having two valves per cylinder, but a slightly shallower 84-degree valve angle. Fred Offenhauser did the castings and most, but not all, of the machining.

The cross-spring chassis Goossen designed to Bowes' limited budget was not up to the power of the engine and the car was a bear to handle. In 1938, Meyer qualified at Indianapolis at only 120.525 miles per hour, more than 5 miles per hour slower than pole-sitter Floyd Roberts, and finished 16th. In 1939, Winfield added an intercooler and upped the supercharger pressure. Meyer then qualified second-fastest, almost 10 miles per hour better than the year before. He crashed on the 197th lap, in his last race at the Brickyard.

Rex Mays put the car on the Indy pole in 1940. At 127.850 miles per hour he was 3 miles slower than Meyer's 1939 speed. He finished second to Wilbur Shaw under a yellow flag. Mays was again second to Mauri Rose at the Speedway in 1941, but at Milwaukee and Syracuse, the only other races on the AAA Championship schedule, Mays and the Bowes car won convincingly, and they took the 1941 National AAA title.

Mays continued to drive the Bowes, and in 1946 he qualified it at Indy at 128.816, behind only the Novi's 133.994. (Neither car made its run on the first day of qualification.) Mays started 14th and went out after 26 laps with manifold problems. He also won dirt track 100-milers at Langhorne, the Indianapolis Fairgrounds, and Milwaukee.

Frank Kurtis built a new chassis for the Bowes car for the 1947 500, and Mays drove it to sixth place. He was 19th in 1948, but in 1949 the old Winfield did not make the race. Bowes' mechanic, Pete Clark, put Mel Hansen in the car in 1949 when the engine was known as a "Meyer-Offy," but Mel was unable to qualify. Bill Cantrell had similar luck in 1950 after which the car was sold to Franklin Merkler. Neither Jimmy Daywalt (1951–1952) nor Jackie Holmes in 1953 could get up to the 135-mile-per-hour speed needed to make the race in those days. After a 12-season career, the Bowes was finally retired.

Rex Mays in the *Bowes Seal-Fast Special* in 1940. The engine was the blown Winfield eight that Goossen designed for Lou Meyer, and which was built, in part, by Offenhauser for the 1938 race at Indianapolis. *Bruce Craig collection/ Indianapolis Motor Speedway*

THE WINFIELD BROTHERS

ED WINFIELD WAS BORN NORTH OF LOS ANGELES IN LA CANADA, CALIFORNIA, IN 1901, and his brother William, always known as Bud to racing people, came along three years later. As youngsters the Winfield brothers thrived on hopping up automobiles. Ed turned a stripped-down Ford Model T into an early hot rod at the age of 11. He went to work in Harry Miller's shop at 14 where he became interested in the design of cylinder heads, cams, and carburetors. He began driving on the local dirt tracks, and his Winfield flathead became famous as the hot setup for low-buck racers of the time. In his book *Ford, The Dust and the Glory*, Leo Levine called him "the father of hot-rodding and its first prodigy."

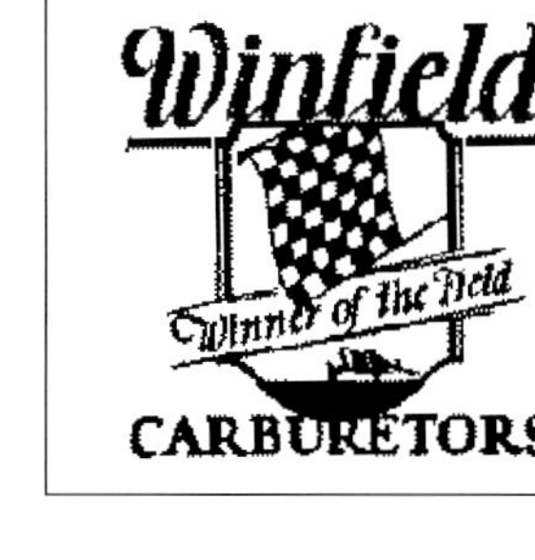

Ed was so successful with fuel flow technology that a series of his carburetors was designed for the hot rod and aftermarket trade. In 1924, a company was organized to build and market them nationally. So good were they that Pete DePaolo used a pair on the Duesenberg with which he won Indianapolis in 1925. "Winfield Carburetors, Winners of the Field" became their slogan, and Winfields displaced Miller carburetors on racing cars for most of the next two decades.

After Ed Winfield retired from the track in 1927, he became something of a recluse. He retreated to his home and worked on his designs for automotive camshafts, seldom going to the races, saying there was no point to his going either to the track or out to Muroc Dry Lake to watch the hot-rodders run. Ed later moved to a place near San Francisco and worked either by himself or with the aid of mechanic Clyde Jones. Marvin Jenkins said many years later that Ed would tell anyone he didn't care for to "go jump in the lake" no matter how much money they were offering for his help.

Despite his genius, Harry Miller had never excelled at cam design, and Fred Offenhauser was practical enough to leave that art to others. Winfield cams became standard on Offenhauser engines, although in various "grinds." There were Winfield 4s, 5s, and other cams for the Offy, depending on the track length and the owner or mechanic's preference. The No. 4 Winfield had a valve lift of 0.400 inch and opened the intake valve at 20 degrees before top dead center (BTDC) while the No. 5 had a lift of 0.375 inch and opened the intake at 24 degrees BTDC. The No. 4 exhaust valve opened at 48 degrees before bottom dead center (BBDC) and the No. 5 at 56 degrees BBDC. The No. 5 was said to be better on paved tracks and the No. 4 on dirt.

Bud Winfield worked as field representative for Winfield carburetors at tracks in the West and at Indianapolis, lending a hand at solving whatever technical problems might arise. Eventually he set up his own shop on Curran Street in La Canada, not far from Ed's place on Alger Street in Glendale. Bud, unlike Ed, was outgoing and friendly. An expert in his own right on cams, engines, and carburetors, with Goossen's help he designed the Bowes eight of 1938, which showed promise, though it never was a winner at Indianapolis. His greatest achievement was with another eight-cylinder engine designed for Lewis W. Welch three years later: the Novi.

The Novi

Ed and Bud Winfield were good self-taught engineers with a successful record in hot-rodding and on the shorter tracks such as Ascot. By the late 1930s they were ready to take on Indianapolis.

The Novi was the most famous of the engines Offenhauser built to a customer's specifications. The Novis, especially when placed in the low-slung front-drive chassis Frank Kurtis built for them in 1946, always brought the crowd at Indianapolis to its feet, particularly after Ralph Hepburn broke the track record by five miles per hour in 1946. The scream of the supercharged Novi engine, turning far faster than the ordinary long-stroke four-cylinder Offy, was frightening in its intensity. The sound alone made the Novis the popular favorites at Indy over all of the 21 years they were entered there.

Lew Welch was head of a company in Novi, Michigan, which supplied parts to the Ford Motor Company. He had worked as a Ford employee in the early 1930s and was a friend of Ray Dahlinger, one of Henry Ford's closest companions. (Dahlinger had been a bodyguard to Ford on the abortive 1915 Peace Ship attempt to stop World War I, a test driver for the Model A, the man who married Ford's alleged mistress, Evangeline Coté, and general handler of "special projects" for the old man.)

Welch ran cars with Offenhauser power from 1937 through 1940. Henry Ford had snapped up and impounded the 10 Miller-Ford cars after the 1935 Indianapolis fiasco, but he allowed Welch to buy two of them. Welch's 1939 entry was an ex-Miller-Ford carrying a 270 Offy engine. Cliff Bergere qualified it 10th fastest at 123.835 miles per hour and placed third in the race. In 1940, Winfield and Welch worked together and the car was sponsored by Bowes Seal Fast. Hepburn spun that car when the steering froze on lap 47.

Somewhere Welch and Winfield found the money for a mighty, new effort in the winter of 1940–1941. The evidence suggests, but does not prove, that Henry Ford offered encouragement and cash to have Winfield design a powerful supercharged V-8 racing engine. At the time the Ford passenger car was the most noted V-8 on the road. Marvin Jenkins, son of Bonneville speed king Ab Jenkins, told the author that Dahlinger supplied money and parts to Welch, but that the Novi was not an official Ford project.

Marv Jenkins was a relief driver for his father at Bonneville in the late 1930s and a pilot for Western Air Lines before World War II. He took instrument training in Los Angeles in 1941 and was pressed into service in his spare time to carry patterns and parts back and forth between the Offenhauser plant and the foundry during the building of the first Novi engine. After the war he worked as a pilot for Welch and as a mechanic on the Novi at Indianapolis.

When Welch asked Bud Winfield to design a supercharged V-8 engine to replace the 270 in the Miller/Ford chassis, Bud and brother Ed proposed the general outline of the engine to Offenhauser, who hired Leo Goossen to do the detail drawings from which the engine was built. Goossen was always willing to design whatever the customer wanted, but he said years later that he had more freedom with the Novi than any other engine. The Winfields and Welch specified it to be a V-8 and insisted on using only three main bearings, but Leo decided on the over-square bore and stroke, valve angles, rod length, port sizes, supercharger diameter, and most other details. He did the drawings in about a month of night and day work in a little pattern shop in Hollywood.

The project was done, as Ed Winfield later told Griff Borgeson, "in one-tenth the time it would take anyone else." The blocks were cast by the Macaulay Foundry in Berkeley. Fred Offenhauser had the Andria Pattern Company make the foundry patterns for Welch and gave him exclusive use of them for a year, after which time Offenhauser could sell the engines to all comers. [23] But no one ever asked Fred to build them their own Novi.

The Offenhauser shop installed the engine in one of Welch's Miller-Ford chassis, which it clearly overpowered. The Novi engine had been designed with a Ford bolt pattern bell housing to drop easily into the old Miller-Ford chassis. In the last prewar race at Indianapolis, Ralph Hepburn brought the Novi in fourth with a block under the gas pedal to keep him from using too much of the engine's tremendous power.

At that time, Winfield's and Goossen's Novi design was only the third American overhead-cam V-8 racing engine built (the first was for the 1932 Miller FWD car and the second was a Riley sohc V-8 built in 1940). It had the advantages of short overall length, compact intake passages and small cylinder size with a relatively larger valve-area-to-displacement ratio than is possible on a similar-displacement four. As such it pointed the way to modern V-8 engines such as the Ford four-cam, Cosworth, and Ilmor Chevy that dominated Indianapolis in the 1980s and 1990s.

Although the resulting engine looked like two Offy midget blocks hung together on a V-8 crankcase—the displacement was about double the midget—the Novi was not just a mix and match of old midget parts. The blocks were bolted to the case differently, and the included angle between the two valves in each cylinder was 84 degrees. There were other relatively small differences, but the engine and the layout obviously owed much to Harry Miller's blown engine idiom of the 1920s.

The Novi was supercharged by a 10-inch diameter centrifugal compressor feeding the intake manifolds through a thin, flat intercooler located on top of the engine. At an engine speed of 8,000 rpm, the blower wheel itself, rotating at 5.35 times engine speed, turned at nearly 43,000 rpm. Abrupt throttle changes impose severe stresses on mechanically driven blower mechanisms and to compensate, Goossen provided a long, somewhat flexible drive shaft, known as a quill, that would twist slightly and absorb the shocks of acceleration and deceleration as in the 1929 Rolls-Royce.

Since the 1935 Miller-Ford chassis proved to be inadequate, in 1946 Welch hired Frank Kurtis to build two new front-drive chassis to Welch's specifications with Goossen doing the drawings. In retrospect it was a mistake to put the Novi engine into a front drive. For his own postwar Indy cars Kurtis built a succession of rear-drive chassis that did very well for him and his customers. The Novi's 700 horsepower, and the great weight of the entire chassis—3,500 pounds fully fueled—put too much stress on the tires of the day. Kurtis urged Welch to let him build a rear-drive Novi but that would have to wait until 1956. Before Welch abandoned them the front-drive cars killed two experienced drivers, Ralph Hepburn in 1948 and Chet Miller in 1953.

The 1935 Miller-Ford chassis in 1941 at the Offenhauser shop where it was modified to accept the Novi V-8 engine. *Gloria Madsen collection*

Ralph Hepburn in the Novi at Indianapolis in 1946 when it set a new track record of 134.449 miles per hour. The engine quit on the 121st lap and Hepburn was credited with 14th place. *Bruce Craig collection/Indianapolis Motor Speedway*

By contrast, Lou Moore, sponsored by the Blue Crown Spark Plug Company, won three successive Indy races, 1947–1949, with Offy-powered front-drives. The Moore cars were superbly prepared and developed and the 270 engines, unsupercharged, probably produced only 300 horsepower. In 1948 and 1949, the Novis qualified faster than the Blue Crowns, but the Blue Crowns won.

Hepburn finished 14th in the Novi in 1946 after the engine stalled on lap 121. Postwar, under Welch, the only good finish the Novis managed was Duke Nalon's third in 1948. Nalon, still around in 1996, was the driver who most nearly tamed the Novi, setting a track record in 1951 of 136.498 miles per hour. He had been severely burned in the Novi two years earlier when the rear axle snapped and he hit the wall. That car has been restored and rests in the Speedway Museum. In 1996, the car that Miller died in was undergoing restoration in Buck Boudeman's Michigan shop.

Speed King Ab Jenkins looks over the Novi equipped with a special streamlined cockpit housing before going to Bonneville for speed-record attempts. Frank Kurtis added the stabilizing fin and wheel discs and built the enclosure. Jenkins, then 66, decided he was not comfortable with the car, and his son Marvin drove it for its record attempts. *Marvin Jenkins collection*

Welch took one of the Novis to Bonneville in 1947 for straightaway record runs under the sponsorship of Mobil Oil. He had Quinn Epperly, a metal man at Kurtis-Kraft, fabricate a large tail fin and an enclosed cockpit. Ab Jenkins, who was then 66, was not comfortable in the car at speed and declined to drive on a record attempt so his son Marvin took the wheel for a late evening run. The results were not overwhelming, as the Novi turned only a 179.434-mile-per-hour average for 10 miles over a circular course. That speed and the intervening one- and five-mile times were Class D records, but fell somewhat short of the 200-mile-per-hour expectations for the screaming supercharged V-8. There were oil pickup troubles and other problems in running an Indianapolis car on a right-hand circular course in sustained full-throttle runs and there was too little time to sort them out, Marvin said.

Also on the Bonneville salt that week was Danny Oakes who drove John Balch's Lesovsky-built, carburetor-equipped Offy midget to a new U.S. midget and Class E record (two liters) of 139.120 miles per hour, breaking Ronney Householder's 1939 midget mark of 123.290 miles per hour. The Balch car was back in 1949 for another attempt, but at the time Oakes was under suspension by AAA for driving in United Racing Association (URA) midget shows. Rex Mays took over the Balch car (then owned by N.J. Rounds) and, using fuel injection, drove 147.095 miles per hour, setting a midget record that stood for 39 years.

Andy Granatelli bought the entire Novi team from Welch in 1961 and went on to race the cars in various chassis through 1965, when they failed to qualify. After he got the cars from Lew Welch, he went to Meyer & Drake to get copies of the Goossen engine drawings, which Meyer sold him for $500. Goossen related that Meyer offered to make copies of the originals, but that Granatelli said he'd just borrow the vellums and make his own copies. "He never brought them back," Leo said.

According to Goossen, after Granatelli rebuilt the engines they failed the first time they ran at Indianapolis because the timing gears had not been heat-treated.

Another, lesser-known Winfield engine that ran at Indianapolis was originally designed for well-known Indy car owner Lou Fageol's Twin-Coach buses. A big, single overhead-cam six, it performed admirably on the streets of Los Angeles. In 1948, Fageol had Bud Winfield hop up the bus engine and stuff it into a Stevens chassis. Bill Cantrell finished 16th with it but a year later, in 1949, it was 0.5 miles per hour too slow to qualify, at 125.055.

Joe Lencki

In the mid-1920s Chicago mechanic Joe Lencki was running the dirt tracks in the Midwest with various Ford-derived engines including one twin-cam "DO" head by Gallivan on a specially cast block and crankcase. After owning a succession of Miller and Offy engines Lencki developed his own ideas about what might win at Indy, and in 1938 went to Goossen to have a DOHC six-cylinder model designed. The first Lencki engine had two valves per cylinder in a hemispherical combustion chamber and a displacement of 270 cubic inches. The Offenhauser plant built the engine, of course, which looked a lot like the standard 270 Offy except for the two extra cylinders, but if you called it a "six-cylinder Offy" Lencki probably would have slugged you.

In 1939, the Lencki six's first year at Indy, the fuel pump went out on lap 188. For 1940 Lencki had a four-valve-per-cylinder pent-roof block made, displacing 260 inches. It threw a rod on lap 52. When he entered it at Indianapolis in 1941 Lencki said the displacement was 265 cubic inches.[24] Emil Andres crashed the car in the northeast turn on lap five in a tangle with Joel Thorne in the Little Six.

Joe Lencki works on his six-cylinder twin-cam engine. The lower cover of the timing gear train is at the right holding at the top half-time gear that reduced crankshaft speed to drive the cams. The engine was designed by Leo Goossen and built by Offenhauser Engineering, but Joe would not hear of it being described as a "six-cylinder Offy." Note the oil tube to the left of the gears that provides lubrication to the cams. *Bruce Craig collection*

During World War II, Lencki worked at a Chrysler plant in Chicago building R-3350 engines for B-29 bombers. He also produced a mysterious fuel additive known as the "Speedway Cocktail" and later an STP-like oil treatment known as Lenckite. It was accepted by the FAA for use in aircraft engines, but its ingredients were never revealed.

Mauri Rose wrecked one Lencki car in 1946. In 1947 Charlie Van Acker crashed another of the Lenckis on lap 24. The magneto in the second Lencki car failed Andres on lap 150. In 1948 Joe and his mechanic George Lyons had both cars, the hemi and the four-valve, out to qualify with Ronney Householder and Cowboy O'Rourke as his drivers, but neither made the field.

He had a new pent-roof six built by Meyer & Drake in 1960 and in 1962 fielded an up-to-date roadster chassis with the 265 engine, but his sponsorship money fell through. In 1963, Lencki's last year, Cliff Griffith went 144 miles per hour in the car in practice, about three miles per hour too slow to make the field.

In the 1960s, Lencki asked Goossen to design a turbocharged version of the Six, but Leo, then well past the usual retirement age and working hard turbocharging the Offy, didn't have time for the project.

Lencki said he spent $200,000 on engine development between 1938 and 1963. He kept all of his cars but one and took all of the drawings and patterns for his engines away with

Joe Lencki looking over a spark plug from his six-cylinder engine at the Packard Proving grounds in Michigan in the spring of 1940. George Connor drove the #10 car in the tests and at the Speedway a month later. *Don McReynolds collection*

Mauri Rose contemplates the wreckage of his Joe Lencki *Blue Crown Spl* after crashing on the 40th lap at Indianapolis in 1946. Though entered with a six-cylinder, Offenhauser-built 265-cubic-inch engine of Lencki's own design, and listed that way in the Indianapolis records, it ran the race with a standard four-cylinder, probably a 270 Offy. Lencki, despite his irascible nature, was able to get top drivers in his cars, including Indy winners Rose, Floyd Davis, and Floyd Roberts, plus Tony Gulotta, Emil Andres, Joie Chitwood, Ronney Householder, Tony Willman, Chet Gardner, and Johnny Sawyer. *Don McReynolds collection*

him, much to the annoyance of Fred Offenhauser. Lencki kept them until the day he died. He was a crusty, difficult man throughout his life. Near the end he offered his cars to both the Smithsonian and the Indianapolis Speedway Museum, but never delivered them. Lencki died in 1994. The patterns and drawings, at this writing, are still in the hands of his longtime aide, Adam Wuchitech.

The Single-Stick and Sampson Midgets

After the Offenhauser shop built the Mighty Midget in 1934, it produced two other midgets on a custom basis. One, built in 1935 to Riley Brett's specification, was designed to be less expensive than the Koetzla model. The other, constructed in 1939, was a beefed-up version of the Mighty Midget intended to remedy all the things left undone in the hasty development of its predecessor. In the end neither the more costly engine nor the cheaper one succeeded.

Brett's much lighter version of the Offy was an 85-cubic-inch single-overhead-cam design. Harry Stephens was the "angel" for the project, and Myron Stevens built a super-light chassis to carry the engine. The original driver was Don Welsh.

The little four-cylinder "single stick," as the engine was known, had a "square" bore and stroke of 3.00x3.00 inches with two valves per cylinder. The intake valves measured 1.575 inches and the exhaust 1.513 inches. These were bigger than the valves of the mighty midget, even larger than the 220 valves that were used in the last midget engines in the 1970s. The first example built had a single downdraft Winfield carburetor. The non-counterbalanced crank ran in tiny 2.0-inch main bearings designed to keep weight to the absolute minimum. The connecting rod journals were 1.75 inches and piston pins 0.75 inches.

Mark Dees says the oil passages in the little crank were too small and it tended to wipe out its bearings, but the tiny size of those bearings undoubtedly played a part in the problem, although the bigger twin-cam midget engine survived with crank bearings of only 2.125-inch diameter. In many details the single-stick was built according to tried-and-true Miller/Offenhauser practice.

The single-stick midget. Designed by Riley Brett for Harry Stephens, it was slightly smaller than the Offy midget and quite a bit lighter. Fred advertised these for sale, but apparently sold only two. The engine was an inexpensive, lightweight version of the Offy midget, in contrast to the Sampson midget engine, which was a much more costly version of the Offy midget engine. According to contemporary reports, Offenhauser put an entire car together to go with the engine, with chassis and body work by Myron Stevens. It is doubtful Offenhauser sold more than one other such engine. At this writing, Robert Binyon and George Parker are building copies from the original drawings. *Mark Dees collection*

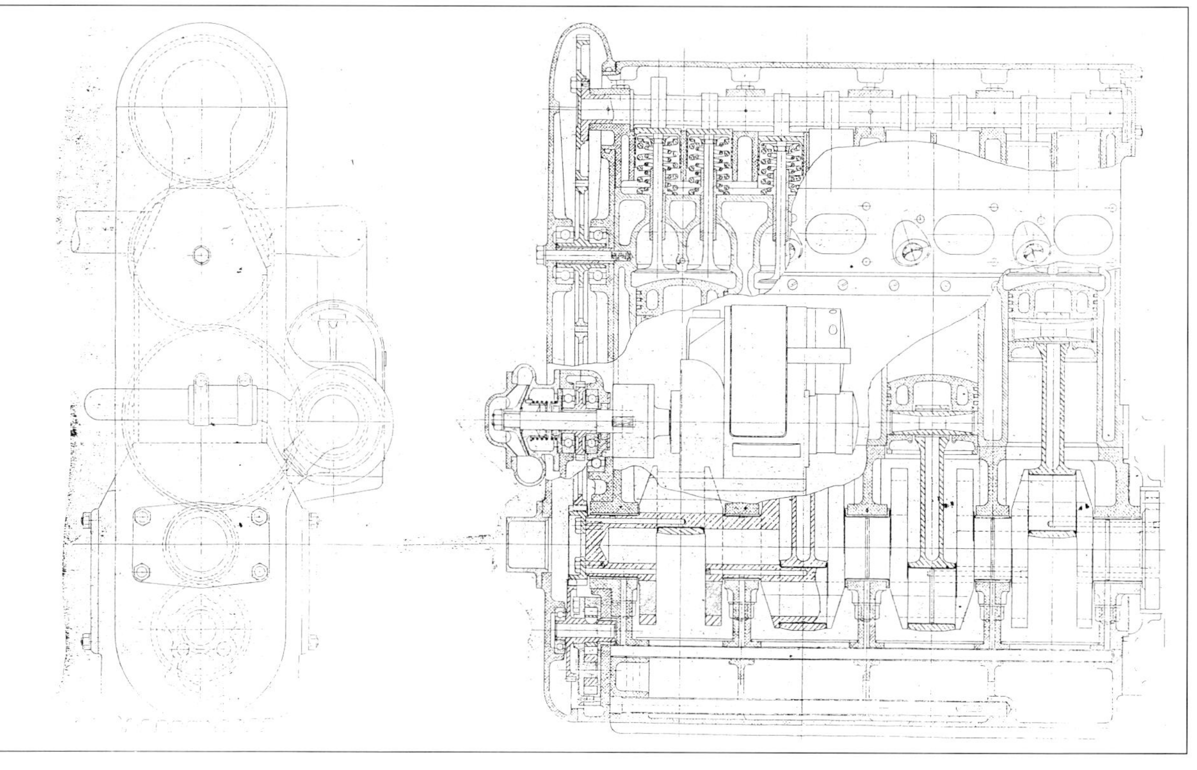

Drawing of the single-stick midget by either Goossen or Riley Brett. Note that it had five main bearings and flat-topped valve cups. (Most Offys had cups with a convex radius that eased the wear on both the cups and the cam lobes.) *Robert Binyon collection*

Stephens little maroon car had a pointed chrome grille and weighed only 510 pounds. Known as the *Packard Bell Radio Special* its displacement was some 13 percent smaller than the regular midget Offys. Even so, Welsh led for 30 laps in its first outing on January 19, 1936, at the road course race at the Atlantic Boulevard Stadium. It finished a creditable second to Karl Young. After two seasons of so-so performance and several bearing jobs, Stephens replaced the single-stick with a standard Offy midget which he hired Bob Swanson to drive. The *Packard-Bell* car was sold to Shorty Hansen and was driven thereafter by Perry Grimm, Andy and Perry Guthrie, Louis Durant (under Cook Ford Company sponsorship), and others. It was later owned by Mel Hanson, and the car reportedly ended its days in Ohio. George Parker and Bob Binyon, a former Meyer-Drake employee, are building improved versions of the single-stick to some of Goossen drawings that turned up after he died.

The 1939 Sampson Midget

In 1939, Riley Brett and Alden Sampson sought to build a winning midget engine that could outrun the Offy. They believed that if the funds were committed to design a new engine from the ground up, they could beat the standard Offy, which was, of course, based on a quick chop job of the old Miller 182. Sampson hired Goossen to draw one up and Offenhauser to help build it.

The result was a five main bearing, four-cylinder gem with four valves per cylinder. Named for its financial angel, the engine was assembled at Sampson's shop with some machine work by Offenhauser.

The Sampson appeared to have more potential for development than the Offy midget, but was quite a bit more costly to build and only two were made prior to World War II. Ronney Householder did very well with one of the engines in 1940. After World War II, Gordon Schroeder bought the drawings, patterns, and five unfinished engines and updated the Sampson to the point that it put out more power per cubic inch than the English Grand Prix Climax engine. Eventually, however, the Cosworth four-cylinder midget engine, designed to wind quite a bit tighter than the Sampson's 7,800 rpm, trumped Schroeder's design on an output per cubic inch basis. (In the 1960s, the Offy midget itself, surprisingly long-lived after more than 30 years, was being twisted to 8,000 rpm and putting out over 210 horsepower on alcohol at 17:1 compression.)

Schroeder, who operated a Burbank machine shop until his death in 1995, never had the money to develop the engine fully. In the 1960s, when it could have been competitive, he attempted to get sponsorship to produce it in quantity but none materialized. At this writing, parts for the Sampson engines still sit on shelves in Schroeder's shop.

Other Midget Projects

Offenhauser built three special supercharged midget engines in the 1934–1946 period, one in 1935, centrifugal-blown, for Stanley Dollar's speedboat and two for the Lou Fageol *Twin-Coach Special* of 1946. All three were designed

The crankcase of the first Novi V-8 engine, just being completed in the Offenhauser shop in February 1941. Ernie Weil has his hand on the case and Fred C. Offenhauser is standing next to a tray of small castings with Heinie Kramer behind him. On the right, in the rear are Frank Smith, Frank Adamson, and Ray Smith at the South Bend lathe. *Gloria Madsen collection*

with 90.88-cubic-inch displacement to meet competition limits. The Twin-Coach engines used Roots-type blowers and the chassis, built by Floyd Trevis and Paul Weirick, had each engine drive its axle separately, connected only through the throttle linkage.

The Offy Remained Supreme

Despite the money and effort invested by competitors, even with the help of Goossen and Offenhauser, engines like the Novi and the Sparks did not do as well as Fred's standard product. Only the Sparks Little Six won at Indy, and only the Bowes\Winfield eight was successful on the dirt tracks. One factor was simply numbers: there were more Offy engines. Unlike most of the other would-be builders of racing engines, Offenhauser was not secretive nor did he reject outside ideas. If a buyer put up money for a new feature, the customer was entitled to a year's exclusive use of it. If it worked, it could be adapted for use in Offenhauser's regular engines. The practice was one of the strengths of the Offenhauser shop. Fred had no interest in a "house" car (Meyer & Drake and Frank Kurtis would be roundly criticized in the 1950s for running their own cars in competition with their customers), and he was willing to sell engines to anyone who would pay for them.

The 1930s were lively with special engines, but after World War II there was only one custom engine for Goossen to design, the Reventlow Scarab, and one stock-block modification, the Utzman-Agajanian Studebaker V-8. The lackluster records of all of the innovative engines emphasized the lock the Offy had on American auto racing.

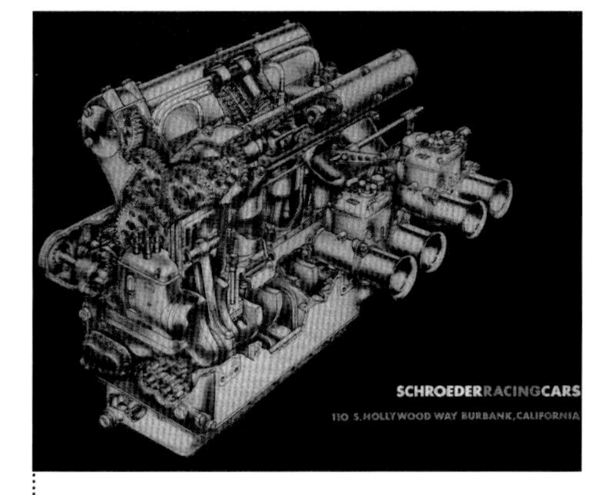

Cutaway drawing of the Sampson midget engine, the design Leo Goossen would have made for the Offy midget if he had had more time and cost was not important. The engine, bankrolled by Alden Sampson III, was eventually taken over by Gordon Schroeder. Note the dual oil pumps at the front of the crankcase. The case, unlike that of the Offy, had a detachable sump and conventional bearing caps. Despite its power, it never became popular, in part because World War II intervened, but also because it offered only a slight edge in performance over the Offy—too slight to justify the additional expense. *Gordon Schroeder collection*

Ray Nestor in the Buck Wheeler #21, Dutch Schaefer in the Golden Arrow #6 and Bill Schindler in the Caruso #2 roar, wheel-to-wheel into a corner on the 1/5-mile track at Middletown, New York, in 1947. All three are Offenhauser-powered Kurtis-Kraft midgets. It was this kind of close, ferocious racing on short tracks that made the midgets so popular. Middletown's Orange County Fairgrounds were built in 1857 for horses and cars have raced there on the dirt since 1917. The smaller paved oval was built in 1946 during the heyday of the midgets just after World War II when the Offy ruled the tracks.
Frank Smith/Author collection

CHAPTER SIX

THE MIDGETS, 1933-1974

INDIANAPOLIS GRABS THE ATTENTION OF RACING FANS AND THOSE PEOPLE who notice auto racing only once a year, and in the South NASCAR stock cars are almost a way of life, but there was a time just before and after World War II when millions of otherwise sane Americans were caught up in a brand of racing known as the midgets. From almost the beginning of the midgets as real racing cars, Offenhauser engines won the majority of those events where they were allowed to compete. The small Offy, dubbed the "Mighty Midget," helped put Offenhauser Engineering in the black in 1934 as Fred struggled to recover from Harry Miller's bankruptcy.

In the 1930s and 1940s, the small cars, modeled after their larger cousins at Indianapolis, raced on tracks in football and baseball stadiums, at county fairs, on quarter-mile ovals specially built for them, even on rough tracks hogged out of cornfields by road graders. In California, the Northeast, Chicago, Texas, and Oklahoma, there were for nearly two decades, midget races seven nights a week and twice on Saturdays and Sundays.

One of the most beautiful eastern midgets was the Cheeseman Offy, piloted here by Al Duffy. *Frank Smith/Author collection*

They were a fad that gripped the nation in the depths of the Depression and held it until television offered alternative entertainment. While they lasted, the midgets trained dozens of drivers who went on to the top level of racing at Indianapolis. One driver who got his professional start in the midgets, Mario Andretti, not only won at Indianapolis and took the American driving championship three times, in 1965, 1966, and 1969, but captured the World Formula 1 Championship in 1978.

Some of the men who either started racing in midgets or who gained most of their early experience in the little cars before going on to Indianapolis fame include Ronney Householder, Duke Nalon, Jimmy Snyder, Henry Banks, Tony Willman, Bob Swanson, Tony Bettenhausen, Freddie Agabashian, Mack Hellings, Duane Carter, Troy Ruttman, Jack McGrath, Walt Faulkner, Jim Rathman, Johnnie Parsons, Mike Nazaruk, Eddie Sachs, Bill Schindler, Bill Vukovich Sr., Rodger Ward, Johnny Thomson, A.J. Foyt, Lloyd Ruby, Parnelli Jones, Johnny Rutherford, and Mel Kenyon. A complete list of the graduates of the midgets would fill many pages.

Midget cars were used originally as playthings and curiosities. In the late 1920s, spurred by articles in magazines like *Popular Mechanics*, enough were built to generate a few pick-up races between owners. There was informal auto racing of all kinds going on in this period, particularly in California. Hot rodders were racing at Muroc Dry Lake and speeding on boulevards in Los Angeles. Elsewhere around the country, youngsters ached to race on tracks like their elders and occasionally did so in vacant lots.

The first recorded organized midget race was at Hughes Stadium, Sacramento, California, on June 4, 1933. (There may have been racing earlier at the Jeffries Ranch outside of Los Angeles.) The drivers were usually youngsters not old enough to drive in regular AAA-sanctioned races. They had so much fun that the idea spread through the teen-age tinkerer groups in California and shortly there were races going on at several small tracks. Dominic Distarce promoted the first professional midget race at Loyola Stadium in Los Angeles on August 10, 1933.

Other promoters realized that there was money to be made with the midgets, and word quickly spread around the country. There were young men everywhere who had or would build some sort of little race car. A group in Freeport, New York, met at the new Municipal Stadium on Sunday afternoon April 8, 1934, to race flivvers that were somewhere between midgets and sprint cars. Ed Hauptner, a speedboat racer from City Island, New York, had been staging motorcycle races and competition between small cars powered by Evinrude Elto outboard engines since 1927. An organized event among cars clearly recognizable as "midgets" was held at Olympic Park, Irvington, New Jersey, on June 10, 1934. Earl B. Gilmore, of the Gilmore Oil Company, was a Hollywood-style showman and his track put the midgets on the map and eventually attracted crowds of more than 18,000. The little cars proved to be a salable kind of cheap, exciting racing. By the winter of 1935

Ronney Householder took the tail off his Offy midget in 1941 and mounted this shield to help Alfred Letourneur, on a Schwinn Paramount, set a bicycle speed record of 108 miles per hour on a road in California. In 1988, at Bonneville, another bicyclist used an Offenhauser-powered Indy car as a windbreaker in an unsuccessful attempt to pedal 150 miles per hour. Note the very large front sprocket and the tiny rear one. *Bruce Craig collection*

midgets were racing indoors in the Chicago Armory and in New York City at the Bronx Coliseum with press coverage in the *New York Times*.[25]

At their best, the midgets were gleaming little cars that raced under the lights on tracks small enough that they were almost in the laps of the spectators. They snarled and roared in a wheel-to-wheel brand of racing more closely competitive than that usually seen anywhere else, even at Indianapolis. Winning drivers and colorful losers became local heros and household names.

Fred Builds a Midget Engine

As noted in chapter five, as a money-making show the earliest midgets had one drawback: most of them were built by backyard mechanics using cast-off junkyard engines that would frequently snort, stall, or catch fire, slowing the proceedings. Gilmore, who had one of

Trio of Daredevils Who Will Seek Midget Auto Racing Crown

Pat Warren working on his four-wheel drive Offy midget. Arnold Krause also had a 4WD midget Offy, but both were eventually banned because they were too successful. *Bruce Craig collection*

This is what the early midgets looked like. The *Nassau Daily Review-Star* gave front-page play to an upcoming midget event at Freeport, New York, on October 7, 1935. Mike Caruso soon switched from the Bugatti power in the car seen here to Offenhauser engines. Johnny Duncan is in the Caruso midget, Ernie Gesell is in the center car and Johnny Peterson is in the Schloeder cycle #10. *Author collection* the best midget tracks anywhere, became fed up with the balky little cars. He sent his racing director, ex-driver Dave Koetzla, to find a reliable midget engine.

Offenhauser and Goossen looked over the possibilities and came up with the Miller engine built for Harry Hartz with which Fred Frame won the 1932 Indianapolis race. They designed a four-cylinder version of 97 cubic inches, based on the front end of the Hartz Miller. The eight was made up of two four-cylinder blocks bolted end-to-end on a single barrel-type crankcase, so Offenhauser could use 183 blocks already on hand, or at least casting patterns for the Hartz engine. The 183 was, as Millers went, relatively simple, that is, inexpensive. It had two valves per cylinder and was unsupercharged. Using half of the 183 crankshaft left the midget engine with only three main bearings but it seemed to work all right.

Gilmore had Curly Wetteroth build a nice chassis for the Offy midget and rolled it out for competition on September 27, 1934. The Mighty Midget was an immediate success at his stadium. It won there and, with one or two exceptions, every other race in which it competed until Offenhauser could put together more of his little engines. A second Offy midget won its first race at Pomona and another at Santa Barbara. Offenhauser produced a torrent of them through 1941 when World War II halted production at serial #101 for Ted Halibrand.

Fred Offenhauser and Dave Koetzla go over Leo Goossen's blueprint for the midget engine in 1937. *Gloria Madsen*

The Offy midgets occasionally ran against the big cars, and defeated them. In 1936 Pat Cunningham in the Fayte Brown Offy midget beat the big cars on the mile track at Oakland and Mel Hansen in the Snyder Offy compounded the insult by finishing second. After that the big car people had AAA impose a *minimum* wheelbase and displacement limit. Danny Hogan and Bob Swanson stretched the Hogan Offy and put 16-inch wheels on it to run in the Vanderbilt cup revival on Long Island in 1936. At one time in the race Swanson was running fifth and Louis Tomei in the Rastelli Offy midget second, but both had problems and finished well back. Tomei in particular, with the short wheelbase, was able to stay with the Europeans on the corners; in fact he shut the door on Italian driver Farina once, to the Italian's vast annoyance.

The Mighty Offy Midget was not as cheap as other engines but owners and drivers had seen the light. Offenhauser sold them for $1,100, or a little less if the buyer expected to finish the assembly process. Five years later Offenhauser advertised complete, ready-to-run engines at $1,175 with magneto, water pump, and a single updraft Winfield Model S carburetor.[26] Offenhauser did not normally offer a fuel pump. General racing practice then was not to use a mechanical pump. Instead, the driver would give a few strokes on an outside-mounted air pump each lap or two, pres-

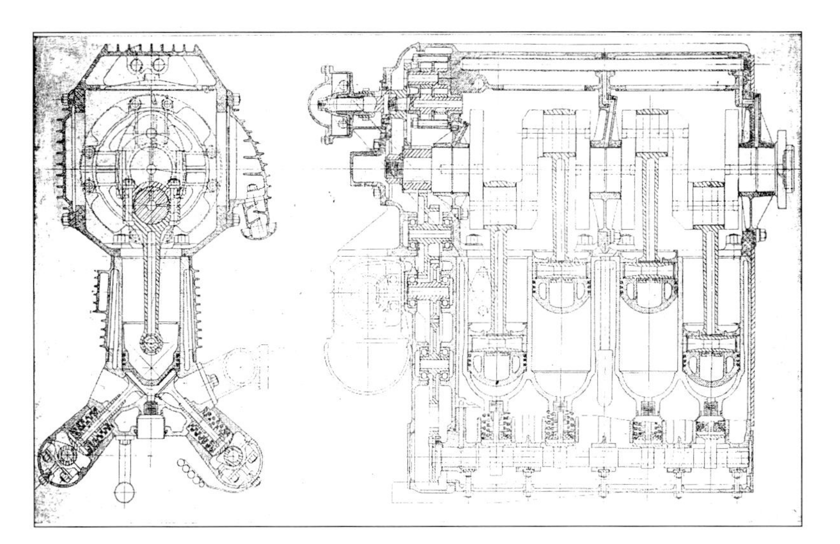

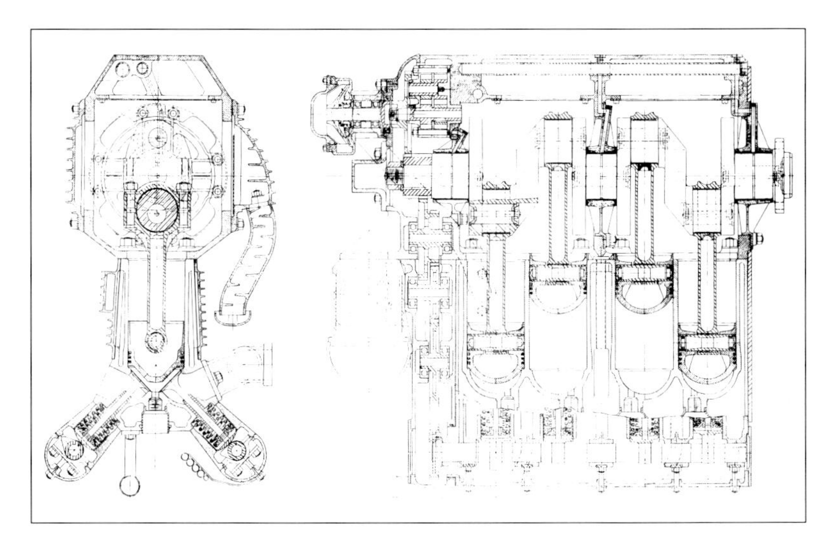

The left drawing shows the Offy midget engine as it was first produced in 1934. It was a close copy of the front four cylinders of the Hartz 183 Indy engine. Note the centrally located spark plugs and the oil pickup tubes in the center of the sump. The right assembly drawing is of the Offy midget engine as updated about 1946. Improvements included offsetting the spark plugs to put more metal between the valve seats to cure a cracking problem and running the oil sump pickup tubes on the right side of the case so that they were better placed to catch oil that tended to be forced to that side of the engine in left turns. *Author collection /Kenneth Walton collection*

Mel Hansen working on the Offenhauser engine in his midget. One of the advantages of the separate block was that a mechanic could service much of the engine without taking the crankcase out of the car. *Bruce Craig collection*

Offy engine in the Caruso midget, 1937. This was one of the early engines with a breather in the center of the block. The space designed to allow for the breather allowed enlarging the cylinder bores over the years. *Bruce Craig collection*

surizing the fuel tank. That was asking a lot of a driver on a quarter-mile track, in traffic, particularly considering that race cars of the day also used a hand brake.

Though probably not the first to do it, Roy Hagedorn, a successful midget owner from Manchester, Connecticut, mounted a surplus Pesco vane-type pump from a Pratt & Whitney R-985 radial aircraft engine on the end of one of the Offy cams.[27] Hagedorn put minimal instrumentation in his cars, only oil pressure and a temperature gauge. "My drivers had enough to do without looking at gauges and pumping the pump," he growled in later years. By the 1950s virtually every midget Offy was using a Pesco, Chandler-Evans, or Hilborn fuel pump, though many owners kept the outside hand pump on their cars to prime the system.

The original Offy midget was offered with a multiple-disc clutch similar to that in the 1928 Model A Ford, and some even came with a cut-down two- or three-speed (two speeds forward and reverse) transmission. Most engines, however, were soon used with a simple in-and-out steel dog clutch made up of the high gear slider from the Ford Model A transmission. This "in-out box" as it was called, was simple, light, and nearly bullet-

One-legged Bill Schindler working on the Offy engine in the Caruso #2, a rail-frame Midget, in 1946 before the advent of the torsion-bar Kurtis chassis. Note the breathers wrapped with rags to keep dust out of the engine on a dirt track. *Frank Smith/Author collection*

proof. It could not accommodate an on-board starter and midgets to this day must be started by using a push vehicle.

The cam drive, a train of spur gears driven off the crankshaft that drives the oil and water pumps, the magneto, and the intake and exhaust cams, was originally copied directly from the Miller 183. The gears had relatively fine, 12-pitch teeth with little heft to them. As the engine's power was increased the fine-tooth gears began to break. The solution in 1947 was to go to gears with larger, stronger 10-pitch teeth. One of the subtle features of the Offy midget is that the number of teeth in the cam gears are such that the same teeth do not mesh with the mating gear on every revolution. This "hunting" feature allows more even wear.

The sanctioning bodies gradually allowed displacements to creep up. That came about on the one hand because owners would rebore worn engines and cheat a little on displacement, and the clubs would let everyone take a "cleanup" overbore. From 100 cubic inches originally, the midget Offy went to 102 inches, and in the 1960s, 110 inches. In fact, the USAC midget circuit was at one time

Danny Hogan and Swede Lindskog work on Hogan's rail-frame Offy midget in 1939. Note the front engine mount, freeing the engine of stress as the frame rails flexed in action. *Bruce Craig collection*

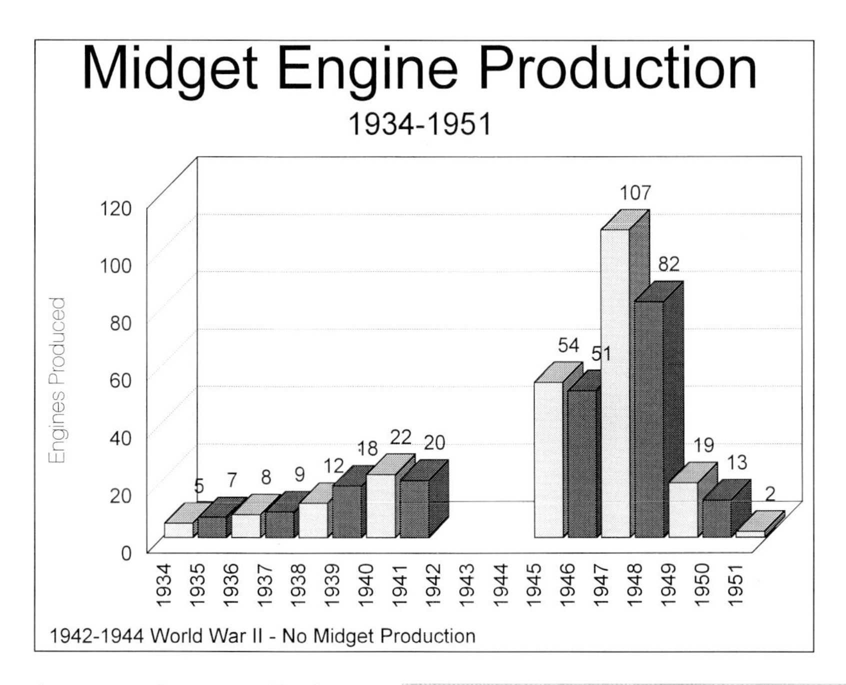

known as the 110 Offy class. A few 85-cubic-inch versions were built in the early years for clubs that limited twin-cam engines to that size.

Through the late 1930s, Offenhauser improved the engines. He improved the ports and modestly enlarged the valves. He added twin carburetors, at first updraft or downdraft Winfields, then, after World War II, 1 1/2-inch sidedraft Rileys. Mike Caruso, one of the craftiest of the eastern owners, had Norden carburetors on Bill Schindler's *Black Deuce* in 1948 when it won 53 feature races. By 1947, the Offy was putting out more than 120 horsepower at 6,000 rpm on alcohol.[28]

Early in the production of the midget engine, the breather passage in the block was eliminated and the spark plug receptacles relocated off-center in the cylinders to deal with a problem of cracking between the valve seats and the plug. In the bottom end the oil pickup tubes were moved from the center of the sump to the right side where oil piles up in left turns due to centrifugal force.

The midgets helped develop several basic racing components including both fuel pumps and the quick-change rear axle. Until quick-changes appeared, changing gear ratios for different-length tracks involved removing the entire ring and pinion assembly in the rear axle and installing a different set. A major job, but not too difficult if races were held a week or more apart. But when you raced every night as the midgets did, it was a major inconvenience.

The solution was to insert a pair of spur gears in the drive line that could be changed with relative ease. The first was the Ambler-type gearbox, just behind the engine, but a better arrangement was the quick-change rear axle.

In 1949, Stuart Hilborn developed his constant-flow fuel-injection system for racing engines. When applied to the midget, injectors increased power by 10 to 15 percent. The first model had a throat diameter of 1 9/16 inches, the same as the Offy's intake ports. Later, Hilborn made

Midget engine as it was produced in the early 1950s with Hilborn fuel injection and a fuel pump mounted on the back of the intake cam. Note the rigid motor mounting plate at the front of this engine, common practice once the tube-frame Kurtis midgets replaced the much more flexible rail-frame chassis. *Gloria Madsen collection*

Roots-supercharged 70.69-cubic-inch Offy midget built in 1969. This was engine #443, sold to Glen Dennee. USAC rules at the time allowed 73.3 cubic inches displacement for blown, overhead-cam midget engines, but it was quickly banned by the midget groups as too competitive. The blower was driven by a toothed Gilmer belt and it had a Hilborn two-hole injection system. The rods were aluminum and bore and stroke was 3.00x2.50 inches. *Robert Binyon collection*

injectors with 1 25/32-inch throats to give more flow. By 1950, Meyer & Drake were getting 132 horsepower at 6,800 rpm on alcohol out of a 102-cubic-inch midget with carburetors and 143 horsepower at 8,000 with injectors.

Offenhauser beefed up the midget crankshafts, but stuck to the three main-bearing design. The later, heavier crank was more robust but supposedly hurt acceleration on the short midget tracks. (The midget Offy has no flywheel, only a light aluminum degree wheel for setting the timing. It is rough at low revs and has to be handled with care when starting off, lest the thump as each piston comes up break parts in the drive line.)

Other improvements made in the midget Offy over the years included higher breathers, insert-type bearings, and improved piston-pin retainers. Meyer & Drake designed a detuned version with a starter, clutch, and transmission to run on gasoline for MG sports cars,[29] but only a few were built and they were only modestly successful. Midget rods have always been offset slightly to match the rod bearings on the crank. Meyer & Drake redesigned the engine to remove the offset but the first two sold went to teams that didn't do well and the idea, Lou Meyer said, fizzled.

As the bigger stock-block engines challenged the midget, it was enlarged to more than 120 cubic inches by providing a new big-bore block, and in 1968, it was supercharged. Both turbo and Roots-blown midgets were built. The Roots model was sold to Glen Dennee of San Jose, California, but may never have been used. There were two turbos built, mounted on the smallest-displacement Offys ever made—63 cubic inches—to fit within USAC rules for blown engines. Bob Higman, of Lafayette, Indiana, an experienced championship and midget mechanic, put one of them into the Shannon Brothers' Kurtis chassis for driver Dave Strickland, one of the top West and Midwest USAC midget drivers of the late 1960s.

As Bob Higman recalls, the car was tricky to drive, generating only 55 horsepower at 5,000 rpm, but more than 200 horsepower at 6,000 as the turbo began to take effect, and on the dyno, a peak of nearly 300 horsepow-

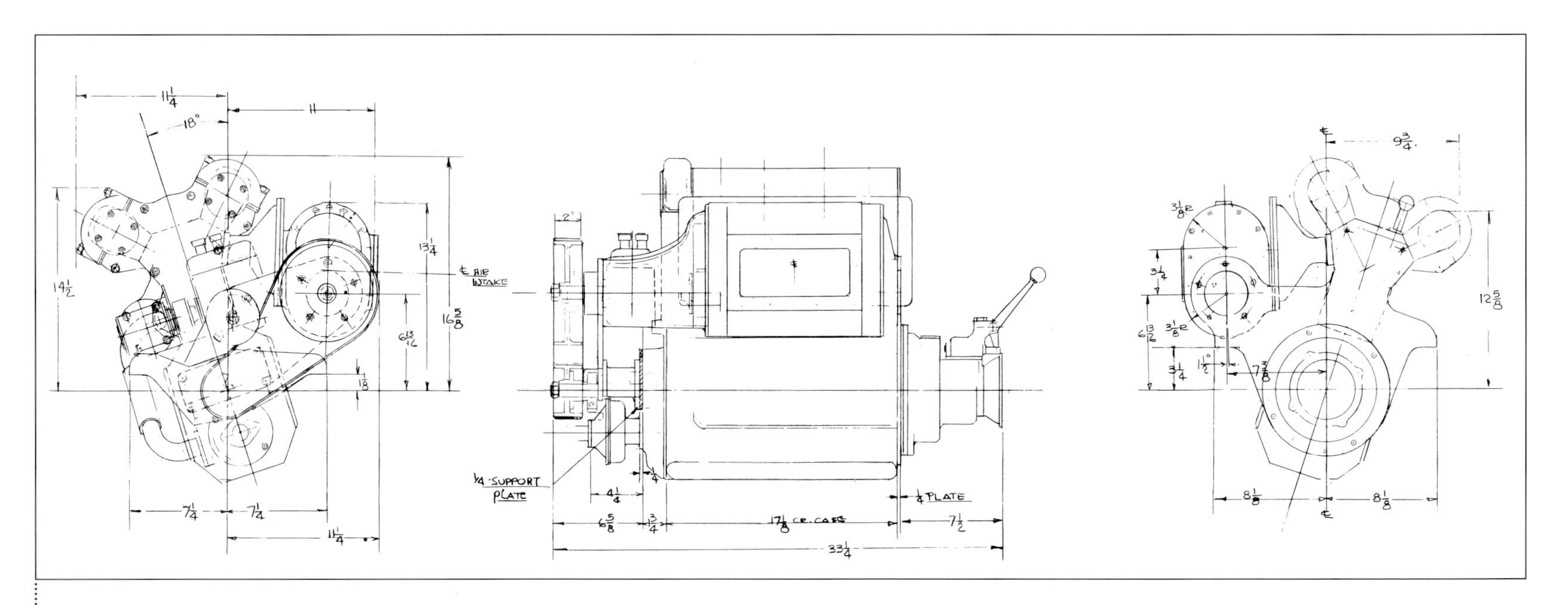

Goossen's assembly drawing for the 70-cubic-inch Roots-blown Offy midget engine. *Kenneth Walton collection*

Bob Higman, a veteran Indiana racing mechanic, had Drake Engineering build this special turbocharged Offenhauser midget in 1969 for the Shannon Brothers Buick Agency. Despite having only 70-cubic-inches displacement (3.00x2.50-inch bore and stroke), it far outpowered conventional engines when it got up to speed. *Bob Higman collection*

er. The engine was almost completely new and few parts would interchange with the standard midget engine. Its bore and stroke was 3.0x2.5 inches. Ironically, most of the turbo components were built by Bendix and came directly from the Ford four-cam, then the big Offy's deadly opponent in Championship racing. The engine cost $9,000, a lot of money for a midget engine then, but a fraction of the price of the Indy turbo powerplants.

Drake spent two years developing the engine and Higman another 14 months adapting it to the midget chassis and getting it in race tune. During 1970 Strickland led the point standings at mid-season, and ended up taking second place overall with nine feature race wins.

"I don't know a paved track we ran that we didn't get quick time with the car," Higman remembered. "In the race Strickland would start in the middle of the field, but on the start he would drop back until the turbo boost came on, then he would just fly right by half the field on the first lap or two. If the race was a clean one we could win, but if there was a late yellow [caution flag] he would lose a lot of places on the restart and might not have time to get them back before the end of the race."

Higman was running a dozen midgets for Midwestern owners at the time and caring for a champ car or two, in addition to farming 440 acres. "We just didn't have time to really sit down and develop it right," Bob said. "By the end of the season the engine was in Bob Rice's car because the Shannons and Strickland were contending for the championship and Rice was not. If the car was not ready to race on a given night Bob didn't care." Higman was working on refinements to the fuel-injection system and an automatic transmission that would keep the engine's revs up where the turbo was effective.

Frankie Del Roy, a USAC technical official at the time, supported the turbo midget, but others at USAC did not. Before the setup was perfected USAC banned superchargers in midgets. The engine was later sold to Tuck Jones, a Drake employee who planned to run it at Bonneville.

Another turbo midget, with timed fuel injection, was being developed by Len Faus when USAC imposed its ban.

Midget Controversy

In its day the little Offy outclassed almost everything on the track. Most of the junkyard engines of the early 1930s quickly disappeared, but their owners did not go down without a fight. When the "Mighty Midget" appeared there were at once efforts to restrict such twin-cam racing engines' size, to 80 or 85 cubic inches. There was talk for a time of a court fight over the engine, but Earl Gilmore controlled the sanctioning group, and the Offy stayed at the 98-cubic-inch size Goossen and Offenhauser had designed.

At first there were only a few midget Offy engines, and most of these in California. Midget racing elsewhere in the early 1930s depended on converted motorcycle engines, mostly with chain drive, converted Elto four-cylinder, two-stroke outboard engines, and after 1937, the little Ford V-8-60 auto engine.

The 60-cubic-inch outboards were light, fast, and incredibly noisy. With twice as many power strokes as the four-stroke engines, they were very competitive. They left a pungent trail of castor oil smoke which made them unpopular in the indoor arenas, and other drivers learned to set a slow pace on the line-up laps so the outboards would foul their plugs.

The motorcycle-powered cars had four-stroke engines of about 90-cubic-inches. They could not match the outboards for power, but being air-cooled were lighter. Early in the midgets' history there were a number of four-cylinder Henderson and Indian motorcycle engines used, then the faster two-cylinder J.A.P. and Harleys. The best cycle engine in the East was a converted Harley known as the *Carlheim*, and in the West it was the water-cooled Harley/Drake conversion.

The 136-cubic-inch Ford passenger car V-8-60s were cheap, fairly solid, reliable engines. They could be bored and stroked a bit and hopped up with special cams, heads, and dual carburetors, generally Stromberg 81s, and they powered the majority of the midgets through the late 1940s. The Ford suffered from being a side valve design which gave up power to the outboards and the Offys, but its worst fault was overheating. Henry Ford designed the exhaust passages in

A young Mario Andretti in one of his first Offy rides, the Mataka Brothers' *Speed & Marine* #11. *Author collection*

Eastern midget driver Tony Bonadies in Anastasis Vatis' Kurtis midget roadster. Frank Kurtis built 10 of the offset roadsters. To accommodate the engine being offset to the left, the blocks on the Offy engines were turned around to put the exhaust on the left side. *Author collection*

his V-8 so that the gasses followed a tortuous path out of the engine, leaving behind a great deal of heat. The Fords were known as "teakettles" and blew hoses regularly, sometimes terribly scalding their drivers.

But some owners and drivers could make Fords fly, generally with a little cheating. Rodger Ward got his early reputation by beating the Offys at Gilmore in a Vic Edelbrock-prepared Ford midget with the help of a little "pop," or nitromethane in the fuel.

The Offenhauser brought a division in the midget ranks between the haves and the have nots. There were many owners who could not afford an Offy, and at the peak of midget popularity there were two circuits operating in some areas, one for the stock blocks and one for the Offys and anyone who cared to challenge them. On the West Coast the United Racing Association had Red and Blue circuits that separated the Fords and others from the Offys. In the East, the American Racing Driver's Club (ARDC) accepted all comers, but there were Ford-only clubs like the American Racing Association and, for a time, the Northeast Midget Racing Association. Some ARDC tracks limited the number of Offys allowed to run.

So fast were the more expensive Offys that they were barred from Freeport in 1947 and for most of 1948. When they were allowed back, Henry Renard, Tony Plakstis' driver, was required to start half a lap behind the field of Ford and cycle-powered cars. He still won.

The bitterness between the Offys and the Fords might be traced to the short tracks and sprint length of most midget races. It was a closer, more personal kind of racing, and pure aggressiveness, acceleration, and guts were more important than at other levels of competition. Whatever the reason, the midget crowd had the loudest, longest arguments in racing.

After World War II the Offy problem was compounded by the development of the Kurtis-Kraft midget. Before the war most frames had been made like those of passenger cars from light and rather flexible sheet steel rails. Tube-frames had been used occasionally, notably by Milwaukee's

Frank Kurtis produced more midget chassis, most of them Offenhauser-powered, than anyone else in history. Though his shop did not really have a production line as this staged photo suggests, at one time he was building a car a day. *Frank Kurtis collection*

Seven Offys: nine midgets race into the corner at Hatfield, Pennsylvania, in 1949. *Bruce Craig collection*

Fred Tomshe, but rail-frame cars predominated. During the war Frank Kurtis sketched out plans for a midget to be built of aircraft-quality 4130 chrome-molybdenum tubing, providing a far stiffer and better-handling chassis.[30]

Kurtis offered a complete midget, painted, the running gear chrome plated, ready to drop in an engine and go racing, for $2,783.72. At the time Meyer & Drake were selling a midget Offy for $2,252.15. Add in a Burbank trailer, some spare wheels at $8.00 each and tires at $9.05, and the proud owner could be out at the track for less than $6,000.00.

To his tube frame Kurtis added torsion bar suspension which reduced unsprung weight therefore allowing the wheels to better follow the track surface. Finally, he used quick-release Dzus fasteners that permitted removal of the entire body in about five minutes, not a help to speed, but certainly a major aid in servicing a car.[31] In 1947, Firestone developed a new and wider tire to replace the skinny three-inch treads that had been used until then. The Kurtis chassis and better tires allowed the Offys to make use of all their power. The Offy midget clearly outclassed its competition in the 1930s. When put into a Kurtis-Kraft it was nearly unbeatable. In fact throughout the midgets' best days the question always was "who can beat the Offys?"

For the fans it was a hard choice. Eventually any driver who proved himself among the Fords hankered to move up to the Offy ranks. The most successful, best-known drivers drove Offys. Every driver wanted an Offy ride.

Some of the best racing in the midgets came about when plucky non-Offenhauser drivers held off the Offys or even beat them. *TIME* magazine called the Offys "brutish," and if you drove anything else, they were. At Freeport, Harold "Pickles" Bicklehaupt would start the feature up front in an aged prewar motorcycle-powered car, the John Schloeder #43, and stay there for 10 or 15 laps before the Offy pilots could make their way from the back of the pack to pass him (they always did) while the fans groaned.

On a given day, one Offy-powered car might be down on power or its driver off his game, but it was seldom that even when the Offys were limited in number they couldn't beat the Fords. There were a few occasions after 1947 when the Offys met their match. Rodger Ward was a tough West Coast driver and his car's owner, Vic Edelbrock, was one of the shrewd California Ford men who pioneered the use of nitromethane. Nitro was tricky to use and hard on an engine, but Ward, in the Edelbrock Kurtis Ford, could meet the Offys on nearly equal terms.

It was even more unusual in the East, but on the night of September 14, 1948, at the Freeport, New York, Municipal Stadium, Ted Tappet (Phil Walters) drove one of the best midget races of all time when his usual Offy ride did not arrive. He jumped into George Dessler's midget, an underpowered, rail-frame car with a flathead four-cylinder Universal Marine engine. Tappet won his heat and finished third in his semifinal. In the feature he started eighth, quickly passed the seven cars ahead of him, and stayed in front of the on-charging Offys to win outright. The car may never have won another race. It was a case of a superb driver on his home track in a well set-up car. (Mike Caruso is rumored to have bought the car from Dessler to see what made it handle so well.)

The last cycle-car driver to win a major feature was Dick Brown, whose feat in August 1952, was considered almost incredible. At Bone Stadium in Pittston, Pennsylvania, in a two-cylinder Carlheim-powered midget, Brown bested a field of AAA Offy drivers that included Bill Schindler, Lee Wallard, Johnnie Parsons, Paul Russo, Len Duncan, Johnny Kay, George Fonder, and Ernie McCoy. Brown started well back in the field but passed some of the hottest pilots in the sport to win the 50-lap feature. The only explanation is that it was a day when all of Brown's biorhythms were in perfect synch. There are occasional rare days when a driver can do amazing things: "the car will go anywhere I put it" as the saying goes. The report in *National Speed Sport News* said the fans were "gasping in utter disbelief" at Brown's victory.

The Kurtis-Kraft Offys were beautiful, streamlined creations. Today, 50 years after Frank sketched them, they still look quite modern. Current midgets and sprints continue to show the Kurtis influence, particularly in the suspension innovations he designed for a group of 10 midget "roadsters" in the 1960s.

But in the 1940s the Kurtis-Offys all looked alike. Worse, they were fairly even in performance. Midget races became parades. Television came along. Fans quit going to the races. Whether it was the power of the Offy engine, the speed and look-alike qualities of the Kurtis, the coming of television, or the inability of the midget drivers and owners to agree on their own best interests, the midget craze sagged by 1948. Midget racing continues but the honeymoon was over by 1950.

Midgets After 1950

As the bloom began to fade from the midgets, stock cars, mostly old Ford coupes, displaced the little cars at many tracks. By 1952 ARDC, had so few races it did not even crown a season champion.

The small cars came back slowly. AAA midget racing continued, largely in the Midwest, with occasional forays to the East, California, and the Southwest, but not on the scale of the golden 1940s. At Meyer & Drake, midget engine orders plummeted in 1949 and by 1950 the company only sold four all year.

Stock-block engines like the Ford V-8-60 had always been given larger displacement limits under the midget rules, since flathead (side valve) engines produce less horsepower than an overhead cam design. As long as the stock blocks were flathead Fords, the Offys could overcome them. But overhead-valve stock blocks were another matter. At first push-rod engines were not well enough developed to challenge the Offys, but in the 1960s and 1970s when engine builders like Wisconsin's Ron Hottels turned stock engines into full-race powerhouses, the Offys were in trouble. Only rarely could a Ford V-8-60 of 140 cubic inches beat an Offy, but a pushrod overhead valve engine of 155 inches, fully race-modified, was tough. Hottels' Sesco (a Chevy V-8 cut in half) or the 160-cubic-inch Ford Falcon permitted by some clubs and the later very light Volkswagen fours as modified by Autocraft were too much for a 110-cubic-inch engine, even a well-designed twin-cam like the Offy.

Under that competitive pressure, Offy mechanics like Johnny Pawl and Ken Hickey pressed Meyer & Drake to design blocks with more displacement. Drake was busy fighting off challenges to the big Offys at Indianapolis, but he had Goossen draft plans for a "120" series of engines. They had the cylinders offset to permit increasing the bore diameters by 1/8 inch.

There were several dozen midget Offy engines converted to 120s in the late 1960s and early 1970s, but according to Drake records, only one complete engine, serial # 452 (the last complete midget sold) was built as a 120. The big-block engines could displace, depending on the crank, as much as 132 cubic inches. By that point the cylinder walls were getting pretty thin, and there was no room for an overbore when wear dictated the need. The later midgets used larger valves out of the 220 sprint car engine and there was some enlargement of the ports, particularly on the intake side.

Competition from stock-block midget engines along with Meyer & Drake's problems at Indianapolis finally brought manufacture of the midget engine to an end. Today John Drake makes a few midget parts and firms such as Mouldex, Carillo, and Venolia will turn out a few Offy cranks, rods, and pistons on a custom basis. Several individuals have made their own parts to restore

Mechanic installing an Offenhauser engine in one of 10 Kurtis midget roadsters built in 1959 and 1960. Note that the engine has had the block reversed, putting the exhaust on the left and the intake on the right. The change involved merely redrilling an oil feed passage to the cams. This Kurtis chassis anticipated most of the suspension technology of later sprint cars. While a winner on pavement, the roadsters were not as successful on dirt. *Frank Kurtis collection*

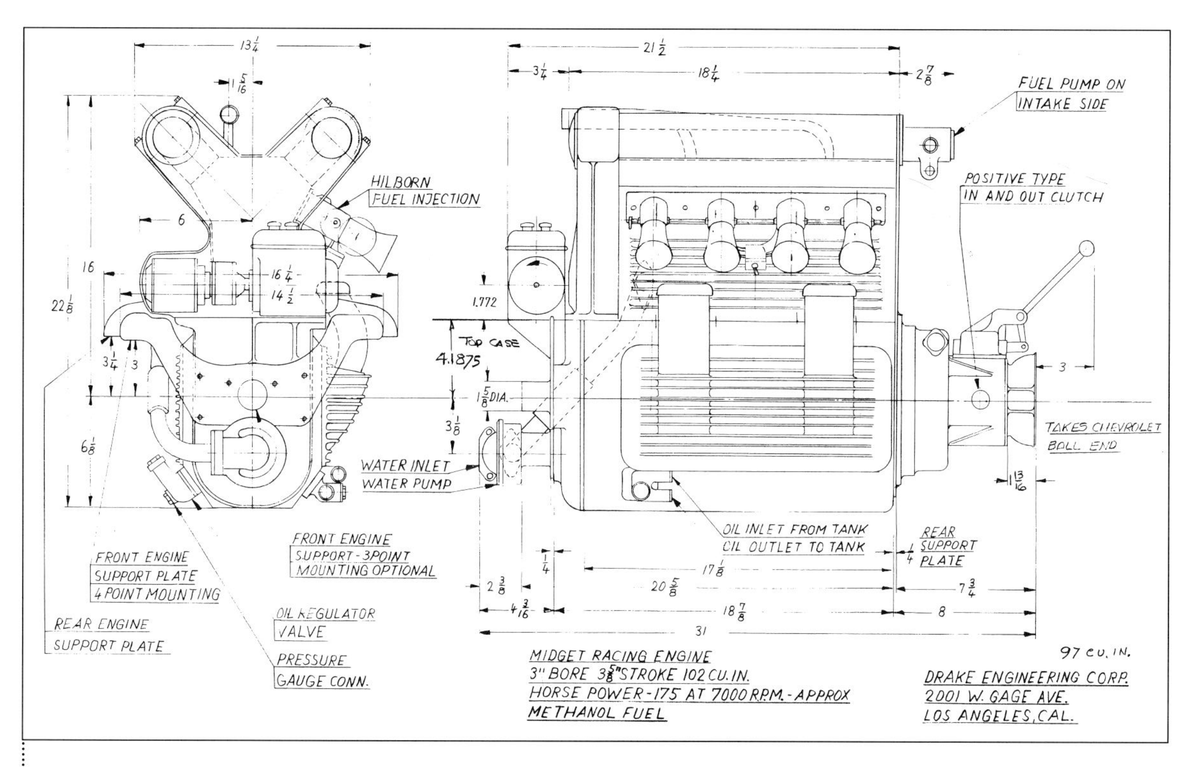

Drake Engineering's assembly drawing for the late Offy midget in 1965. *Drake Engineering*

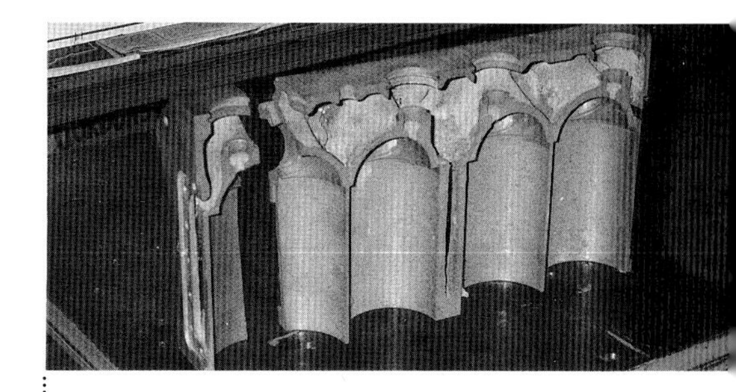

Ken Hickey cut up this Offy midget block to see if there was a way to get larger cylinder bores. Note the #4 cylinder, so close to the back of the block that the cooling jacket is a separate plate bolted on. The plugs are offset radically in this big, 120 block. *Author*

damaged engines. With luck, cash, and determination one could still put together an Offy engine.

Midgets on the Salt and on Road Courses

Midgets ran several times for straightaway records at the Bonneville Salt Flats in Utah; at Muroc Dry Lake, California; Daytona Beach, Florida; and on Nantasket Beach, Massachusetts. Ronney Householder, Rex Mays, and Danny Oakes, all in Offys, held the record at various times. Mays' 147-mile-per-hour mark at Bonneville in 1949 in the Balch Offy, then the West Coast AAA championship car, was the longest-standing record. The story of the author's Bonneville experience is related in the epilogue.

Midgets VS. Sports Cars

One of the most dramatic Offy midget victories was won by Rodger Ward in Ken Brenn's Kurtis Kraft on the 1.5-mile sports car road course at Lime Rock, Connecticut, in 1959.

Ward had won Indianapolis in May. That spring USAC and the ever-more-professional sports car ranks decided it would be a moneymaker to put together cars and drivers from several different types of racing and run a series of

Danny Oakes at Bonneville in the Jack Balch #8 Offy midget. The car, built by Lujie Lesovsky, was the Pacific Coast champion in 1948. Oakes, using Riley carburetors, set a new midget speed record of 139.436 miles per hour. Two years later Oakes had been suspended by the AAA, so Rex Mays drove the Balch car, then equipped with Hilborn fuel injection and without the large windshield, 147.307 miles per hour, a record that stood for 39 years. *Marvin Jenkins collection*

George Constantine in his Aston Martin DBR2 #49 led Rodger Ward's #24 Ken Brenn Offenhauser-powered Kurtis midget for a few laps at Lime Rock, Connecticut—a twisty, right-hand road course—in the July 25, 1959, Formula Libre race, but not for long. Constantine's car failed to finish and Ward defeated the cream of U.S. sports racers two heats out of three with drum brakes and only an in-out box clutch. *Author collection*

History of the Midget Record Straightaway Speed Attempts 1930–1989

Date	Driver	Engine	Cu In	Site	Speed (mph)	Remarks
1930	Arlen, Don	Harley	90	Muroc	112	
1933	Woodman, Hap	4-cyl Indian	90	Muroc	114	U.S. cycle record
1935	Betteridge, B.	Elto 4-60 outboard	60	Bonneville	120	U.S. outboard record
1/37	Bailey, F.	Adams J.A.P.	90	Nantasket Beach, MA	112.40	
4/37	Householder, R.	Householder Offy	98.3	Muroc	123.290	
8/47	Oakes, D.	Balch Offy	102.49	Bonneville	139.12	
9/49	Mays, Rex	Balch Offy	102.49	Bonneville	147.095	
2/54	McGrath, S.	Tadlock Offy	102.49	Daytona	131.19	
2/54	Arnold, C.	Offy	102.49	Daytona	130.33	
2/54	Hart, B.	Ford V-8-60	140	Daytona	117.810	U.S. Ford record
2/54	Fonoro, N.	Allen Offy	102.49	Daytona	127.240	
2/55	Orlando, S.	FordV-8-60	140	Daytona	102.433	
2/56	Rodee, C.	Hardwood Door Offy	102.49	Daytona	133.090	
2/56	Arnold, C.	Brenn Offy	102.49	Daytona	119.087	
10/88	White, G.	Tassi Vatis Offy	121.5	Bonneville	156.902	U.S. midget record
8/89	White, G.	Tassi Vatis Offy	121.5	Bonneville	153.123	F.I.A. 2,000-cc record

formula libre, or "run what ya brung" races. They invited Ward, John Fitch, who had raced sports cars in Europe driving a Cooper-Monaco, Chuck Daigh with a 3.5-liter Grand Prix Maserati, Pedro Rodriguez in a 3.0-liter Maserati, George Constantine in a 4.2-liter Aston Martin DB2-R, Lance Reventlow in a Formula II Cooper, Denise McCluggage in a Porsche, Jokko Maggiacomo in a 4.9-liter Ferrari, and Tony Bettenhausen, Russ Klar, Bert Brooks, and Duane Carter in Kurtis Offy midgets.

Ward tried to get a ride in a Cooper, but the owner refused, sneering that Ward was a roundy-round driver and might not be competent to drive such an important sports car.

Chris Economaki, publisher of *National Speed Sport News*, a midget fan who was midwife to the formula libre idea, persuaded Ward to drive a midget. It seemed almost a joke. Run a single-speed, no-transmission car designed to turn left with less than outstanding brakes, against the cream of European sports cars on a road course with seven right turns and only one to the left? But Economaki persuaded Ward to try and hooked him up with Brenn, whose Offy had won the eastern midget championship in 1958.

As it turned out Lime Rock was a pretty fair midget track. Aside from its single long straight, its curves were not unlike those on an average midget oval. Its "big bend" corner was no tighter than a 1/4-mile midget track, and Ward was able to accommodate turning right instead of left. In practice he broke the Lime Rock track record. In the race he smoked the sports cars, including one daring move off the pavement onto the dirt inside the left-hander to get by Daigh. It was the midget's finest hour and perhaps their last hurrah.

Ward became intrigued with putting a midget up against the sports cars. He later ran in Formula Libre events in Florida and Illinois but never matched his Lime Rock performance. Ralph Wilke provided Ward one of the Leader Card Kurtis Offys to drive at the U.S. Grand Prix in Florida later that year. Sebring had far longer straightaways than did Lime Rock which put the midget at a great disadvantage even though Wilke said that Ronney Householder calculated from the revs that Ward might have been running as fast as 148 miles per hour on the straight stretches.

Ward drove the Leader Card Offy at Meadowdale, Illinois, using a two-speed Casale rear axle. Wilke recalled that Ward used 3.78 and 4.56:1 ratios in the Casale. "The clutch lever broke," Wilke said. "Ward tossed it into the pits as he came by. Fortunately it was in the high ratio when it broke." The Offy's multiple-disc clutch was not made for constant up and down-shifting and it ground itself apart. Perhaps the sports car drivers learned something at Lime Rock but most likely no other track offered the kind of course a midget could negotiate competitively without shifting. Ward returned to Lime Rock in 1989 for a re-creation of his victory but the Brenn car, restored as an antique, was not so competitive. Most of the 1959 players were there, but Ward's car fell out with oil pressure problems. At the dinner afterwards Rodger's remarks recounting the 1959 affair made up for the lack of verisimilitude on the track.

There were a few more victories for the Offy midget in the 1960s but its day was largely past. Lime Rock was its last shining moment. Today the midgets run with far larger engines than the old 110 Offy "growler." Four-cylinder Pontiacs and Cosworths have overtaken the Falcon, Sesco, Chevy II, Autocraft VW, and Pinto engines of the 1960s and 1970s. Midgets on some circuits sprout sprint car style wings. But still, very rarely, an old Kurtis Offy may creep out on the track to contest, bravely if futilely, as the "Mighty Midget."

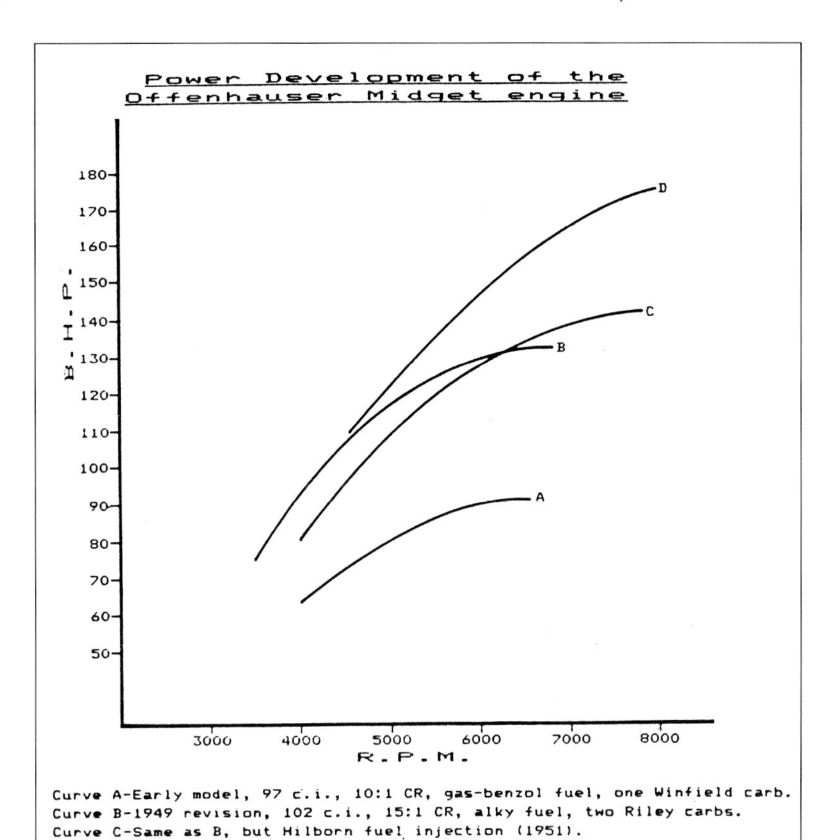

Dyno runs from Meyer & Drake on four generations of the midget engine:
- Curve A is the original design, 98-cubic-inch, 10:1 compression, single updraft carburetor, on gasoline. The peak was about 90 horsepower at 6,700 rpm.
- Curve B is the postwar improvement, about 1948, with two side-draft Rileys, 15:1 compression ratio, burning methanol. Note that the horsepower jumps to more than 130 and the rpm peaks slightly higher at 7,000.
- Curve C is a 1951 curve with Hilborn fuel injection but no other changes. Better breathing lifts the rpm peak to 8,000 and horsepower to more than 140.
- Finally, curve D is the 1965 Offy midget at 115-cubic-inch, 16:1 compression ratio, more radical Schneider cams, the late, larger Hilborn injection, and other improvements. The engine could then produce 175 horsepower at 8,100 rpm. With the even larger 120- to 127-cubic-inch blocks the midget pumped out more than 210 horsepower, but it was not able to overcome the 155-cubic-inch "stock block" engine competition once they were fully race-prepared. Even so, it was a remarkable showing as the little Offy more than doubled its power output while increasing its displacement only 25 percent. *Meyer & Drake*

Some of the Meyer & Drake staff posed with the red # 99 car when it was rolled out of the plant in 1949. Seen here are, left to right, unknown, Eddie LaVoie, Bob Binyon, George Salih, Takeo "Chickie" Hirashima, (front) Dale Drake, Lem Drake, and Ole Pearson; (in back) Ron Pearson, Hank Mahler, Al Doig, and Jack McCracken. Lou Meyer is in the driver's seat. The car was painted a deep blue the following year after it was sold to Murrell Belanger but still carried the number 99 when it won the Indianapolis 500 in 1951.
Robert Binyon collection

CHAPTER SEVEN

MEYER & DRAKE BUY OUT OFFENHAUSER

THE END OF WORLD WAR II IN 1945 LEFT AMERICANS BOTH EXHILARATED and exhausted, but racing resumed with characteristic enthusiasm and huge crowds everywhere as soon as the guns were silent. Fred Offenhauser, however, was tired. Defense production for Lockheed had been a long grind for his shop, and much of his plant's machinery was worn out. He had made money in racing during the Depression and had done well in war work. Now he felt it was time to retire. He had a certain uneasiness that his heart might give out, but that was a momentary misgiving, as he was to live on for another 27 years. As to the business, the midgets were booming, but in the last prewar years his championship engines had been challenged by the Maseratis and the Winfield-Bowes. He remembered what had happened to Harry Miller 13 years earlier and decided it was time to get out.

Meanwhile, Lou Meyer had come to the conclusion that the Ford engine-rebuilding business was no longer interesting and sold his share to his partner, Lew Welch, the owner of the Novis. With the proceeds Meyer bought into a machine shop on Wilcox Avenue in Bell, California, with his old racing mechanic, Dale Drake.

Welch thought adding Offenhauser's operation to his engine plant in Vernon, California, would make a good combination, and he made Fred an offer for the business. But Welch, though well-known through his Indianapolis efforts, was not one of the racing crowd. He spent more time on his businesses than socializing with the boys, and he was not particularly well-liked. Although Offenhauser wanted to be bought out, he didn't necessarily want Welch as the purchaser. Fred went around to see his old friends Dale and Lou. They were interested, and in spring 1946 a deal was completed. By the time he left the company Offenhauser had produced just over 180 midget engines, about 30 220's and some 50 larger engines for Indianapolis and the championship trail, plus special jobs like the Novi and the Lencki.

Louie Meyer and Dale Drake, his future partner, teamed up in 1932 in the *Sampson Special*. It was the third year that riding mechanics had been back at Indianapolis since they were dropped in 1924. (In 1923 only one driver, German Christian Lautenschlager, in a Mercedes, used a mechanic, Jacob Krauss.) In 1930, Meyer's sponsor, Alden Sampson III, rode with him, and in 1931 Winton Crow was his mechanic. *John Drake collection/Indianapolis Motor Speedway*

Meyer and Drake paid Offenhauser $75,000 in cash of which he took $60,000 to his brokers and told them to invest it in blue-chip stocks. Drake became president of the new company and oversaw the shop, while Meyer was made vice-president and dealt with suppliers and customers. Meyer & Drake rode to the crest of the Offy's success. The engines they produced absolutely dominated Indianapolis and the 100-mile dirt track championship races for the next 19 years. It was a vindication of Miller's original vision and Fred Offenhauser's and Leo Goossen's skills and determination.

Lou Meyer

Lou Meyer was a mechanic who wanted to drive race cars. In fall 1926, Fred Wagner, the AAA starter, thought young Meyer too inexperienced a driver, but in less than a year and a half he won the Indianapolis 500. Dale Drake, the son of a blacksmith, was in the engine valve business when he met Meyer, and after sponsoring one of Meyer's rides at Indianapolis became his riding mechanic. They remained friends after they both retired from active racing. When Offenhauser told them he

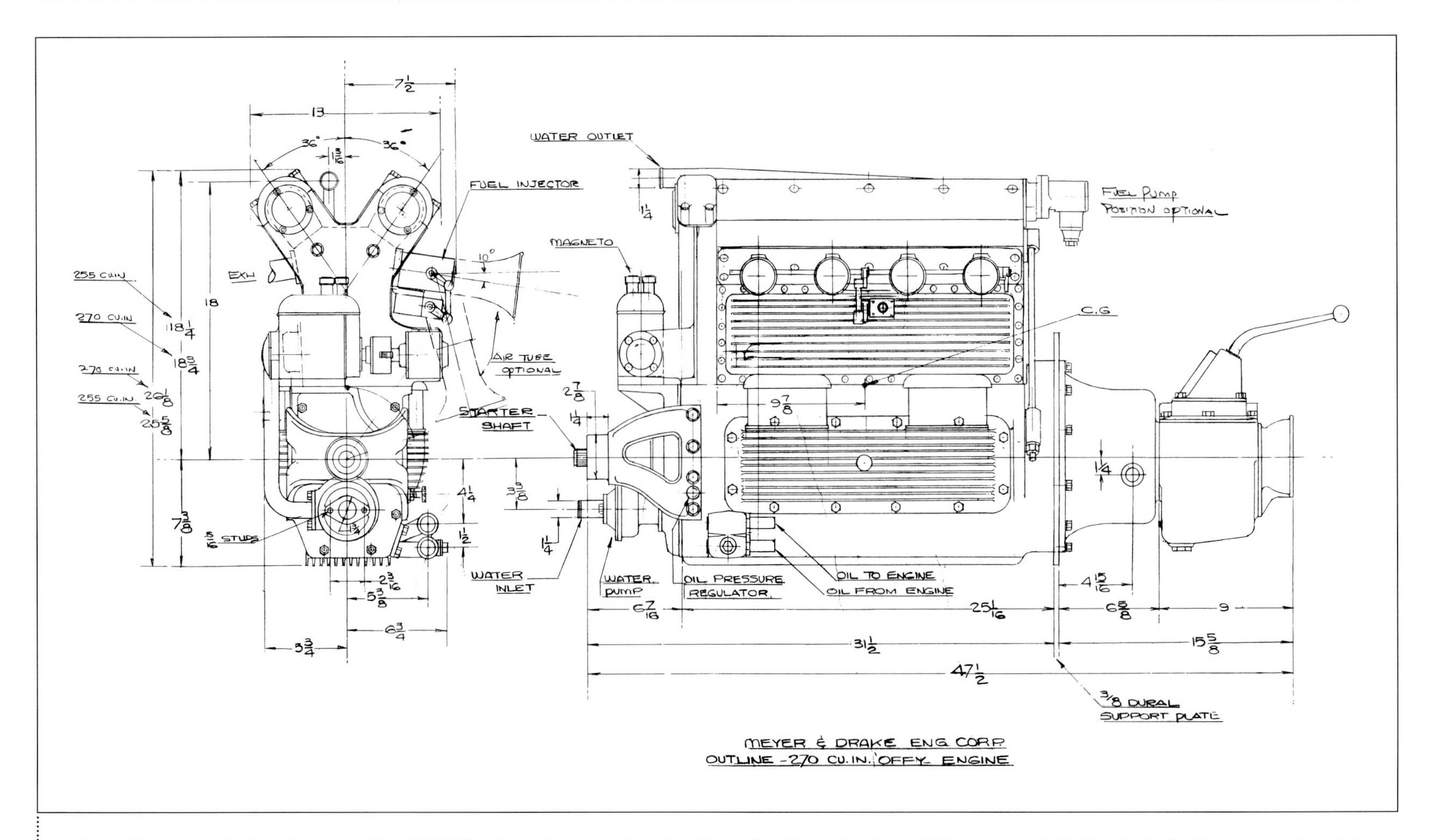

Assembly drawing by Leo Goossen of the 270 Offy, the engine that reigned in Championship racing from 1947 through 1956. This is the fuel-injected version. When the engine size was cut back in 1957 from 274 to 255 cubic inches, Meyer & Drake simply reduced the internal dimensions of the 270 slightly. Chickie Hirashima and A. J. Watson went further. They trimmed the block height of the engine, shortened the stroke, and thus increased the rpm. Goossen's drawing of the 255 had external dimensions identical to the 270. A typical 270 might have a bore and stroke of 4.375x4.500 inches and displace 270.6 cubic inches, while a 255 might have a bore and stroke of 4.28125x4.375 inches, displacing 251.9 cubic inches. There were other common combinations such as 4.3125x4.625. *Kenneth Walton collection*

wanted to quit the engine business they jumped at the chance to return to the sport they knew best.

Meyer was born in New York City in 1904. His father, Eddie Meyer, Sr., had been a champion bicycle racer in Europe before emigrating to the United States. In this country, the senior Meyer became a barber to the wealthy. His family went with the tycoons of the day to the horse races at Saratoga in the summer and to Miami in the winter. Shortly after Lou was born, the family followed the trail to California, settling in Redlands.

His brother Eddie, 11 years older, began driving race cars on California dirt tracks around 1919 and Lou worked as mechanic on Eddie's cross-spring Rajo at Legion Ascot Speedway on Valley Boulevard near Lincoln Park. In 1921, given his first chance to drive, Lou promptly spun the Rajo down Ascot's front stretch. Two years later, despite his apparent lack of driving skill, his mechanical abilities landed him a job with Frank Elliott caring for Elliot's rear-drive Miller 91. Elliott finished sixth at Indianapolis in 1926 and Lou accompanied him on the racing trail, occasionally getting to warm up the car at tracks such as Altoona and, in July, at Atlantic City.

His first chance to drive came in a card of AAA sprint races on the board track at Charlotte, North Carolina, November 11, 1926. Race starter Wagner told the 22-year-old Meyer he was there to race strictly for the experience and not to pass anyone. Lou obeyed orders, and after just over a dozen laps Elliott's Miller quit anyway. Meyer qualified in the Elliott car again at Culver City on March 6, 1927, but Wagner bumped him from the field as too green to run a 250-mile race at more than 144 miles per hour.

"I never cared much for Pop Wagner," Meyer told the author. "Val Haresnape and Eddie Edenburn (AAA officials) were okay, but Wagner was too tough on new drivers." Despite his problems with Wagner, Meyer never ran "outlaw" or non-AAA sanctioned races as some drivers did.

At Indianapolis in 1927 Meyer hoped to get a chance as a relief driver for Elliott who by then tended to tire in longer races. Elliott, however, sold his Miller (the car Jimmy Murphy had been killed in at Syracuse) to Skinny Clemons, who had Wilbur Shaw as his driver. Relieving a young charger like Shaw seemed a remote possibility. (Clemon's sponsor for the race was a tire-sealing compound named Jynx, a name that seemed a little ominous when painted on the side of the car.)

Meyer helped prepare the car, which started 19th. Shaw had it up to ninth at 300 miles when suddenly he came in, exhausted. Fritz Holliday, another of Shaw's sponsors, put Meyer in the seat and sent him out in the Indianapolis 500, the first really competitive race Lou had driven. Over the next 41 laps, as Lockhart, Bauman, Kreis, and Schneider dropped out, Lou improved the car's position from ninth to sixth. Shaw took over for the last 40 laps and finished fourth. At Rockingham later in the year Meyer drove relief for Eddie Hearne in one of the Duesenberg cars and earned an offer from the Duesenbergs to drive for them at Indianapolis in 1928.

The Duesenberg ride fell through when the team could get only four of their five cars ready in time. Red Shafer, who had rear-drive and front-drive Millers—one of which he was preparing for Shaw—lost the sponsorship of Albert Champion, the spark plug king, and offered Meyer his choice of the two cars if he could come up with an appropriate sponsor.

At the Atlantic City board track race in July 1926 Meyer had met a wealthy young racing fan of about his age from Tippecanoe City, Ohio, Alden Sampson III. Sampson had inherited a $6 million trust fund when his father died in 1909, and he came into the principal in 1923 when he turned 21. Sampson invested part of the money in a Chrysler and Maxwell dealership in the little town just outside of Dayton and had enough left over to indulge his racing fancies.[32] It was while running a Chrysler in a stock car event at the Atlantic City track in Amatol, New Jersey, that he met Meyer.

When his Indy ride evaporated, Meyer told Sampson and talked him not only into sponsoring one of the Shafer cars, but into buying it outright. Sam wired his mother in Massachusetts for the money and paid Shafer the cash the next day. Meyer's choice of the cars was the golden number 14 Miller he had seen Shafer drive to fourth place at Atlantic City.

Dale Drake, riding mechanic Lawson "Useless" Harris, and Lou Meyer look at the 18-mm Champion spark plugs in Meyer's *Ring Free Spl* with which he was to win his third 500 in 1936. The engine was a 255 Miller built by Lou with Fred Offenhauser's help. As did most of the top drivers, Meyer used an old eight-cylinder Bosch magneto with four leads grounded out. *John Drake collection/Indianapolis Motor Speedway*

Lou tore down and rebuilt the supercharged Miller eight and qualified it 13th at 111.352 miles per hour. In the 500 he drove at an unspectacular but steady pace. Faster drivers broke down in front of him, and in the first race he ever finished, Lou Meyer won the Indianapolis 500 at a speed of 99.482 miles per hour. Shafer's front-drive Miller placed sixth. After the race Sampson bought Meyer the ex-Lockhart rear-drive Miller that Tony Gulotta had been driving, and in that car Lou won a 200-mile race at Altoona in August and went on to capture the 1928 AAA Championship. At 23 he was the youngest man to win the national title, a feat he repeated in 1929 and 1933. He was to win the 500 twice more in 1933 and 1936.

In 1931, with sponsorship by the J. A. Drake & Son's Company, Meyer had Myron Stevens build a two-man chassis powered by a 230-cubic-inch Miller eight. It was the beginning of a 34-year association. Meyer didn't drive the *Jadson Special* himself, but put Myron Stevens in the car while he handled the supposedly faster *Sampson Special*. The *Sampson* expired on the 28th lap. The *Jadson* was running 20th when Stevens pitted and Meyer replaced him. In a tough charge over the ensuing 127 laps, Lou brought the *Jadson Special* up to a 4th place finish.

The Bowes-Winfield Eight

In 1933, with brother Eddie twisting the wrenches, Meyer won his second 500 in his own 255 Miller. Late in that year he had a brief business association with Fred Offenhauser's machine shop after Miller went bankrupt, but driving was his business and the partnership—if that is what it was—was short-lived. Lou took a third Indianapolis victory in 1936 with a 255 he and Offenhauser built. In 1938, under Bowes Seal-Fast sponsorship, Meyer built his own car, the supercharged 179-cubic-inch eight-cylinder powerplant designed with the help of Bud Winfield and Goossen. It was to be the last straight-eight American racing engine.

"I assembled most of it myself in my garage at Walnut Park," Lou related. "Fred Offenhauser had the patterns made, poured the castings and did most of the machine work."

For 1939 Winfield changed to an alcohol fuel blend and designed a new intercooler to reduce the temperature of the fuel mixture downstream from the supercharger. The change added about 100 horsepower but made the car even more of a beast to handle. In the race, Wilbur Shaw was Meyer's chief competition. Lou took the lead at 250 miles and held off his fuel stop longer than did Shaw. After Wilbur pitted he made up a minute's lead by Meyer and passed him on lap 182. Lou nearly lost control of the ill-handling Bowes attempting to repass Shaw, and blew a front tire, forcing him to stop, but he charged back after Wilbur who then ran out of fuel and coasted into his pit for a quick splash, returning just a straightaway ahead of Meyer. On the 197th lap Meyer, driving furiously, was closing in on Shaw when he spun in the oil slick from Floyd Roberts' earlier crash. The Bowes car took out 200 feet of the inside wooden fence on the backstretch, tossing Meyer out before it came to rest right side up.

Meyer was only shaken and bruised, but he was rushed to a nearby hospital for a checkup. The ride in the ambulance, he said, was almost as frightening as the crash. When he got there he found his wife, Junie, his brother, Eddie, and Henry Ford. He had about decided to retire from racing, but Ford cemented the decision, telling him it was time to quit while he was still alive. Ford invited Meyer to Detroit to discuss a job with the Ford Motor Company.

Henry Ford wanted to move the engine rebuilding business out of the Rouge factory complex in Dearborn, and suggested that Meyer set up a plant in California to handle Model A, B, and V-8 rebuilding. Meyer said he told Ford, "fine, but I will need capital."

"Stay away from financiers," Ford warned him. Ford said he would put a friend, Lew Welch, into the business to supply the necessary money. Together Welch and Meyer set up a Ford engine remanufacturing plant in California, just before World War II.

The Meyer & Welch plant in 1946; the company rebuilt Ford engines. Seen here are flathead V-8s of vintages from 1932 to 1946. The big electric motors were used to run-in the rebuilt engines before shipping them to customers. *Marvin Jenkins collection*

Lem Drake driving the *Drake Special*, a Fronty-Ford, in 1919, with his brother Dale as mechanic. *John Drake collection*

Dale Drake

Dale Drake was born in 1902 in Reedley, a small town in California's Central Valley. His father, J. A. Drake, was a blacksmith who, with Dale's brothers, developed a high-quality forged valve for automobiles at about the time of World War I. Harry Miller was one of the customers for their valves which were sold under the JADSON trade name.

Dale was more interested in flying, particularly in gliders, than in racing cars. In fact he won considerable renown as a glider pilot, culminating in 1928 in a world distance record for towed glider flight.

With the rapid development of flying that followed Charles Lindberg's epic flight from New York to Paris, federal officials in late 1928 instituted licensing rules that required pilots to be judged by federal inspectors who were not pilots themselves. Dale, for whom flying was a romantic calling, felt that was unreasonable and he never flew again. His brother Lem was already involved in racing and, left without a consuming interest, Dale gravitated to the race track as well.

Jadson had been putting up small amounts of sponsorship money since 1922 when Frank Elliott won 50- and 100-mile races at the Cotati Speedway with their valves. With his brothers Dutch and Lem, Dale put Jadson money behind Lou Meyer's Miller. A year later he became Meyer's crew chief and riding mechanic at the 500. He was also Meyer's chief mechanic in 1933 and 1936 when Lou won his second and third races at Indianapolis.

In 1937 J. A. Drake and Sons was sold to Thompson Products Company and Dale and Lem Drake set up their own machine shop at 8355 Wilcox Avenue in Bell, California, where they made small runs of specialty valves that Thompson did not want to bother with. With a machine shop at his disposal, Lem had designed a Drake motorcycle, something like the British J.A.P. that was winning speedway races, but he never found enough money to

The Jadson (J. A. Drake & Sons) Valve Company, about 1934. This was Dale's family business. *John Drake collection*

The first Drake racing engine was a conversion of the Harley-Davidson motorcycle engine to water-cooled cylinders and other modifications. It was quite successful, particularly in the non-Offy circuits in California. Bill Vukovich earned his spurs with a Drake in the Fresno area. *Robert Binyon collection*

produce it. In 1937 Dale, with Leo Goossen's help, began work on an air-cooled horizontally opposed two-cylinder midget engine, but ended up modifying a Harley-Davidson engine by adding watercooled cylinders.

The two-cylinder Drake, with an 89-cubic-inch displacement, was 10 percent smaller than the Offy midget, but was lighter and produced more torque. It was rough, but it got better traction on slick dirt than the Offy. Later, Drake was fond of saying "the only thing better than a four-cylinder racing engine for dirt would be a three."

The Partnership and the Product

During World War II everything was put on hold. Racing was suspended and the Drake shop concentrated on defense work. When racing resumed after V-J Day, both Meyer and Drake were caught up in the enthusiasm. Meyer wanted to get out of the by-then rather routine business of rebuilding old Ford engines. After the Drakes wound up their wartime production, Lem retired and Dale sold the Drake midget engine business including the patterns, parts, and drawings, to Fred Gerhardt for $4.500.00 in 1941(these eventually ended up with ex-driver Edgar Elder).

Charlie Andrews in his #10 Carlheim-powered *Bardahl Special,* a Kurtis-Kraft midget, at Lonsdale, Rhode Island, September 28, 1952. The air-cooled Carlheim was the eastern version of a re-designed Harley motorcycle engine. In this car Dickie Brown beat the Offys at Pittston, Pennsylvania, July 29, 1952, probably the last cycle-powered midget to accomplish that feat. Al Pillion is in the other car, the Wen Kelley Ford. *Frank Smith/Author collection*

When Offenhauser's business was offered to Meyer & Drake, their first plan was to absorb it into the Drake Machine Corporation. They made plans to redesign the large engines and produce a 91-cubic-inch blown version for Indianapolis and international competition. A "top engineer from the Allison Company" [33] was to be brought in, and the patterns for all the engines were to be redesigned. The midget was to be put into special sports car chassis to be built by Frank Kurtis. In reality, however, the market for midget engines absorbed most of that energy, and the blown engine was put off until 1948. The midget was adapted for sports car use (as will be detailed in chapter eight), but no complete vehicle came to pass. The company name became

Lou Meyer, Leo Goossen, and Dale Drake look at Leo's upgrade for the 10-year-old 270 Offy in 1947, shortly after they bought Fred Offenhauser's racing engine business. *John Drake collection*

Meyer & Drake and "Offenhauser" remained on the letterhead. To meet the demand for engines, Dale and Lou kept both the Drake shop and Offenhauser's place on Gage Avenue.

In 1946, Fred had between 20 and 25 workmen at the West Gage Avenue plant. At the time Offenhauser had a backlog of 50 engines, mostly for the midgets, with a value of more than the amount Meyer and Drake paid for the company. Fred had been using old machinery, some of it from Harry

When Meyer & Drake put up their own sign, they kept the Offenhauser name on the Gage Avenue building. *Bruce Craig collection*

Miller's plant. In some respects a job shop, Offenhauser let customers work on their own engines and his plant was always a winter home for the racers. Other than the modernization required for his war work, Offenhauser had not bought much equipment, and in the rush to build midget engines, he had not been able to keep up with the demand. Crankshafts and other parts were being made by outside suppliers at high cost.

When Meyer & Drake took over they made the Offenhauser shop more businesslike. Walt Sobraske was still with Offenhauser and he was to become the shop's foreman. Lem Drake came out of retirement to design tooling to make the manufacturing process more efficient, faster, and more accurate. Where Offenhauser turned out hand-built engines that in some cases did not have good interchangability, Meyer & Drake were able to deliver a ready-to-run engine that was built to stricter specifications. Dale, who ran the shop, added turret lathes and other modern equipment and hired four or five new men to deal with the backlog.

As they had planned, Meyer & Drake built a blown midget in 1949 and ran it in a championship car, but few owners at the time wanted to work

Lou Meyer, Dale Drake, and engine man George Salih at work on the Meyer & Drake dynamometer with the blown 107-cubic-inch Offy, 1949. *John Drake collection*

with superchargers. Although their sports car was never built, engine accessories including a flywheel, starter, and bell housing were designed and a few castings made for a handful of ambitious owners.

Leo Goossen stayed on with Meyer & Drake as chief engineer, and although as he would say, there were no new Offy engines built for a decade, there were incremental improvements and suggestions from drivers and mechanics. The first change Meyer & Drake made in the Offy engine was to design inserts to replace the hand-babbitted main and rod bearings that had been used since Harry Miller's days. Since babbitt bearings had to be line-bored whenever they were replaced, the use of inserts greatly speeded up engine building and repair. In Milwaukee, William Schoof had discovered that with some minor machine work a White Diesel Truck insert would fit the main bearings on a 270 crank. Clevite, in Cleveland, Ohio, made the first reliable production inserts for the Offy. For economy's sake Meyer & Drake altered the 220 Offy to the same diameter bearings (2.375-inch mains, 2.125-inch rods) as the 270. (Mechanic Clint Brawner later found some Chrysler bearings that could be made to fit the older 220 cranks.) They also beefed up the cam drive gears from 12 to 10 pitch in June 1947. The midget crank was redesigned slightly to accommodate inserts beginning April 15, 1948, with engine serial number 347.

Midget engines poured out of Meyer & Drake in 1946 and 1947. According to Offenhauser records midget number 102 was the first produced after World War II. By December 1947 Meyer & Drake had sold number 313, a rate of three engines a week. During 1948, the last good year for the little cars, they sold 84 midget engines.

The first production records for Meyer & Drake for larger engines start with engine number 71 on February 28, 1947, a 220 sprint-car engine for Henry Meyer of Indianapolis. Through May 4, 1965, they sold 160 finished engines, with the last of the unsupercharged Offys, serial number 231, a 255.6-cubic-inch engine, going to Ted Halibrand. (No records exist for the turbo Offys, but John Drake has estimated that Drake Engineering built about 20 per year between 1965 and 1976.)

Champ cars on the pace lap at Milwaukee, June 10, 1956. Johnny Boyd is on the pole in the *Bowes Seal-Fast* Kurtis roadster #15 carrying a 270 Offy and Pat O'Connor is outside in the Sumar dirt car. Frank Kurtis downsized the design for his subsequent midgets. *Venlo Wolfsohn collection*

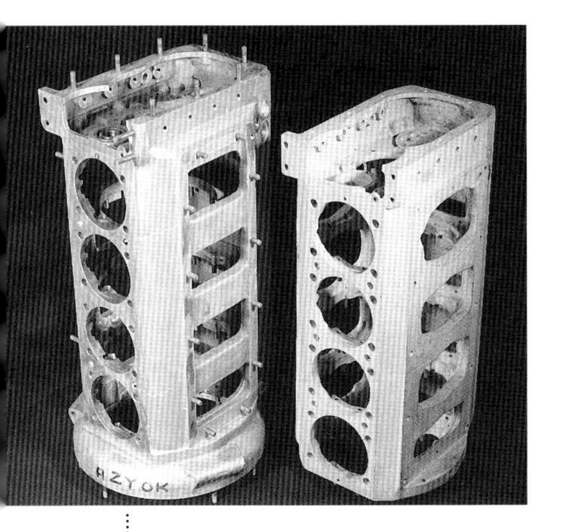

Old- and new-style Offenhauser crankcases: On the left is the style that was introduced in 1951 to strengthen the case against cracking and the lifting of the back of the block. On the right is the older "flat-back" case. Drake returned to the flat-back design with the turbos. *Kenneth Walton collection*

This 107-cubic-inch midget engine was supercharged by Meyer & Drake for competition at the championship level. Frank Kurtis built for it what was essentially the first "stretched midget" with a wider tread and longer wheelbase. The supercharger installation was virtually identical to one Fred Offenhauser made for a 1935 midget installed in Stanley Dollar's speedboat, though it used a diffuser type impeller. *Robert Binyon collection*

This stack of crankcase patterns in the Meyer & Drake shop is a testament to the number of variations it made over the years, at relatively low cost, to upgrade the engine as customers suggested. In the 1960s, Dale Drake started to toss the old wooden patterns into a dumpster and employee Bob Binyon salvaged a large number of them. *Gordon Schroeder collection*

The Offy's Golden Age

During the eight years that Fred Offenhauser built Indy engines under his name, Offys won five Indianapolis races. There was an average of 11 Offys each year, a third of the field, yet Meyer & Drake were to do even better, winning for 18 years in a row, and 24 of the next 30 years at the Brickyard. Never emotional about engines, Meyer was content to leave them as "Offenhausers." In fact, the only engine ever to be called a "Meyer" was the 1938 Winfield-Bowes, which after Lou had retired from racing, was entered at Indianapolis as a "Meyer-Offenhauser."

Over the 34 years that Meyer & Drake and then Drake alone built the Offys, Indy race fields averaged 24 Offenhauser-powered cars plus a few Drake-Goossen-Sparks or Drake-Offys. It was an amazing record of domination of the world's most important race and a tribute to the Miller, Goossen, and Offenhauser crew that established the basic design in the 1920s.

At the beginning of the postwar period 19 different makes of engine vied for places in the 33-car Indianapolis field. By the mid-1950s only the Offys remained. Few other engines were entered, almost none of them with a serious chance of making the show.

Lou Meyer confirmed in 1995 that Meyer & Drake did not make many changes in the engine they inherited from Fred. "We didn't have the [research] equipment engine shops have today," Meyer explained. But during the reign of Meyer & Drake, the Offy continued to benefit from the input of racing mechanics. "Our testers are in the field," Meyer said of both drivers and dealers. He would go to the race at Indianapolis and the 100-milers at

Chickie Hirashima installing a crank in an Offy. In the old-style cases (1932–1965) the crankcase was heated to expand it; the bearing webs mounted on the crank; and the whole assembly lowered into the case, passing the ears on the webs through notches in the bearing mounting bulkheads, then bolting the webs in place. On the early Bill White/Art Sparks 220s and on the late cases (both late midgets and 159 turbos) there were no notches and the webs had to be inserted through the access holes in the side of the case—a much longer process. *Author collection*

Sacramento and Del Mar, California late in the season and ask mechanics what they thought would improve the Offy. He would take their ideas back to Los Angeles and with Leo Goossen's help see if they made sense. Some were as minor as relocating the oil pressure fitting, others involved changing the bore-stroke ratio.

Goossen fretted under the relative inactivity. He said years later he would have replaced the costly old Miller-style tubular connecting rods with I-beam rods, but that Drake would have none of it. "They don't break, so don't change them," he told Goossen.

Challenges on and off the Track

In the late 1950s, changes in competition and manufacturing began to challenge the Offy. Meyer & Drake looked at ideas to upgrade its engines, but aside from incremental improvements, it saw no reason to change its product. It did work with supercharging in the late 1940s, but other ideas were discarded. Briggs Cunningham's museum curator, ex-racer John Burgess, intrigued by Jimmy Frankland's Hal, suggested that the Offy could benefit from Hal Hosterman's stagger-valve layout for sprint car engines, in which there were an exhaust and an intake valve on each side of the cylinder. Burgess interested Goossen in the idea and the two did a layout of the top end of such an engine with vertical exhaust ports. Drake was unimpressed and refused to build a stagger-valve Offy.

There were numerous manufacturing challenges to be met. While the Offys generally used Winfield camshafts, getting delivery from the reclusive Ed Winfield became a problem. Meyer & Drake eventually solved it by buying profiles from Clay Smith and grinding their own cams. The quality of block castings deteriorated, partly because the Macaulay foundry began to use scrap iron rather than virgin ore. When they went to aluminum blocks, there were serious problems of porosity and voids in the metal, difficulties that England's Cosworth Engineering was also having, and which took years to correct. Raw-iron block castings cost Offenhauser $38 in 1946, Meyer said. By the 1960s, Meyer & Drake was paying $400 each and not getting the same quality.

Meyer said Dayton Steel bet him they could do the Offy block for a fraction of the Macaulay price, but after a year conceded that the complex block casting was more difficult to make than they had thought.

"We found in the 1960s that we could save a lot of money by casting 220 and 255 camshafts [as they had done for years with midget cams] rather

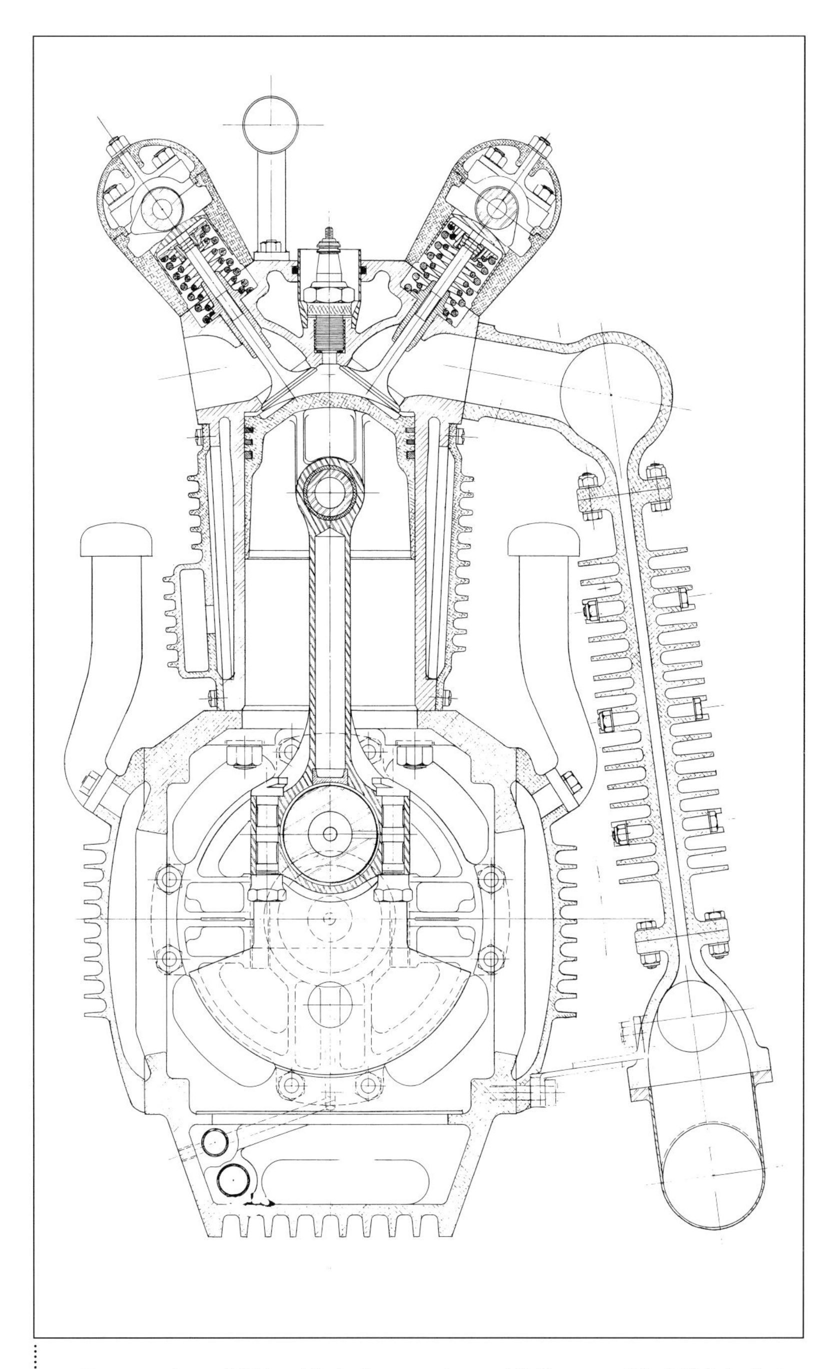

Cross-section of 176-cubic-inch supercharged Offy, a modified 220, built by Meyer & Drake in the 1950s. It was destroked to 176 cubic inches to meet the rules and did not have as much torque as the big 270-cubic-inch Offy, and although it put out more top-end horsepower, race teams abandoned it before it was fully developed—it did not seem worth the added trouble and perceived unreliability of supercharging. *Kenneth Walton collection*

Lou Moore looking over work on his three *Blue Crown* cars before the 1949 race at Indianapolis. *Gordon Schroeder collection*

than grinding them from billets," Lou said. "There was a foundry in Glendale that cast meehinite blanks for us, but they moved and we couldn't get another single usable one from them. They lost the men who knew how to do the pouring."

More than a dozen rough-machined crankshafts that were sent out for heat treating came back with cracks. Meyer said he only found out why when he was playing golf with the heat treater's salesman who admitted they had gotten the parts too hot. "They offered to pay us $400 for the material, but that didn't cover much more than the steel; it didn't begin to cover our labor. I just told Dale to drop that company."

Eventually they bought a second dynamometer and tested every engine before it was shipped. For most of the 1950s and early 1960s, Meyer & Drake continued to operate both their old shop at 8355 Wilcox Avenue in Bell as well as the Offenhauser plant on Gage Avenue with about 20 workmen at each place. In 1965, after Meyer left, the Drakes consolidated their operation at a new plant at 17502 Daimler Street in Santa Ana, California.

In 1949, Dale Drake and George Salih, then a Meyer & Drake employee, worked on a "floatless" carburetor, after they discovered that the floats in the rather simple Riley carburetors were beginning to become troublesome as engine revs climbed. John Drake recalls his father running an engine on the dyno with the top off one of the carburetors. He touched the rapidly vibrating brass float with a pencil and the tip ate right through it. The system they devised bore some resemblance to certain pressurized aircraft carburetors, with both supply and scavenge pumps driven off the cams. One supplied fuel to the carburetors, while the other was attached to vertical standpipe tubes with the open ends at the desired fuel level. The arrangement worked well enough, and Murrell Belanger (who provided the "mules" for several Meyer & Drake experimental developments.) used the floatless carburetors at Indianapolis in 1949. By that time, however, the Hilborn injec-

Dale Drake watches as Chickie Hirashima sets the cam timing on a 270 Offy. *John Drake collection*

Hilborn fuel-injection unit, perfected between 1949 and 1950, gave the Offy engines a horsepower boost of about 15 percent. *Kenneth Walton collection*

tion system had been invented, with its simpler, more easily adjusted bypass "pill."

The Offy continued to win, despite technology that was three decades old. It was there. It had a reputation. Once it proved it could win, racing mechanics, often extremely conservative, stuck with it until something else proved conclusively that it was better. The engine had four valves per cylinder, cams that were state of the engine art, and it was strong. Most of all the Offy had that marvelous torque. That acceleration won races and it gave a driver the confidence to drive out of tight places. The Offy was highly developed. The normally aspirated engine was nearly bulletproof if maintained well and not too badly abused. The engine had no particular weakness. It could survive horrendous piston speeds, severe vibrations, even liberal doses of nitromethane for qualifying. When turbocharged it would hang together under pounding that would destroy stock-block engines and the Ford four-cam of the 1960s.

It was the engine for its age. Meyer & Drake carried it through the years of the Kurtis and Watson roadsters, those marvelous dinosaurs of the fabulous 1950s. Boring they may have been to some at the time, but who would not give much to see and hear Flaherty or Foyt, or Vukovich or Parnelli, blasting down the Indy bricks today in a Kurtis or a Watson Offy?

National Championships Won with Offenhauser Engines 1947–1974

Year	Driver	Car	Engine
1947	Ted Horn	T.H.E. Spl	Offy (270)
1948	Ted Horn	T.H.E. Spl	Offy (270)
1949	Johnnie Parsons	Kurtis-Kraft Spl	Offy (270)
1950	Henry Banks	Blue Crown Spl	Offy (270)
1951	Tony Bettenhausen	Belanger Spl	Offy (241)
1952	Chuck Stevenson	Springfield Welding (Paoli) Spl	Offy (263)
1953	Sam Hanks	Bardahl Spl (K-K 4000)	Offy (270)
1954	Jimmy Bryan	Dean Van Lines Spl	Offy (274)
1955	Bob Sweikert	John Zink Spl (K-K 500C)	Offy (270)
1956	Pat Flaherty	John Zink Spl (K-K 500C)	Offy (270)
1957	Jimmy Bryan	Dean Van lines Spl (Kuzma)	Offy (252)
1958	Tony Bettenhausen	Jones & Maley Spl.	Offy (252)
1959	Rodger Ward	Leader Card Spl.	Offy (252)
1960	A. J. Foyt	Bowes Seal-Fast Spl.	Offy (252)
1961	A. J. Foyt	Bowes Seal-Fast Spl. (Watson)	Offy (252)
1962	Rodger Ward	Leader Card Spl. (Watson)	Offy (252)
1963	A. J. Foyt	Sheraton-Thompson Spl. (Trevis)	Offy (252)
1964	A. J. Foyt	Sheraton-Thompson Spl. (Trevis)	Offy (252)
1968	Bobby Unser	Leader Card Spl.	Offy (168T)
1972	Joe Leonard	Samsonite Spl.	Offy (158T)
1973	Roger McCluskey	Lindsay Hopkins Spl.	Offy (159T)
1974	Bobby Unser	Olsonite Eagle	Offy (159T)

National Championships won with Offenhauser engines, 1947–1976. After Meyer & Drake bought Offenhauser Engineering, the 270s and 255s simply made every other engine an also-ran in the 100-mile championship contests for the next 18 years. When the turbo Offy came back, it won four championships between 1968 and 1974. *Author*

The Offy Network

Offenhauser Engineering Company enjoyed customers who both provided suggestions to improve the Offy and served as its dealer network. While some drivers and mechanics gave technical feedback from the track to both Miller and Offenhauser, others did what would today be called field service and stocked engines and parts.

Clint Brawner and Jimmy Bryan were at the circular mile track at Langhorne, Pennsylvania, in 1955 with Al Dean's dirt championship car. Bryan qualified well, but Bob Sweikert took the early lead. Near the 40-lap point Bryan's Offy began to run rough and it looked as though it wouldn't finish in the money. On the 45th lap rain began to come down hard. Jerry Hoyt spun on the rain-slick dirt and Johnny Thomson hit him, going end over end. Thomson survived, but the proceedings were halted. Since the race had not reached the halfway point it could not be "official," and Shorty Pritzbur, the AAA supervisor, postponed the finish for a week.

Although the cars were supposed to be impounded, Brawner whisked the Dean car away to a Chrysler dealership where he knew the mechanic and could borrow a shop stall. He tore into the engine and discovered a broken guide and a bent valve. Calling on the Offy network, he dropped by Ken Hickey's shop in nearby Ambler, Pennsylvania, bought a new valve and guide, and repaired the engine. The following Sunday Bryan took the lead on the restart and became the first man to win a 100-miler at Langhorne two years in a row.

Ken Hickey

Ken Hickey is one of a handful of men around the country who acted as dealers for Offenhauser and Meyer & Drake, some of them for Kurtis-Kraft. Others included Frankie Del Roy, Bob Wilke, Bob Higman, Buster Warke, Johnny Pawl, and even for a time Ted Horn.

Ken was born in Tupper Lake, New York, April 28, 1912. He moved to Philadelphia In 1934 and went to work as a mechanic at a Ford dealership. In 1939 Zeke Meyer, an Indianapolis driver who had piloted a Gulf Miller car in his last effort at the Speedway, was running a Ford V-8-60-powered midget on local tracks. Meyer wanted out of midget racing and he sold his midget to Hickey.

Hickey quickly became a master racing mechanic, his cars both reliable and quick. He hired Charlie Breslin as his driver and won a feature the first time out at Sanatoga, a new 1/5-mile paved track near Pottstown, Pennsylvania. Hickey, Breslin,

Johnny Pawl holds the crutches for Bill Schindler, who lost his left leg in a big car crash at Mineola, New York, in 1936, as Bill prepares to climb into the #35 Van Nostrand Offy midget in 1939. *Johnny Pawl collection*

Master Offenhauser Mechanic Ken Hickey works on the Traylor Offy in 1955. *Bruce Craig collection*

and Shorty McAndrews were so successful with the car in 1940 and 1941 that Hickey had Doc Shanebrook of Allentown, Pennsylvania, build him a new chassis. He had just six months to run it in the 1942 season before racing was shut down for the duration of World War II.

Hickey and his #19 Ford returned to racing in 1945. His and Roscoe "Pappy" Hough's Fords were able to run with the Offys until new wider tires and the torsion-bar Kurtis-Kraft midgets came to the East in 1947. When the state-of-the-art Kurtis chassis outmoded his rail-frame cars, Ken bought his first Offy, the ex-Gib Lilly Offy, an early Kurtis, from Ed Bourgnon. Hickey's postwar drivers included George Fonder, Larry Bloomer, and Len Duncan. He owned Offy midgets for more than 30 years and last raced at Bloomsburg, Pennsylvania, in 1981, where Duncan, by then in his 70s, finished fourth in the feature.

When the midgets began to fade in the 1950s, car owners asked Hickey to stretch their Kurtis-Kraft midget chassis into sprint cars, putting wider axles under them and installing 220 Offy engines. In 1952, he built such sprinters for Jake Vargo and Sam Traylor. A year later he helped Traylor wrench a Kurtis 2000/Offy at Indianapolis for driver Al Keller. The accident that killed Bill Vukovich knocked the Traylor car out of the race.

Hickey built his current Ambler, Pennsylvania, shop in 1955. Over the years he bought, overhauled, and resold many Eastern cars. Probably half the cars running in ARDC, NEMA, and UMA in the 1960s passed through Hickey's hands. In 1953, he bought the last 220 Offy engine sold in the East by Meyer & Drake.

As the larger stock-block engines began to make life on the track difficult for the 110-cubic-inch Offy midgets, Hickey and Johnny Pawl pushed Drake to make larger blocks. Ken sawed an Offy block in half to see what was necessary to allow bigger bores and worked with Goossen to get castings large enough to get more than 130 cubic inches in the little midget engine. The largest midget block in Drake records had a bore of 3.3125 inches that, with a 3.750-inch crank, gave a displacement of 129.268 inches. Most of the 120 series midgets were actually built by putting big blocks on older engines. (When new cases were required, Drake beefed them up and went to "notchless" web bulkheads.) Hickey recalls buying between 20 and 25 120 blocks to upgrade the small Offy. He still ministers to eastern Offys in his scrupu-

Mechanic Frankie Del Roy working on the 270 Offy engine for Johnnie Parsons' Indianapolis car. *Bruce Craig collection*

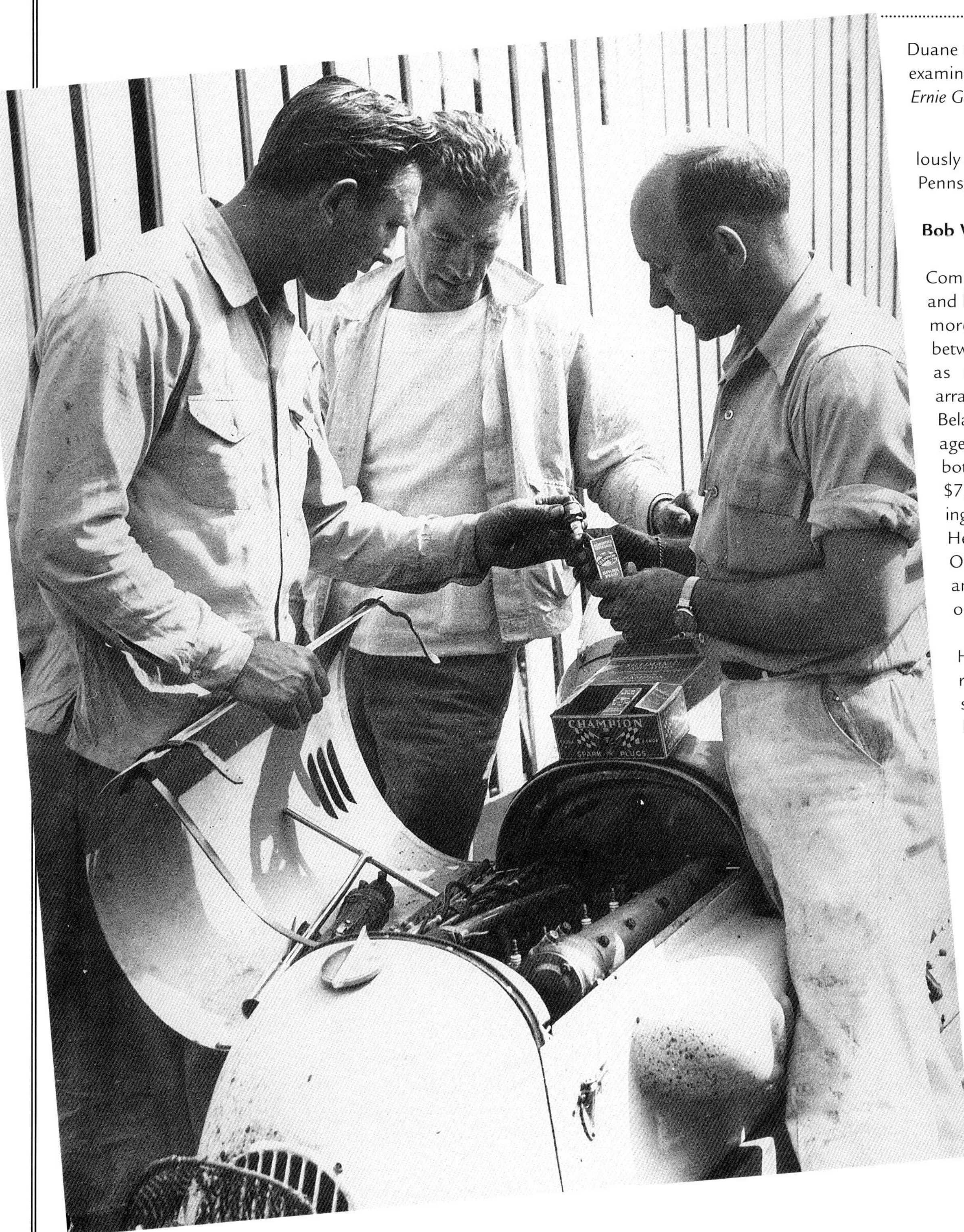

Duane Carter, Ted Duncan and Johnny Pawl examine the plugs from the Pawl #17 Offy. *Ernie Gesell/Johnny Pawl collection*

lously clean shop on Bethlehem Pike in Ambler, Pennsylvania.

Bob Wilke and Johnny Pawl

Bob Wilke of Milwaukee's Leader Cards Company was Offenhauser's first engine dealer and he sold 60 or 70 Offenhauser engines and more than 20 unfinished Kurtis chassis between 1946 and 1949. At the end of 1948, as the midgets' popularity faded, Wilke arranged for Crown Point auto dealer Murrell Belanger to buy his Kurtis and Offenhauser agency and set Johnny Pawl up as a dealer for both. Three years later Pawl paid Frank Kurtis $7,500 for his midget chassis business including fixtures, jigs, and several unfinished cars. He also bought out Frank Spillar's Offenhauser and Kurtis dealership in 1955 and, shortly thereafter, M. A. Walker's race outlet in Kansas City.

Wilke died on November 24, 1970. His son recently sold the CART franchise and retired from racing, though Leader Cards still keeps A. J. Watson on the payroll, and he runs some USAC Silver Crown events.

Johnny Pawl was born Johnny Pawlowicz in Trenton, New Jersey, August 21, 1917. In 1932, he went to see the Jimmy Cagney movie *The Crowd Roars*, and on his way home happened to pass an auto dealership where Fred Frame, Lloyd Vieaux, and some other race drivers were headquartered. He went inside, met the racers, and became hooked on the sport.

Pawl quit school at 16 and rode the circuit as a mechanic with Vieaux in Paul Bost's Miller. After Vieaux was killed at Lakewood Speedway in Atlanta, Georgia, in a Cragar 122 on July 8, 1934, Pawl worked for driver Bob Sall. A small man, Pawl was in demand as a riding mechanic in the days of the two-man cars, riding with Babe Stapp in a 100-mile race at Syracuse in early 1935, at Atlanta with Wilbur Shaw, and at Langhorne with Fred Winnai. (A riding mechanic watched for overtaking cars, examined the right-side tires for wear, transfered oil if needed, and pumped pressure into the fuel tank.)

Pawl had lined up an Indianapolis ride in May 1935 with Johnny Hannon, the Eastern AAA big-car champion. He was supposed to travel from Langhorne, in eastern Pennsylvania, to Indianapolis with Hannon but he and Winnai crashed and Johnny was knocked unconscious. When he awoke in the hospital, Hannon was gone. Pawl, who had no car and no money, hitchhiked to the Speedway. When he arrived Hannon was just going out for his first practice run with another mechanic in Leon Duray's #45 Stevens-Miller. On his first lap Hannon went over the northeast wall to his death.

Although he worked at Indianapolis as a mechanic after the end of the two-man cars, Johnny gained more fame as a midget owner. He passed up the Speedway in 1939 and 1940 to work with Ruth Rastelli's midget (one of the ex-Don Lee Offys) in the East, then with Rudy Adams' #23 J.A.P. midget driven by Henry Banks. He also worked with the Van Nostrand Offys, driven by Bill Schindler, and finally, just before the war, with Mike Caruso and the famous Black Deuce Offy which Schindler drove so successfully.

Pawl spent World War II in the Coast Guard at San Diego, building a new Offy-powered midget in his spare time. When the war ended he towed it east, racing along the way. Early in the popularity of the new Kurtis-Kraft midgets, Pawl built a Kurtis chassis for Bob Wilke, beginning his long association with Leader Cards Racing. When the torsion-bar Kurtis-Kraft chassis outmoded Pawl's rail-frame Offy, he bought a Kurtis. In 1947 Pawl won the 100-mile midget championships at Milwaukee, DuQuoin, and Toledo with Ted Duncan driving, and at Langhorne with Mike Halloran. During the 1950s, Pawl also worked as a chief mechanic at Indianapolis.

Pawl serviced the midgets at his Crown Point, Indiana, shop as long as the Kurtis chassis and Offy engines were competitive, and in later years worked with many restorers of vintage racing cars. St. Louis car owner Ed Walsh also served as an Offenhauser and Kurtis dealer just after WW II. He also sold his Offenhauser business to Pawl in the 1950s.

Frankie Del Roy

Frankie Del Roy, of Paterson, New Jersey, was another ex-riding mechanic who went into business as an Offenhauser Engineering and a Kurtis-Kraft dealer.

Del Roy (whose real name was De Rosa) was born in Philadelphia, Pennsylvania, on November 7, 1911, and began driving at the age of 19. In the early 1930s he raced (without much success) at the old Alcyon Speedway, a half-mile dirt track in Pittman, New Jersey. Norris Friel, a promoter and AAA Contest Board official, is credited with convincing Del Roy that he was a far better mechanic than driver.

Like Johnny Pawl, Del Roy was a small man and, consequently, in demand as a riding mechanic during Indianapolis' two-man years. He rode with Jimmy Gleason at Altoona, Pennsylvania, and they placed second in the last race on that board track in July 1931. Del Roy rode at Indianapolis in 1935 with Louis Tomei and in 1936 with Floyd Roberts. He was with Bill Cummings in 1937 when Cummings put the Boyle front-drive 255 Offy on the pole at 123.445 miles per hour.

Cummings' great mechanic, Cotton Hennings, taught Del Roy about racing engines. Del Roy rode at the 1937 Vanderbilt Cup race with Hennings' driver Jimmy Snyder, then struck out on his own. By 1939 he was chief mechanic on the Marks Indianapolis car, a 255 Offy. In 1940, Del Roy was with the Marks car again—then with a 270 Offy—but the engine broke a crank on the 32nd lap, putting driver Tommy Hinnershitz into the wall. Del Roy worked with Lou Moore, in 1941, on the Mauri Rose/Floyd Davis Noc-Out Hose Clamp Spl. Through Rose, Del Roy met an up-and-coming driver named Ted Horn.

He went to work for Horn, who became AAA national champion from 1946 to 1948. In the 1940s, Horn and chief mechanic, Dick Simonek, kept a shop on 29th Street between 17th and 18th avenues in Paterson, New Jersey, in a block of rented garages known as Gasoline Alley. Many racers made their eastern headquarters and at Willie Belmont's tavern. A skilled and careful mechanic himself, Horn was at the time an eastern dealer for Offenhauser.

Horn was killed at Du Quoin, Illinois, in October 1948 when a spindle broke on Beauty, his ex-Haskell championship car. Del Roy suggested that Simonek put Schindler, the one-legged midget ace from Freeport, New York, into Horn's old sprinter, Baby. This marked Schindler's re-entry into the big cars after 10 years with the midgets.

Del Roy became a chief mechanic at Indianapolis and his best year was in 1951 with the Jim Robbins car. He overhauled the year-old Offy and put Mike Nazaruk, a Long Island midget star, in as driver. Nazaruk finished second, the best showing by a rookie since Louie Meyer's victory in 1928.

Frank Spillar

Frank J. Spillar, Sr., and his son were dealers in Cleveland, Ohio, for Kurtis-Kraft and Meyer & Drake They got started in racing before World War II as pit crewmen for some of the drivers who came east during the racing season—men like Ronney Householder, Sam Hanks, Duane Carter, Paul Russo, and Roy Sherman who were top drivers but who didn't have regular traveling crews. When the midgets ran at the Rubber Bowl in Akron, Ohio, and at other Ohio tracks in Toledo, Canfield, and Ft. Miami, the Spillars found there was a demand at the tracks for tires, parts, fuel, and other necessities.

After the war the Spillars opened Midwest Racing Equipment Company and became dealers for other speed parts manufacturers including Halibrand, Firestone, HAL, and others. In 1955 they sold their Offenhauser and Kurtis-Kraft business to Johnny Pawl. Frank Spillar Sr. died in 1983.

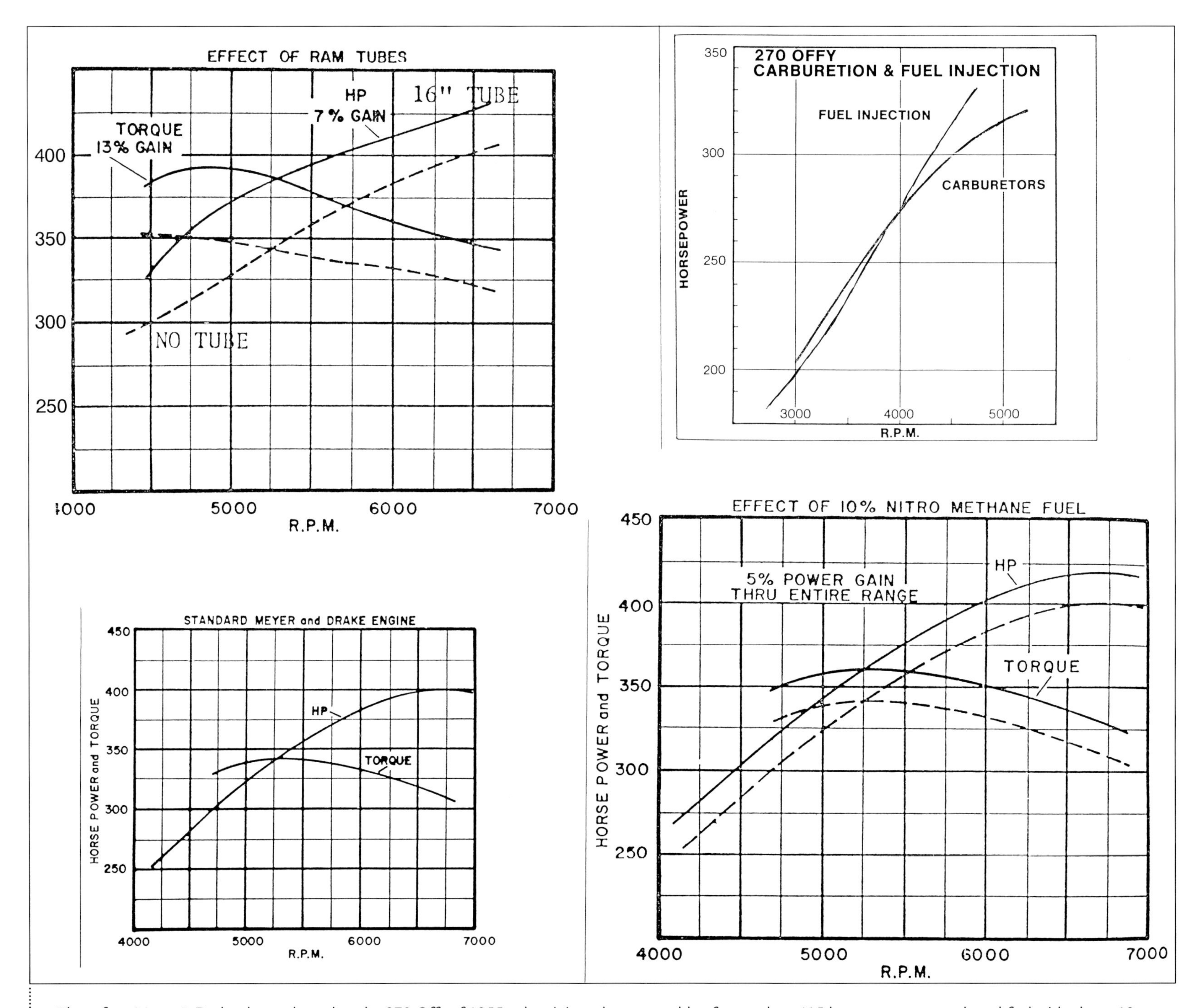

These four Meyer & Drake charts show that the 270 Offy of 1955, when injected, was capable of more than 415 horsepower on methanol fuel with about 10 percent nitro. A "standard" 270 with carburetors produced about 325 horsepower at 5,000 rpm. Injectors alone added 40 or more horsepower through better top-end breathing. Tuned ram tubes helped power, too. Using a 16-inch tube gave a 13 percent torque gain and a 7 percent horsepower increase. When Meyer & Drake added 10 percent nitromethane to the methanol fuel it got a 5 percent power increase throughout the rpm range. When all of these improvements were made to an engine they did not add as much power increase as they showed individually on the dyno. *Meyer & Drake*

Who said there was no innovation in the 1940s? Pat Clancy designed this six-wheel chassis and had Frank Kurtis build it. It was equipped of course with a 270 Offy. In 1948 Billy DeVore qualified it at Indianapolis at 123.967 miles per hour and finished 12th, 10 laps behind winner Mauri Rose. A year later Jackie Holmes qualified it at 120.087 miles per hour and finished 22nd after a drive shaft broke on his 65th lap. It was an attempt to get more rubber on the ground for cornering, but the added weight more than offset the rubber advantage. This was an innovation that did not pan out, although the car qualified twice, which was better than some experimental ideas fared at the speedway. *Indianapolis Motor Speedway*

Body and chassis builder Emil Deidt looks at the layover 220 Offy as it was being installed in the Scarab. The Offy used in the first Scarab Grand Prix car was a fairly conventional 16-valve 220 engine, modified, as had been the 255s at Indianapolis, to run as a layover. It had a 4.00-inch bore and a stroke reduced by 0.875 inches to give a displacement of 182.2 cubic inches to meet the 183-inch Formula 1 limit. Compression ratio was 10:1 so it could run on high-test gasoline. There were no counterweights on the crank and it was mated to a Chevrolet Corvette bell housing and transmission and a Chevy starter. *Preston Lerner/Dean Batchelor collection*

CHAPTER EIGHT

Offy, Meyer & Drake Sports Car Specials

In the years just before World War I, the states closed most public roads to auto racing and thereafter most American motor competition took place on oval tracks of wood, pavement, or dirt. The competing cars became entirely adapted to racing on such closed courses and their design diverged sharply from European competition which remained on roads or road-like circuits. In the late 1930s, a few American amateurs with knowledge of European-style road racing and access to European cars began a revival of road racing in the well-to-do suburbs of New York City. In those early days of sports car racing, many of the competitors put together "specials" using Ford or other passenger car engines in light chassis. These would have been called hot rods if they had been built in Southern California by boys who made their living pumping gas rather than in the East by somewhat better-heeled scions of wealthy families. In the early 1950s, with the success of Offenhauser engines at Indianapolis, on the dirt tracks, and among the midgets, it was natural that sports car builders would look to the Offy to power road racing specials. Meyer & Drake were more than willing to help them.

Offy midget engine described by Meyer & Drake as set up to go in George Beavis' sports car. Note the bell housing adapter to the MG transmission and the twin SU carburetors. The rear of the intake cam has a special fitting for both a tachometer take-off and a lever-type fuel pump. Beavis had both 91-cubic-inch and 106-cubic-inch versions of the engine. *Robert Binyon collection*

Briggs Cunningham and Offy Power

Briggs Cunningham was one of the most noted builders to try running an Offenhauser engine in a sports racing car, although in the end his effort was defeated by the poor quality of the French pump gasoline he was required to use at Le Mans.

Briggs Swift Cunningham, Jr., is one of the great American sportsmen of the 20th century. He won the America's Cup in the 12-meter sailboat *Columbia* at the same time his teams were running cars at Watkins Glen. He has been involved with sports cars since before World War II, and his prewar

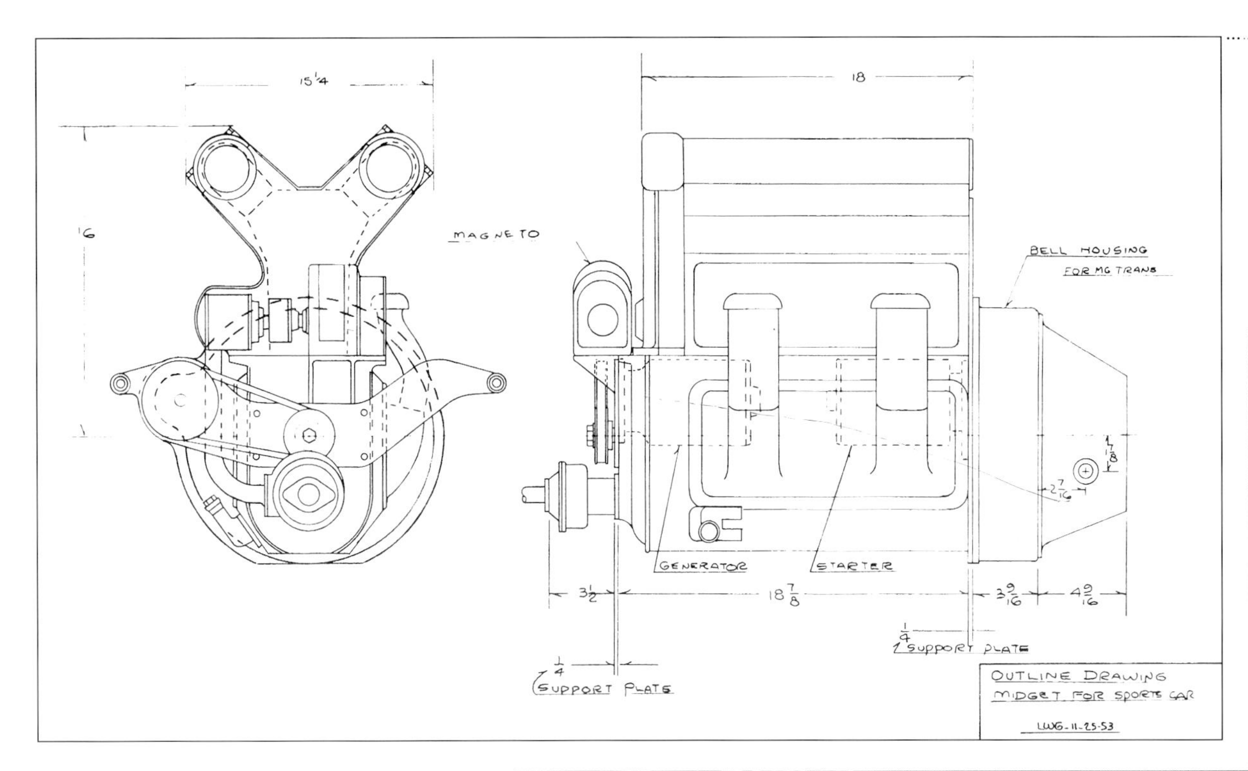

Leo Goossen's 1953 drawing for an Offy midget adapted to sports car use. Note the provision for a starter and a belt-driven generator. *Kenneth Walton collection*

Front view of the C-6R chassis in the Cunningham shop just after installation of the modified 220 Offenhauser engine. Destroked to 180 cubic inches (2,942 cc) and inclined to the left 12 degrees, it was a neat installation. Its two Weber 50DCOE3 carburetors were fastened to the frame and attached to the engine by flexible plastic tubing. Next to the radiator beside the left front wheel is the oil cooler. The transmission was a four-speed ZF model that failed at Le Mans. *Collier Historic Motor Cars*

Bu-Merc was precisely the kind of hot rod that would have been appreciated in Los Angeles. It was a Buick chassis powered by a straight-eight, Buick rocker-arm "Red Ball" engine modified by Charles Chayne and covered by a New York body shop with the sheet metal from a wrecked Mercedes. The Bu-Merc looked a trifle crude, but it went pretty well and Miles Collier Sr. was doing a good job in it at a race at the New York World's Fair in 1939 until he hit a lamp post.

In 1950 Cunningham decided to take an American challenge to Le Mans, the premier sports car race in the world. He tried a Cadillac V-8, then a Chrysler Hemi in specially built Cunningham chassis. Although the cars won a number of races, Cunningham thought the Chrysler engines were too heavy. In 1954 he determined to try something else, a much lighter, de-stroked 220 Offenhauser (bore and stroke of 3.97x3.63 inches for a displacement of 179.73 cubic inches) in a special chassis to be known as the C-6R, the fourth racer in a series of beautiful blue-and-white sports cars. This displacement qualified the car to run in the 3.0-liter (183 cubic inch) Le Mans class with cars like Aston-Martin.

Briggs S. Cunningham at speed at Le Mans in the C-6R. By then the car had not only a headrest but a fin, making it look somewhat like a D-type Jaguar. Note the Halibrand, "kidney"-style, Indianapolis magnesium wheels with knockoff hubs. As was typical racing practice, on the right side of the car the threads were left hand, and on the left side they were right hand. This was supposed to counteract any tendency to loosen the nuts on acceleration. This was the Offy's only run at the world-famous French sports car course. It ended when the ZF transmission lost all gears but high and, lugging off a corner, the Offy burned a valve on the poor-quality French pump gasoline. *Collier Historic Motor Cars*

The 220 (serial number 170) was originally delivered from Meyer & Drake in late 1954 with track-type Hilborn fuel injection. On the Cunningham dynamometer at West Palm Beach, it put out 220 horsepower with American high-test gasoline. Phil Walters (known as "Ted Tappet") and Bill Frick (a midget car owner who later gained fame for his "Fordilac," a 1949 Ford with a Cadillac V-8 stuffed neatly under the hood) exchanged the constant-flow injectors for Weber 50DCO3 carburetors and put a Lucas distributor in place of the Joe Hunt-converted Bendix magneto and got a dyno reading of up to 270 horsepower.

The engine was installed in the very light Cunningham chassis (#5422) at a 12-degree layover angle using a special bell housing provided by Meyer & Drake to accommodate a flywheel with a Cadillac ring gear and starter. At its first outing at Sebring in March 1955 the C-6R did well until the flywheel bolts—loosened under the stress of repeated clutch use.

The worst problem Cunningham would face at Le Mans was the poor quality French pump gasoline the C-6R would have to use. The Offenhausers had for years been run on gasoline blends hopped up with benzole and other additives, then spiked liberally with a dose of tetraethyl lead. Art Sparks had used alcohol on the dirt tracks since 1928 and at Indianapolis since 1938. By comparison, for all its antiknock quality the French gas might have well been kerosene. The engine had to be modified with lower-compression pistons which reduced its power. Worse, the cam and ignition timing, engineered for alcohol, had to be modified.

Methanol has a far higher latent heat of vaporization than gasoline, meaning that it has a refrigerating effect in an engine. Fed poorer stuff, the Cunningham Offy overheated, particularly around the exhaust valves. There was not time to redesign the water passages, and after a few minutes on the dyno the power would fade.

Despite the fuel problem, Cunningham took the C-6R to France and ran it at Le Mans in 1955. Briggs and Sherwood Johnson were able to get a top speed of 141 miles per hour and to turn laps averaging a respectable 106 miles per hour. During the race they got up to 13th place but the four-speed ZF transmission lost second and third gears. Lugging corners in high, the Offy burned a piston, ending the effort. The C-6R with the Offy repaired was run last at Elkhart Lake, in September, and again lost a piston.

Cunningham sold the engine to a friend of Bill Frick, Long Island sprint car owner Frankie Cal. Cal had Offy specialist Ken Hickey get parts to reconfigure it to run on methanol and he campaigned it with some success in the East in a stretched Kurtis-Kraft midget.

Midget Offy-Powered Sports Cars

Several years ago the author was showing his Kurtis Offy midget at a car show in central New Jersey when a man walked up and examined the engine unusually closely, then disappeared. An hour later he reappeared, carrying a scrapbook and two Offy cams. It was, I believe, Jim Matthews, and the photos he showed me were of a stripped-down little Italian Bandini sports car with an Offy midget under the hood.

My own recollections had been that only a few Offys had done well in sports car racing, but Matthews had a raft of 1954–1955 clippings to prove that *his* Offy had been one of the successful ones. It won a lot of races and held the 2.0-liter record at Thompson Speedway in Connecticut. Its success was probably attributable to the care with which Dave Michaels of Belleville, New Jersey, adapted the Offy to the sports car chassis, and to the Bandini itself, which was light and had excellent road-holding ability.

Matthews started out with the Offy engine (which belonged to Fred Sinon) in an MG-TD before going to the Bandini. Much of the adaptation to the Italian chassis was done at Paterson's Ken-Mar Engineering. The change from midget use to the road courses involved adapting a Bosch variable-advance magneto in place of the fixed 38-degree advance of the original Joe Hunt-modified Bendix magneto. The compression ratio was cut to 10.4:1 and the engine was adapted to a five-speed Fiat gearbox through some tricky machining using MG and Fiat parts. The Offy crank was altered to put the thrust bearing on the rear main instead of the center crank bearing.

There were several other small sports cars with Offy midget engines in the under-2.0-liter class of the SCCA. Meyer & Drake had Leo Goossen draw up an engine with the necessary accessories, but the market was never large. Some sports Offys were competitive, but it was difficult and expensive to fit the engine to a sports car's chassis. One of the sports Offys went into a modified Kurtis midget roadster chassis that Jack McGrath helped design for Jack Hinkle by widening the torsion bar car to provide the SCCA-required passenger seat. The 88-cubic-inch midget engine (#422) was a special one equipped with two spark plugs per cylinder and Italian Marelli ignition. After trying Solex carburetors Hinkle settled on a pair of Webers.

The Meyer & Drake #4 cams were not well-adapted for road racing so Hinkle had Winfield prepare a special grind that woke up the little engine in the lower rev ranges. Hinkle drove the combination to 1,500-cc class wins against chiefly Italian OSCA competition, but the 1956 Porsche eventually outclassed it in SCCA.

George Beavis tried a used 106-cubic-inch Offy midget engine in SCCA racing on the West Coast. His first engine was equipped with dual British SU carburetors, a mechanical fuel pump, and a special bell housing that adapted it to an MG clutch, flywheel, and transmission. He worked with Meyer & Drake to build a special low-tower midget block displacing 91 cubic inches and using a timing chain. At first his car had lights, fenders, a door, and a spare tire as the rules required. Eventually he had Autocraft make a tube-frame Formula II car, #52, not greatly unlike the Kurtis-Kraft midgets that were running then, and installed the low-tower Offy as a laydown with his own special sump and the other alterations required in a laydown. He won at least five races with it including (with a 106-cubic-inch block) the SCCA 2,000-cc event at Palm Springs in 1954, defeating a Ferrari Mondial. With the Offy in 91-cubic-inch trim he won 1,500-cc events at Santa Barbara, Torrey Pines, and twice at Willow Springs. The car was far and away the most successful Offy-powered competitor in the West at that time.

Bill Lloyd was another who installed an Offy midget engine in a sports car—a Lester MG chassis, with twin British SU carburetors in place of the Rileys.

One of the most professional sports Offys was the supercharged *Pesco Special*, assembled on a Cisitalia chassis by engineers at Borg-Warner, manufacturer of Pesco aircraft fuel pumps and Roots-type superchargers. The Cisitalia had excellent road-holding properties for its day. At the time, in 1950, the Offy in all its variants was unbeatable on American oval tracks and it seemed a natural combination with the underpowered tube-frame Cisitalia. It took a reported 4,000 hours of work, but the little 88.9-cubic-inch Offy was reported to be putting out 160 horsepower with SU carburetors taken from an XK-120 Jaguar, a variable-advance Vertex magneto, and as usual, a cam shaped to give more low-end power.

The original cast-iron flywheel broke up and was replaced by a steel version with a Ford-pattern ring gear, most likely from a V-8-60. Other changes included an electric fuel pump, a 12-volt generator, electric radiator fan, and a Ford transmission. The blower was belt-driven at the front of the

Jack Hinkle's Offy midget engine as adapted to a sports car installation. This is engine serial #422. It was de-stroked to 3.125 inches to displace 88.36 cubic inches. The crank had special large journals and it was equipped with a Lucas distributor driven through a special 2:1 reduction unit. The block was mounted with 12 studs, and the crankcase was drilled to match. This engine had two spark plugs per cylinder and breathed through Weber carburetors. *Kenneth Walton collection*

To avoid the high cost of designing and cutting a special train of gears to drive the cams in his sports Offy, George Beavis used timing chains when he cut the block height. *Karl Ludvigsen Archive*

Beavis had Meyer & Drake make a special low-tower midget block and shorter rods for his 91-cubic-inch engine. *Karl Ludvigsen Archive*

engine. Pesco engineer Bud Middendorf said he thought that with the addition of a centrifugal blower for two-stage supercharging the engine might be capable of producing 200 horsepower or more.

Ken Brenn, a New Jersey contractor, went the other way in 1960, adapting a sports racing chassis to oval track competition. Brenn put the engine from one of his Kurtis-Kraft Offys into a rear-engine Cooper Formula Junior. Aspiring driver Mark Donohue had Tippy Lipe, a Cooper racer, set up the suspension and the combination won a Lime Rock midget race, Donohue's first important track victory.

220 and 270 Offy Sports Cars

There were others including William Escherich (Simca) and Allen Le May (Lotus), who put 91-cubic-inch Offenhauser midget engines into sports cars to run in the smaller SCCA classes, but few attempted to use the larger engines which were fairly costly to acquire. To some degree, the Indy Offenhauser's displacement was a problem. The largest available Offy was the 270, and the cheaper Ford and Chevrolet V-8s had from 289 inches to over 400. As always, there was no substitute for cubic inches.

In 1954, Ted Cannon and Jim Seely stuffed a retired Indy 270 Offy into a "special" 97-inch wheelbase chassis at Cannon's North Hollywood engineering shop. Using a Halibrand quick-change center section and Ford and Lincoln driveline parts, they built what could have been the ultimate 350-horsepower hot rod of the day. They mounted the big Offy as a laydown (to the left) and ran dual Stromberg carburetors with a standard Ford V-8 distributor driven off the intake cam. They added a Lucas 12-volt generator which drove a Pesco aircraft fuel pump off the back end, a Ford starter, and a Chrysler Six water pump.

The car's record was spotty, chiefly because of problems with the brakes, fan, and radiator. The engine itself ran satisfactorily, but with a minimal gearbox carrying only two useful ratios, they were lugging down to 1,700 rpm at 30 miles per hour—far too slow for the Winfield #4 cams in the Offy. It won a class victory at Bakersfield in 1955 and ran at Torrey Pines but lost an oil line to the dry-sump tank and at March Field put the fan through the radiator. Its subsequent history is unknown. It is believed to be the only effort to run a 270 in sports car competition, a displacement class where it faced truly awesome competition.

Another sports car effort with a large Meyer & Drake engine was George Tilp's Aston-Martin Offy, and later, his Ferrari Offy. Tilp bought a 179.6 cubic-inch sports Offy version of the 220 (serial number 165) in 1954 to put in his Aston-Martin coupe. Tilp's Offy was next put into a Ferrari and mated to the four-speed transmission, a Delco-Remy starter on the left (exhaust) side, a Vertex magneto, #4 cams and, originally, Weber carburetors, but a Mercedes shop subsequently swapped the Webers for Bosch direct fuel injection in a very neat installation. The compression ratio, to operate on pump gas, was 8.6:1. Walt Hansgen drove it at Sebring and some other SCCA events, blowing the engine in a race at Cumberland Airport, Maryland.

The 220 Offy that George Tilp stuffed into his Ferrari. The Offy was destroked about 1/8 inch and sleeved 1/2 inch to displace 179.64 cubic inches. Thus, keeping the bore and stroke ratio reasonably close to that of the standard 220. *Karl Ludvigsen Archive*

The 270 Offy engine in Lou Senter's hot rod, complete with dual Weber carburetors and an alternator. *Kenneth Walton collection*

At least two 270 Offys were put into hot rods on the West Coast with street cams, and are run quite happily today. Lou Senter has a 270 in a 1923 Ford T roadster and Bob Anderson has one in a 1929 Ford.

Buster Warke helped Fred Maier put a 255 Offy with a 4.5-inch crank into a Jaguar coupe in the 1960s and Maier ran it on the streets in Pennsylvania for 10 years. Warke reduced the compression from 13.5:1 to 10:1. (Most Offys in street cars had too much compression.) and replaced the fixed magneto with a variable-advance ignition. He adjusted the cam timing for street use and replaced the fuel injection with Solex carburetors.

Maier drove the Offy/Jaguar until Amoco high-test gas with benzole was no longer available, then sold the engine to collector Vic Yerardi who used it to replace the engine in the Dean Van Lines Watson roadster he restored. Buster said the only problem he found in the Offy (driven many more miles on the street than any racing car was ever driven on the track) was that the bearings in the gear tower had loosened in their seats and the tower needed to be replaced. He related that the first street ignition he used on the engine was a British Lucas, but that it did not keep its timing. Maier's engine had an alternator and starter, used the Jaguar bell housing and a flywheel adapted to the Offy crank. Its only routine trouble was broken springs in the mag drive pack.

Scarab

The most ambitious effort by far to use an Offy derivative in a sports car was Lance Reventlow's Formula One Scarab of 1958.

In 1957, the Federation Internationale de l'Automobile (FIA) had decreed an engine displacement limit of 3.0 liters (183 cubic inches), thus eliminating the 283-cubic-inch Chevy V-8 from international events. Reventlow asked Jim Travers and Frank Coon of Traco Engineering to adapt a 3.0-liter Offy to one of his current specially built Scarab models as the only American engine likely to be remotely competitive with the Europeans under the new limit.

As Cunningham had found, downsizing the 220 Offy to 183 inches without redesigning the ports put them out of proportion for proper flow into the smaller cylinders. The Hilborn constant-flow injectors were great for oval tracks but not so good for road courses. Adapting the needed accessories like a starter and generator was, as usual, difficult. On gasoline the Offy's legendary torque was lacking and it usually did poorly in sports car events. The engine was sold to Vince Conze for a pittance and ended up in Dick Jones' and Bob DeBisschop's shop where it became the mule used to develop supercharging for the Indianapolis Speedway Offy.

Reventlow's Chevy-powered team demolished its U.S. competition in 1958, and Lance decided to go racing in European Formula 1 the next season. He wanted to do it state of the art, no matter the cost, and although the 183 Offy had not done the job he was convinced that a specially designed

Lance Reventlow in his Grand Prix Scarab with 18-degree layover 220 Offy, a stand-in for the desmodromic Reventlow engine Leo Goossen was then designing. The photo was taken at Reventlow Automobiles Inc. in Culver City, California. *Gordon Schroeder collection*

improvement on the Offy would be a winner. He asked Warren Olson to arrange for Goossen to draw a world-beating engine, and Olson went to Meyer & Drake to actually carry out the project. Unfortunately, among other errors, Travers and Coon told Leo to give it desmodromic valve gear.

Desmodromic operation involves cams that both open and close the valves mechanically without relying upon springs. Theoretically, desmodromic valve action eliminates the power wasted in overcoming the friction of the springs, which can be considerable. By eliminating valve float, the designer can rev the engine higher without worrying that the valves will hit the pistons. On

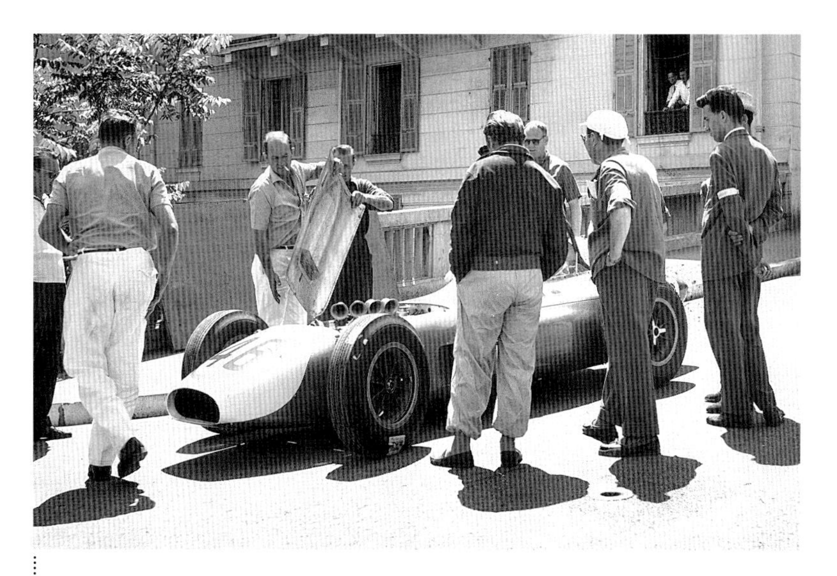

The Reventlow F-1 Scarab is rolled out for the first time at Monaco. Reventlow has his back to the camera while Tom Barnes holds the hood. Remington is at the front of the car in white pants and W. Olson is wearing dark glasses. *Dean Batchelor collection*

Leo Goossen at his drafting table working on the special opening and closing cams for the desmodromic Reventlow engine. *Bruce Craig collection*

Jim Travers, top, and Frank Coon, pointing out the complex dual-lobe cam for the desmodromic engine they had Leo Goossen design for the Scarab. The small square objects on the cables to each cylinder are temperature probes. Although the engine looked like an overgrown Offy, it was too complex and was not properly developed. *Preston Lerner/Mrs. Dean Batchelor*

The Offy engine that Dave Michaels mounted in a Bandini chassis for Jim Matthews. The engine, formerly run in an oval-track midget, was quite successful in eastern small-bore sports car racing in the mid-1950s. *Karl Ludvigsen Archive*

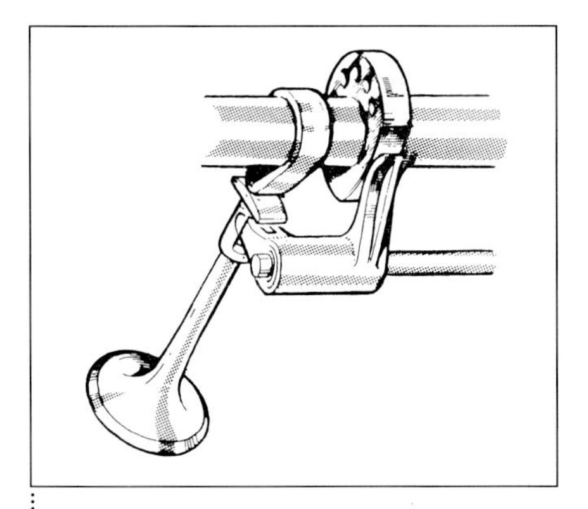

Desmodromic valve arrangement of the 300 SLR, inspiration for the Reventlow Scarab's valve gear. *Author collection*

the other hand, in modern times only Mercedes among large auto makers, and at least one Italian motorcycle manufacturer, Ducati, have been able to make a desmodromic engine work and Mercedes gave it up in 1956.

Travers and Coons had examined, in fact had disassembled and reassembled a Mercedes 300SLR desmo engine in the Henry Ford Museum at Greenfield Village and had made drawings of it. They, at the time among the top racing development engineers in the country, became entranced with desmodromic valves and infected Reventlow with the disease. Goossen at first would have none of it. Reventlow, however, insisted. Goossen said years later that the Reventlow group were "boy racers," with more enthusiasm than experience. Left to his own desires, Goossen would have built an engine far closer to the Miller mold.

Even reverse-engineering the Mercedes desmodromic design was daunting. With the cams closing the valves, clearances were more crucial than on an ordinary valve gear. Coefficients of expansion of the different metal parts were key to a valve not quite closing or closing too sharply and breaking. Making everything work at high revs was going to be tricky. Goossen drew a two-valve per cylinder in-line four in Offy fashion but with a removable cylinder head, starter, and other accessories. The engine was installed at an 11-degree layover and the drive-line was angled horizontally so the driver could sit alongside it as was being done at Indianapolis in the roadsters in those years.

One of the problems the engine had at first, Goossen said, was that the outside machine shop that ground the cams failed to follow his profiles for the closing ramps at the transition points and they stretched all the valves. Then Travers and Coon had trouble synchronizing the positive and negative cams correctly.

Meyer & Drake squeezed building the Scarab engine into a spring busy with Indianapolis projects, and it fell behind schedule. Although the engine swallowed a valve the first time it was started, the desmodromic gear actually worked fairly well, though its power was about 25 percent below expectations. Travers and Coon worked it over until they got 230 horsepower at 7,500 rpm.

Reventlow's 1960 Formula 1 effort was a disaster. Unlike 1957 and 1958 when the Americans blew away the Europeans at Monza, the foreign cousins had learned a lot and were no longer the ones chasing the power curve. The Scarabs looked good but were about three years behind the Europeans, who

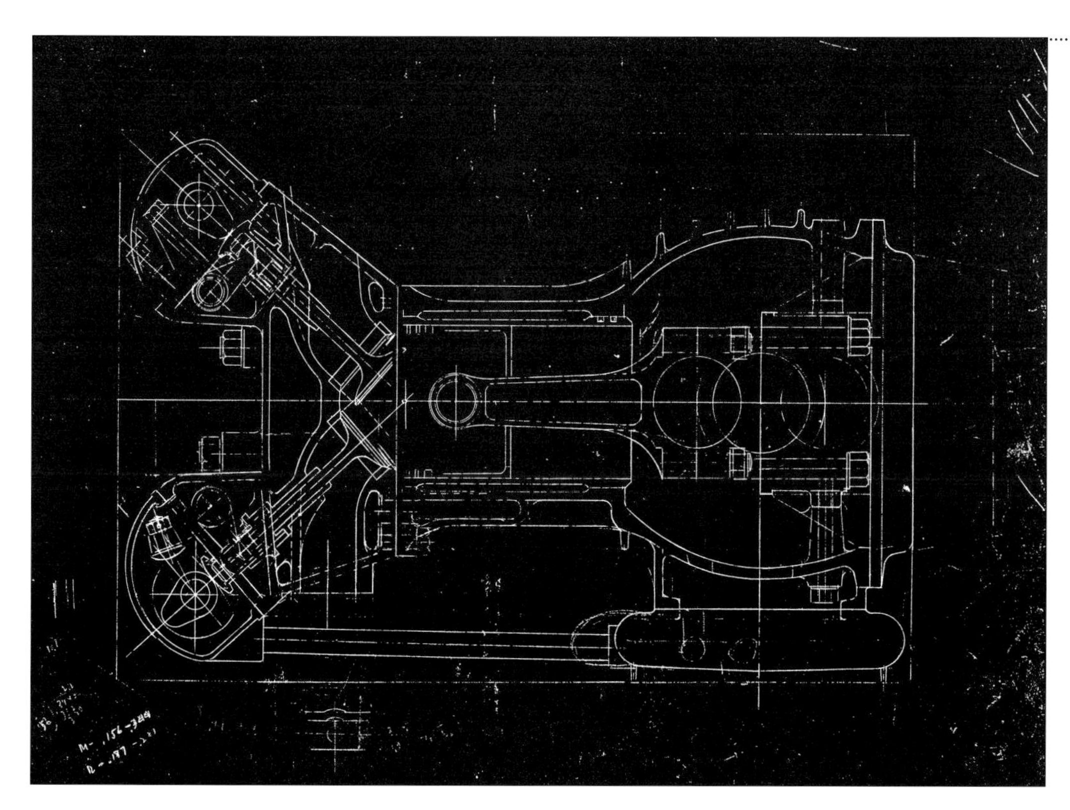

Sectional view of the desmodromic Scarab engine, by Leo Goossen. *Kenneth Walton collection*

by then were producing 400 horsepower from their well-developed 3.0-liter engines. Worse, the Scarab chassis didn't handle. All told, the desmo engine and the Grand Prix chassis were simply very costly failures.

Goossen discussed building a new head for the engine using a straight Offy-like four-valve setup, and in fact did rough layout drawings, but by that time Reventlow had exceeded the limit of cash that even his very wealthy mother, Barbara Hutton, was willing to let him burn on the project.

The Brisko FWD

One of the most successful Offy engines in sports car events involved a Miller/Offenhauser, or at least that is the way Frank Brisko described the 255 he installed in the Miller FWD Indianapolis car. The engine was built in 1934 from castings obtained several months after the bankruptcy of Harry A. Miller Inc. It used many parts including crankshaft, rods, cams, timing gears, cam towers, and pistons that Fred Offenhauser machined himself. The original Miller 308-cubic-inch V-8 had shown serious problems in its oiling system, wiping out its bearings and throwing connecting rods. Its oil and fuel consumption made it noncompetitive at Indianapolis under the 1934 fuel and oil limits, leading Brisko to replace it with the 255, assembled at the FWD Company plant.

Although the car continued to have troubles at Indy, chiefly with the Goossen-designed transfer gears between the front and rear driveshafts, when it ran it proved very fast on the rough Indianapolis bricks with the skinny, high-pressure (45 psi) tires of the day. In 1936, it started Mauri Rose on his way to the National AAA Championship with a fourth at Indianapolis at a 107.272-mile-per-hour average. Mauri drove the Burd #32 the rest of the season, but the points he earned at Indy in the FWD helped him to a 20-point margin over Lou Meyer for the title.

But after World War II William Milliken of the Cornell Aeronautical Lab, driving for the FWD Company, developed the car as a potent competitor in SCCA hill climb and road-racing events. Running on 100-octane aviation gasoline, the 255 Miller/Offenhauser gave Milliken no trouble at all. A skilled engineer, Milliken developed the 18-year-old car's handling sufficiently that he was fully competitive at Pikes Peak, Watkins Glen, and other SCCA events and won the May 21, 1950, Mount Equinox Hill Climb in record time over George Weaver's Maserati, and XK-120 Jaguars driven by Bill Spear and Briggs Cunningham. Milliken proved that when intelligently developed, the four-banger Offy was a powerful competitor on courses ranging far from the original intent of its designers.[34]

The FWD four-wheel drive Miller chassis of 1932 originally had a 308-cubic-inch Miller V-8, but after Miller's bankruptcy Frank Brisko replaced that engine with a 255. The car helped carry Mauri Rose to the National Championship in 1936 and William Milliken to a course record at the Mt. Equinox Hill Climb in New Hampshire in 1950. *Indianapolis Motor Speedway/Dean Butler*

Hard-luck Eddie Sachs in the 255 (252-cubic-inch) Offy-powered *Dean Van Lines Special* in 1961. This was a Ewing copy of a Watson roadster. *Vic Yerardi collection*

CHAPTER NINE

Indy and the Championship Trail

THE DECADE JUST AFTER WORLD WAR II WAS TRULY THE AGE OF THE OFFY'S dominance. Offy midgets were running and winning almost everywhere. AAA and IMCA Sprint car racing drew huge crowds and the Offenhauser 220s and 270s would shortly force the Ford B block engines into also-ran status. In 1948, there were 21 Offys in the field at Indianapolis; by 1950 there were 32 Offys at Indy and they were contested only by the Cummins' diesel entry which was more of a corporate promotion than a real challenge to the Offenhauser's reign. Soon there would be years when every car in the 33-car field was Offy- powered.

After its success in the 1930s, the Offy had had a ragged postwar start, but that was definitely not a portent of things to come. The 500 resumed on May 30, 1946, with a field of cars left over from before the war, some from the early 1930s. It was a grab-bag of engines and chassis: three Alfa Romeos, five Maseratis, cars built by Adams, Stevens, Wetteroth, and even three old Millers. The only new cars built in time for the race were the *Twin-Coach Spl* Paul Weirick and Floyd Trevis built[35] for Lou Fageol and two by Frank Kurtis for Ross Page and Lew Welch. In the other Kurtis, powered by Welch's Novi engine, Ralph Hepburn electrified the Speedway with four qualification laps at an average of 133.944 miles per hour, a new record by more than 3 miles per hour. On race day, Hepburn's Novi engine quit on the 121st lap and he finished 14th. Mel Hansen qualified the Page Offy at 121.431 miles per hour and finished a respectable 11th in the race

There were 18 Offy engines among the entries, two of them 91-cubic-inch, Roots supercharged midgets in Fageol's ill-fated *Twin Coach* car, which crashed on its 16th lap. George Robson won the race in Joel Thorne's car with the supercharged six-cylinder engine Art Sparks had built in 1938. The race was disappointing for Offenhauser, but changes were coming for 1947. Meyer & Drake had taken over the Offenhauser plant just weeks before the 1946 race, and their reorganization of the shop and modernizing of the machinery had just begun. There were to be no major modifications to either the midgets or the larger engines until 1951.

Five 100-mile championship races were run for the AAA Championship in 1946, all on mile dirt tracks. Rex Mays continued his prewar form, driving the supercharged *Winfield Bowes Special* to victories

A full field of Indianapolis cars roars into the first turn in the 1954 race—every one of them powered by an Offenhauser engine. It was the culmination of two decades of increasing power and reliability for the Offy, a domination destined to continue nearly unchallenged until 1964. According to Indianapolis entry forms, 32 of the 1954 starters had 270s (the engine in Jimmy Bryan's Al Dean car displaced 274 cubic inches). Meyer & Drake sold only three new engines before Indianapolis that year, each 270.6 cubic inches, plus several spare and replacement blocks. *Indianapolis Motor Speedway*

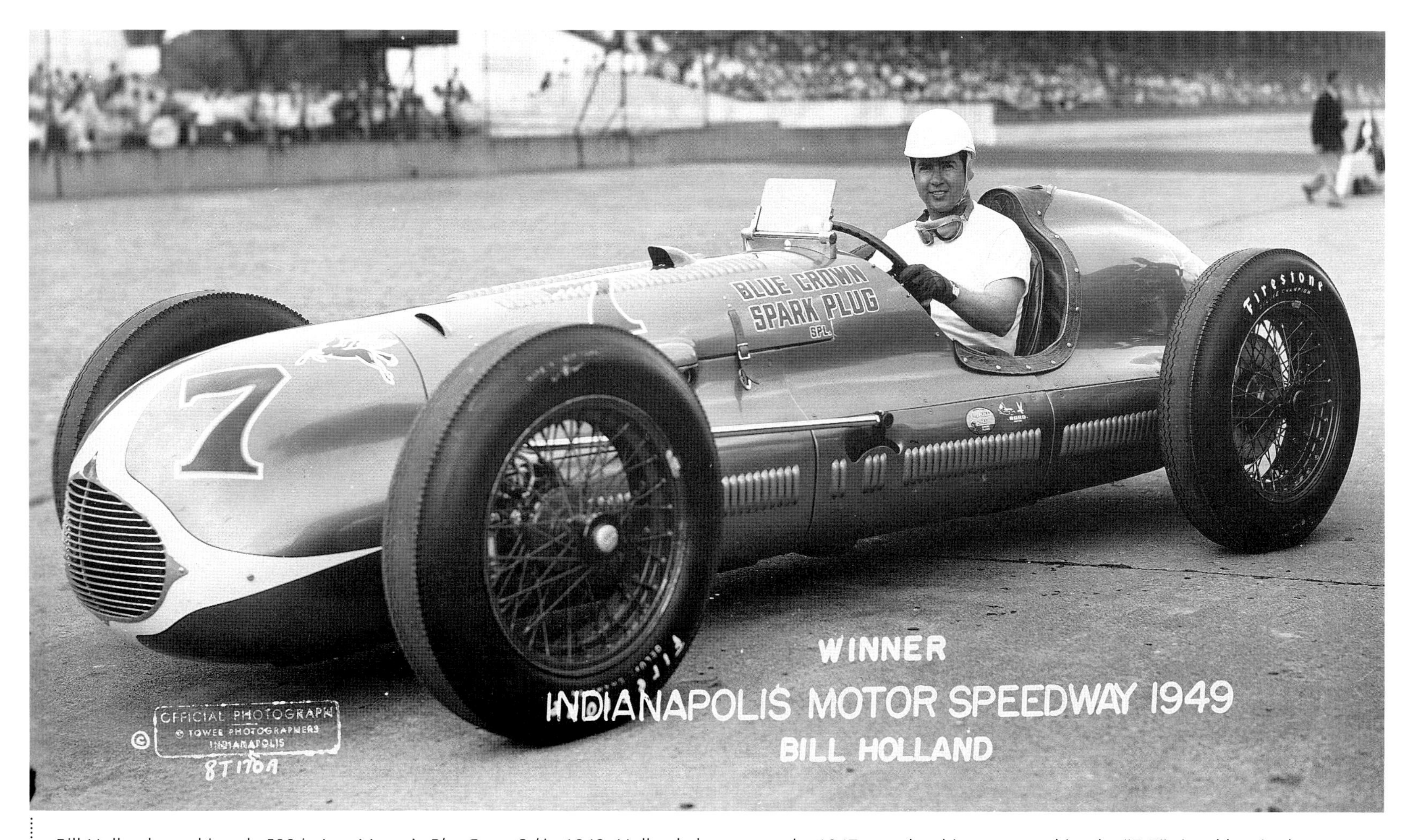

Bill Holland won his only 500 in Lou Moore's *Blue Crown Spl* in 1949. Holland almost won the 1947 race, but his crew gave him the "E-Z" signal late in the race and he allowed Mauri Rose, in the other *Blue Crown*, to pass him. Moore is reported to have used special eight-valve hemi-head blocks in the *Blue Crowns* to get better fuel mileage. *Indianapolis Motor Speedway*

Frank Kurtis and his shop crew in 1948. Left to right, Joe Ward, Carl Blackman, Rod Schapele, Johnson, Don Allen, Quin Epperly, Tom Barnes, Tony Coleman, and Lou Salzgaber. Harry Stephens is seated in the car, a KK-2000, and Frank Kurtis is behind him. *Mark Dees collection*

at Langhorne, the Indianapolis Fairgrounds, and Milwaukee. George Connor won at Atlanta and Tony Bettenhausen at Goshen, New York, both with 270 Offys. The consistent, Offy-mounted Ted Horn had enough high placings to go with his third in a Maserati at the Brickyard to be named the 1946 Champion.

In 1947, the first two 270s Meyer & Drake built went to Lou Moore and with them he began his remarkable string of three Indy victories in a row. The Blue Crown front-drive cars had been designed during the war by Leo Goossen, and Moore built his cars to be as reliable and as economical on fuel as possible in order to reduce the number of pit stops. The engines had a 13:1 compression ratio and ran on the 115-octane aviation gasoline that had been developed during the war. The secretive

The factory's Kurtis shown in the Kurtis shop crew photo without its body panels, showing the installation of the 270 Offy engine. Tommy Hinnershitz, the eastern sprint car champion, drove it to ninth place. *Mark Dees collection*

Moore is believed to have used eight-valve blocks with hemispheric combustion chambers for better fuel-efficiency. They were superbly prepared by Moore and fulfilled his plan to the letter.

At Indianapolis in 1947 Mauri Rose started on the outside of the front row and won after Moore gave his other driver, Bill Holland, an "E-Z" signal from the pits. Holland had been leading comfortably and thought he was a lap ahead of Rose when he let Mauri go by, seven laps from the end. Third behind Moore's cars, Horn gave the Boyle 8CTF Maserati a steady, competent drive, then came Herb Ardinger in the Novi, followed by Jimmy Jackson in Jim Hussey's rebuilt old Miller chassis equipped with an Offy engine. Of the 11 cars still running at the end, five were Offys.

On the mile dirt tracks there were nine 100-mile AAA races that year and 255 and 270 Offys took them all. Louis Unser did win Pike's Peak with a Maserati, however.

In 1948, 40 Offy-powered cars were entered at the Speedway. It was a vote of confidence in Meyer & Drake, but there was no stampede to buy new engines. Most of the entries had been running for years and had been rebuilt many times over. Meyer & Drake records show they built only 13 new large engines between January 1947 and May 1948, three of which were 220s for the dirt tracks. As was typical, owners and mechanics held on to existing engines as long as they could, upgrading them with new blocks at a fraction of the cost of an entire engine. Twenty-one Offys qualified, making up two-thirds of the field. Rose in a Blue Crown won the pole at 129.129 miles per hour and he and Holland finished one-two again.

On the Championship trail in 1948 there were 12 dirt track races, and Offy-powered cars won them all, 11 by 270s while Lee Wallard took the 100-miler at Du Quoin, Illinois, in Lou Meyer's old 1938 chassis carrying a 220 bored out to 241 cubic inches. Horn had already clinched the Championship for a third time when he lost his life in a then meaningless race at Du Quoin, in October.

The Offys continued to win. They were reliable and easy to service. By contrast, the prewar Maseratis, Mercedes, and Alfas were difficult and expensive to overhaul. Ironically, when no one else was able, Meyer & Drake overhauled Maserati engines on at least two occasions, replacing bearings and making special parts. In 1949 at the Drake machine shop on Wilcox Avenue in Bell, Meyer & Drake pulled the Maserati engine out of one of the Harry Schell 8CTF chassis and installed a 270 Offy. Danny Kladis tried unsuccessfully to qualify it at Indy for R. A. Cott in 1950. Although five of the Maseratis kept coming back, ultimately repowered with either 270 or blown 180 Offys, they finished far back and after 1951, were never able to qualify.

The immediate postwar years established an Offy dynasty that would shortly become boring to many race-watchers. There was no lack of innovation, but the innovators simply were not competitive. Art Sparks had two entries powered by his own engines in 1948, and they finished 25th and 26th. The Novi, the most innovative of all, came in third, one of its best finishes ever, but the Novis were too heavy and too hard on tires and the increasing speeds only accentuated their tire problems.

Technology or Sport?

Some observers said the 1950s saw little advance in racing science, but was that true, and if it was, what did it mean? Was speed alone the criteria? Racing had been a testing-ground for improvements in tires, fuels, metallurgy, and other areas of automotive technology, but only a few fans were interested in such esoterica. Most wanted to see good, close, dramatic racing, which the period provided in plenty.

Between 1920 and 1928, driven by the competition between Miller and Duesenberg, speeds increased by 21 percent, but the racing was described as boring. Between 1930 and 1941, under the restrictions of the

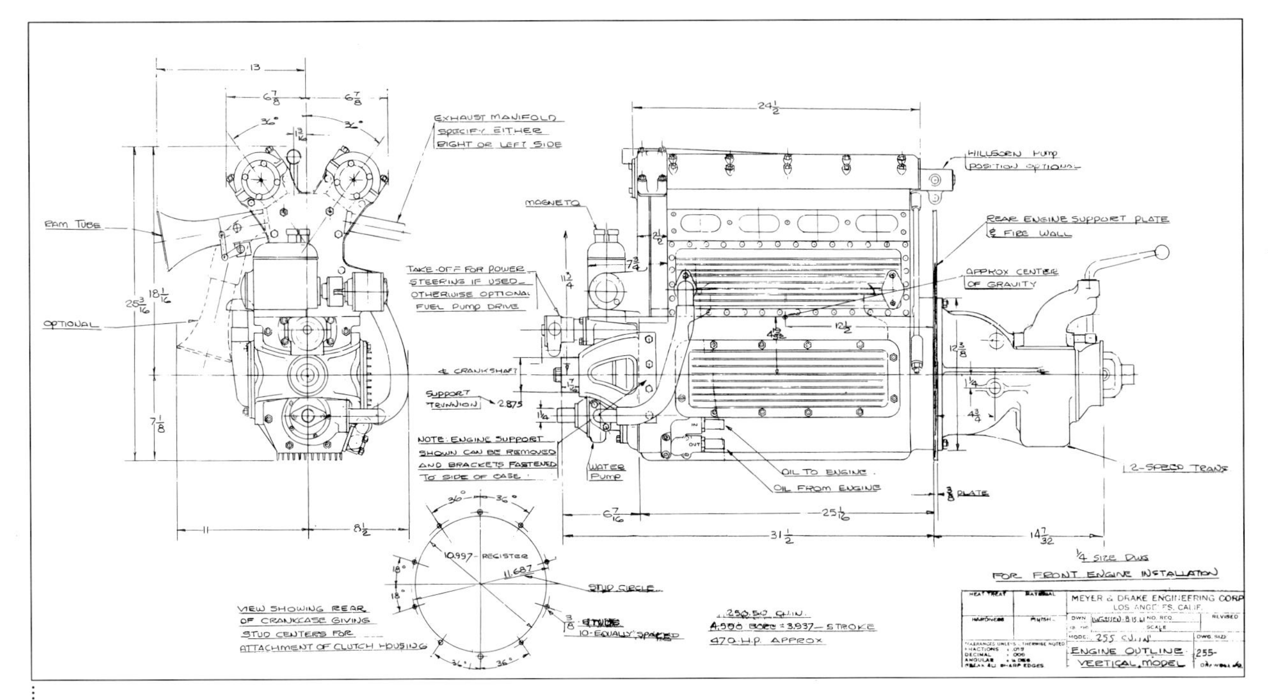

Drawing of upright 255 Offy. *John Drake collection*

junk formula, there was a great deal of experimentation and the racing was more interesting to the fans, but speeds went up only 5 percent. In the 1946–1963 era, the racing was close and qualifying speeds climbed 19 percent in 18 years.

"Unfair" Competition

At the Speedway in 1949, two-thirds of the 66 entries were Offy-powered and 28 Offys made the 33-car field. Bill Holland gave Lou Moore another victory for the Blue Crown Offy front-drives as Rose fell out on lap 192 with a loose magneto. Offenhauser-powered cars swept the first 19 places.

On the dirt, 1949 was again an all-Offy season, and Meyer & Drake's own supercharged Offy midget engine in a lightweight Kurtis chassis carrying the number 99 powered Tony Bettenhausen to a pair of victories. So successful was the #99 that other car owners complained mightily that the factory was giving them unfair competition, and Meyer & Drake sold the car to Murrell Belanger. Belanger replaced the supercharged midget with a slightly undersized 241-cubic-inch Offy. The other 10 races of the season were won with 270 Offenhausers with no one successfully challenging what an unsentimental Lou Meyer was fond of calling "the ol' air compressors."

Early in 1950, Meyer & Drake were still experimenting with superchargers and they had Goossen design a centrifugally blown 220, sleeved to the allowable 176.9 cubic inches. It incorporated everything Leo had learned about blowers in 30 years of designing racing engines. He used a gear-type drive with its own cushioning system mounted on the crankshaft flange. Four of the blown 220s were completed and entered at the Speedway, and three qualified. First to finish was Duane Carter in 12th place, some five laps off the pace when rain cut short the race. Belanger ran one of the blown engines in his old #18 Stevens chassis and although it qualified at 131.666 miles per hour, fuel feed problems put it in the pits too often to be competitive. Unfortunately, the blown 176s Meyer & Drake were never fully developed and only ran twice more at Indianapolis, both times in uncompetitive chassis. Herb Porter, who worked with the Belanger, said the blown engine produced 80 inches of boost (about 25 psi) and on alcohol at 6,000 rpm the engine would make 425 horsepower or better.

The Offy's winning ways continued in 1950 as Parsons won the 500 in the same car he had driven to second place a year before. Kurtis was stung by the same kind of criticism that Meyer & Drake had heard a year earlier about the factory competing unfairly with its customers, so he sold the car to Jim Robbins after the race for $9,500. Kurtis also sold his other Indy car and all his racing equipment to Ed Walsh of St. Louis for $10,000.

Lee Wallard won the 1951 500 in the Belanger #99, by then carrying a 241-cubic-inch Offy using a 270 block and a 220 crank. In one of the first jobs he did in his own shop, managed to squeeze the big engine into the #99 (which had been built to carry a much smaller, 107-cubic-inch, blown midget Offy). Wallard, who was from

Dale Drake, Lou Meyer, and Sonny Meyer with one of the laydown 255s on the assembly bench at Meyer & Drake. In the laydown, engine oil would collect in the low-side cam box thus requiring special drain tubes. The sump was built into the crankcase side cover. *Jim Etter collection*

Bill Vukovich, in a KK-500A chassis powered by a 270 Offy, is congratulated on winning the 1953 500 by Johnny Moore of Firestone and mechanics Frank Coons and Jim Travers. *Firestone/Author collection*

Albany, New York, beat another New Yorker, Mike Nazaruk, by about a lap despite losing two shock absorbers and half his tailpipe. Nazaruk was driving the Offy Parsons had won with in 1950.[36] There were 56 Offy-powered cars entered at the Speedway and 31 qualified, plus two Novis. Meyer & Drake had built 13 big engines between the 1950 and 1951 500s, and the rest were the usual rebuilds from earlier years. It was the last year that the old so-called "high-tower" prewar design 270s were made.

Hardly anything but Offys contested the championship dirt track races in 1951. The Belanger #99 with Bettenhausen at the wheel won eight of them with ease. (Lee Wallard was badly burned in a sprint car race at Reading, Pennsylvania, four days after winning the 500 and never got to enjoy the fruits of his victory. He tried once more in 1954 to qualify for the 500, but failed. He died in 1963.)[37]

At the time there was really no competition for the 270 Offenhauser at the Speedway. Alberto Ascari qualified a factory Ferrari in 1952, but broke a wheel hub. The two Novis were back, but both suffered supercharger shaft failures.

The powerful but unsuccessful Novis were continually plagued by problems throughout their 21 years at the Speedway, a story that is beyond the scope of this book (it should be noted, they killed two experienced drivers, Chet Miller and Ralph Hepburn). Duke Nalon came the closest to taming the beasts, finishing third in a Novi in 1948, their best. Nalon drove the Novis through 1954, despite nearly being incinerated by one in the 1949 race. As bizarre as it sounds, at one time the Novis were equipped (according to both Duke Nalon and Marvin Jenkins) with small spray nozzles to spread a fine mist of oil on the front tires in an effort to reduce their wear!

The Cummins Engine Company had Frank Kurtis build a chassis for one of their diesels. Frank had tried an offset engine in a midget in 1936. Then, for Cummins, he designed the first Championship "laydown" chassis to carry the big 401-cubic-inch truck diesel, since it was far too tall to be run in an upright position. Freddie Agabasian took the pole at 138.010 miles per hour in the Cummins but went out after 71 laps with a clogged supercharger. Kurtis installed a 270 Offy with the engine tilted to the left 36 degrees in another 1952 car, his first 500A, for Jim Travers and Frank Coon, the Howard Keck "roadster" that Bill Vukovich drove.[38]

Of the 58 Offenhauser-powered cars entered at Indy in 1952, 29 qualified. Under-age Troy Ruttman won in J. C. Agajanian's #98 dirt track car powered by a 263-cubic-inch Offy, the last year a dirt-tracker would be competitive. As in 1951, 270 Offys won all ten of the dirt track championship races.

Meyer & Drake weren't the only builders experimenting with supercharging during this period. Herb Porter constructed his own supercharged cars in the 1950s, but he had constant troubles with them. According to John Laux, the Porter cars would run like a scalded cat for 40 or 50 laps, then dirt would get into the supercharger or the blower shaft would break. By 1952 supercharging appeared unacceptable to the majority of car builders, and the unblown engine ruled the track. Porter, a supercharger fanatic, soldiered on with his ideas. He ran a blown engine in a Lesovsky chassis in 1957 and Rodger Ward won a 100-miler with it at Milwaukee. The most important thing to come out of these experiments was the Hilborn diaphragm-controlled fuel-flow regulator.

Stuart Hilborn had started the design of a constant-flow fuel-injection system during the war and tested it on hot rods at El Mirage. Once perfected, injectors produced about 15 percent more power than carburetors with better throttle response. Indianapolis mechanics used Hilborn set-ups first in

The full-laydown Offy in the Lindsay Hopkins roadster. *Kenneth Walton collection*

1949 and the first Offy to be equipped with injectors at the factory was bought by Russell Snowberger in August 1950. By 1951 most racers were using the Hilborn system.

Meyer & Drake were continually trying to make a blown Offy competitive. They tried running a Roots-type blower on another 176-cubic-inch, sleeved-down 220 engine, but the blower unit couldn't take the engine's full rpm and the experiment was dropped.

The roll of Offy drums continued. In 1953 and 1954 Bill Vukovich won Indy with a 270 and he was leading the race again in 1955 when he crashed to his death. Bob Sweikert with another 270 Offy-powered car won that race. Though it became boring for some to see only Offys at Indy, the racing itself was often close, dramatic, and dangerous. Safety had not kept pace with the power of the engines, and in the mid-1950s several great drivers lost their lives. Drivers like Bettenhausen, Bryan, and Vukovich were exciting players on a deadly stage. Mike Nazaruk and Jimmy Bryan died on the turn at Langhorne known as Puke Hollow, and Bettenhausen died at the Speedway in 1961 testing a car for Paul Russo.

With the Offy the standard engine, most innovations in oval-track racing were in the chassis. Frank Kurtis' roadsters, with the engine offset to the left and laid over 36 degrees, had superior torsion-bar suspensions and

Jimmy Daywalt in the #48 *Sumar Spl* and Ed Elisian in the #25 *Lutes Truck Parts Spl* dicing at the 100-mile Championship race at Milwaukee, Wisconsin, June 6, 1955. These were typical Offenhauser-powered champ cars of the day, equally at home on dirt or pavement. Johnny Thomson won this particular race in a Kuzma Offy at 98.80 miles per hour. The Milwaukee race has followed the 500 by a week since 1949. Daywalt finished ninth at Indy that year in Chapman Roots' *Sumar* car, but Frank Bardazon's *Lutes* car had failed to qualify at the Speedway. *Venlo Wolfsohn collection*

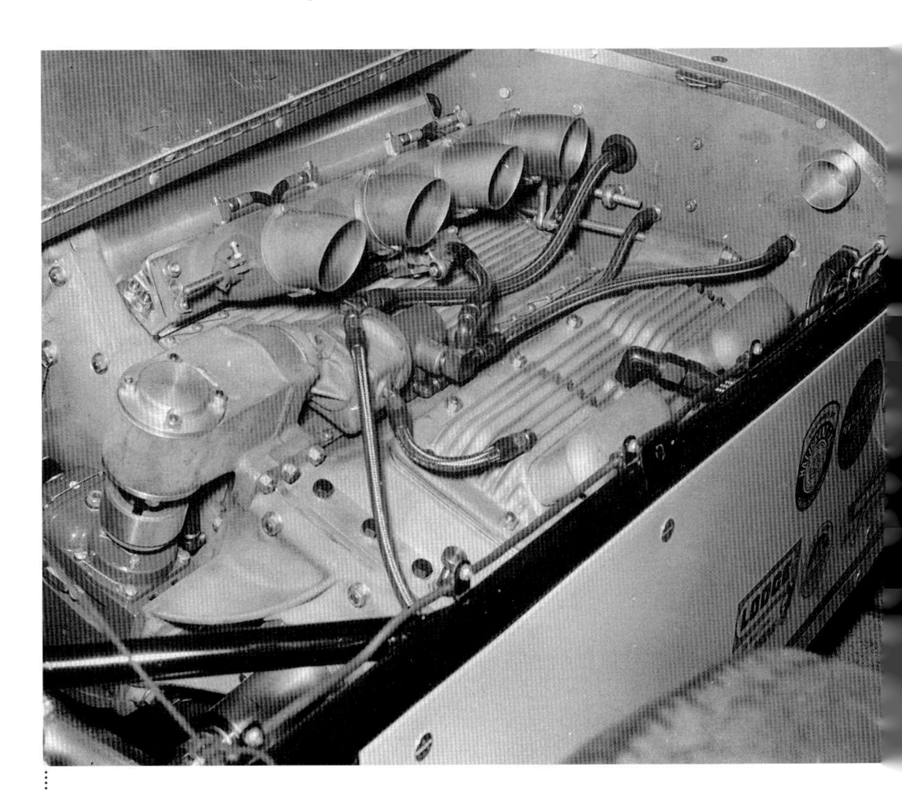

The 270 Offenhauser engine in the Salih laydown car, 1957. The oil sump, the drain-back lines from the engine, the breathers on the high side, and the fuel pump were all relocated by Meyer & Drake for the laydown engines. The fuel pump was driven off the magneto drive primarily to make it more accessible. The engine was put together of odd parts in the Meyer & Drake plant because Salih couldn't afford the price of a new engine. Salih had been Meyer & Drake's engine man, so he knew how to make even reject parts reliable. *Gordon Schroeder collection*

Sam Hanks in the Salih laydown car, the *Belond Exhaust Special* a Quinn Epperly- built chassis, which won the 500 in 1957. Although Frank Kurtis had built a laid-over chassis for the *Cummins Diesel* in 1952 the idea did not catch on until Salih tried it five years later. The Salih car also won the race a year later, in 1958, with Jimmy Bryan at the wheel. *Indianapolis Motor Speedway*

lighter, stiffer tubular frames. (Torsion bars—essentially just a spring—were developed by Mercedes-Benz before World War II. An appropriate-diameter steel bar was attached to the chassis at one end while the other end, held in a bearing, supported the wheel. As the wheel moved up or down it twisted the bar. Frank Kurtis was the first to apply the torsion bar to race cars in any quantity in the United States. Its advantage was lower unsprung weight and ease of adjustment compared to leaf or coil springs.) Kurtis' full-laydown design did not catch on immediately. It was difficult to make the oiling system work with the engine laid over, and until George Salih came along, no one would make the effort.

Despite the Offy's dominance, there were always attempts to run new engines at Indianapolis. In 1953 when AAA considered allowing a 335-cubic-inch stock block class, Chrysler built up a 331-cubic-inch, passenger-car Hemi V-8 and tested it at the Speedway in Roger Wolcott's Kurtis. Joe Sostillio pushed the car to more than 134 miles per hour, which would have won the 1952 race. Though the Chrysler actually ran no more than 20 laps at any one time in its testing, rumor got around that it had run nearly 500 miles with only routine pit stops. The demonstration led to opposition within the ranks of AAA car owners and the stock-block formula never came to be, as the Hemis downsized to 270 inches were not competitive. Willie Utzman, with J. C. Agajanian's money, had Goossen design a pretty four-cam setup for the Studebaker V-8, but broke a crank in practice, and the effort died.

The Rise of USAC and the Laydown Cars

The Vukovich crash, Alberto Ascari's death at Monza, and the 1955 disaster at Le Mans led to the AAA abandoning racing and the creation of the United States Auto Club (USAC). There followed one of those periodic attempts to slow the racing speeds, and USAC decreed that the displacement limits for the 1957 season would be 4.2 liters (256.2 cubic inches). Meyer & Drake delivered the first new "255," engine #180, to Jones & Maley on November 30, 1956.

George Salih finally took the plunge in 1957 and designed a full laydown car. The idea was to put the engine's mass as low as possible, reducing frontal area and lowering the center of gravity while at the same time shifting it to the left to counteract the car's tendency to roll outward in the turns. So compelling was the logic that Lou Meyer staked the cash-short Salih an engine (built of parts from the plant's scrap pile) and driver Sam Hanks offered to invest some of his own money in the car. The Salih laydown, powered by 255 engine #185, with an actual displacement of 251.5 cubic inches was finished on March 26, 1957. Making it work involved replumbing the oil return flow from the top of the engine and building a new sump on the low side of the crankcase. Machinist Al Long at Meyer & Drake made six modifications of the sump design before they got one to work. The Salih car started a scramble by racing mechanics to build their own laid-over engines. There were laydowns to the right and left, with special engine parts to match. Meyer & Drake built 11 such engines over the next four years with the last sold as serial #209 in March 1961. Hanks won with Salih's laydown in 1957 and Jimmy Bryan repeated in 1958, using the same engine but that was all the laydowns would win.

Other mechanics thought it was not necessary to tilt the engine so far as Salih had. It was sufficient, they thought, to offset an upright engine to the inside, run the driveshaft by the driver's elbow, and lower the seat as much as possible. A. J. Watson was the prime exponent of the upright roadster, building his first one for John Zink. Bob Wilke of Leader Cards hired him after the 1958 race and Watson more than proved his point. He built 23 roadsters all-told and his cars won the 500 seven years out of nine between 1955 and 1964.

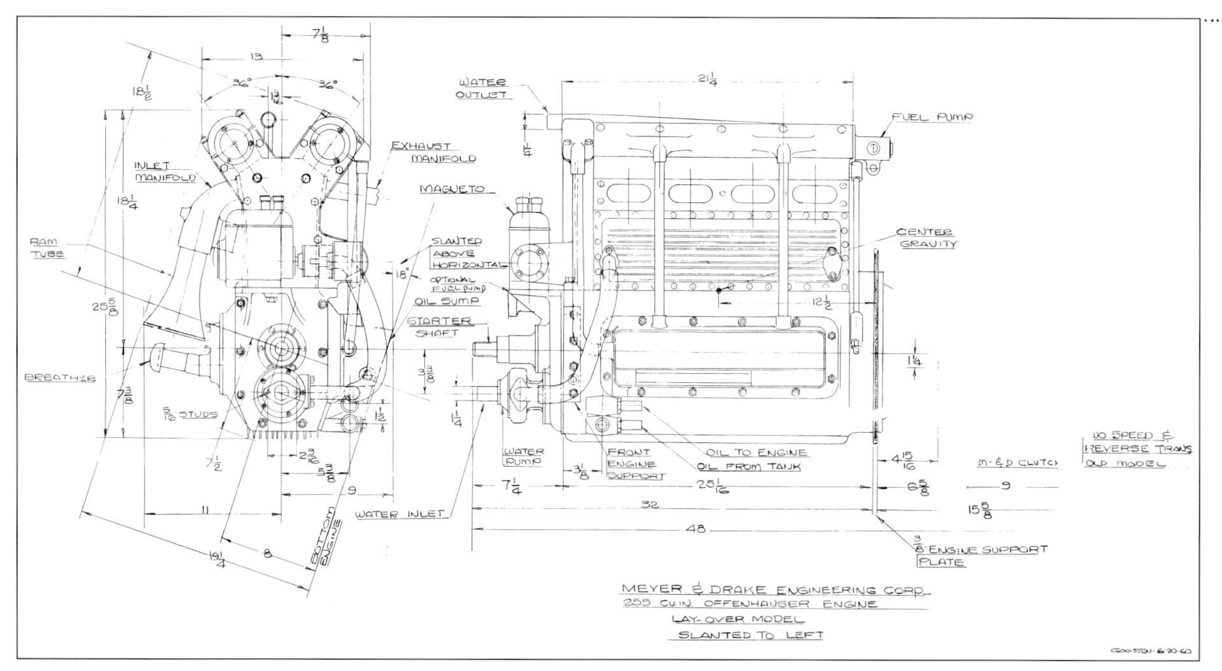

Goossen's drawing of the "laydown" Offy, put together in 1957 for George Salih along lines suggested by Frank Kurtis as early as 1952. This version is a well-developed 255, drawn by Goossen in June 1960. *Kenneth Walton collection*

Victory at Monza

In the 1950s the supposedly obsolete Offy was so dominant as to be intimidating, and in its most impressive moment outside of Indianapolis it simply demolished European competition at Monza, Italy. The "Race of Two Worlds" was conceived by the builders of a new 2.66-mile, high-banked, concrete speedway at the Monza Autodrome near Milan, long the site of important European races. In 1929, Leon Duray set records on a flat oval there in his Miller 91 front-drive cars. Two decades later the Europeans wanted a rerun. The Americans had accommodated the European Grand Prix cars with a road course at the Vanderbilt Cup revival, and Italy would repay that hospitality with an American-style oval course.

There was considerable opposition to the match-up on the part of the European racing drivers. They knew from a few bitter experiences that their cars were not designed for continuous high-speed competition like that at Indianapolis. In 1957 only three Jaguars, unsuited to high-speed ovals, would meet the Americans who were mounted chiefly in A. J. Watson-designed Offy roadsters. Jimmy Bryan took two of the three heats in the Dean Van Lines car at an average speed of 259.424 kilometers per hour (161.103 miles per hour). Troy Ruttman and Johnnie Parsons finished second and third ahead of the Jaguars, while the rest of the Americans dropped out, as speeds near 170 miles per hour and the rough Monza concrete nearly shook apart the American cars. The following year was a repeat with Rathman the winner at 166.720 miles per hour, though the Europeans were a bit more competitive.

Technical Details

During the late 1940s Meyer and Drake made only incremental changes in the Offy engines—such things as putting stronger 10-pitch gears in the cam drives, beefing up the crankcase a bit and going to insert-type main and rod bearings. Their quality control tightened up, but there were no major improvements in either the midgets or the larger engines, nor would there be until 1951.

Until 1957 the Championship rules at Indianapolis and on the mile dirt tracks allowed 4.5-liter displacement (274.5 cubic inches). Most of the Offys were run at about 270 inches, in part because bore and strokes measured in inches and fractions easily produced that number. A bore and stroke

continued on page 141

Another way to offset an Offy at Indy: an angled installation in the #8 Lesovsky roadster that Rodger Ward drove for Roger Walcott in 1957 and 1958. *Indianapolis Motor Speedway*

Color Gallery

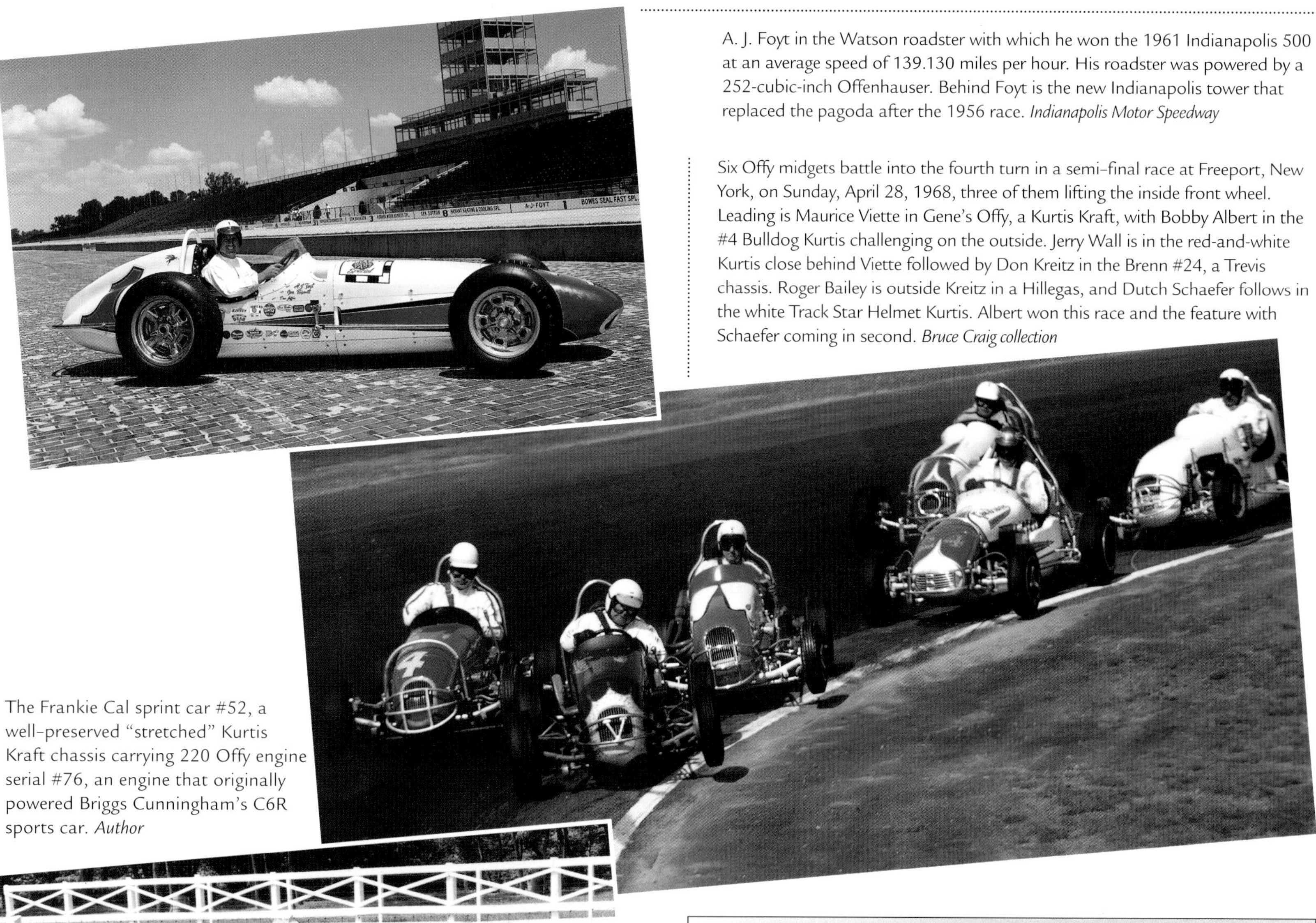

A. J. Foyt in the Watson roadster with which he won the 1961 Indianapolis 500 at an average speed of 139.130 miles per hour. His roadster was powered by a 252-cubic-inch Offenhauser. Behind Foyt is the new Indianapolis tower that replaced the pagoda after the 1956 race. *Indianapolis Motor Speedway*

Six Offy midgets battle into the fourth turn in a semi-final race at Freeport, New York, on Sunday, April 28, 1968, three of them lifting the inside front wheel. Leading is Maurice Viette in Gene's Offy, a Kurtis Kraft, with Bobby Albert in the #4 Bulldog Kurtis challenging on the outside. Jerry Wall is in the red-and-white Kurtis close behind Viette followed by Don Kreitz in the Brenn #24, a Trevis chassis. Roger Bailey is outside Kreitz in a Hillegas, and Dutch Schaefer follows in the white Track Star Helmet Kurtis. Albert won this race and the feature with Schaefer coming in second. *Bruce Craig collection*

The Frankie Cal sprint car #52, a well-preserved "stretched" Kurtis Kraft chassis carrying 220 Offy engine serial #76, an engine that originally powered Briggs Cunningham's C6R sports car. *Author*

The author's Tassi Vatis Offy on its run to an international 2,000-cc record of 153.198 miles per hour at the Bonneville Salt Flats on August 23, 1989. A year earlier the Vatis Offy went 156.902 to set the U.S. midget record. *Author collection*

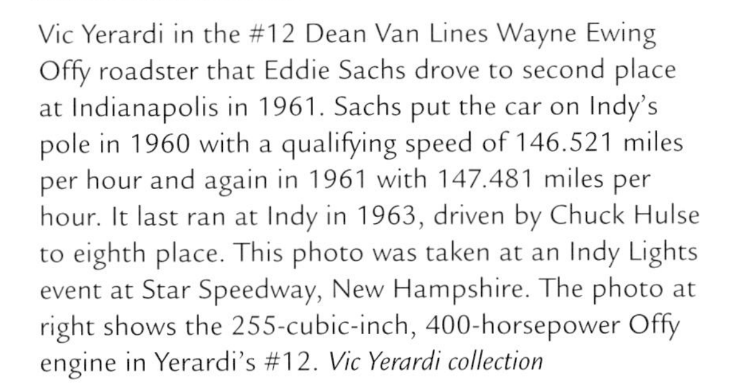

Vic Yerardi in the #12 Dean Van Lines Wayne Ewing Offy roadster that Eddie Sachs drove to second place at Indianapolis in 1961. Sachs put the car on Indy's pole in 1960 with a qualifying speed of 146.521 miles per hour and again in 1961 with 147.481 miles per hour. It last ran at Indy in 1963, driven by Chuck Hulse to eighth place. This photo was taken at an Indy Lights event at Star Speedway, New Hampshire. The photo at right shows the 255-cubic-inch, 400-horsepower Offy engine in Yerardi's #12. *Vic Yerardi collection*

Jim McWithey in the #26 Bob Estes 270 Offy setting a new International Motor Contest Association 25-lap record of 20 minutes, 20 seconds on the half-mile at the Minnesota State Fair in St. Paul, August 24, 1958. McWithey also won at St. Paul on August 26, 27, and 31 and was second there to Pete Folse on August 28. *Larry Jendras collection*

Troy Ruttman won the Indianapolis 500 in 1952 in this Kuzma dirt track car, powered by a 270 Offy. With him is car owner J. C. Agajanian (right) and mechanic Clay Smith. *Indianapolis Motor Speedway*

Veteran driver Dee Toran in his gold-and-blue "7-11" Kurtis Kraft Offy midget at the Seekonk, Massachusetts, track in 1949. *Himes Museum of Motor Racing Nostalgia*

Johnnie Parsons takes his time trial at Reading, Pennsylvania, in 1951 in his own Autobright Special, an Offenhauser-powered sprint car. *Bruce Craig collection*

The Novi Grooved Piston Special #54 as Duke Nalon drove it in 1948 at Indianapolis, finishing third. *Indianapolis Motor Speedway, Ron McQueeney*

Mark Donohue lines up in the Ken Brenn "pusher," a Cooper with a rear-mounted Offy, at Lime Rock, Connecticut, in 1960. The Cooper was well-adapted to the twisty, right-turn road course and in it Donohue won his first major event. He went on to win at Indianapolis in a rear-engine Offy-powered McLaren in 1972. *Bruce Craig collection*

Buster Warke gets ready to take the Wolfe # 77 championship car out for a run at the New Hampshire International Speedway at a 1992 vintage meet. The Wolfe car, a KK-2000 equipped with a 270 Offy, finished 5th at Indianapolis in 1950 with Joie Chitwood driving and 10th in 1952 with Bill Schindler at the wheel. *Author*

Tommy Hinnershitz, the great eastern champion, in the Miracle Power #2, a Hillegass Offy, leads Speed McFee in Dutch Culp's Hillegass equipped with a 220 Offenhauser engine at the Ted Horn-Bill Schindler Memorial race at Williams Grove, Pennsylvania, in 1955. It was McFee's last race before he retired. *Lou Ensworth collection*

The Offy engine in the restored Ruth Rastelli pre-World War II rail-frame midget sports two updraft Winfeld carburetors. *Frank Gudaitis*

Look at the size of the tires these cars had to power through the wind! Their aerodynamic drag was three or four times that of the car itself. Here Bobby Unser in the Leader Cards turbo-Offy/Eagle #3 leads A. J. Foyt driving the blown Ford four-cam/Coyote #1 at the USAC 250 at Hanford, California, November 3, 1968. Unser won the Indianapolis 500 in another Eagle-Offy that May and Foyt finished 20th with rear axle failure, but Foyt and his four-cam V-8 Ford won this Hanford race at 134.416 miles per hour. *Bob Tronolone*

Gordon Johncock driving a Turbo-DGS/Wildcat at Phoenix in March 1978. This was the penultimate Offy victory. The last time an old four-banger—Offy, Drake, or DGS—would see victory lane in an American Championship race would be at Trenton, New Jersey 36 days later when Johncock, in this car, would win for the final time at an average speed of 129.033 miles per hour. *Bob Tronolone*

Gary Bettenhausen with the Sherman Armstrong DGS/Wildcat II in which he finished third at Indianapolis in 1980, the last year that an Offy, Drake, or DGS would make the field. Drake Engineering quit producing parts in order to concentrate on a V-8 engine that never became competitive. Bettenhausen gave the old Offy a great last ride at the Speedway, coming from 32nd starting spot to nearly win the race. *Indianapolis Motor Speedway*

Offy Big Engine Production

1947 - 1965

0 2 4 6 8 10 12 14 16

1947 1948 1949 1950 1951 1952 1953 1954 1955 1956 1957 1958 1959 1960 1961 1962 1963 1964 1965

220s
270s
255s
252s
176s

Engines shown by approximate displacement, not "series"

Graphics by Tyler

Jerry Sneva drove the last Offy-powered car to take a green flag at Indianapolis in 1981. He turned an average of 187.784 miles per hour in Rolla Vollstedt's Escort Radar Detector car #17. That was fast enough to make the race, but Sneva was disqualified because a competitor thought the popoff valve had been jammed. John Martin drove the car a year later but spun in practice and did not take a time trial. Seen here is the Vollstedt # 17 in 1982. Left to right are: Bruce Vollstedt (in front), Bob Sowle, Larry Harris, Rolla Vollstedt, Steve Farakally and Martin. The mechanic on the right is unidentified. *Monte Shelton/Indianapolis Motor Speedway collection*

The 251-cubic-inch Offy in the *McKay Spl* at Indy in 1957. Don Edmunds drove the car to 19th place. *Gordon Schroeder collection*

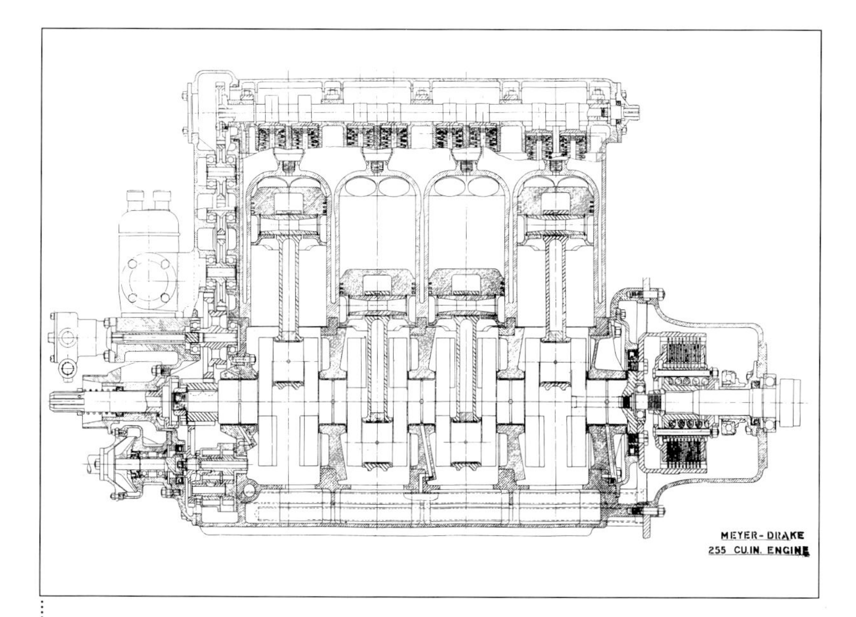

Drawing of the new "low-tower" Offy. Chickie Hirashima and A. J. Watson cooperated to reduce the stroke of the Offy by cutting down the 270 block to fit the 220 timing tower. The result gave higher rpm and less wear. Note the multiple-disc clutch, used since the 1920s. *Mark Dees collection*

continued from page 132

of 4 5/16x4 5/8 inches gave a displacement of 270.3. It also allowed a little room for cleanup with a boring tool in case a cylinder were damaged. On dirt tracks enough dust could be inhaled in 100 miles to scour a few thousandths from the cylinder walls.

The 270 had been designed by Goossen for Fred Offenhauser in 1937 to allow the use of a longer stroke crankshaft and longer rods (8 1/4 inch) than the 255. Owners of 255s had been using long strokes and large bores, but they were having clearance problems inside the case. The 270 was given a taller block (11.1 inches) and of necessity a higher gear tower to match it and a widened crankcase to provide clearance.

Blocks from the 255 and 270 engines would interchange if the timing gear tower was changed, though with later blocks the stud holes in the case might have to be redrilled. As almost always with Offenhauser engines, a mechanic could mix and match many parts from different engines if he was familiar with the subtle differences involved.

A. J. Watson

ABRAM JOSEPH WATSON WAS THE SON OF A MACHINIST. BORN IN Mansfield, Ohio, May 8, 1924, he served in the Air Corps during World War II and went to college in California on the GI Bill. In 1947 he started racing midgets in Glendale, and a year later was at Indianapolis as a mechanic with Bob Estes. In 1949, he built a 270 Indy Offy out of discarded parts for the City of Glendale Special, but the car broke a crankshaft in the race. In 1955, John Zink hired Watson as chief mechanic for his Indianapolis cars, and with a Kurtis 500C roadster, Watson and Bob Sweikert won the 500 and the last National Championship under AAA sanction.

Watson built his own Indy roadster in 1956. With careful attention to detail he made the John Zink car 200 pounds lighter than anything else in the race and Pat Flaherty won the 500 for him going away. A. J. split with Zink in 1958 when the owner objected to Watson's selling copies of the roadster to other teams. In the interim, of course, George Salih won two Indianapolis races with his Quin Epperly laydown, a trend Watson refused to join. When Bob Wilke hired Watson and driver Rodger Ward in 1959 the "Flying Ws" won Watson's third 500, followed by a fourth in 1962 and a fifth in 1968 with Bobby Unser in a rear-engine Offy. In 1996 Watson still worked for Ralph Wilke and fielded an occasional USAC Silver Crown car.

The Low-Tower Block

One of the best-known Offy modifications was A. J. Watson's low tower block (not a return to the 1937 block, but a lower version of the 1952 270). Both Takeo Hirashima and Watson reasoned that shortening the stroke would get more revs out of the 270 Offy with little sacrifice in power. A shorter stroke indicated a shorter block, so Watson machined the bottom of his 270, reducing its height to 10.953 inches. (He subsequently had Meyer & Drake cast blocks with more metal around the bottom of the bores, and Meyer & Drake later made such blocks with cylinder bores that extended down into the crankcase.) When USAC cut the displacement limit from 274 inches to 256 in 1957, almost everyone opted for the Watson low-tower block to reduce their engine's size.

The low-tower block matched the gear tower for a 220 Offy, so the change was not terribly expensive. Meyer & Drake was actually quite accommodating about making such special parts at a minimum cost. It

Rodger Ward in his Indy-winning 1962 252 Watson/Offy. *Indianapolis Motor Speedway*

was apparently just part of the development process for its product. Imagine trying to get a change in the block height today on a Cosworth or Ilmor engine! The 1957 Watson 255 produced more than 360 horsepower on methanol fuel at 6,200 rpm. It could be geared to turn 6,500 rpm for qualifying.

Incremental Improvements

While the 270 was larger and stronger than the 255, it was heavier. Some mechanics felt the added weight was not worth the gain in strength. The heavier 270 crank was a handicap particularly on dirt tracks, where quick acceleration was more important than it was at Indianapolis with its long straightaways, Meyer & Drake sold the engines as a standard item, but if you wanted special features, like a lighter crank or Winfield, McGurk, or Plaisted cams, you could mention them to chief engine builder Takeo (Chickie) Hirashima and get them installed.

The pounding of the Offy's big pistons tended to lift blocks and crack the case at the rear of the engine. Murrell Belanger had an engine break the last two studs at the back of the block. The earlier flat-back crankcases were at first bolstered by a steel plate that bolted into the rear of the block, sandwiched between the case and the bell housing. In 1951, to solve a case-cracking problem, it was strengthened by making the front portion of the bell housing part of the main casting. The studs again began to break. In order to hold the block down, the "bustle back" engines were equipped with splayed reinforcing rods that ran from the top of the block to the outer sides of the bell housing. Goossen later laughed when he recalled that they found the cause of the problem was just that the studs had not been relieved below the threads.

"When we undercut them just a little below the threads they stopped cracking. They didn't need the rods, but people kept asking for them because they were the latest thing." Later, in the turbo era, Drake Engineering dropped the reinforcements then brought them back to handle the 1,000-horsepower pounding the turbo engines took.

As time went on, Meyer & Drake had Winfield grind cams with more lift than the long-running #4s, requiring cam housings to be opened up for clearance over the lobes. Build-sheets show Winfield #131s and 133s first being installed in 1959. Some chief mechanics went to more exotic grinds than that, with steep opening and closing ramps that were hard on valve springs, so spring pressures went up, demanding better materials and design. The new cams required even greater clearance inside the cam covers and late in 1959 Goossen drew up a new wider cover with better seals. These can be identified by their double row of studs, similar to those on Art Sparks' sixes. Some 1960 and 1961 engines were built with the old-style cam covers, but after mid-1961 almost all Offys had the double row.

Sparks himself contributed to both improved valve springs and pistons for the Offy. Using German technology he picked up in Europe, he had a run of ForgedTrue Offy pistons made out of 2018ST aluminum which helped eliminate weaknesses in the cast pistons that Meyer & Drake had been using. He and Tim Witham also supplied the Offy with better quality valve springs under the S & W trademark.

Frank Curtis, of Hewlett, Long Island, was chief mechanic of Carl Hall and Barney Martin's *Hall-Mar Spl* #71. Here Bob Luscomb snugs down the block in the car's 255 Offy. Chuck Arnold drove this car to 15th place in 1959. Note the turnbuckles used to hold down the block, a trick Bruce also used on other engines. This engine has the fittings for the tie-down rods, but no rods are in place. Curtis made a steel plate to hold the block on his 220 sprint engine, but Meyer & Drake were seeing cases cracked at the back and they extended the casting that made it no longer possible to use the plate as a reinforcement. When Wally Campbell drove Sam Traylor's 220 and blew the block off, Traylor went to Meyer & Drake and asked them to do something—the solution was the bracing rods, later adapted to both the 220s and the 270s. *Indianapolis Motor Speedway*

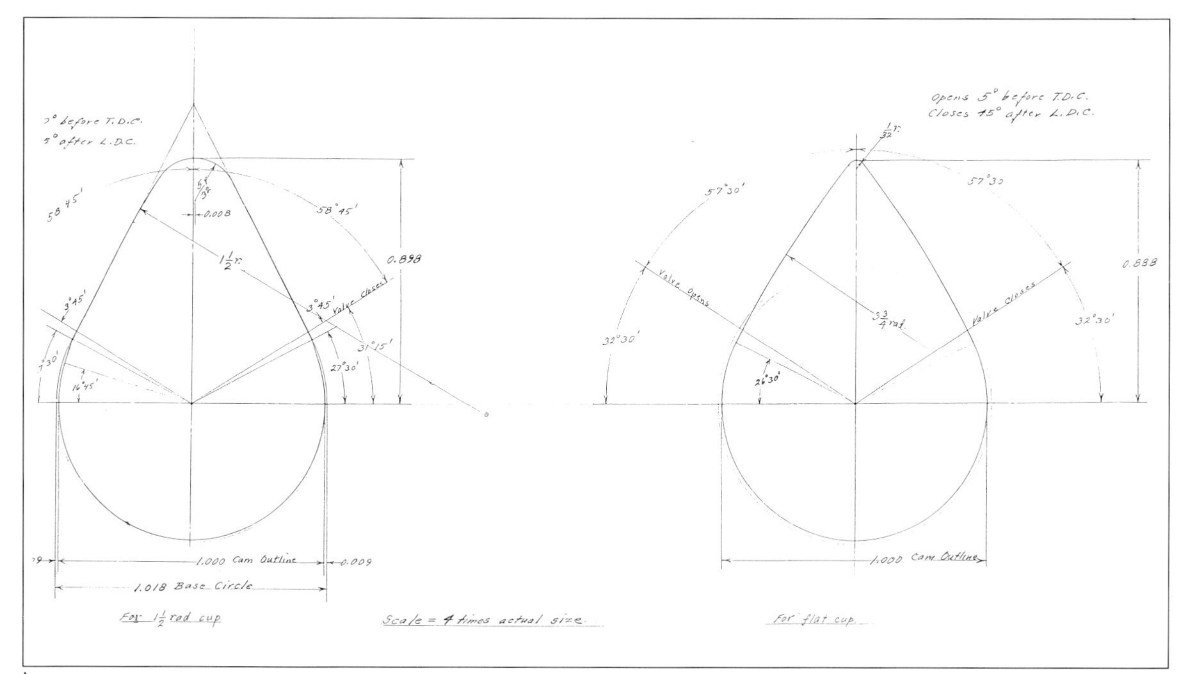

Drawing of cam profiles for the flat and radiused valve tappet cups. The radiused cups had a raised convex top. On the left is a standard Offy cam profile for the radiussed cup tappet. Note that it opens the valve at 10 degrees before top dead center. On the right is a cam for a flat-type cup and it opens the valve at 5 degrees before tdc. All of the cups were hard-chrome plated for wear resistance. *George Parker collection*

There was no shortage of ideas to improve the engine. During 1954 Meyer & Drake tested models with two and even three spark plugs per cylinder. When word got around, there were a dozen orders for the blocks with multiple plugs, but in dyno tests Meyer & Drake found that an eight-plug engine got no more power than a four-plug setup. Nevertheless, the Jack Hinkle team used an eight-plug block in Jack McGrath's Kurtis 500C in 1955. The car went out of the 500 with magneto failure on lap 54. Hinkle also bought at least one multiplug midget block for his sports car.

Flat valve cups were tried in 1958 and, according to some users, produced considerably more power than the radiused tappets by forcing the valves to open faster. The flat-topped cups required a much more pointed cam profile and were not only hard on valve springs, but wore the hard-chrome plating off the cups in short order. Despite that, mechanic Buster Warke was a believer in the flat cups. Buster said that whatever the problems, "We sure went faster with them." Better and higher-pressure lubrication was devised to try to make the flat cups last longer, requiring better O-ring type seals on the cam covers. At the time the flat cups could not be made reliable and Meyer & Drake kept the radiused style standard.

A weight-reduction program was devised for the Offy engine in the 1950s, with sleeved aluminum blocks but they leaked and were unsuccessful. Magnesium was adopted for side plates and unstressed parts, and aluminum for crankshaft webs. Mechanics were pushing the Offy as hard as they knew how, and even as the engine size was reduced from 270 to 255 inches, qualification speeds at Indianapolis climbed from 128.756 miles per hour in 1947 to 158.416 in 1965. To achieve the higher speeds meant running ever closer to the brink of failure. Mechanic Clay Smith mused that the Offy had reached the point where when pushed until it broke, anything could let go: pistons, rods, cranks, gears. From an engineering standpoint there was no single most likely point of failure in the engine.

There were fuel rules at Indy in the mid-1950s, but they were not tightly enforced. Nitromethane began to be commonly used as an additive. Although it sounds explosive, nitro is a clear liquid that is, effectively, a form of supercharging; it increases the amount of oxygen in the mixture. When using nitromethane, the amount of fuel must be increased so the mixture's fuel-oxygen ratio remains the same. Until mechanics realized they could not just pour a little nitro or "pop" in the tank, they burned a lot of pistons. Horsepower output for a 270 Offy on straight methanol was around 345 at 5,500 rpm in 1952. On a stiff dose of pop, a mechanic could get more than 400 horsepower, at least for short bursts such as a four-lap qualifying run. George Bignotti, wrenching the #6 Bowes car, a 252, for Bill Boyd, squeezed 30 additional horsepower out of a mixture of 4 1/2 gallons methanol, 1/2 gallon nitromethane, 77 cc polyoxide (an oxygen-bearing lubricant), 20 cc benzol, and enough blue cake dye to make it look like Blue Sunoco gasoline!

A Decade of Dominance

Bryan, 1958; Ward, 1959; Rathmann, 1960; Foyt, 1961; Ward again in 1962; Jones in 1963; Foyt in 1964—the roll of drivers who won Indianapolis was long and spectacular. In 1956, 1957, and 1958 the only non-Offy competition was from the Novis. Every championship race, most half-mile dirt track races, and virtually every open midget race was an Offy preserve. It seemed as if it would never end. But after an absence of three decades, racing was beginning to attract the major manufacturers. The Offy would shortly face challenges from the small-block Chevy and an entirely new engine built by the Ford Motor Company.

Author, Graphic by Tyler

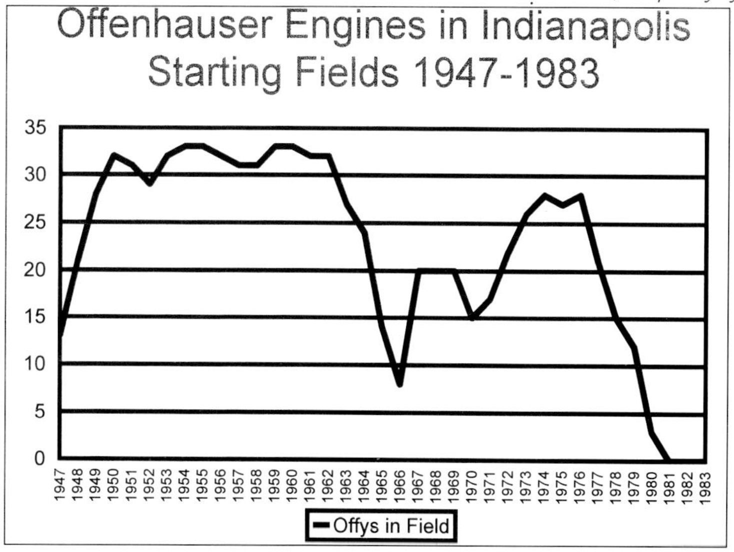

Offenhauser Engines in Indianapolis Starting Fields 1947-1983

Offys in Field

Sprint cars on the half-mile dirt track at Reading, Pennsylvania, in 1957. Bearing down on the Fords of Donald Woods (in an ex-Wally Campbell #84), and Jim Ryder in the #44, are Rex Records in Ed Stone's white # 5 Offy, Herb Swan in the ex-Hinnershitz #1 Miracle Power Offy, Joe Mattera in the Deer Lake Inn Ford and Hank Rogers in the Steffen #6 Offy. Hinnershitz, who was almost unbeatable at Reading, his home track, sold the Miracle Power car early that year and drove the Pfrommer Offy. This race, ironically, was won by Joe Barzda in his Chevy-powered #33 stretched Kurtis midget, the first-ever Chevy win in the east. The big Chevy, while fast, generally overheated, but rain cut the race short while Barzda was leading. *Venlo Wolfsohn collection*

CHAPTER TEN

THE BIG CARS, 1930s TO THE 1960s

WHILE INDIANAPOLIS AND THE BOARD SPEEDWAY CHAMPIONSHIP RACES took the national headlines in the 1920s, there was a lower rung on the racing ladder: the half-mile dirt ovals and the country fairgrounds. Races run on smaller tracks were sometimes classified as for "light cars", but generally they were just "race cars." AAA called these "big cars" until 1955 when the Contest Board was abolished, and the International Motor Contest Association (IMCA) called them "speedway cars" until 1959. After World War II, the racing press tagged them "sprint cars", the name they are known by today. This indigenous dirt track racing was the training ground for men like Frank Lockhart, Wilbur Shaw, and A. J. Foyt, and it was the kind of racing most people watched.

The shorter dirt tracks like Ascot in California, Williams Grove in Pennsylvania, and the country fair ovals were the backbone of American racing between the world wars until the midgets attracted huge followings. Men who drove the half-mile dirt tracks brought racing to those who were never going to see a race at Indianapolis and for whom the board tracks were a faded memory. Around the country there were hundreds, possibly even a thousand cars built and campaigned in this type of racing at any one time. There were never enough Miller or Offy fours to dominate these circuits as completely as they did at Indianapolis, but from 1928 until 1960 the top drivers consistently drove cars with the DOHC Miller and Offy engines.

The AAA had short-track displacement limits in the 1930s that ranged from 200 cubic inches to 366, but they were occasionally ignored. If the AAA needed cars for a particular race they were known to bend the rules a bit. On the tracks controlled by the IMCA, the top racing was in the "free-for-all class" and any engine could run. IMCA records show the Schrader and Wilburn 255- and 318-cubic-inch engines were virtually the only Offys in that circuit for most of the prewar years and those two won every IMCA championship from 1937 until after World War II. The California Roadster Association (CRA), when it went from a roadster group to a sprint car organization in 1957 (then called California Racing Association), was a "run what ya brung" club that also had no engine limit. On the other hand, Ohio-based Central States Racing Association (CSRA) had at least a nominal 250 limit on twin-cam engines, but effectively no limit on stock-blocks or the low-revving converted aircraft engines such as the Hisso or Curtiss.

From the fragmentary records that survive, there may have been 30 to 40 Miller and Offy engines running on the shorter tracks at any one time, and for three decades those engines won races out of all proportion to their numbers. At first the Miller engines that were available to the nonchampionship racers were usually older 183s or 122s and the four-cylinder engines built for boat racing. The "marine" engines of 151 cubic inches could be bored out or stroked to 200 cubic inches rather easily and outrun most—but not all—of the Ford Model T and Model A-and B-based cars.

IMCA payoff sheet, Shreveport, Louisiana, October 19, 1941, from the last race Gus Schrader finished, a seven-lap semi-final in which he beat Jimmy Wilburn. Schrader, driving the #5 *Riverside Offy* was on the pole and Wilburn in the outside position in the *Morgan* #39 Offy. The six others in the race were Ben Shaw in his #9 Curtiss; Ben Musick in Schrader's other car, the *Riverside Offy* #1; Lyle Christie in his #43 Miller; Dave Champeau in the *Wonder Seal Hal* #6; Herschel Buchanan, a local, in *Hal* #2; and Buddy Callaway in the *Wonder Weld* Curtiss #64. In the final, feature race Schrader and Wilburn tangled on the first lap and Schrader was killed. *IMCA/Author collection*

Depression-Era Racing

It is important to remember that during the Depression there was money to be made on the 1/2- and 5/8-mile dirt tracks. California's Ascot was packing in the crowds, and before it closed in 1936, the payoffs there were good. There were also a dozen other groups that ran on the short dirt tracks. The previously mentioned IMCA was the largest of what AAA called the "outlaws." There were also the National Motor Racing Association, Garden State, Central Penn, Southern Tier, AMAR, ARA, and several other local associations where the money was good enough to attract an occasional Miller or Offy.

The fair circuit provided a decent living for the traveling troupe of IMCA drivers. IMCA had come into being after a particularly arrogant group of AAA Contest Board members made enemies among the managers of several large state fairs. The flash point came in fall 1914, when the AAA barred the Michigan Fair from holding an AAA race because the Fair had permitted an unsanctioned cycle car race on the Fourth of July. The head of the Michigan Fair Board was livid and he got other fair managers together to set up their own racing group known as the International Motor Contest Association. They immediately set about hiring promoters to provide cars and drivers for a series of dirt track races.[39] IMCA also ran a few races in Canada justifying the "international" in its name, but most of its events were in the United States, many of them far from the bright lights of the big cities.

This first 318 Offy was built for broadcaster Tommy Lee for his sports car. The engine later went to his partner, Willett Brown, and after Brown's death it was bought at auction by Jan Voboril of Topanga, California. This 318 was larger than any of the other Miller or Offy four-cylinder engines built and Lee's 318 was obviously experimental. Note the double row of cam cover studs; the distributor ignition facing left rather than right, as on the 220 and 270; the high cam tower necessary to accommodate the long, five-inch stroke; the wide case; and the long block. If the engine was run with the two 1 1/2-inch updraft Winfield carburetors, as shown here, it is no wonder it was not particularly successful. *Jan Voboril*

J. Alex Sloan soon became IMCA's promotional major-domo. During the late summer fair season, he sometimes had three circuits going at once. A practical man, Sloan put on entertainment. A look at the association's records show that he got along just fine with 10 to 15 traveling cars and drivers plus an occasional local or two. Owners and drivers were expected to cooperate with the promoter and do what they were told, even if that meant setting somewhat specious records or agreeing beforehand who was going to win the day's race. They would make it look good, but most of Sloan's events before World War II were going to be won by the Offenhausers of either Emory Collins or Gus Schrader.

Collins and Schrader were on salary from Sloan. They would have the usual "grudge" race on a given Saturday or Sunday but the guarantee was larger than the prize money. They were expected to have their cars shiny with chrome and fresh paint, and if they looked unbeatable, all the better. Schrader and Collins both drove bored-out Miller Marines through the 1935 and 1936 seasons. At the end of 1936 Schrader sold his Miller to Bob Sall and ordered a 255 Offy to go in a new chassis being built at Curly Wetteroth's Los Angeles shop.

Collins had been cast to come in second to Schrader most of the time, but apparently that paled for Emory in 1937. After Schrader cleaned up in IMCA once more in his new 255, Collins went to Offenhauser's plant and asked for the biggest Offy that could be built. Goossen had just designed a 270-cubic-inch version of the 255 with a beefed-up crankcase for Indianapolis, and he proceeded to top that with a monster 5.0-inch stroke, 4.5-inch bore version of 318 inches for radio scion Tommy Lee. Offenhauser sold Collins the second 318 which he used to finally beat Schrader to take the 1938 IMCA crown. Schrader bought himself a 318 in 1939, so the two were back on even terms and Schrader retook the championship in 1939.

If the 318 was not the largest Offy that could be built, it was close. At one time Collins reportedly had an Offy of 326 cubic inches, but according

IMCA Championships Won with Offenhauser Engines 1937–1962

Year	Driver	Car
1937	Gus Schrader	Schrader 255 Offenhauser
1938	Emory Collins	Collins 318 Offenhauser
1939	Gus Schrader	Schrader 318 Offenhauser
1940	Gus Schrader	Schrader 318 Offenhauser
1941	Gus Schrader	Schrader 321 Offenhauser
1942–1945	***No Racing during WWII***	
1946	Emory Collins	Collins 318 Offenhauser
1947	Emory Collins	Collins 318 Offenhauser
1948	Emory Collins	Collins 270 Offenhauser
1949	Frank Luptow	Luptow 270 Offenhauser
1950	Frank Luptow	Luptow 270 Offenhauser
1951	Frank Luptow	Luptow 270 Offenhauser
1952	Deb Snyder	Snyder 270 Offenhauser
1953	Deb Snyder	Snyder 270 Offenhauser
1954	Bob Slater	Slater 270 Offenhauser
1955	Bobby Grim	Honore 220 (218 ci) Offenhauser
1956	Bobby Grim	Honore 220 Offenhauser
1957	Bobby Grim	Honore 255 Offenhauser
1958	Bobby Grim	Honore 255 Offenhauser
1959	Pete Folse	Honore 270 (263 ci) Offenhauser
1960	Pete Folse	Honore 270 Offenhauser
1961	Pete Folse	Honore 270 Offenhauser
1962	John White	Dizz Wilson 270 Offenhauser

Between 1937, when Gus Schrader replaced his Miller with a 255 Offy, and 1962, IMCA Champions rode behind Offys, and the larger the better. *Author* to later IMCA star Bobby Grim, the bigger block could not handle the pounding of the four coffee-can-sized Offy pistons. Schrader is supposed to have had three 318s, Collins two, and Ralph Morgan one for Jimmy Wilburn to drive on the IMCA circuit. There may have been one or two more. With their long stroke, the 318s could be wound only to 5,000 rpm, but with the right gears they were fearsome beasts on a dirt track and a handful for anyone but a Wilburn, Schrader, or Collins.[40]

IMCA drivers would sometimes compete against locals who were usually driving T-based Fronty Fords or Model A blocks hopped up with Riley or Cragar heads. While the Fords were lighter, and on a slick surface like Ascot might be competitive, one reason for the success of Schrader and Collins, outside of their giant engines, was the contract IMCA had for the preparation of the tracks where it ran its events. The promoter would plow the surface deeply enough that only the Offy engines had the power to slog through the heavy dirt. The big 318s usually made it no contest against Fords on such tracks.

Although Schrader, Wilburn, and Collins put on a hippodrome show much of the time and the rivalry was friendly, there is a tale that things changed when Schrader got married in 1940. Wilburn was already married and Eunice Schrader and Irene Collins started arguing about whose man was better and deserved the most money. Pretty soon Wilburn, Collins, and Schrader were *really* racing their 318s. Schrader and Collins were friendly rivals, but Wilburn didn't get along as well with Schrader and the competition got rough. On October 22, 1941, at Shreveport, Louisiana, Wilburn and Schrader started the feature side by side. On the first lap neither man would back off and Schrader was killed.

Hank Rogers in the *Steffen Offy*, a 220, takes the inside route while Mike Nazaruk in Mike Caruso's supercharged, stretched midget #36, and Ottis Stine in his own #2 Offy take a higher groove at Williams Grove, Pennsylvania, in 1950. *Author*

The Dirt Half Miles—220 Offy Territory

Although until 1941 the AAA allowed much larger engines to compete, the smaller Pacific Coast rules between 1933 and 1936 made the 220 the more or less standard half-mile engine. Indeed, the 220 was often preferable on a slick track with skinny tires that could not handle the torque of a larger engine. At HoHoKus, New Jersey, in 1934, Mauri Rose slid all over the track with Joe Marks' 255, and a 220 won the feature.

There were more of the big engines outside of California: the Hank O'Day Offy was a 270 and Emil Andres drove a 255 to the Midwestern championship in 1940. Joie Chitwood said that when O'Day sold his Offy to Ben Musick in 1942 it had a 310-cubic-inch engine in it. Despite a 214-inch limit in the CSRA circuit where he was racing, Chitwood drove the 310 anyway, being careful not to run so far out front that he would get protested and the engine measured. John Burgess, an early dirt-track racer, said it was a period when people were getting away with all sorts of things. "You had to put up protest money to tear an engine down and we couldn't afford it."

The chief competition for the Millers and later the Offys was the Ford Model A with a wide variety of special conversions: flatheads, four-port Rileys, Dreyers, D. O. Hals, McDowells, Cragars, and a dozen others. A very few Rileys and Dreyers were built with specially reinforced crankcases. In the 1940s and 1950s, some mechanics tried the flathead Ford V-8 engine with modest success and there were Chevys, Hupmobiles, and all manner of stock-based engines. One of the most formidable was the Hisso, usually one bank of the huge World War I Hispano-Suiza V-8 aircraft engine—a producer of enormous torque.[41] Later, Ben Shaw drove a car powered by half of a V-12 Curtiss, and after World War II six-cylinder Ranger aircraft engines raced in the IMCA ranks.

The Miller engines were wearing out in the 1930s, and the Offys

Displacement Limits. Unsupercharged engines, Big Cars/Sprint Cars, 1930–1960

Years	Sanctioning Group	Displacement
1930–32	AAA[1]	Local rules prevailed. Essentially no limits for non-Championship events.
1933–37	AAA	366 ci for all engines except 205 ci in Pacific Coast circuit 1934–36
1938–40	AAA[2]	274.6 ci; 183.07 supercharged
1941–45	AAA[3]	205 ci for OHC; 183 ci supercharged
1946–51	AAA[4]	210 ci for OHC; 183 ci supercharged
1952–55	AAA	220 ci for OHC engines[5]
1956–60	USAC	220 ci for OHC engines[6]
1961	USAC	236.9 ci for OHC engines[7]
1962	USAC	222.7 ci for OHC engines
1963–64	USAC	256.3 ci for OHC engines

1 Contest Board, American Automobile Association.
2 IMCA had no displacement limits before WWII.
3 CSRA had limits ranging from 214 to 274 ci over the years.
4 IMCA adopted a 274.6-ci limit after WWII.
5 Stock-block 305 ci; supercharged 138 ci.
6 Stock-block 336 ci.
7 Stock-block 366.9 ci.

The American Automobile Association's Contest Board set the rules for big car (later sprint car) racing on half-mile dirt tracks it sanctioned from the 1930s through 1955, when the AAA quit racing and the United States Auto Club took over big-time racing. *Author*

Jimmy Wilburn in the *Wright* Offy, a 318 running with CSRA, about 1939. *Author collection*

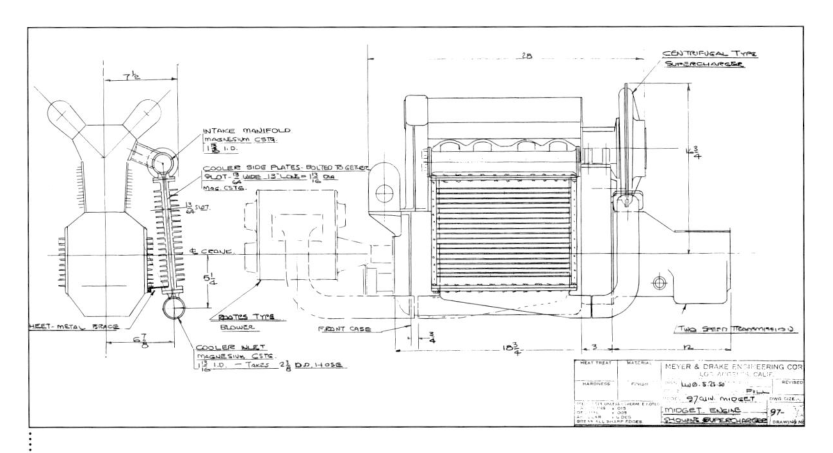

Assembly drawing dated May 26, 1950, of the supercharged midget for sprint car use. This Goossen drawing suggested using either a Roots blower, as Mike Caruso did, or a centrifugal supercharger with an intercooler. *Kenneth Walton collection*

Hal Cole in the #2 *Offenhauser Spl* big car about 1937. This car carried a 220 Offy engine. It was one of a very few cars actually known as "Offenhauser Spl." *Gloria Madsen collection*

replaced them as they retired. The top combinations in AAA racing usually involved an Offy: Joie Chitwood in the Peters, Bill Holland in Ralph Malamud's #29, Mauri Rose in the Hank O'Day car, Harry McQuinn in the Marks, Ted Horn in his *Baby*, and Tommy Hinnershitz—all drove Offenhauser engines by the time they became champions.

Ascot shut down in 1936, but there was good, close half-mile dirt track racing on tracks in the Midwest and the East. One of the best was Jungle Park, in Rockville, Indiana, which opened in 1920 and had its best years in the 1930s. Frank Funk's speedway in Winchester, Indiana, became well-known after it was given high banks of oiled dirt in 1938. Ted Horn, in his 220 Offy, held the record there at the time of his death in 1948. Williams Grove Speedway, built by Roy Richwine in 1939 and touted as the "Ascot of the East," became the most popular track in the nation as the decade ended. Though Ford conversions made up most of the cars that raced there, the winners were usually Offys, since the Grove attracted huge crowds and the payoffs were rich. At the last big car race there before World War II, 31,374 fans packed the stands.

The Fifties and "Stretched" Midgets

When in the 1950s the short-track midgets no longer provided enough competition to support top drivers and owners, a number of mechanics "stretched" their Kurtis Kraft chassis by welding the appropriate amount of tubing into the frame rails, installing wider axles and 16-inch wheels and dropping in a 220. They made light and fearsomely fast cars that killed several drivers.

Meyer & Drake built its last 220 for the dirt tracks in 1955. The four-banger was being challenged by the much larger stock blocks, and Joe Barzda, who operated the California Speed Shop in New Brunswick, New Jersey, is credited with running the first competitive V-8 Chevy in the East. "Gentleman Joe," ever the experimenter, drove a very clean black #33 Kurtis Ford during the heyday of the midgets. When they fell out of favor he stretched his midget, mounted a supercharger on the V-8-60 engine, and ran it as a sprint car. When Chevrolet introduced its small-block V-8 Joe pulled out the Ford and stuffed in a Chevy. By 1958 he was able to run with the 220 Offys.

AAA/USAC Big Car/Sprint Car Championships 1936–1960

Year	Driver	Car/Owner	Engine	Division
1936	Rex Mays	Poison Lil	239 Spark/Miller[1]	Midwest
1936	Frank Bailey		210 Hal	Eastern
1937	Rex Mays	Poison Lil	269 Sparks/Miller	Midwest
1937	Frank Beeder		237 McDowell	Eastern
1938	Ted Horn		233 Miller	Midwest
1938	Duke Nalon		239 Dreyer	Eastern
1939	Rex Mays		233 Miller	Midwest
1939	Joie Chitwood	Hank O'Day	274 cu in Offy[2]	Eastern
1940	Emil Andres	Foley	255 Offy	Midwest
1940	Joie Chitwood	Peters	233 Offy[3]	Eastern
1941	Duke Nalon	Poison Lil	220 Miller	Midwest
1941	Bill Holland	Malamud	210 Offy[4]	Eastern
Note: No racing during WWII, 1942–194				
1946	Elbert Booker	Lawrence Jewell	210 Hal 210 cu in	Midwest
1946	Ted Horn		210 Offy	Eastern
1947	Johnny Shackleford	Charlie Engle	220 Offy	Midwest
1947	Ted Horn		220 Offy	Eastern
1948	Spider Webb		210 Vance	Midwest
1948	Ted Horn		220 Offy	Eastern
1949	Jackie Holmes		233 Dreyer	Midwest
1949	Tommy Hinnershitz		220 Offy	Eastern
1950	Duane Carter		220 Offy	Midwest
1950	Tommy Hinnershitz		220 Offy	Eastern
1951	Troy Ruttman		220 Offy	Midwest
1951	Tommy Hinnershitz		220 Offy	Eastern
1952	Joe James		220 Offy	Midwest
1952	Tommy Hinnershitz		220 Offy	Eastern
1953	Pat O'Connor		220 Offy	Midwest
1953	Joe Sostillio		220 Offy	Eastern
1954	Pat O'Connor		220 Offy	Midwest
1954	Johnny Thomson		220 Offy	Eastern
1955	Bob Sweikert		220 Offy	Midwest
1955	Tommy Hinnershitz		220 Offy	Eastern
1956	Pat O'Connor		220 Offy	Midwest
1956	Tommy Hinnershitz		220 Offy	Eastern
1957	Elmer George		220 Offy	Midwest
1957	Bill Randall		220 Offy	Eastern
1958	Eddie Sachs		220 Offy	Midwest
1958	Johnny Thomson		220 Offy	Eastern
1959	Don Branson		220 Offy	Midwest
1959	Tommy Hinnershitz		220 Offy	Eastern
1960	Parnelli Jones	Fike Plumbing	305 Chevy	Midwest
1960	A.J. Foyt		220 Offy	Eastern

[1] A 220 Miller with Sparks' improved block and other changes.

[2] This engine was a 274 at the start of the year. For some races there was a smaller displacement limit. AAA reduced the national limit for "big cars" to 205 ci beginning in 1941.

[3] Chitwood said the Peters car had a 310 ci Offy in it at one time.

Walt Davison, left, watches as Spider Webb prepares for a rope-tow start at the AAA big-car races at Trenton, New Jersey, in April 1947. Floyd Dreyer built the #36 car for Fred Johnson. Behind Webb in the *Malamud* #29 is Bill Holland. Both cars were powered by 220 Offys. *Bruce Craig collection*

In USAC racing, Don Branson drove the last Offy to win the Midwest title in 1959, and A. J. Foyt was the final Offy champion in the eastern circuit a year later driving A. J. Watson's car. The *Fike Plumbing Chevy* took Parnelli Jones to the Midwest championship in 1960. A year later when the circuits were combined, Jones was again crowned champion, the Chevy having vanquished the Offy strictly because it had more cubes and cost fewer dollars.

In IMCA racing, the Offys were of the 270 breed and they staved off the Chevrolet V-8s a little longer. Johnny White, in Dizz Wilson's #71 Offy took the 1962 championship, but in 1963 Sid Weinberger of Atica,

The Roots-supercharged midget Offy engine in Mike Caruso's stretched midget sprint car, about 1950. The blower was driven off the front of the crank. This was formerly the Caruso #3 midget. If you look closely you can see the welds where the hood and frame were lengthened and the location of the original front radius rod mount. Note the Scintilla mag, Pesco aircraft fuel pump, and the cloths wrapped around the breathers to keep out the dust of the dirt track. *Bruce Craig collection*

National Championships Won with Offenhauser Engines 1935–1976

Year	Driver	Car	Engine
1935	Kelly Petillo	Gilmore Speedway Spl	Offy (260)
1936	Mauri Rose	F.W.D. Spl	Miller (255)
1937	Wilbur Shaw	Gilmore Special	Offy (255)
1938	Floyd Roberts	Burd Piston Ring Spl	Offy (270)
1939	Wilbur Shaw	Boyle Maserati	Maserati
1940	Rex Mays	Bowes Seal-Fast Spl	Winfield (Offy-built)
1941	Rex Mays	Bowes Seal-Fast Spl	Winfield
1942–1945 ***no racing during WWII***			
1946	Ted Horn	Peters Offy	Offy (270)
1947	Ted Horn	T.H.E. Spl	Offy (236)
1948	Ted Horn	T.H.E. Spl	Offy (236)
1949	Johnnie Parsons	Kurtis-Kraft Spl	Offy (270)
1950	Henry Banks	Blue Crown Spl	Offy (270)
1951	Tony Bettenhausen	Belanger Spl	Offy (241)
1952	Chuck Stevenson	Springfield Welding (Paoli) Spl	Offy (263)
1953	Sam Hanks	Bardahl Spl (K-K 4000)	Offy (270)
1954	Jimmy Bryan	Dean Van Lines Spl	Offy (274)
1955	Bob Sweikert	John Zink Spl (K-K 500C)	Offy (270)
1956	Pat Flaherty	John Zink Spl (K-K 500C)	Offy (270)
1957	Jimmy Bryan	Dean Van Lines Spl ((Kuzma)	Offy (252)
1958	Tony Bettenhausen	Jones & Maley Spl.	Offy (252)
1959	Rodger Ward	Leader Card Spl	Offy (252)
1960	A.J. Foyt	Bowes Seal-Fast Spl	Offy (252)
1961	A.J. Foyt	Bowes Seal-Fast Spl (Watson)	Offy (252)
1962	Rodger Ward	Leader Card Spl. (Watson)	Offy (252)
1963	A.J. Foyt	Sheraton-Thompson Spl (Trevis)	Offy (252)
1964	A.J. Foyt	Sheraton-Thompson Spl (Trevis)	Offy (252)
1968	Bobby Unser	Leader Card Spl	Offy (168T
1972	Joe Leonard	Samsonite Spl	Offy (158T)
1973	Roger McCluskey	Lindsay Hopkins Spl	Offy (159T)
1974	Bobby Unser	Olsonite Eagle	Offy (159T)

Michigan, fielded a 327-cubic-inch big-block Chevy with which Gordon Wolley took the title. Pete Folse in the Hector Honore Offy finished in second place in 1963 and the Lempelius, McDonald, and Johnson Offys took three of the top eight placings, but the Offy could no longer overcome a 20 percent displacement handicap. In 1965, even Honore had a Chevy, and in 1968 George Wilkins' #37 was the last Offy in IMCA records. As Dale Drake said, "there is nothing cheaper or more effective than displacement."

The big 270 Offys were also allowed to compete with CRA on the West Coast. Bruce Bromme's Andy Gump sprinter carried a 270 and Paul Jones won the CRA title in the Bromme car in 1965. Alex Morales' *Tamale Wagon* kept the Offy in the hunt, and when Morales' turbocharged the *Wagon's* 255 in 1972, it was a fearsome beast indeed.

After the shutdown of Drake Engineering's production of sprint car engines and the full development of the big- and small-block Chevys, the Offy was finished on the shorter dirt tracks. There were a few miles to go yet at Indianapolis, but the dynasty was winding down.

When the rear-engined Cooper showed promise and the British Lotus in 1963 came near to winning at Indy, Americans jumped on the rear-engine bandwagon. This is the prototype Halibrand Shrike, wrenched in 1965 by George Bignotti, at left. It was powered by a normally aspirated Offy. Among those working on the car are, Wally Meskowski, in front of Bignotti, and Ted Halibrand at the upper right.
Gordon Schroeder collection

CHAPTER ELEVEN

FROM THE HEIGHTS TO THE DEPTHS, 1965-67

AS HAPPENED WITH HARRY MILLER'S THOROUGHBRED EIGHTS 30 YEARS earlier, the very success of the four-cylinder Offy engine and the Indy roadsters in the mid-1950s bred opposition. The Offy fours not only dominated Victory Lane at Indianapolis and the winners' circles at almost every championship, sprint, and midget oval track race, but they were in almost every car that qualified at Indianapolis between 1953 and 1964. Over seven years, 97 percent of the cars that qualified at Indianapolis were Offys and most years the remaining cars were the Novis derived from the Offy bloodline.

Despite the nostalgia with which the Indianapolis roadsters of the 1950s are now regarded, the Offy-powered Frank Kurtis, A. J. Watson, Eddie Kuzma, Lujie Lesovsky, and Quinn Epperly cars looked too much alike for some tastes. On the shorter tracks the Kurtis-Kraft Offy midgets were also, to some, boringly alike. The Offy-powered sprint and champ cars of that period were only slightly different from one another. It is not an uncommon complaint. Many people in the 1990s have found the aerodynamic rear-engine Indianapolis cars depressingly similar.

The outlook for the Offy looked bleak indeed in the mid-1960s. Lou Meyer had gone over to Ford as sales and service representative for the Offy's competition, the four-cam Ford V-8, and the Ford was beating the Offy on the race tracks. It would take strong measures by Drake Engineering to come back, along with the the basic Offy design's inherent strength. *Jim Etter collection*

The *Rounds Rocket*, a rear-engine Offenhauser-powered car, tried at Indianapolis in 1949 by N. J. Rounds. It was an idea that was ahead of its time, but Billy Taylor could not get it up to qualifying speed. It took another 12 years before Jack Brabham tried another rear-engine at Indy, and Brabham's Cooper-Climax started a rear-engine revolution. *Indianapolis Motor Speedway*

This was A. J. Foyt's 1964 Indy-winning Watson roadster, a front-engined Offy known as the *Sheraton-Thompson Special* and entered by Ansted-Thompson racing. Powered by a 252-ci Offy, Foyt averaged 154.672 mph in qualifying. A nearly similar Watson, the Weinberger Homes #76, driven by Gordon Johncock in his rookie year, 1965, was the last roadster to finish a full 500 miles at the Speedway. *Indianapolis Motor Speedway*

In a June 1959 *Road & Track* magazine article Bob Thatcher wrote, "Chassis details . . . while possibly quite different to the experienced eye, will appear to the casual observer to be designed and built by the same man. Unfortunately, this is truer than we like to admit."

Thatcher went on, "Most of next year's new cars will be copies [of this year's winner]."

He concluded, "This leads to a stagnation of design and a sameness that dulls the interest to a greater degree than the event deserves. . . . One old hand at the Speedway says that he no longer goes to the Memorial Day race because all the cars sound alike and even look somewhat alike except for color."

It was not that other engines and other chassis had not tried at Indianapolis and elsewhere. Harry Miller built dramatically different rear-engine cars for Gulf Oil just before World War II, but they were not successful. Lou Fageol tried a dual-engine four-wheel drive car in 1946. Billy DeVore qualified Pat Clancy's six-wheeled Offy in 1948, but it was too heavy to be competitive. Billy Taylor could not qualify in the rear-engined *Rounds Rocket* in 1949. A variety of engines had been tried over two decades but none could match the Offy.

The Offy and the roadster were too well-developed, tested, and perfected at the top level of American oval-track racing to be dethroned easily. There seemed to be no way for challengers to break that monopoly at Indianapolis. Ferrari tried in 1952 but fell short. Jack Brabham brought a Cooper chassis with a British Climax engine to the Speedway in 1961, but it did not win, nor did it much disturb the existing order of things. The roadster's builders tended to copy success. They developed the offset and the laydown engine designs and had raised qualifying speeds from 126 miles per hour in 1946 to 158 by 1964. They did it largely without any advance in tire technology by the long-time supplier, Firestone. Until a well-developed rear engine chassis could be mated with a competitive engine, the roadsters were going to keep winning, and there was no reason to replace the Offenhauser engine. Even so, the 1960s were a period when the nation's cultural values were becoming antagonistic to tradition, and many race-watchers—particularly those who enjoyed sports cars and road courses over open-wheel oval track racing—liked to jeer the Offy.

Changes Were in the Wind

It took a concatenation of events in the early 1960s to successfully challenge that engine. One was corporate pride at the Ford Motor Company. Ford, and its chairman, Henry Ford II, had grown tired of being beaten by General Motors and Chrysler. Despite an Auto Manufacturers' Association agreement banning participation in racing, both Chevrolet and Chrysler were supporting their makes through thinly veiled subsidies and technical assistance, most particularly in NASCAR racing (as was Ford to a much lesser degree). Finally, in June 1962 Ford issued a statement withdrawing from the agreement. Lou Meyer wrote Henry Ford II offering Meyer & Drake's help in a Ford return to racing.

Leo Beebe was appointed head of the Ford competition effort that Ford's Don Frey had quietly sustained during the AMA ban. Frey suggested to Beebe that the company build an aluminum-block V-8 that might run at Indianapolis and Henry Ford II gave Frey the go-ahead to hop up the Fairlane passenger car engine.

Coincidentally, racing driver Dan Gurney[42] and Colin Chapman, head of the British Lotus racing car company, went to Frey with a proposal for a Ford Indianapolis effort that would to become Ford's first direct factory involvement at the Speedway in 28 years.[43] Gurney had made his way from the hot rod ranks (his family moved from New York to California in the early 1950s) to big-time sports car racing. He was driving in Europe at the time the Americans and their Offys went to Monza and blew away the competition. Later he watched Chapman's cars revolutionize Grand Prix racing, and he reasoned that it might be possible for the rear-engined chassis that had taken over European racing to do well at Indianapolis.

Jack Brabham in his little rear-engine Cooper #17 leads the roadsters of Shorty Templeman, #7, and Parnelli Jones, #98, at Indy in 1961. A. J. Foyt won this race and Brabham finished ninth. His underpowered Cooper-Climax could go through the turns faster than the roadsters, but would lose the advantage on Indy's long straightaways. *Bruce Craig collection*

Jack Brabham's 1961 Indianapolis effort in his rear-engine Cooper with an underpowered Climax engine gave Gurney and Chapman more food for thought. They discussed rear-engine design and concluded that such a car, properly powered, could win at the Brickyard. Gurney brought Chapman to Indianapolis in 1962. He drove Mickey Thompson's rear-engine Buick-powered car and went out of the race with gear failure, but he showed that a rear-engine design did have promise on the bricks. Many roadster men thought otherwise. A. J. Watson shrugged, "Why build a rear-engine car? They haven't beaten me yet."

One of the first things Ford's people did when they started work on their new engine was to order an Offy from Meyer & Drake for study. In August 1962, Ford's Autolite division bought engine #215, a then-current 252-cubic-inch Offy. The engineers at Dearborn had no technical manual on the engine (one did not exist except in the minds of the Offy mechanics) and did not know how to disassemble the engine or get it back together. They contacted Lou Meyer for help. While it might seem suicidal for Meyer & Drake to give up secrets to a potential competitor, Meyer dispatched Chickie Hirashima to Detroit to help.

There was no time for Ford to design and build a completely new Indianapolis engine in nine months. It was a large corporation with many committees and Ford didn't have the services of Leo Goossen. They probably did not know that back in Harry Miller's day, Goossen and Offenhauser designed and built a 1,113-cubic-inch V-16 for Gar Wood in two months. For the 1963 season Ford put together a 255-cubic-inch V-8 that was basically a hot-rodded passenger car engine with an aluminum block. To gain an advantage by making fewer pit stops than the methanol-burning Offenhauser-engined cars, the Ford was designed to burn gasoline, giving it better mileage though it ran hotter. The use of the more-flammable gasoline would have terrible consequences in 1964.

While Ford was contemplating a possible chassis for its engine, Gurney and Chapman showed up with their ideas for a rear-engine car. There were several starts and stops to the Ford-Gurney-Chapman effort, but by May 1963 Ford had produced a pushrod V-8 racing engine and had financed a Chapman Lotus chassis that was competitive at the Speedway.

Ford Engine Development

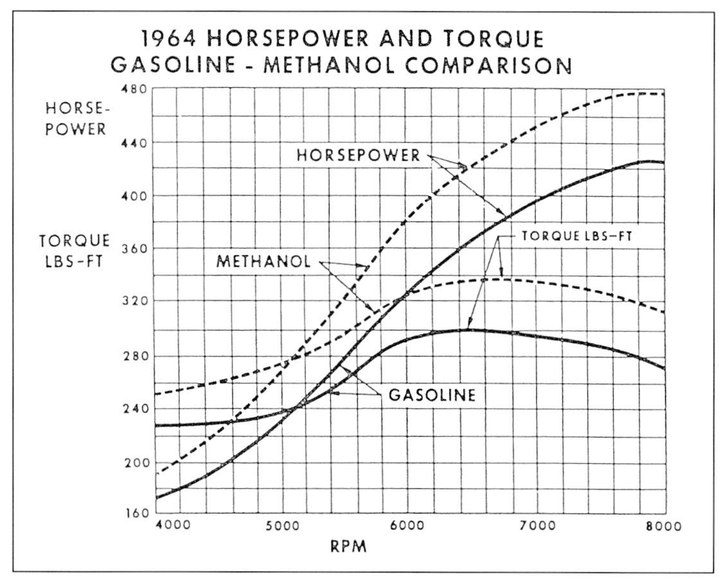

This Ford chart shows the development of its V-8 engine over three years. In 1963, it was a pushrod version, essentially a hot-rodded Ford Fairlane of 256 cubic inches. It showed good midrange torque but ran out of breath at 7,100 rpm. In 1964, Ford engineers had finished the four-cam heads for the engine, copied largely from the Offy. Breathing improved and the horsepower peaked above 8,000 rpm, while the absolute torque stayed the same, though moved up about 2,000 rpm. For 1965 Ford pushed peak horsepower up about 5 percent through redesigned cam profiles and other small tweaks. *FoMoCo*

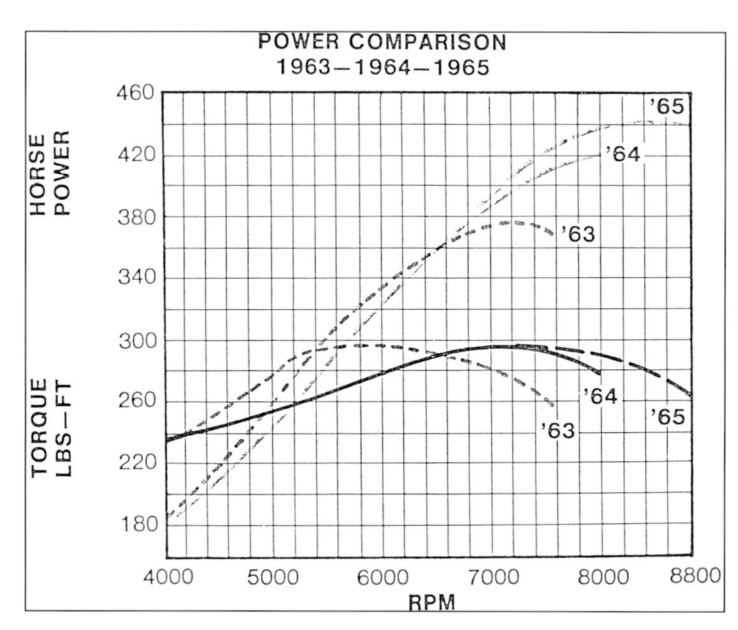

The Lotus was designed with wide 15-inch wheels for which Firestone built special tires. When the car proved to be fast in practice, other teams, including Sonny Meyer, George Bignotti, A. J. Foyt's mechanic and others objected, saying the smaller, fatter Firestones were unfair. After they lost that fight the Indy regulars demanded 15-inch wheels and tires, too. In the chaos of the Lotus effort, Firestone, which had for 40 years supplied all the tires at Indianapolis, was unable to build enough 15-inchers for all those who wanted them. Bignotti called Goodyear, which was supplying tires to NASCAR teams, and got a set of Daytona tires which he mounted on special Halibrand wheels, picking up a quick three miles per hour. An angry A. J. Foyt grabbed Herb Porter's phone, called Akron, and shouted at Goodyear's Tony Webner that his company ought to get into Indianapolis racing, for so long a Firestone monopoly. It was a momentous fit of pique.

The rear-engine Ford Lotuses proceeded to run as fast or faster than the front-engine Offy roadsters. Eddie Sachs found he could go four car lengths deeper into the Indy turns with a rear-engine Lotus than he had with a Watson roadster, and the mid-chassis location of the fuel tanks made the Lotus easier to handle with varying fuel loads than the tail-tank roadsters.

Parnelli Jones won the 1963 Indianapolis 500 and $150,000 in prize money in J. C. Agajanian's Watson Offy roadster but Jimmy Clark in his Lotus Ford was second, and it seemed possible Clark might have won it. Jones was clearly faster but his *Ole' Calhoun* roadster developed an oil leak late in the race and there was a huge controversy over whether to black-flag him. The Clark camp said there was a "stream" of oil behind Jones. Agajanian said it stopped, which it eventually did, and Parnelli won. Englishman Clark, however, won the USAC 100-miler at Milwaukee and both the roadster and the Offy found themselves in deep trouble.

The Tire Wars Heat Up

Jim Loulan, Goodyear's rep, shipped several sets of tires to the Speedway in 1964 but they were not as

Eddie Sachs drove a Halibrand chassis with one of the new Ford four-cam V-8 engines in 1964, only to die in a fiery crash on the first lap. *Bruce Craig collection*

fast as the Firestones and despite much testing with Foyt, who was paid in excess of $100,000 by Goodyear for his work, they were still a bit slower than the Firestone product. Foyt won the 1964 race on Firestones, but Goodyear worked furiously, invested millions, and eventually Firestone, defeated, pulled out of racing, unwilling to invest the money needed to compete in the suddenly much more expensive business of racing. They would not return for 20 years.

These developments were causing tension at Meyer & Drake. The Drakes had been unaware that Lou Meyer had written to Ford in 1962 congratulating him on Ford's reentry into championship racing and also suggesting that Meyer & Drake could be acquired by Ford to help carry out its racing program. Drake was ready to fight rather than switch. In 1963, he had Goossen draw up an installation to mount the Offy in a rear-engine chassis. They worked with teams that were building copies of the Lotus chassis in the belief that Offy power in the smooth-handling rear engine setup would be the way to go. Rolla Vollstedt bought the first such rear-engine Offy, serial #224, on March 28, 1964. The *Bryant Heating Special*, built by Volla and Grant King, was the first rear-engined Offy out at the Speedway that May. With old roadster pilot Len Sutton at the wheel, the car qualified eighth-fastest at 151.813 miles per hour. Sutton's qualifying speed was *two miles an hour faster* than Parnelli Jones had gone to win the pole the year before in his front-engine car. On race day Len finished 15th after the fuel pump quit on his 140th lap.

Ford replaced the interim pushrod Fairlane with a modified aluminum-block V-8 topped by specially designed-for-racing dual-overhead-cam heads that cost the company $10 million to develop. The four-cammer used most of the design basics of the Offenhauser four but with the inherently better valve area and fuel economy (particularly on gasoline) of the V-8 layout and the short-stroke ability to wind to 9,000 rpm. The 1964 Ford engine was the first V-8 designed for American racing since the birth of the Novi in 1941[44], and it foreshadowed the Cosworth, Ilmor, Honda, and other V-8 engines that in the 1990s rule Indianapolis and the CART (Championship Auto Racing Team) circuits in the United States and the Grand Prix courses in Europe. Lou Meyer continued to allow Meyer & Drake to work with Ford, producing parts for the four-cam such as the radiused cam cups (borrowed directly from the Offy midget).

In 1964 a front-engine Offy roadster driven by Foyt and riding on Firestones eked out a final victory, but Rodger Ward was second in a rear-engined Watson Ford. The race was marred tragically by a first-lap crash and subsequent fire fueled by gasoline from the Fords' tanks, killing Dave MacDonald and Eddie Sachs.

For Meyer & Drake it was, on balance, a good year as the Offys nailed down 14 of the first 16 places.

Clark's Ford-powered Lotus (ironically, considering the claims of superiority that Colin Chapman and some of the other British were spouting) was running on English Dunlop tires that started to disintegrate during the race. Clark's suspension was disabled as one of his tires failed and Chapman withdrew both cars from the race. Gurney, in the other Lotus, (still running at the time), was credited with 17th place.[45] Despite the tire fiasco there was a rush by the Americans, including roadster guru A. J. Watson, to develop more rear-engine chassis. (Whatever part the smaller and wider tires on the Mickey Thompson car of MacDonald's had played in the crash, they led to a rule that in effect required everybody to run tires of approximately the same size.)

The combination of the rear-engined Lotus chassis and the Ford four-cam V-8 was fast, though perhaps the Ford engine was not quite so strong as it may have appeared. A. J. was able to win 10 of 13 USAC championship races, half of them on dirt, driving Bignotti's Watson Offy, but race drivers and mechanics are notorious for following the leader, and now the Ford-powered rear-engined cars seemed the ticket. After all, the screamingly fast Novi was a V-8, and Lotus seemed to have licked the chassis problems that had defeated the Novis. Even Foyt made a deal with Ford to use one of its engines, and suddenly everyone wanted one of the new Ford four-cams.

Lou Meyer Goes Over to Ford

When Ford set up its V-8 racing organization in 1965 the company hired Meyer to run it. Lou was a businessman and less-nostalgic about the Offy engine than Dale Drake. His relationship with Ford went back to 1938 when he went into the Ford passenger-car engine rebuilding business. He had kept his contacts at Dearborn, and in 1964 Ford President Lee Iacocca offered Meyer & Drake the business of merchandising and servicing the four-cam V-8 and supplying spare parts to the racing mechanics.

For a brief period in early 1965 Meyer & Drake, at Meyer's insistence, actually was made a sales agent for the Ford four-cam. Ford sent four engines to Los Angeles along with three engineers, but according to John Drake, the Ford men were chiefly interested in getting help with a valve spring breakage problem. Meyer & Drake never sold any engines for Ford. Meyer went east to Indianapolis in May and the Drakes began to hear rumors that Lou was saying the Offy was finished.

At Indy Meyer told *National Speed Sport News* that the Ford four-cam was so overwhelming that the Offy—he called it "the old truck motor"—was dead and that none would be built for the 1966 race—a premature burial as it turned out.

Relations with the Ford people deteriorated at the Meyer & Drake plant in Los Angeles . The Ford engineers told anyone who would listen that they were going to win Indianapolis because they were going to spend as much money as it took. Dale, who wanted nothing to do with being a small business tied to a major motor company like Ford could see his beloved Offy slowly twisting in the wind. He finally told the Ford men to take their engines and get out.

Meanwhile, to the Drakes' dismay, Meyer accepted Ford's offer to sell and service its engine. According to John, "Lou and Sonny went back to Indy, made the deal, and we read about it in the papers. My dad called Lou to find out what was going on and he said 'you'll be getting a letter in the mail that will explain it,' and when the letter came it was an offer to sell his share of the company." Thirty years later, Meyer told the author that it was simply that Ford had a better engine and it was time to get on board or quit the race engine business. "Ford had more money than we did," Lou said. If they wanted to spend it they could. Ford offered us a very good deal and if we hadn't taken it somebody else would have."

To the mechanics, car owners and drivers who had long worked with and treasured the Offy it seemed a little unfair of Ford and Meyer. Still, many of them rushed to adopt the Ford engine. Later, when the turbo Offy made its comeback, Dale had *Drake-OFFY* cast into its cam covers to let everyone know that it was the old Offy that defeated the Ford. Lou Meyer's brother, Harry, elected to stay on with the Drakes at the shop which in 1969 became simply Drake Engineering and Sales, established at a new location on Daimler Avenue at MacArthur Boulevard in Santa Ana, California.

Ford was certain that its money and expertise would conquer Indianapolis and that nothing could stand in its way. According to Meyer, the Ford engineers forced some ideas on the four-cam engine that he and Sonny knew were not sound. "We lost some arguments with them," he said. "Specifically, the engine never really had a racing block designed from scratch. The bore and stroke were wrong, and Ford copied the top end of the Offy engine so closely that the four-cam's ports were too large." Some parts from the Offy went directly into the four-cam engine.

The 255 series Offenhauser engines were selling, ready to race, for $12,000. The Ford four-cam cost the company over $30,000 apiece to build. At first Ford gave the engines to selected racing teams, something Drake could not afford to do. As time went on, in order to keep its engines on the race tracks, Ford swallowed half the cost and delivered the engines for $15,000. Later, in some degree of quantity production, the Ford V-8 was assembled by Meyer in Indianapolis at a selling price of $22,500 each.

The Roadsters Outmoded

The end for the roadster and the unblown Offy came in 1965. Although John Drake does not recall that any paid-for engines were canceled, orders for the 255 engine fell off. The Drakes built their last unblown championship engine—a 252, serial #231—for Ted Halibrand early that May. At the Speedway two-thirds of the entries were rear-engined: Brabhams, Watsons, Halibrand Shrikes, Gerhardts, copies of Clark's Lotus, and others. There were 24 Ford four-cam V-8s among the entrants, and 17 Fords would be on the starting grid.

The Offy men tried valiantly. There were 10 rear-engine chassis with Offenhauser power. As May 1965 moved toward the first qualification weekend, the stage was set for a shoot-out between the Fords and the Offys.

Armed with Fords were Clark, A. J. Foyt, young Mario Andretti, Parnelli Jones, Dan Gurney, and a clutch of old roadster hands: Don Branson, Al Unser, Lloyd Ruby, Len Sutton, and Roger McCluskey.

Arrayed with the Offy were Chuck Stevenson, Jim McElreath, Gordon Johncock, Jud Larson, and Mel Kenyon. It looked like an uneven battle at the O.K. Corral from the start.

Andretti went out in his Ford and turned 158.849 miles per hour, a new record. Clark, next, did his four laps at 160.729, the first man over 160 at Indianapolis. Foyt, driving a Ford-powered Lotus in which Bignotti had installed special Winfield cams, outdid them all with a speed, good for the pole, of 161.233 miles per hour.

The Offy's best was Billy Foster, a rookie driver from Canada in Jim Robbins' and Rolla Volstedt's rear-engine car at 158.416 miles per hour.[46] Bob Veith qualified at 156.427 miles per hour, Jim McElreath at 155.874, and Walt Hansgen, a sports car driver, at 155.662 miles per hour. Rookie Gordon Johncock was in at 155.012 in a clearly obsolete front-engine Watson roadster sponsored by Weinberger Homes. Foster's outside second row starting position was, in truth quite a high placing under the circumstances, but it was nearly 5 miles per hour off Foyt's speed. In 500 miles that difference could equal three-and-a-half minutes, or about eight miles—more than three laps around the Indianapolis track.

It turned out to be more than that, but Foyt and Foster were not the players. After a few laps, Jim Clark in his green Lotus motored easily away from A. J., giving the lead back only on his fuel stop. The Woods Brothers, hired by Ford to run Clark's pit, had Jim in and out in less than 20 seconds. Foyt took 44 seconds.

Foyt was leading when, ignoring Bignotti's plan to come in for fuel, he ran out of gas on the 68th lap. A. J. trashed the transaxle on the backstretch trying to slop the last drop from his tank and jump-start the engine. In the end, Clark beat the second place car, Parnelli Jones in another Ford, by about two minutes with Andretti close behind. Johncock, first of the Offys in his old front-engine roadster, was fifth, about three minutes farther back, an amazing performance, given the speed disparity between the roadster and the rear-engine cars.

Jimmy Clark, the giant killer, who with a Lotus rear-engine chassis and the new Ford four-cam V-8, defeated the Offenhauser after 18 straight years of victory at Indianapolis. *Indianapolis Motor Speedway*

OFFENHAUSER IN RETIREMENT

FRED OFFENHAUSER CONTINUED TO WATCH OVER THE ENGINE he had saved in the 1930s. Most years he drove east to Indianapolis in May. There, often dressed in a colorful Hawaiian shirt, he schmoozed with other old-timers, including Harry Hartz and Lou Meyer and talked about the old days. He was made Honorary Starter at the Speedway one year, and the Indianapolis Old-timers Club gave him a special award for service to the sport.

In retirement Offenhauser assumed the role of sage. When asked who he thought were the 10 best drivers of all time he looked at the interviewer and ticked off the names: Rex Mays, Ralph DePalma, Earl Cooper, Tommy Milton, Jimmy Murphy, Frank Lockhart, Lou Meyer, Wilbur Shaw, Mauri Rose, and Bill Vukovich. Mays, he said was the best of them all. In 1949, he was called by the government to testify in the fraud trial against Preston Tucker, telling a Detroit federal court that, contrary to Tucker's assertions, Preston had never helped design Miller cars or engines.

Fred and Ethel traveled to Honolulu in the 1950s and Fred danced a few steps with a lei-clad Polynesian beauty while staying at the Royal Hawaiian Hotel on Wakiki Beach. *Gloria Madsen collection*

Offenhauser fished, hunted occasionally in Nevada with Lou Meyer and entertained the racing crowd when they were in town. The drivers and mechanics gathered at the Offenhausers' place the night of November 5, 1949, before a race to be held at Bing Crosby's Del Mar horse track. During the evening Rex Mays worried aloud about the race and repeated his insistence that lap belts were a hazard; they might trap a man in a burning car. The next day Mays flew his Beech Bonanza down to Del Mar. Though he wore a belt in the plane he refused to wear one in the racing car. During the race Rex was thrown from the flipping Wolfe Special and died under the wheels of an oncoming car. His own car came to rest on its wheels, virtually undamaged. A saddened Marvin Jenkins flew May's Bonanza back to Glendale the next day. Rex had often said, Jenkins recalled, that he did not like being a pall-bearer at racing friends' funerals, but it was better to be a bearer than the pall.

Most years Fred Offenhauser would visit the Indianapolis Speedway and schmooze a bit in the pits with old friends like Jean Marcenac and Harry Hartz. *Gloria Madsen collection*

Offenhauser traveled to Europe during the summer of 1951, visited the family home in Nordlingen, inspected the Nurburgring, where he spoke with European champion Juan Manuel Fangio, and toured the International Machinery Exhibit in Paris for some shop talk. He remarked that six years after the devastation of World War II two-thirds of the machines on display were German.

At home, Fred raised camellias and roses and made pickles, his sister Agnes said, from tiny cucumbers he grew in his garden at 3211 78th Street near the Los Angeles-Inglewood boundary. Occasionally he would go fishing for Marlin out of the marina at Balboa with J. C. Agajanian, Dale Drake, or Danny Oakes.

Fred Offenhauser liked to hunt and fish in retirement. He is seen here with one of the trophies he caught off Balboa. *Gloria Madsen collection*

Len Sutton drove the Vollstedt rear-engined Offy to fifteenth place at Indianapolis in 1964. Seen here behind the Vollstedt car is Dave MacDonald's ill-fated Thompson "roller skate." *Bruce Craig collection*

It was a very convincing win for Ford, and the line-up of engines on the Indianapolis grid in 1966 confirmed it: 24 Fords. Thirty-eight Offys filed entry forms. Only nine qualified. Jackie Stewart's Ford was leading comfortably at 491 miles when it broke a rod allowing Graham Hill to win in a Lola-Ford.

The Ford Triumphant

The Ford four-cam and the Lotus chassis revolutionized Indianapolis—in fact, all championship-level racing. Virtually overnight they brought the rear-engine chassis to success. Inadvertently, through Foyt, it got Goodyear into a tire war with Firestone that led to long-term improvements in racing tire design and thus to much higher racing speeds. Because rear-engine cars were unsuitable for dirt tracks, they and the four-cam led to Langhorne, Phoenix, and Atlanta being paved—and for many, spoiled. Tracks that remained dirt, like Syracuse and Du Quoin, were dropped off the championship racing schedule in 1970.[47]

The Ford also turned race engine maintenance from a hands-on process to a factory job. In 1965, a lot of Ford V-8s were racing at Indianapolis and 17 Fords made the race. These engines had been provided to the racers by Ford at little cost and still belonged to the factory. In Ford's opinion the former Offy mechanics were not qualified to handle such high-tech engines.

One of the secrets of the Ford's power output was its much higher rpm compared to the long-stroke, 6,600-rpm Offys. Winding the V-8s in the vicinity of 9,000 rpm required a new degree of care and cleanliness. Though the Offy wrench-twisters were undoubtedly talented, the Offy was a tough brute. It would take a lot of abuse, from both drivers and mechanics. The new V-8 was another story. After the 1965 qualifications the Ford men grabbed up most of their engines at the Speedway and whisked them back to Detroit to be rebuilt, run on a dynamometer, and then returned.[48]

Thus began the process, now followed by almost every engine supplier at Indianapolis and in the top rung of championship racing, of in effect, leasing engines to teams but not allowing them to do overhauls or even any serious internal servicing. The result was to drive costs into the stratosphere. It also eliminated the dozen or more small independent shops where American racing engines had been rebuilt since World War II, shifting that business instead to rigidly controlled corporate facilities.

The Offy, restricted since 1957 to 255 cubic inches, had until then met every challenge through development by mechanics that Ford said couldn't time the cams of its new V-8. Meyer & Drake and the Offy wrenches had boosted the engine's output from 360 horsepower on 270 cubic inches in 1956 to 420 horsepower out of 255 inches in 1959. According to mechanic Clint Brawner in 1964, the Offy still produced slightly more horsepower than the Ford, but it was to no avail. In 1965, a week after Indianapolis, A. J. Foyt drove a Lotus Ford at Milwaukee. Bignotti watched sadly from the pits with his Offy on the trailer. He and A. J. had finally split over Foyt's fuel incident at the 500.

Defeated by the better Lotus rear-engine chassis, the coming of Goodyear into championship racing and the high-revving new Ford engine, the normally aspirated Offenhauser engine was on the ropes. It had been deserted by Lou Meyer, its 20-year co-producer. By 1967 the Offy mustered less than a quarter of the Indianapolis field. A. J. Foyt won in a Ford, the third 500 victory for both. The first Offy finished seventh.

Offy's Losing Out Everywhere

By the mid-1960s, the Offy midget was on the ropes as well, suffering stiff competition from much larger stock-based engines. In 1969 George Benson won the midget Offy's last Turkey Night championship in Los Angeles behind the wheel of an Oliver Johnson car. In 1970, Tommy McAndrew took the last Offy championship in American Racing Driver's Club (ARDC) in the *K & G Shell* car. Mike McGreevy won the last USAC Offy division title in 1966 in the Kenyon Offy. By then USAC had changed the circuit's name to the "Compact Sprint Car Division."

In AAA, URC, CSRA, and most other sprint car racing on the half-miles the 220 Offy held sway just to the end of the 1950s. Late in that decade when it was challenged by the Chevrolet V-8, a 220 Offy generally could make short work of a mildly-hopped-up push-rod but when the 440-cubic-inch big-block Chevy was fully developed, as scores of owners were doing, it was another thing. In an attempt to help, USAC allowed Offy owners to run 255's, but it was no use.

As the sun set at Indianapolis and on the dirt tracks in the mid-1960s, the nation itself was changing, many traditions abandoned. It seemed also that the old Offy that had evolved from the speedboat engine of 1926 was finished at last. Louis Meyer had gone over to Ford, and Dale Drake was left, with Leo Goossen, to struggle with an aged, over-the-hill engine.

Bobby Unser, in a Leader Cards, turbo, 168-cubic-inch Offy Gurney/Eagle, won at Indianapolis after three years of Ford V-8 victories. Only four turbo Fords were able to qualify and the best of them, driven by Jerry Grant, finished 23rd. Only two Fords, both normally aspirated, were able to crack the top 13 positions.
Gloria Madsen collection/Indianapolis Motor Speedway

CHAPTER TWELVE

RENEWAL AND VICTORY

THE 1964 RACE AT INDIANAPOLIS WAS THE SWAN SONG OF THE ROADSTER and nearly that of the Offenhauser engine. Jimmy Clark hammered the coffin all but shut in 1965 with his rear-engined Lotus and the more powerful Ford four-cam V-8. Clark finished five minutes ahead of the closest Offy, Gordon Johncock's obsolete front-engine roadster. By 1965, defeated at Indianapolis for the first time since 1946, down on power against the Fords, with Lou Meyer working for the opposition, the Offy did not appear to have much chance of revival.

Ironically, the events of the 1964 race brought rules changes that helped the Offy to return in another form: supercharged. The MacDonald-Sachs crash that killed both drivers in a horrendous first-lap gasoline inferno led to requirements that all but forced the use of methanol as a fuel (methanol has a higher flash point than gasoline and is considered safer), forbid cars from carrying more than 75 gallons, and required at least two mandatory pit stops. At a stroke these changes took away the Ford four-cam's advantage of greater fuel economy.

The USAC formula at the time permitted a supercharged engine 170 cubic inches of displacement against 252 inches for an unblown engine. Given the state of the supercharging art even in 1966, that was heavily weighted to the blown engine, at least if fuel economy were not part of the equation. Surveying the Offy's problems at the time Leo Goossen, said "We've got a lot of places we can go" to catch up with the Ford.

Meyer & Drake had been trying to interest teams in supercharging for years. Welch had built the Novi, Art Sparks had run his big and little sixes, there had been the Bowes-Winfield eight, and Harry Miller had been supremely successful with supercharging in the 1920s. The drawback of the supercharged engine was that it was less reliable and more difficult to work with, and that had turned off A. J. Watson and other experienced Offenhauser mechanics.

To get back in the fight, the Offenhauser needed an ally or two. One result of the Ford four-cam's victory was that Ford's Autolite brand spark plugs could be advertised as Indianapolis winners. The Champion Company had been supplying the racers for years, but now Autolite was making the most of its Indianapolis success, and even in midget racing its decal began replacing the Champion oval. Firestone tires had ruled the Speedway almost as long, but now Goodyear was encroaching on Firestone's Indianapolis turf. Both Champion and Firestone rushed to help the Offy battle the Ford.

Champion had a dynamometer facility in Long Beach, California, not 10 miles from the Drake shop. There Dick Jones, the Champion company's auto racing troubleshooter, was already experimenting with a Roots-blown 220

The turbocharged Offenhauser of 1967. Four years later this well-developed engine, with its boost unlimited by the rules, produced more than 1,200 horsepower from 159 cubic inches. Although the normally aspirated Offy had lost its laurels to the Ford four-cam V-8 in 1965, the turbo engine recovered and by 1972 had the Ford on the ropes. It was only a combination of changed rules and the new Ford-Cosworth engine that finally defeated the Offy in 1977. *Bob DeBisschop/Gloria Madsen collection*

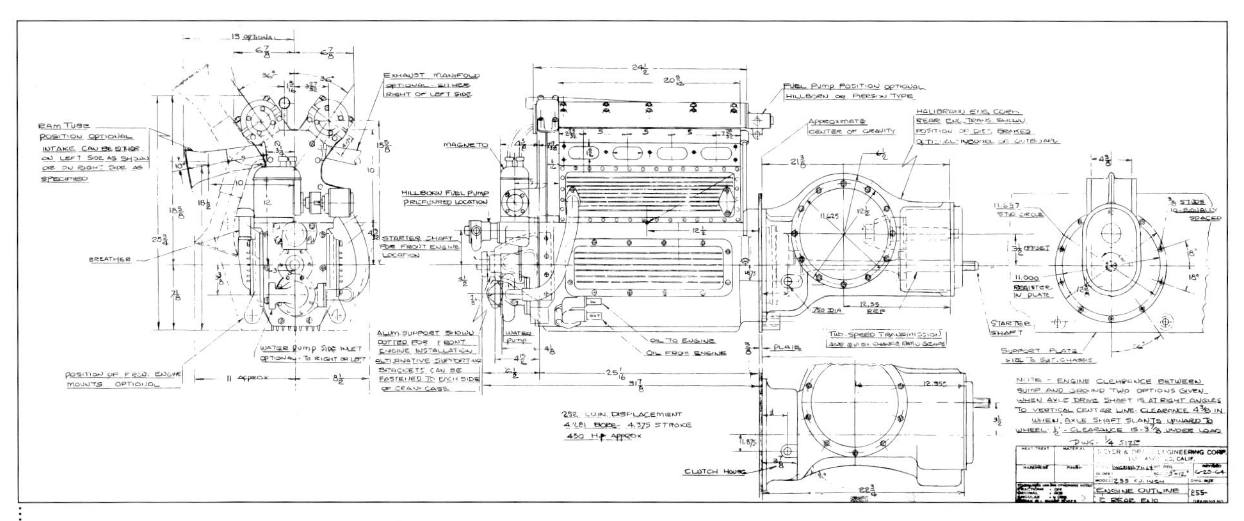

Naturally aspirated, fuel-injected 255 Offy set up for a rear-engine chassis in 1964. *Kenneth Walton collection*

Dale Drake setting an exhaust cam on the 168-cubic-inch Roots-blown Offy, 1965. *John Drake collection*

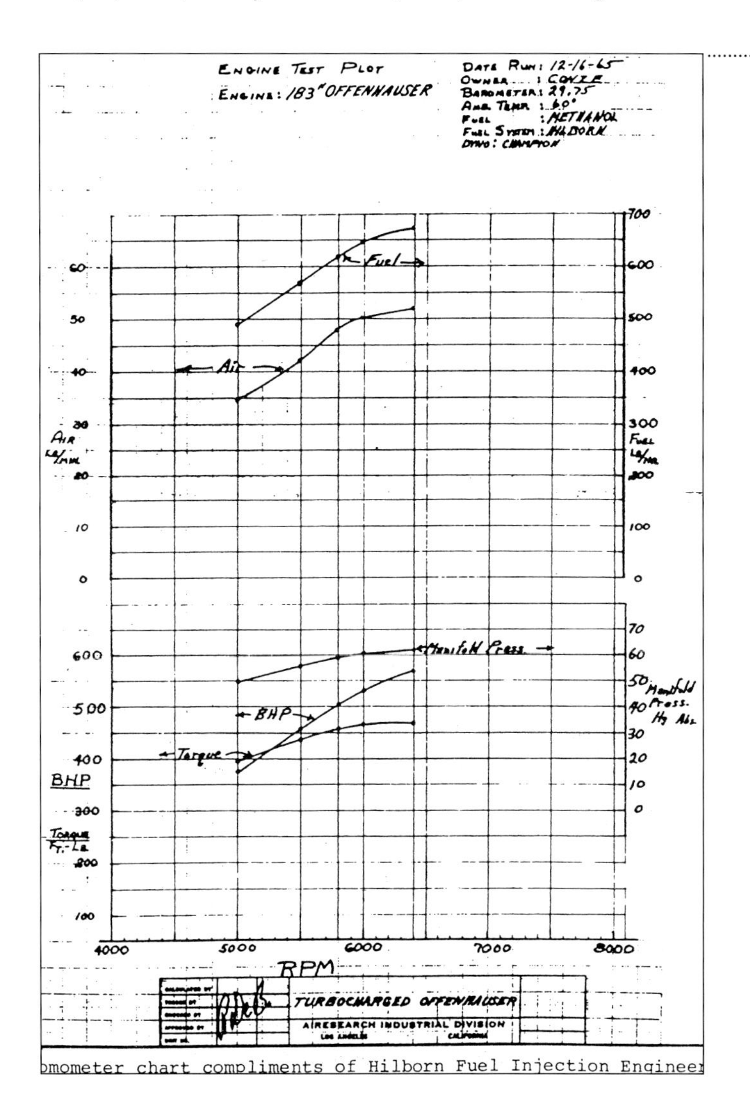

By the end of 1965 the test Offy, borrowed from Vince Conze, was making more than 600 horsepower at 6,400 rpm. *Kenneth Walton collection*

Offy borrowed from Vince Conze. The engine, serial #187, had been in Lance Reventlow's first Grand Prix car in 1958 and Conze, who collected all the old Miller and Offy material he could find, had bought it when Reventlow quit. For a while Firestone did its part by using Offy-powered cars in testing to develop its latest rubber compounds then Goodyear jumped in on the Offy's side.

There were then two types of mechanically driven superchargers in common use. The *Roots* blower is a positive-displacement air pump, using closely fitted rotors. Like a piston pump, it pushes lots of air at low rpm. Roots blowers are commonly used on top fuel and other drag cars where off-the-line acceleration is crucial. They take a lot of power and require strong, and therefore heavy, mechanical drive systems. Unlike *centrifugal* blowers they usually run at less than crankshaft speed, so are less affected by rapid rpm changes. Both Miller and Duesenberg used centrifugal superchargers, a kind of fan that does not give much boost at low speeds. At Indianapolis where cornering speeds are high the centrifugal blowers work better than the Roots, but centrifugal superchargers have to be turned far faster than the positive-displacement Roots type, leading to drive problems as the rapidly-spinning blower accelerates and decelerates.

Sonny Meyer Offers Solution

Many Meyer & Drake employees worked at the plant during the winter and then went to Indianapolis as mechanics or chief mechanics, including Chickie, George Salih, and others. Lou Meyer's son, Sonny who had done almost every job in the Meyer & Drake shop from sweeping the floor to running the old Van Norman mill, stooged at Indy for Salih on the Jones & Maley KK500C Offy roadster in 1956 and in 1957. When Salih had his own car, the laydown, Sonny became chief mechanic on the Jones & Maley car, driven by Bob Christie.[49]

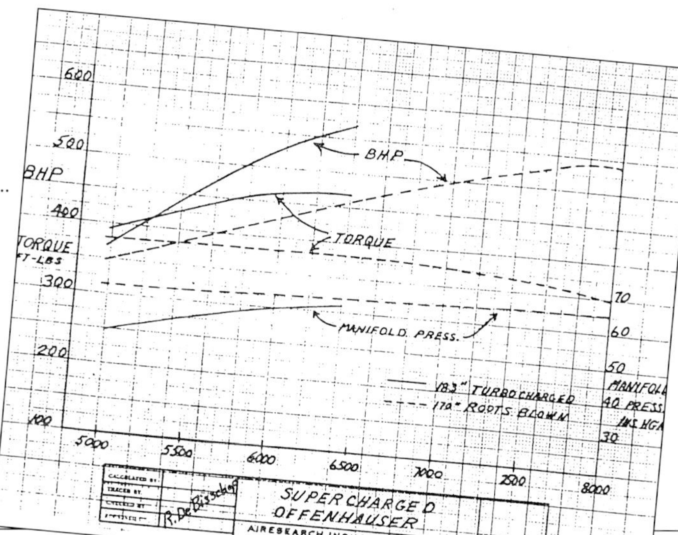

An AiResearch dyno test by Bob De Bisschop of both a 183 turbo and a 170 Roots-blown Offy showed the turbo, even early in its development, could put out nearly 570 horsepower at 6,400 rpm compared to 450 for the Roots. The turbo's run was not carried past that point, but in practice it actually improves. In fact, the turbo has an advantage of some 90 horsepower at 6,400 rpm. At higher rpm the Roots supercharger becomes less efficient. A lower-rpm chart would show the Roots with an advantage in the 2,000 rpm area because it is a positive-displacement pump mechanically geared to the crankshaft, whereas the turbo is driven by exhaust gas. *John Drake collection*

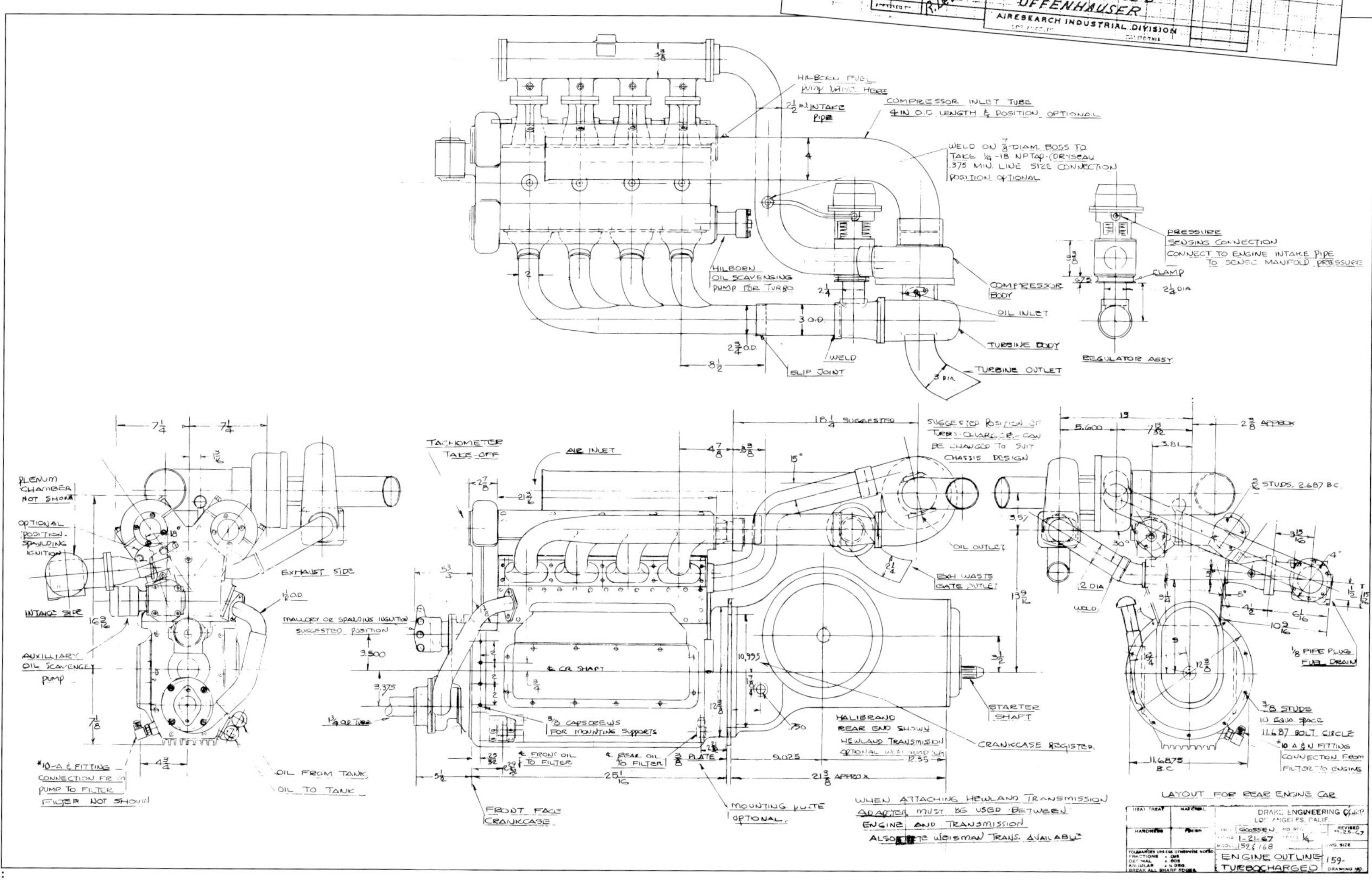

The early turbo-Offy as drawn by Goossen in January 1967. At that time, the popoff valve was merely a waste-gate on the exhaust side. *Kenneth Walton collection*

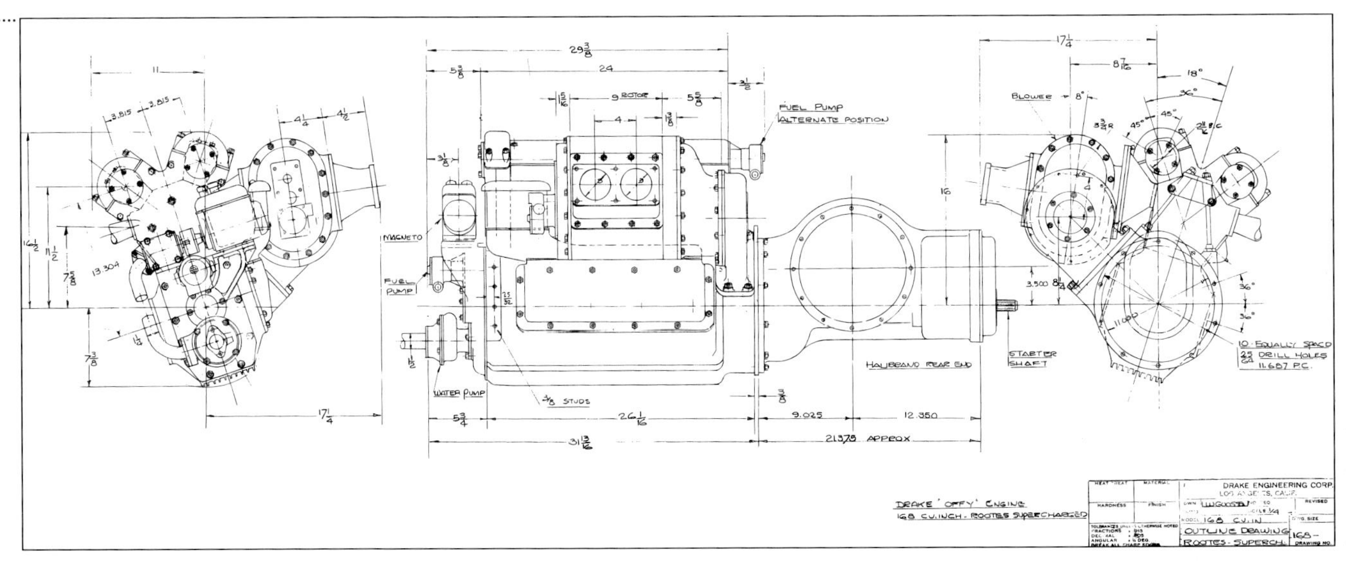

Goossen's drawing for Drake Engineering ("Meyer" has been erased from this drafting sheet) of the Roots-blown 168-cubic-inch Offy. (Leo labeled it "Rootes," which is incorrect.) *Kenneth Walton collection*

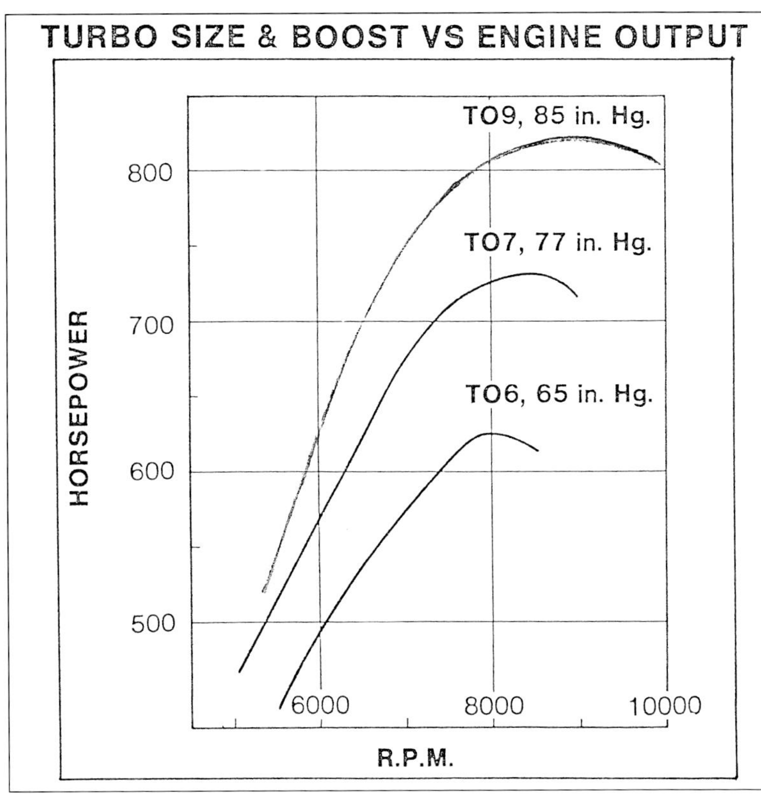

The size of the turbo blower and the amount of boost allowed are crucial to the output of a turbo engine. The larger blower takes slightly longer to "spool up" because of weight and inertia, but where the small TE-06 made 625 horsepower at 8,000 rpm and 65 inches of boost, the big TH-08 could produce 820 horsepower at 8,500 rpm and 85 inches boost on the same engine. Late Drake-Offy and D-G-S engines absorbed more boost and actually showed in excess of 1,200 horsepower for qualifying at Indianapolis in 1973. *John Drake collection*

After the events at Indianapolis in 1964 Sonny suggested to Dale that they build an engine combining the advantages of both the Roots and the turbo, a two-stage supercharged engine (two-stage supercharging had been used on aircraft for years). It would have the Roots for acceleration off the corners and the turbo for top-end speed down the straights. They would have to shorten the stroke of the 252 Offy and they had no forged rod blanks of the right size. Sonny recalls that Dale went to Fresno to look for a blacksmith who could make the blanks but couldn't find anyone who would do it.

At Champion, Jones had Bob Strahlman bolt a GMC 4-71 Roots-type diesel truck blower driven by a toothed Gilmer[50] belt to the 171-cubic-inch 220-series Offy. Jones used a two-port Hilborn fuel injection unit that produced 540 horsepower at 7,900 rpm on the dyno with about 15 pounds boost.

He built a second prototype Roots-blown Offy for Paul Goldsmith that produced 545 horsepower at 9,000 rpm. Though Jones carried out most of the testing he was constantly in touch with Drake and Goossen over its progress. When the Roots Offy had been developed sufficiently, Drake had Goossen design a special crankcase for it as a 168-cubic-inch low-tower version of the 220. On the production model the supercharger was gear- driven and used an automotive blower built by the Miehle-Dexter Company.

Parnelli Jones tested one of the Roots-blown Offys at Phoenix in February 1966 and set a new track record of 123.49 miles per hour, which was also, at the time, the fastest anyone had ever turned a one-mile track. In tire testing for Firestone at Phoenix, Jones went on to run 50 miles at an average of 122 miles per hour. His best lap was more than a mile faster than Mario Andretti had done there three months earlier with a four-cam Ford. Parnelli said the Offy was the stronger engine, and he drove one himself in a Shrike chassis at Indianapolis in May. Dale Drake and Leo Goossen, were overjoyed at Jones' success with the blown engine, seeing it as repudiation of predictions that the Offy was dead. In production the new Roots-blown Offy sold for $12,000, and Drake built 17 of the engines for Indianapolis in 1966.

Two other men familiar with superchargers, Herb Porter and Robert De Bisschop, entered the Offy's corner in 1965. Porter had been building and running supercharged Offys for 20 years with mixed results. His cars were fast but often failed to finish. The established Offy mechanics were amused, but took his efforts as proof of the unreliability of superchargers.

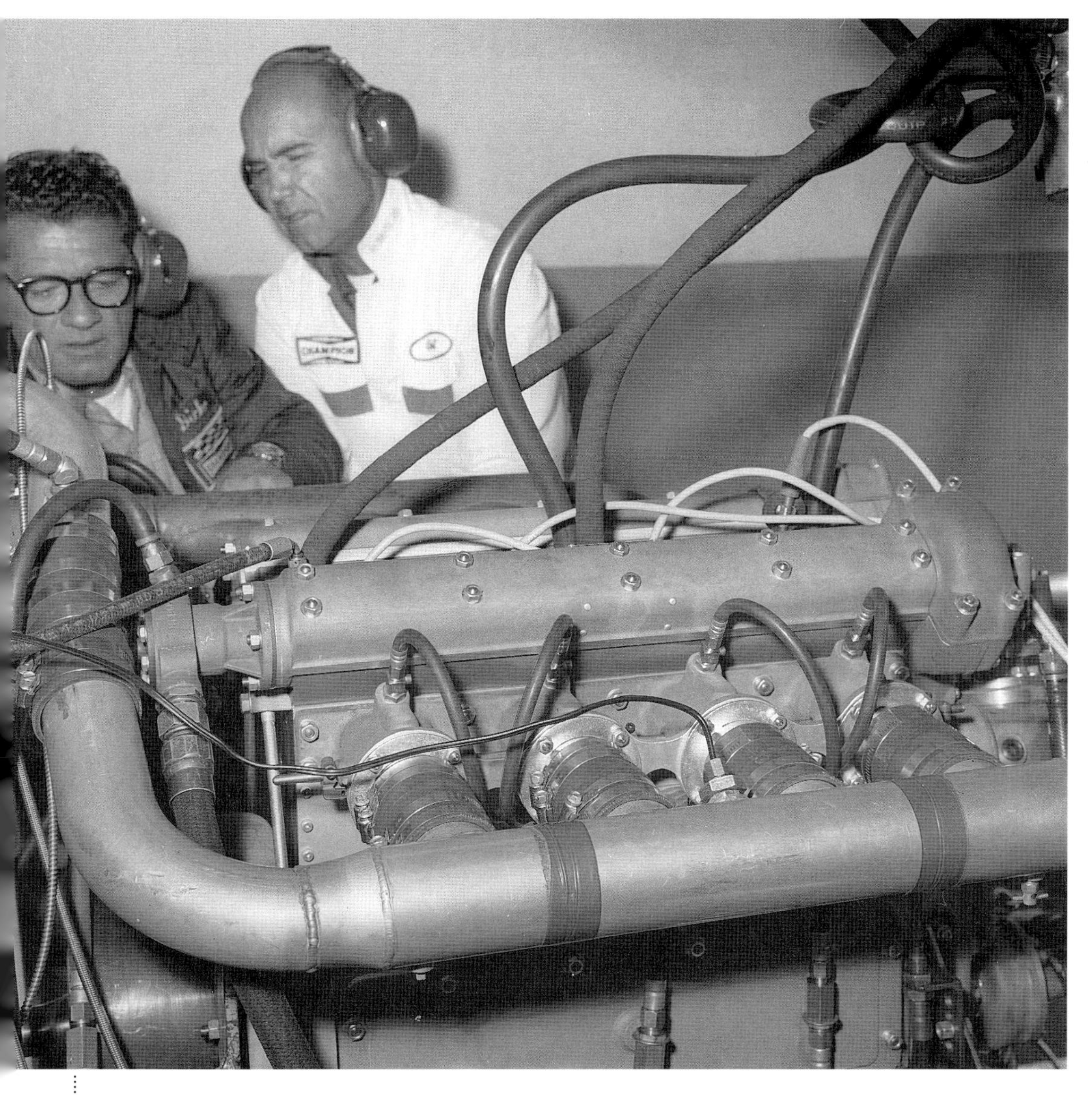

Dick Jones, of Champion, and Art Lamey, using the Champion Spark Plug Company's dynamometer, run a test on a turbo Offy in 1968. *Gordon Schroeder collection*

One of the turbo supercharger units built by the AiResearch division of Garrett Industries. The tiny turbine wheel on the right is driven by the exhaust gas and forces the air-fuel mixture into the engine with the rotor on the left end of a common shaft. The turbo eliminated the supercharger drive-line problems that bedeviled Harry Miller and the other original developers of supercharged engines. *Gordon Schroeder collection*

In 1949 Herb, with help from Stu Hilborn, built a stretched-midget, Roots-supercharged sprint car at about the same time Mike Caruso was running one in the East. Porter went to a centrifugal supercharger for his next sprint car engine, which gave him practical experience with two kinds of blowers. De Bisschop, then working for the AiResearch division of the Garrett Company which manufactured turbochargers for aircraft, wanted to try a turbo on an Offy. After Watson declined to participate in such a project, De Bisschop turned to Porter. Garrett financed much of the work and supplied the turbo units and wastegates as Porter, De Bisschop, and Drake undertook an effort paralleling that of Jones.

Though production turbos were the same length as the 270, the new turbo-Offy was originally based on the 220, the 1931 design that updated the Miller Marine 151 for land use, and the turbo displacement limit of 168 cubic inches (bore and stroke of 4 1/8x3 1/8 inches) was only a little more than 10 percent larger than the 1927 Marine engine—in a sense the clock had been turned back nearly 40 years. The unblown Offys were effectively laid to rest. Some were updated, but the demands of turbocharging would shortly leave them with no place to run competitively, except at Bonneville and in vintage events.

Turbo Superchargers

Turbochargers are simply centrifugal superchargers driven by an engine's exhaust gasses. The Besasie Engineering Corporation built an exhaust-driven supercharger for Chevrolet engines in 1939 and it remained a Chevy hop-up item into the late 1940s,[51] but the design was not adopted by racing mechanics. During World War II turbos had been used on engines such as the Wright R-3350 radial that powered the B-29 bomber and later the DC-7 and Super Constellation airliners.

As we have seen, the 1952 Cummins Diesel was turbocharged. In the 1960s turbos were used chiefly on high-performance small aircraft piston engines and diesel trucks. Since they do not have a mechanical belt, gear, or shaft-drive system they are lighter than traditional blowers and have no mechanical drives to break. Driven by energy from the exhaust that is otherwise largely wasted, turbos draw much less power from the engine. On the other hand, they do suffer from "turbo lag," and like all centrifugal blowers, "wet manifold."[52] Back-pressure tends to keep heat in a turbocharged engine, another problem. Engine lubrication is critical, and in the 1970s some owners—Dan Gurney for one—had Drake make special crankcases with two oil pumps. Most of the late turbo cases were, in fact, double-pumpers.

Bobby Unser drove this turbo-Offy, Huffaker-chassised car to eighth place at Indy in 1966, the highest-placed of the three turbo-Offys in the race. That's Wally Meskowski with the glasses on the right. *Mark Dees collection*

Bobby Grim in Herb Porter's experimental turbo Offy roadster at Indianapolis in 1966. The turbo and its plumbing were add-ons hung out the left side of the car. Bobby ran practice laps as high as 160 miles per hour, as fast as a roadster ever went at the Brickyard, and qualified at 158.367. A first-lap pileup that took 11 cars out of the race ended Porter and Grim's day at the starting line. *Indianapolis Motor Speedway*

Turbos require careful design. Porter said that at first his high-revving supercharged engines would run only about 35 laps until the blower bearings fell apart.

Because of the tremendous power increase, the Offy crankcase had to be beefed-up. The bell housing was again cast as a separate piece, as it had been before 1951. The case was by then being heavily stressed and Porter suggested returning to the notchless crankcase of 1931. Eliminating the notches in the bulkheads to which the bearing webs bolted strengthened the case. Inserting the crank into the case became a more time-consuming job as the entire assembly could no longer be dropped in; the webs had to be inserted from the side. The block was cast asymmetrically for the first time since the Sparks Little Six, with separated exhaust ports and better cooling around the exhaust valves. Despite the difficulties, Drake sold some 20 $3,500 kits to upgrade existing engines to work with turbo blowers.

Increasing the revs from the 5,200–6,500 range the Offys had been running for so many years imposed new requirements for closer manufacturing tolerances. Crankshafts and bearings became less forgiving. Just centering the bearing webs became critical and finishing crank journals for rotational speeds in excess of 10,000 rpm required grinding them to tolerances much closer than in the old Miller days. New heat-treating methods were necessary to avoid embrittlement of parts. It was a measure of Drake's skill and ability to keep up with the new sciences in a shop lacking the resources of a Ford Motor Company.

Among other fixes to the Offy, the oiling system in the top of the engine was changed from the scavenge side of the oil pump as it had been plumbed since Harry Miller's day, to the pressure side. The new setup pumped cleaner oil to the cam towers (an oil filter had been added to the Offy in the 1960s for the first time). Porter also added an oil cooler to the lubricant plumbing.

Goodyear Gets Into the Act

The original turbo unit was a model used on Allis-Chalmers diesel tractors. A. J. Foyt was the first driver to track test it on an Offy. Porter put the prototype engine into Ebb Rose's obsolete Watson roadster and took it to a Goodyear tire test session at Phoenix in April 1966, two months after Parnelli's test of the Roots-blown engine. After Porter had warmed up the car, Foyt took it out, but a puzzled A. J. quickly shut down and coasted back into the pits. The engine had popped and sputtered; A. J. thought it had blown something. Porter looked it over and found nothing wrong. Foyt went out again, and after going fast enough for the turbo boost to become effective, the engine ran well enough to be encouraging.

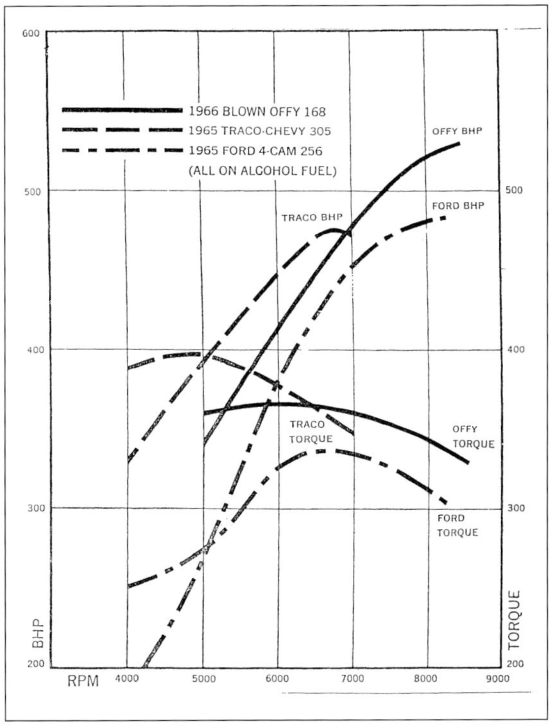

Then John Poulesen, Foyt's mechanic, crashed Foyt's car. A. J. had to go back to Houston for repairs, and Porter hired Don Branson to drive the Rose roadster. By the end of four days the sputtering in the turbo transition stage was eliminated. Goodyear's tire session had proved that given unlimited boost, the turbo Offy could beat the four-cam Fords. With encouragement from Goodyear Racing Director Leo Mehl and Foyt, Goodyear continued to help develop the Offy. The company put Porter on its payroll as the engine man for tire testing and bought him a half-dozen turbo Offys for the job.

Porter took the Rose roadster to Indianapolis in 1966 more as an experiment than as a serious entry. Bobby Grim, the IMCA champion, undertook to drive it, and Porter and Grim decided they might have a competitive car even though the roadster chassis was clearly obsolete.

First Turbos in Competition

The 1966 race at Indianapolis was frustrating for both the Roots and the turbo Offys. The first production Roots engine kit was sold to Cave Buick in Fresno, California, for a Gerhardt chassis. Driver Bob Wente was unable to get the car up to speed. Eleven 1966 Indy entries were powered with the Roots-blown iron-block Offys, but only three made the race. For the three steel-sleeved, aluminum-block turbos there were problems of expansion rate differences in the blocks, sleeves, and valve seats. Bobby Unser blew turbo engines in Gordon Van Liew's Vita Fresh car more than a dozen times in practice.

Grim qualified at 158.367 miles per hour and turned a practice lap at more than 160 miles per hour, the fastest a roadster ever ran at the Speedway. Grim's ride was the next to the last roadster to make the race (an honor that went to Jim Hurtubise in 1967). At the start, the car, with only a two-speed gearbox, was not able to accelerate as rapidly as the more modern four-speed Lolas and Lotuses. When another car spun Grim was unable to avoid it, and his race ended after 750 feet in a first-lap wreck that eliminated Foyt, Gurney, and eight other cars before they got to the first turn.

Parnelli qualified his 1966 Agajanian Roots-blown Offy fourth behind three Fords at 162.484 miles per hour but went out with a bad wheel bearing on lap 87. Graham Hill won the race in a Lola-Ford wrenched by George Bignotti. In 1967 Lloyd Ruby's Offy-Mongoose qualified at 165.229 mph, up until that time the fastest a turbo-Offy had ever gone, but suffered a broken valve from an incautious shift on the third lap of the race.

Turbo Lag and Casting Problems

Turbo lag was a continual problem for the drivers. Not only did the blower take time to spool up under throttle application, when a driver shifted gears at or near full-throttle, the inertia of the turbo spinning at 80,000 rpm would continue to force the fuel mixture into the engine, the waste-gate would stutter, and over-revving would result. One solution was to use as small, and therefore as light, a turbine unit as possible to reduce the time it took for the turbine to accelerate or decelerate. Eventually Stu Hilborn solved the lag problem with injector improvements.

A comparison of torque and horsepower figures was done by Drake Engineering on the 1966 blown Offy, the 1965 Ford four-cam, and a Traco Chevy 305. At that time the turbo Offy had a 40 horsepower advantage and more torque, particularly in the lower rpm range, than the other engines. *John Drake collection*

The Roots blower was not able to provide more than 52 inches of boost. Beyond that it was, according to Porter, "just pumping heat into the engine." Looking critically at the 1966 results and the power the Roots blower required, Porter and Drake decided the turbo was a better bet.

There were also serious problems with the castings for the aluminum turbo blocks. Macaulay, the long-time Miller-Offenhauser-Meyer & Drake foundry, was not used to working with aluminum and its blocks were not satisfactory. As Cosworth and General Motors had found, casting large forms in aluminum was not a perfected science, even as late as 1966. There were voids and porosity in the metal that often were not discovered until much expensive machine work had been done on a piece or until the engine was run. The searing heat of a turbocharged engine could cut through a thin spot in a combustion chamber in short order.

Roots Fade and Turbos in Rear-Engine Chassis

In 1967, Ronnie Duman in a J. C. Agajanian-sponsored Halibrand Shrike chassis qualified the only Roots-blown Offy at Indianapolis. He lasted until lap 153 when he went out with fuel feed problems. There were seven turbo Offys that May, and fuel problems plagued them all until Stu Hilborn worked the bugs out of his diaphragm-controlled bypass system. Porter and Grim had a new rear-engine Gerhardt chassis, but it broke an axle half-shaft and Grim spun on his 187th lap, also taking out Chuck Hulse in the fastest of the Offys. The crash came just as Foyt in his Ford was heading for the checkered flag on his last lap. A. J. managed to thread his way through the melee to win his third 500. Fords took the top five places and during the season Offys won only 5 of the 21 USAC races, a low point for them indeed.

The aluminum-block casting problem nagged continually at Drake, Ford, and Cosworth, which was making Formula 1 engines in England. The difficulty involved cooling of the liquid metal in the foundry form in such a way as to eliminate gasses that were leaving bubbles in the finished pieces. The way the metal was poured and the position of the flask during cooling was critical. The problems were not solved until engineers who were not foundrymen took a completely new look at the process. Drake eventually got acceptable castings from the Turner Company, in Bell, California. Even so, every block had to be sonic and pressure tested before it was machined.

Despite the improvements, there were continual problems in the engines. As revs rose above 9,000, magnetos faltered. Outside air had to be piped in to cool the mags to prevent breakdown of coils and condensers. Joe Hunt, the traditional supplier, worked hard to keep up, but eventually magnetos were replaced by crank-triggered Mallory distributors. Among block modifications, the traditional siamesed oval ports were altered to separate the porting for the two valves in each cylinder. Hilborn also developed an injector kit for the turbocharged Offy that incorporated dual nozzles, one for running at low revs and a second set that kicked in as the boost came on.

Ford Plays Catch-Up

Porter worked closely with Jud Phillips and DeBisschop on turbocharging the Offy for the Leader Card car to be driven by Bobby Unser in 1968. Unser's car was tuned to produce 625 horsepower in qualifying and 590 in the race where fuel economy was important. Although Ford was aware of the Drake turbo work, the company was reluctant to authorize the development necessary to turbocharge its four-cam.

When the first Drake turbo engine appeared in 1966 Louis Meyer got in touch with Jacque Passino, Ford's director of racing, for money to turbocharge the V-8. Passino was sympathetic, but told Meyer that the corporate higher-ups said that no one would ever see a turbocharger in a passenger car so Ford was not interested in spending the money on such an exotic and costly project. Ford had spent a pretty penny to win at Indy and to assuage Henry II's ego. Lee Iaccoca's Mustang was a fantastic success in the showrooms and Fords were still winning at Indy and in road racing with Carroll Shelby, so turbocharging did not seem necessary to the Ford corporate higher-ups.

Drake was about to prove them wrong. With the help he was getting from Porter, DeBisschop, Champion, and Goodyear, the turbo Offy was gaining strength and reliability.

Dan Jones, Clay Smith's nephew and a former dry lakes and URA midget driver, was the liaison between Ford's Dearborn headquarters and the racing teams, and he realized what was happening. He didn't want the Ford engine to die, as it was obviously about to do, so in the best tradition of sub-rosa corporate encouragement of racing he took things into his own hands and stretched his mandate as far as he could, which was quite a bit. He persuaded Ford to make cranks and some of the other necessary parts for the turbo engines.

The first turbo Fords used Hillborn and AiResearch parts, but at the same time Lou and Sonny Meyer went to Louie Schwitzer's company, an auto parts manufacturer in Indianapolis[53], to get one of its 3MD turbocharger units and to Elmer Haase[54] at the Bendix Corporation's fuel-injection division in South Bend for other parts, including a venturi-controlled air-metering system and engineering assistance to help them turbocharge the Ford. (Lou Schwitzer had been a racer himself who won the first race ever held at the Indianapolis Speedway, a five-mile sprint in 1909 with a Stoddard-Dayton). Meyer got Schwitzer to help by marching into his office and reminding him of a certain debt. At Indianapolis in 1929 Meyer had been leading the race at 157 laps in Alden Sampson's rear-drive Miller 91 when Schwitzer (then Technical Committee Chairman at the Speedway) noticed a small oil leak from Meyer's car and had him black-flagged. The leak (according to Meyer) was minor, and was quickly fixed, but the hot Miller failed to start and it took seven minutes to get him back in the race. By then Ray Keech had taken a commanding lead and despite Meyer's frantic charge he could only finish second, 6 minutes and 24 seconds behind. Recalling the incident, Schwitzer told Meyer "my factory is yours" and assigned his chief engineer, Bill Wallenhaber, to work with them on the four-cam.

Bignotti had two Lola chassis that would only accept the Ford engines, so he had to make the Fords competitive. Jones was able to pry three development engines out of Ford, and he, George Bignotti, and Sonny Meyer did the initial work on Bignotti's dyno in Indianapolis. It was tough and costly sledding without Ford's full support. Bignotti said (and Meyer agreed) the Ford cams and ports were fine for normally aspirated engines but didn't flow worth a damn for the turbos. "They didn't have any torque," Meyer said. The first one George got to run, Ford grabbed and gave to Foyt, who won a Trenton race with it, beating Bignotti's older Ford entry (which broke a fuel pump while leading).

The Offy Revived!

With its late start, Louis Meyer Inc. was only able to supply seven turbo Ford engines to the Indianapolis teams in 1968. There were still difficulties to be worked out in fuel mixture distribution in the Ford's convoluted intake tract and the engines suffered from overheating problems never really corrected throughout their life-span. Just four Fords made the race and only Mario Andretti qualified well. None of the Ford turbos finished.

George Bignotti, right, and Jim Dilamaiter, work on the four-cam Ford engine in Bignotti's Indianapolis entry in 1969. *Gordon Schroeder collection*

Bobby Unser, on the other hand, qualified at 169.507 miles per hour and won the 1968 race in his Eagle/Offy, the first victory for the old engine in four years and Offy-powered entries took 9 of the first 11 places. In dramatic fashion the competition from Ford had driven Indianapolis speeds up by 24 miles per hour in eight years.

Dearborn still refused to pay attention, and Offenhauser-powered cars won 15 championship races that year to Ford's nine. Ford drivers started switching back to the Offy as Mario Andretti did at Trenton that September.

"The 255 Ford doesn't seem to get the job done," Andretti needled Ford before the Trenton race. "When they get the turbo Ford to where it's competitive I'll go back . . . and when they do," Mario added, "the Offy will be history."

Only later, when Al Unser set a new Trenton track record in qualifying Bignotti's Retzloff turbo Ford and led for 40 laps (until an O-ring in the fuel system failed) did the power of the turbo V-8 become clear. Sonny Meyer said that "woke up Ford to the potential of turbocharging the four-cam and they got behind the program." Louis Meyer Inc. immediately had orders from racing teams for 35 turbo four-cam engines or kits to upgrade its existing normally aspirated Fords that were by then being walked-over by the rejuvenated Offys. Lou Meyer said Ford, embarrassed by their 1968 defeat, poured $10 million into developing the turbocharger. As well it might, that money paid off over the next three years. Ford and Bignotti improved the Ford sufficiently that Andretti was able to win Indianapolis in 1969 and five of the first 10 cars to finish were Fords. A Ford won Indy again in 1970 for Al Unser, Sr., and the four-cam took 15 championship races in 1970 and 1971.

The aluminum block turbo Offys were still having problems traceable to bad castings, and Drake ordered a run of iron blocks as an interim measure. He had tried a flat-back case design but dropped it and went back to the stronger integral bell housing and bracing bars. The blocks were cut down yet again for a shorter stroke.

USAC's reduction in the size of supercharged engines to 162 cubic inches in 1969 was a futile gesture to trim speeds and did not slow things down significantly, although the pole speed did drop by 1/2 percent—one mile per hour. Despite the 10 percent displacement downsizing, crew chiefs simply adapted larger turbos—an AirResearch TE-0-69 was most often used—and horsepower increased for both the Ford and the Offy. Goossen designed a 159-cubic-inch engine, and small-bore sleeves to convert the 1968 models.[55]

Goossen was a little contemptuous about the four-cam. "It was a miserable engine to work on," he would say before he died, and "it has a lot more frontal area than the Offy." Goossen only saw one of the Ford engines close up, and in 1973 he finally had a chance to ride behind one when Jim Toensing went around to the Drake shop with a GT-40 into which he had put a by then obsolete Ford four-cam. Leo was nearly overwhelmed by the power of the racing engine in the streetable GT-40. "I can't get over it," he told Toensing again and again. It was the only time in his long life as a race engine designer that he rode with a race engine.

Ford finally decided it had spent enough money on its V-8. In December 1969, Henry Ford II announced Ford's withdrawal from racing. There was no appropriation to continue developing the engine. They cost Ford about $16,000 more in parts and assembly than they were selling for, and according to Meyer, some of the casting patterns for the engine were worn out while others were missing. Although the Fords were still winning, the operation had begun to run down. Al Unser, Sr., took the pole at Indianapolis in 1970 in a Ford at 170.221 miles per hour and won the 500 with Mark Donohue second in another Ford, but the engine was six years old. It clearly was not as strong on torque[56] as the turbo Offy was after Drake, Goossen, and the others had spent four years developing it. If the Ford four-cam was going to stay in business it needed even more costly work. Ford executives estimated that they would have to spend $35 million to improve it sufficiently to stay ahead of the turbocharged Offenhauser.

George Bignotti said, "Louie Meyer was the most honest person I have ever seen. Ford wanted him to buy them out [for $250,000] and take over the parts for ten engines to build and sell and recover his investment. One of the engines would have to be made up from used parts which had run on the dyno and Louie didn't want to do that." Lou Meyer said, 25 years later, "It needed $1 million just to keep it going" (meaning to keep the doors open at the shop in Indianapolis). He told the author that he was glad to drop the four-cam. "Ford was losing a lot of money," Bignotti said, "and Lou didn't have the Meyer & Drake shop to supply the parts and help control the cost. So they gave it all to [A. J.] Foyt and he made a couple of million dollars on [the] deal."

A. J. Foyt had wanted the Ford four-cam engine since 1965 when the Meyers were struggling to turbocharge it. "Foyt wanted it real bad," Meyer said in 1995. "Ford sold the entire setup—patterns, tooling, drawings, parts and spare engines to him at a giveaway price. And he didn't do anything with it."

That's not entirely accurate. Foyt did quite a lot with the four-cam himself, but he was never successful in selling engines to other teams. He came in third at Indianapolis with a Ford four-cam in 1971, a race that Al Unser, Sr., won with a Ford, but without the Ford Company's money Foyt had a hard time keeping up. He had none of the manufacturing expertise nor the facilities of Drake, and it was a wonder that Howard Gilbert, his engine man, did as well as he did, getting 825 horsepower from it at 9,600 rpm with 80 inches of boost. In 1972, the first year the engine ran under his name, Foyt was able to find only half a dozen customers for engines. He suffered from the same problem that Meyer & Drake faced in 1950: selling engines to competitors. Whether or not it was true that Foyt kept the best engines for himself, he was the only driver ever to win a race with the Foyt four-cam in its eight-year history. Only Dick Simon, Eldon Rasmussen's Rent a Racer Incorporated, Foyt's own team, and one or two others fielded Foyt V-8s.

George Bignotti

George Bignotti was born in San Francisco in 1918. For a time he ran a florist shop, but he found his true calling in 1954 at Indianapolis with Freddie Agabasian and the #77 Merz Engineering Special, a KK500C with a 270 Offy in it. George became the chassis man while Frankie Del Roy twisted the engine wrenches. In 1956 he worked for Frank Kurtis on the roadsters, and by 1961 A. J. Foyt was his driver. Bignotti and Foyt won the 500 twice, in 1961 and 1964, before splitting in 1965. Bignotti went to work for John Mecom, followed by Vels-Parnelli Jones, and then in 1973, Pat Patrick. His last Indianapolis victory was with Tom Sneva in 1983.

The Offy Back on Top

Without the Ford factory subsidy behind the V-8, the field was once again wide open to the Offy. The championship teams went back to it in droves after 1971, and the four-bangers once more dominated the Speedway's line-ups. The years 1972–1976 were a reprise of the Offy's golden years. The engines had about a 10 to 20 horsepower edge on the Fords and were far more durable. They made up from 67 to 85 percent of the Indianapolis qualifiers and won there in 1972, with Mark Donohue's Penske McLaren Offy averaging 162.962 for the 500 miles. Offys took four of the five top positions, beginning a run of five Indianapolis victories that proved the engine still had staying power after 40 years, a tribute to the work of Leo Goossen, Fred Offenhauser, and the Drakes. In 1972, there were 22 Offys in the field to one Ford and 10 Foyt four-cam V-8s. Under the lash of the Ford-Offy competition the pole speed jumped 15 miles per hour in a single year. Offys won 10 championship races in 1972, 14 in 1973, and 13 in 1974. Foyt had his own best year in 1975 as he won seven championship races, more a tribute to his driving than the strength of his engine. The four-cam was all but finished by then, with Foyt the only driver able to win with it, though he did very well, taking a total of 19 races before he retired it in 1979.

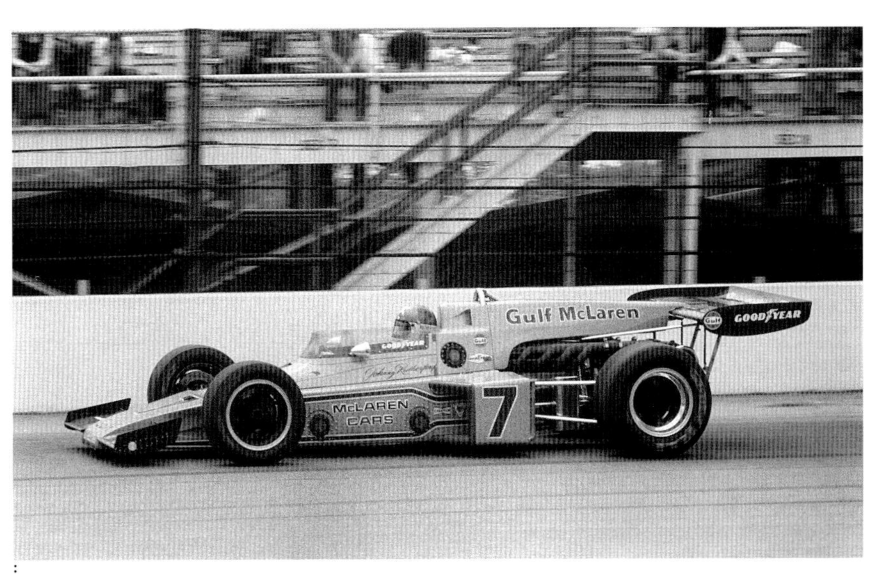

Johnny Rutherford as he qualified his turbo-Offy McLaren in 1973 at 198.413 miles per hour (one of his four laps was over 199). At this time boost for qualifying was essentially unlimited. His was the high-water mark of the Offenhauser engine; restrictions on both boost and fuel consumption would later hobble the Offy until the Ford-Cosworth was able to challenge it successfully. *Indianapolis Motor Speedway*

Lou Meyer returned to the Offy camp and worked with some of the teams headquartered in Indianapolis, even offered to handle the Drake engines in Indianapolis. Bignotti built 1972 Offys with even shorter-stroke cranks of 2.60 inches and had Goossen design the lowest tower of all: 0.369 inches shorter than the 1970 version; the lower piston speed allowing rpms to exceed 10,000. Other teams experimented with four different strokes and five bore sizes that would fall within the 162-cubic-inch limit.

Bignotti and Patrick worked furiously to update the Drake-Offy. Patrick, one of the Offy's staunchest supporters, helped finance Drake's development work in the 1970s, and Gordon Johncock won the 1973 500 for him in a turbo Offy/Eagle. Turbo Offy entries made up three-quarters of the cars that came to the Speedway in May 1973.

In November 1972, Lou Meyer sold his share of Louis Meyer Inc. to Bignotti and retired to his 100-acre Indiana farm. Bignotti, a brilliant mechanic with many strong ideas, carried on with his own version of the turbo Offy, building, (with the help of Goossen) his own 157-cubic-inch version which became the D-G-S. At the same time Bignotti became head mechanic for Patrick's racing team, using modified Gurney Eagle chassis. At Gurney's own shop John Miller was developing Offy engines for Dan's All American Racers. That team would win the 500 in 1975 with Bobby Unser in an Olsonite Eagle-Offy.

Drake and Goossen continued to beef up the engine to handle higher boost pressures. They strengthened the case yet again and once more refined the oil and cooling systems, making the Offy able to handle boost pressures in excess of 110 inches. The Ford/Foyt at the time would overheat if its boost exceeded 80 inches.

In 1972 Dale Drake died suddenly of an aneurysm, leaving the Offy legend to his son, John, his widow, Eve, Leo Goossen, and shop foreman Walt Sobraske. Under John and Leo's guidance 159-cubic-inch Offys were run to remarkable power levels at boost pressures above 40 psi. Connecting rods became a problem, and Gurney's team replaced its tubular Miller-Offy style rods with H-section Carillos. The Carillo rods were a few grams heavier, and also had problems surviving. One puzzling problem cropped up: AAR's Miller found in 1970 that an erratic magneto was causing an ignition spike slightly out of time. The resulting misfire put enough force on the rod to break it. John Miller eventually went back to the Drake rod. There was also a return to the flat-top valve cups by some teams as better top-end oiling and the end of running on dusty dirt tracks coincided with a renewed need for lighter spring pressures and higher rpms. There were some experiments with sodium-filled valves, which can cool the valve head several hundred degrees, but Goossen said Drake never needed to use them in its engines. The Fords had a serious exhaust valve problem, but the Offys did not unless they were run too lean.

Driver Mark Donohue took the Offy back to Victory Lane at Indy in 1972 in this Penske McLaren. *Mark Dees collection/Indianapolis Motor Speedway*

Rod lengths varied slightly for Gurney, Bignotti, and Jud Phillips, with Bignotti's the shortest at 5.5 inches, 2 1/2 inches shorter than they had been in the old 270 Offy. Rod bolts and nuts were a problem for a time. In Miller's day they had been secured by cotter pins. Fred Offenhauser used clinch nuts, but Goossen found that the best solution was a plain nut, tightened until the bolt stretched 0.005 inches, effectively clamping it tightly enough to endure all the vibration the turbo engine could put out. For a while Drake bought rod bolts from SPS, but he found that the supplier was not holding dimensions to tight enough tolerances—within 0.0005 inches.

The 159-cubic-inch turbo Offy developed more horsepower per cubic inch—about 7.5—than any other engine the world had then produced. Turbos can actually put out almost unlimited power. Exhaust flow goes up with engine speed and so, therefore, boost pressure. John Drake related that while John Miller was running a turbo Offy on the All-American Racers dyno the waste gate froze shut. The engine's revs jumped to 10,200, and the engine put out nearly 1,400 horsepower—about that of the Merlin engine used in the World War II P-51 Mustang fighter. Even that run did not reach the Offy's absolute torque peak. "I don't know how long it could have run that way," Drake said. They cut the engine after about a minute and a half, so fearsome was the power it was putting out. By 1972 the turbo Offy was producing prodigious gobs of power on the track; perhaps 1,200 horsepower. The Offy was running 115 inches of boost in qualifying trim and 85 inches in the race.

At the time, John Drake said, Drake Engineering was building as many as 20 turbo engines a year. They also produced between 400 and 500 replacement blocks during the decade—a measure of the casualty rate from high boost pressures and nitro for qualifying.

Boost continued to climb and there were continuous problems to be solved at high turbo pressures. One was that during caution flag periods one of the injector stages might shut down, lean out the fuel mixture, and burn a piston. However, with careful testing and development Drake was meeting the challenges. If the fuel and boost rules had remained unchanged, the Offy might well have remained competitive for years. Indeed, without fuel limits the Cosworth challenge might never have appeared at the Speedway.

Johnny Rutherford's 198.413-mile-per-hour qualifying run in the McLaren M-16C turbo Offy in 1973, with essentially unlimited boost (turning one lap at 199.071 miles per hour), stands as the all-time high for the Miller-Offy-Drake engine. That year saw the Offy win 13 other championship races, but never again would the old four-banger do so well.

Engine man Marvin Clifton, right, of Pendleton, Indiana, and Bob Sowle, left, of Indianapolis, prepare the turbo Drake-Offy in Rolla Vollstedt's A. J. Watson-built chassis. Note the popoff valve on top of the intake plenum. This car was a copy of a Vollstedt version of the March that Leader Cards ran with Offy power for Billy Vukovich in 1980. Rusty Schmidt was not able to pass his driver's test in time to qualify the car in 1982. Sowle and Clifton were longtime volunteers on Vollstedt's crew.
Mark Dees collection

CHAPTER THIRTEEN

Final Defeat

In 1973 the Arab oil embargo struck the Western world, and there was an outcry for fuel economy. A national speed limit of 55 miles per hour was enacted, and there was virtual panic at gas stations. Some in Washington and the media called for a halt to auto racing (ridiculous, in view of the fact that the racers were burning not gasoline but methanol, which could be made from renewable resources) and sponsors recoiled, cutting or eliminating racing budgets. The political scare talk and fear about Indy speeds nearing 200 miles per hour led to limits on boost and fuel consumption. Overnight the new rules shifted the balance to the V-8 by about 50 horsepower.

Fuel Crisis Slows All Racing

In 1974 Indianapolis entries dropped to 68 and a year later to 59, the fewest in five years. The loss of sponsorship money hit Drake hard, as orders for new four-cylinder engines and even parts dried up and the company was forced to suspend production for several months, severely restricting the Drakes' ability to develop a new engine. New USAC rules in 1974 to "conserve scarce resources," reduced the boost limit to 80 inches of mercury, about 25 psi above atmospheric pressure, limited fuel tanks to 40 gallons and consumption to 280 gallons of methanol or 1.8 miles per gallon. (Methanol has a much lower heat content per gallon than gasoline, thus nearly twice as much must be burned per mile driven.) Those rules dropped the pole speed to 191.623 miles by Foyt's turbo—nearly seven miles per hour slower than the previous year. Despite the restrictions, 1974 was another Offy year, as Rutherford won the 500 and 11 of the first 12 finishers were turbo-Offys.

In 1974 to beat the boost rule, George Bignotti, always a thinker, put an oversize TH-08 turbo on Wally Dallenbach's Eagle Offy. The idea was to put out more volume than the mandatory popoff valve could pass. After much discussion Bignotti was allowed to use the big turbo on Dallenbach's and Gordon Johncock's Patrick cars to qualify, and he was required to keep them on for the race as well. Dallenbach burned a piston early in the race and Johncock finished fourth.

The fuel restrictions hit the Offy far harder than the Ford/Foyt V-8. In order to keep pistons in the Offy from melting, mechanics had been running the engines rich. At 1.6 miles per gallon, they were burning about 312 gallons of alcohol in 500 miles, well within the 1972 USAC 350-gallon limit. With the new fuel rule, however, they were running dangerously lean. They needed something as effective as Fred Offenhauser's 1935 trick of turning off the idle jets in Kelly Petillo's Offy!

Lean mixtures and high rpms led to more durability problems. Better cooling and oiling had to be designed, with oil pressure pushed to 150 psi, double that of the old Offy. Centrifugal force in the oil passages in the crankshafts and cams was holding the lubricant away from the bearings, requiring a

Looking at these two engines—the 255 in 1946 in Jimmy Jackson's old Miller chassis, the other a 159 turbo Offy in Sheldon Kinser's Watson rear-engine car in 1978—can you believe that under all that intake hardware they began, essentially, as a 220 Offy, the same machine that grew from Harry Miller's marine engine of 1926? *Indianapolis Motor Speedway/Mark Dees collection*

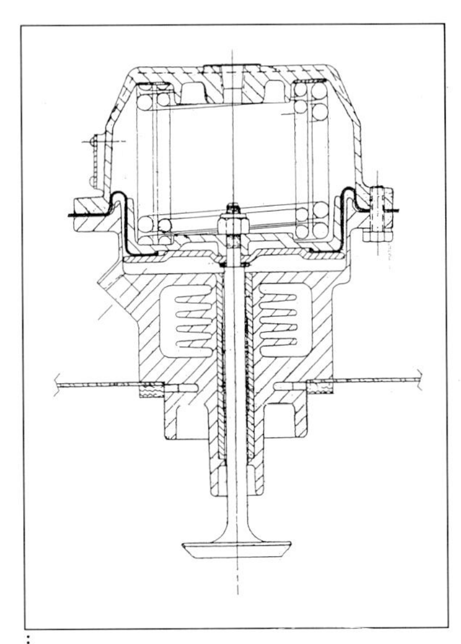

A manifold pressure valve, similar to the notorious popoff valve. Adapted from an U.S. Air Force jet engine pressure-relief valve, these units were used to enforce the boost limits at Indianapolis and wherever else racing officialdom imposed such rules. They were designed to allow pressure in the intake tract to be vented at a predetermined level via a spring-loaded outlet. As with many mechanical devices, early versions were unreliable, and even the best do not always release at precisely the same point. Use of the popoff valve to limit boost doomed the Drake-Offenhauser four-cylinder engine. *Kenneth Walton collection*

Two Offy crankcases. The one on the right is the old "notched" style that allows the bearing webs to be assembled to the crank and lowered into the case. The ears on the webs can be slid through the notches and rotated to line up the retaining bolts. The case on the left has no notches. The intermediate webs must be inserted through the access holes in the side of the case. This is done while the case is hot enough that the aluminum has expanded so the webs will seat. *Kenneth Walton collection*

redesign. The external, cam-driven, oil pumps being used on some engines were cavitating because of vibration harmonics from the valve-trains. Cam oiling had to be changed from internal in the shaft to a pressure spray inside the housing in order to be reliable at 10,000 rpm. Fuel pumps also cavitated and had to be moved. Cooling at the exhaust ports was revised with an external water manifold.

Art Sparks, who since the 1920s had been a thinker and innovator, was still producing ForgedTrue aluminum racing pistons. In Germany, where he was having pistons made for him by the Mahle Company, he met European engine designers who brought him up to date on their ideas, which held that shallow valve angles allowed for a more compact, more efficient combustion chamber than the Offy's 72-degree valve-included-angle. Bignotti and the Meyers had done intensive flow-bench work on the turbo Offy and also proved to themselves that the old 72-degree valve-included-angle was obsolete. A shallower angle dictates nearly flat-top pistons, giving better intake flow and flame-travel in the cylinder. Bignotti also worked directly with Goossen after his own heavier (9/16-inch versus 1/2 inch) diameter rod bolts gave trouble. Goossen said it was mandatory to make the bolts out of the highest quality 4340 vacuum-melt steel machined to aircraft tolerances. Bignotti added that even then the Drake bolts stretched too much under heavy power output and did not return to their original length. He had specials made by Delco Grinding in Indianapolis.

Keith Duckworth and Mike Costin at Cosworth Engineering in England, had already given their four-cam V-8, the Cosworth FVA, a 40-degree valve-included angle, and followed it with the double four-valve with a valve angle of 32 degrees. The Cosworths quickly dominated European Grand Prix racing. In fact, the Cosworth in a Lotus 49 chassis took the pole position at Zandvoort, Holland, its first time out, won the race, and took every pole on the Formula One circuit for the next year. Duckworth claimed then, and since, that his shallow valve-included angle was a new benchmark, equal almost to the invention of the twin-cam.

Meanwhile, in Los Angeles, the next Offy engine was, according to Bignotti, his brainchild. Bignotti, who was frequently at the Daimler Avenue plant to consult on a revised turbo-Offy, gave Goossen and Sparks a great deal of advice and input. Sparks added his word on pistons and the benefit of his soundings around Europe. During the winter of 1973–1974 Leo drew plans for the new version of the Offy christened the Drake-Goossen-Sparks (Bignotti says he chose the name to give credit to Drake for machine work, Goossen for drafting, and Sparks for the pistons). It was the most major change in the Miller-Offenhauser engine in 40 years, with a valve angle of 42 degrees and intake valves and ports made smaller for better velocity. The timing gears were also re-designed and accessory drives eliminated. The D-G-S had a 4.281x2.750 inch bore and stroke and displaced 158.3 cubic inches.

"It was an amazing engine," Bignotti remembered in 1996, "once we got the patternmaker to correct the pattern. He left out the hole [cooling passage] between the exhaust valves. I had Sonny cut one up and even went out to Drake's to check the print. Goossen had it on the print, and he and I went to the patternmaker. Once that was corrected, there weren't many failures, but the fuel (restrictions) and boost (limit) to eighty inches took away its potential."

In September 1974, Bignotti and Sonny built a turbo Offy for USAC Silver Crown dirt racing, more for the fun of it than for anything else. Jackie Howerton, a sprint car driver, had fast time in the car at the Hoosier Hundred, setting a new track record. He led the race from the pole to the checkered flag while Bignotti rubbed his hands in the infield. Before the race was over USAC voted to ban turbos from the dirt tracks.

Just as the D-G-S engine was being completed Goossen fell ill. At the age of 82 he had been working four days a week, living in a motel near the plant in Santa Ana to shorten the drive from his Los Angeles home. An amazing designer of vast influence, he had told colleagues a few months earlier, "It's fun to meet the challenges." Goossen worked at Drake Engineering until 10 days before he died on December 4, 1974. Over 53 years at his drawing board he had designed 25 competition engines and 12 racing cars. With his passing three pillars of the Offy tradition, Fred, Dale, and Leo, had gone in just three years. Lou Meyer, Sr., would outlive them by two more decades.

At 80 inches of boost, the D-G-S gave 150 more horses than the older turbo Offy, developing 800 horsepower at 9,000 rpm under the USAC 75-inch limit. While the D-

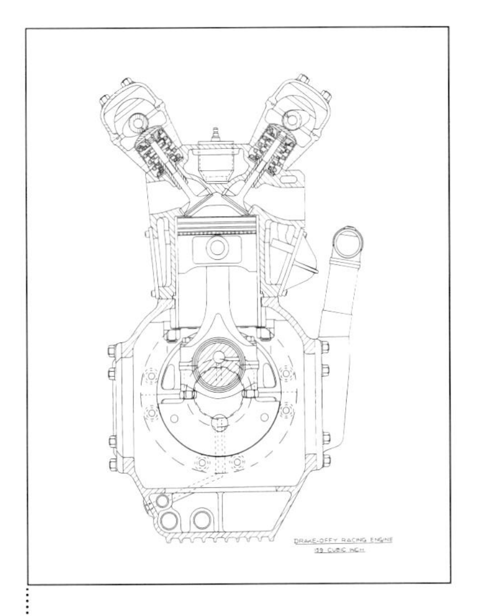

Section drawing of the late turbo-Offy with a low-tower block, asymmetrical head, and no notches in the crankcase bulkheads. *Kenneth Walton collection*

Late engine with Drake-Offy cast into the cam covers. By this time a Mallory or Spalding ignition was driven off the half-time gear rather than the old magneto mount. *Kenneth Walton collection*

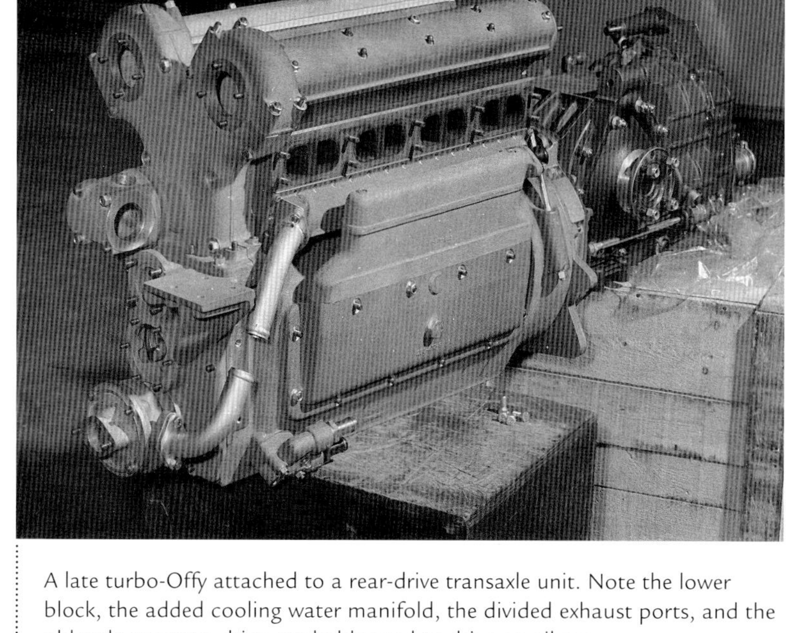

A late turbo-Offy attached to a rear-drive transaxle unit. Note the lower block, the added cooling water manifold, the divided exhaust ports, and the old-style magneto drive, probably used to drive an oil scavenge pump. *Gordon Schroeder collection*

G-S engine was strong, as with all new designs, it suffered teething problems. Drake built 15 D-G-S engines in 1974–1975 with financial help from Patrick under the usual agreement that gave him a year's exclusive use of the design.

In order to have engines for other customers Drake had to come up with his own updated Offy for 1975. After Goossen died, Hank "the Crank" Bechtloff (who was Drake's outside crankshaft supplier) suggested that John Drake talk to engineer Hans Hermann about taking over as draftsman and engineer. It was not possible to *replace* Goossen, who had been present at the creation of every important American racing engine since the Miller 183 of 1921, but Drake needed someone to work up the Drake-Offy and Hermann was an experienced draftsman and designer.

Not only was he called upon to replace a legend, the young Hermann was also thrown into a shop filled with older men, some of whom had worked with the engines for 50 years. There was a clash of cultures. Sobraske and other old hands did not easily accept Hermann's foreign education and European background. Despite that, Hermann completed the work Goossen had begun on the design for the Drake-Offy engine, reduced the valve angle to 38 degrees and finished Leo's redesign of the port layout. Pistons were flat-topped and the valves were made even smaller than on the D-G-S, though many of the D-G-S dimensions were carried over. On the dyno, the Drake-Offy, which had its name cast into the cam covers, appeared to have a small edge over the D-G-S. Complete engines sold for $20,000, and blocks and valve gear could be bought as kits to put on existing turbo cases.

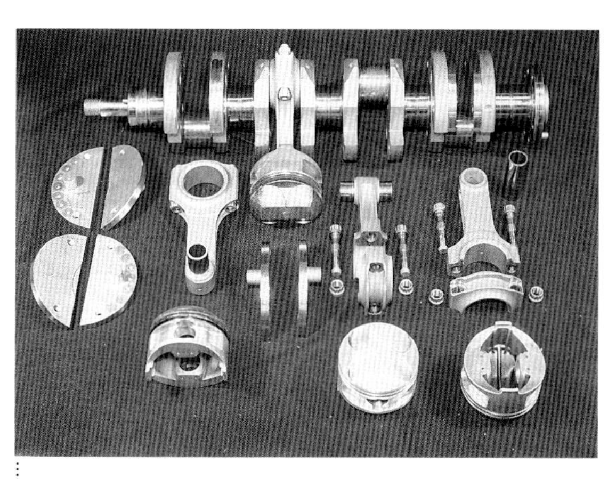

Late turbo Offy crankshaft with Carillo rods, Sparks pistons, and bronze counterweights. *Kenneth Walton collection*

The Drake engine put the Offy back on top again at Indianapolis in 1975. In a banzai effort, Foyt took the pole with one of his V-8s at 193.976 miles per hour, but Bobby Unser won the race in a Gurney Offy. Gordon Johncock qualified a D-G-S second-fastest at 191.652 miles per hour, but went out with ignition failure. Wally Dallenbach put his D-G-S in the field at 190.648 miles per hour and finished ninth. Twenty-nine of the 33 starters, or 88 percent of the field were Offys, Drake-Offys, or D-G-Ss. John Miller said that in 1975 Gurney's turbo Offys produced about 870 horsepower at 9,000 rpm at 75 inches of boost. With no boost limit for qualifying they turned out 1,200 horsepower at 10,000 rpm.

The boost and fuel limits continued to hound the Offys. USAC officials cut the allowable boost again for 1976. That move dropped the qualifying speeds significantly, with Johnny Rutherford taking the pole in 1976 at 188.957, some 5 miles per hour slower than Foyt's 1975 speed.

Ford Casts Another Shadow Over the Offy

The first Cosworth DFX V-8 appeared at Indianapolis in 1975, brought there by Vel Miletich and Parnelli Jones. Miletich was a wealthy Ford dealer from Torrance, California, and with the Ford Motor Company's resources, he began to develop the unblown Grand Prix engine into a turbo powerhouse for U.S. racing. The engine had been financed by Ford in Britain as a Formula 1 competitor, and until Jones took it in hand, no one had thought of trying it at Indianapolis. Al Unser, Sr., and Mario Andretti took the Vels-Parnelli Cosworth

The Cosworth DFS V-8. It was the DFX, a slightly earlier version of the Ford-financed Grand Prix engine that, with the help of the rules, finally defeated the mighty Offy. *Author*

car out for trials at Indianapolis in 1975 but it did not make the race.

In 1976 the Cosworth shadow grew larger. The new turbo V-8 made the show at Indianapolis in 1976 and with one Al Unser, Sr., finished seventh. A Ford-Cosworth scored its first American Championship victory at the Pocono 500 on June 27, 1976. In that year 38-degree valve angle Drake-Offy engines would win six USAC races, the 44-degree D-G-S three, and the new Ford- Cosworth V-8 three.

By 1977 the Cosworth was ready. It had timed fuel injection for better mileage, better intake ports, better cooling, and a smaller aerodynamic profile than the Ford/Foyt four-cam. To deal with its lower torque output the Cosworth was given a four-speed gearbox. Able to run all day at 10,500 rpm, it had a 50 horsepower advantage over the Foyt and 100 horsepower over the Offy at 80 inches of boost. At the 48-inch limit in effect in 1977 its advantage was even greater. The Offy might have equaled it at 110 inches if that had been allowed, but under the rules the Cosworth was clearly stronger. The fuel efficiency of the new Ford was already apparent, and USAC officials were squeezing the boost regulations tighter and tighter finally to 42 inches (22 psi). Under those limits the four-cylinder Offy was in serious trouble.

Johnny Rutherford won the 1976 Indianapolis race with a Drake-Offy in a McLaren chassis. Foyt was second with one of his four-cam V-8s, and Patrick's two D-G-S-powered entries took third and fourth with Johncock and Dallenbach driving. Eighty-five percent of the starters were Offys of one stripe or another. Rutherford drove a Drake-Offy-powered McLaren to win the Texas 200 on October 31, 1976, in what would be the last championship victory for the old engine in Drake-Offy form.

Patrick's D-G-S Wildcats took three races on the Championship Trail in 1977: Wally Dallenbach at Trenton in May, then Gordon Johncock at Michigan in July and at Phoenix in October.

The 1978 season started off well for Patrick's D-G-S team as Johncock took the Phoenix 150 in March and the Trenton 200 in April. At the Speedway in May, however, there were 10 Ford-Cosworths. Lindsay Hopkins put a Drake-Offy in a Lightning chassis and with it Johnnie Parsons finished 10th, but under the tightened boost restrictions the Drake and D-G-S efforts were not enough. Though Johncock and Steve Krisiloff finished third and fourth in their D-G-S Wildcats, Al Unser, Sr., would win his third Indianapolis 500 in a Ford-Cosworth with Tom Sneva right behind him in another Ford.

The Drake V-8

At Drake Engineering, John Drake and Hans Hermann were working on their own Indy V-8. Hermann saw it as the basis for a modular series of engines, using one bank of the Vee as a sprint or midget engine of varied displacements. With Drake trying desperately to survive, John turned all the shop's efforts to building the new engine and stopped production of most parts for the earlier Offys—the midgets, 220s, and four-cylinder championship engines—making it difficult for Offy teams anywhere to keep their engines running.

Pat Patrick and his friends, including Leader Card's A.J. Watson, put down deposits to help finance building of parts for 20 DT-160 V-8s, the first of which ran late in 1978. Drake assembled a dozen race-ready engines at a price of $30,000 apiece. Watson and Bignotti got two each for testing, but the engine was hampered by persistent breakage of its Uniroyal timing belts. When a belt broke the pistons would hit the valves, wiping out the top end of the engine. Bignotti and Sonny Meyer went to the trouble of building an Offy-style gear train to drive the cams. After a year of belt failures—one even broke in the pits during starting—Bignotti finally persuaded Goodyear, their tire supplier, to build a belt that would hold up. "It wasn't easy," George noted later. Drake went to the Goodyear belt, but the wasted time had hurt.

Bignotti, while trying to help with the Drake V-8 was not pleased with it. He recalled going to Drake's shop with Lou Meyer to look at the engine before the first one was put together. "I was shocked to see the crank, as they had built a small crankcase and the crankshaft diameter was too small—couldn't be balanced. I told them I had experienced the same thing years earlier trying to balance a Ford V-8-60 crank for a midget—it could not be balanced. We put mercury weights on it to help, but the Drake V-8 kept knocking out the main bearings, which is why we had to give up on that engine."

Still, in 1979, despite all the problems, success for the Drake V-8 seemed to be within reach. It was finishing races, if not yet winning, but Offenhauser and Meyer-Drake had never been able to put enough money aside for engine development which for years had been done largely by the racers. After 1965 Drake Engineering had had its hands full trying to keep the big four-cylinder Offy alive on a veritable shoestring, and there was neither the time nor the money needed to develop an entirely new and highly sophisticated engine. Still, as fast as events were moving, Drake was giving it a good try.

"The Drake V-8 was built like an Offy," John Drake said. "If anything, we built the bottom end too heavy in order to be strong. The Cosworth couldn't get the horsepower we could, and its bottom end was weaker. Like the Ford it couldn't survive at high boost levels. We built ours that way [strong] because we expected the rules on boost would be relaxed after the oil embargo was lifted."

Drake and Hermann were sitting in the restaurant at the Speedway Motel in 1976 when Keith Duckworth came over to their table and suggested that they might want to handle sales and servicing of the Cosworth engine. John and Hans had just seen Johnny Rutherford win the race with a turbo-Offy. If the boost and fuel limits were lifted they expected to be in the engine business for quite a while. They told Duckworth they weren't interested.

Later Drake thought they might have made it if they had been able to sell the four-cylinder engines for a year or two longer to support the V-8 development, but it was not to be. The boost limits were not lifted, at least partly because many owners had already invested in Cosworths. Some of Drake's Offy customers were at odds with the officials, and to make things even more difficult, the race community was divided between USAC and CART.

Finally, in 1979, the money ran out. There were no more teams willing to put cash into the Drake V-8 when the Cosworth was readily available. The effort to keep the engine alive did not appear to be paying off—it had no edge on the competition. When there was no money in Drake's till to continue work on the V-8, John Drake closed it down. As an epitaph on the efforts to replace the old Offy, Lou Meyer told the author: "We wanted to develop a new engine, perhaps a V-8, as early as

1957, but the rules at the Speedway were always changing. We had to wait to see what their decision was going to be. We did not have the money or the time to undertake something of that size without knowing we could use it."

Sonny Meyer and George Bignotti went on to build a flat six, with Mahle pistons from Sparks. Bignotti had it on his dyno making the first full-power run when Kay Bignotti came in and told them USAC had lowered the boost to 48 inches. They had to scrap it.

"We built it to run unlimited boost, "George said. " At 10,000 rpm it was smooth as glass, producing 800 horsepower at eighty inches of boost. We didn't even get to put it in a car as it was designed to run with eighty to ninety inches. We had built a six so as to meet the previous rule change on the fuel limit." The engines went to the Speedway Museum.

Offy at the End of the Road

A.J. Watson's Drake V-8 still sits in his Indianapolis shop. He entered one at the Speedway for Leader Cards, in 1979 but George Snider was not able to qualify it.

There were 12 Offys in the 1979 field at Indianapolis plus Herb Wysard's D-G-S. Twenty-two other Offys failed to find the speed to qualify. Twenty of the 33 cars that qualified were Cosworth-Ford powered. The four-cam Foyt was already history and A. J. was driving a Cosworth. Without support from Drake, the four-cylinder engine could only stagger on briefly. In 1980 Offys were still a third of the entries but only three qualified. The last Offy to finish well at Indianapolis was Gary Bettenhausen's Armstrong Mould car, a rebuilt Bignotti-Patrick Wildcat wrenched by Paul Leffler, which placed third, amazing under its handicaps.

The last Offy: Mark Alderson waits for a chance to take his trial at Indianapolis in 1983 in Rolla Vollstedt's #17 turbo-Offy. Though Alderson passed his driver's test and was running practice laps over 190 miles per hour—fast enough to make the race—time ran out. *Indianapolis Motor Speedway*

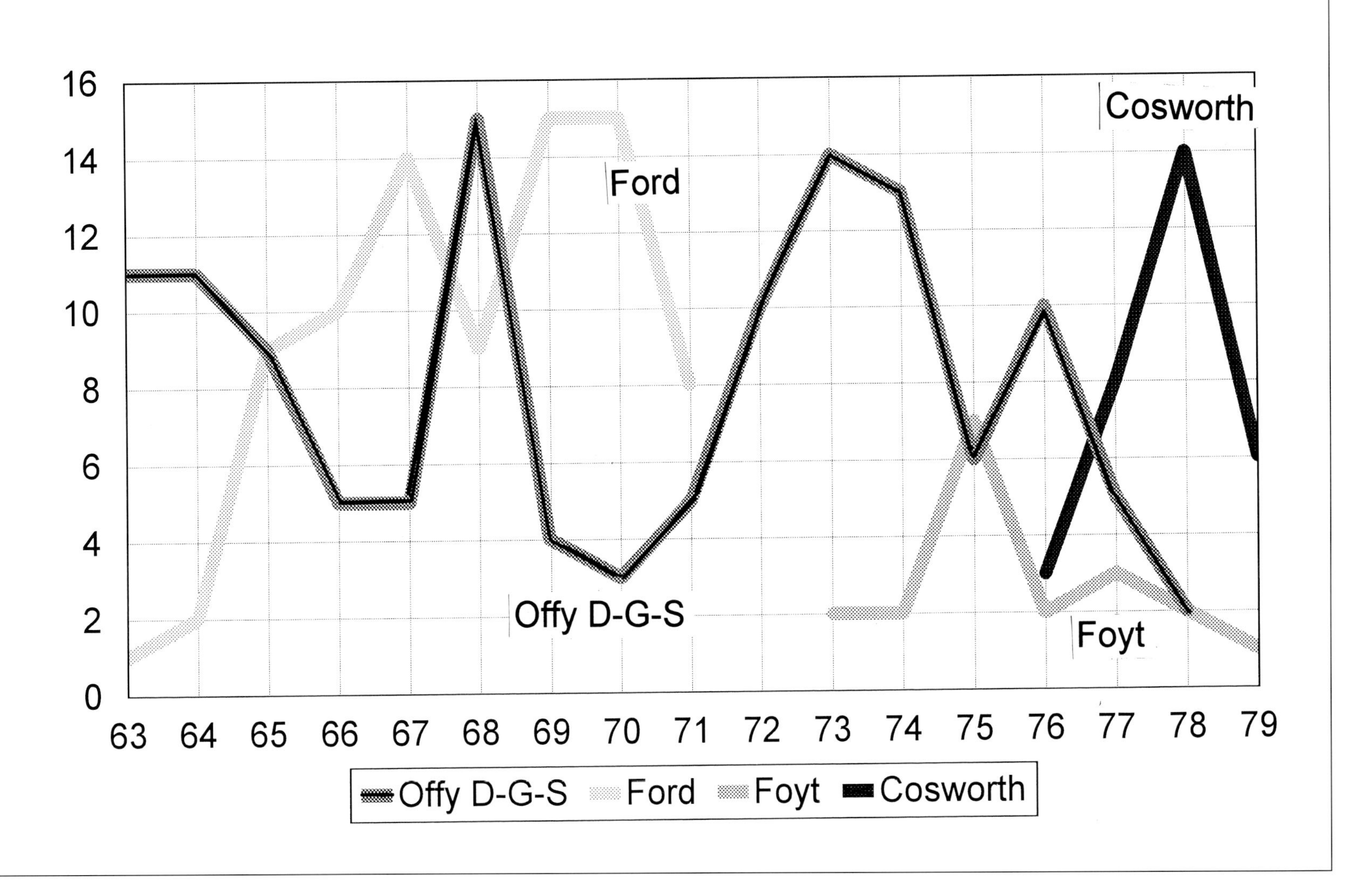

This chart shows the victories by Offenhauser, Ford four-cam, Foyt, and Cosworth engines from 1963 through 1979. While Ford had dramatic success from 1964 through 1966, it failed to realize how well Drake and its friends Porter, Jones, and the rest were doing at turbocharging the Offy. In 1968, the Offy won at Indianapolis and took 14 other Championships races as the race teams deserted Ford. George Bignotti's turbocharging of the V-8 paid off in 1969 and 1970, but then Ford dropped it. When A. J. Foyt bought the engine, only he won races with it. Increasingly restrictive boost and fuel limits hurt the Offy at the end of the 1970s, and Drake's inability to develop a fully competitive V-8 of its own allowed the more sophisticated Ford-backed Cosworth engine to take over American racing. (The decline in the number of Cosworth victories in 1979 reflects the fact that there were only seven Championship races that years.) *Author, Graphics by Tyler*

In July 1980, Bignotti and Sonny Meyer sold the race car shop in Indianapolis to Patrick Racing. On the verge of retiring, Bignotti, instead, became a car owner, mating Cosworth engines to March chassis. Three years later, Tom Sneva won the Indianapolis 500, marking Bignotti's seventh victory there as a mechanic and owner. Sneva's win at Milwaukee a week later was Bignotti's 87th Cart/USAC victory. At the end of the season he sold his interest in the team. In semiretirement he served as a consultant to Mobil Oil and designed special cams, pistons, and valves for selected race teams.

In qualifying in 1981 the last Offy took a checkered flag at Indianapolis: Jerry Sneva turned four laps at 187.784 miles per hour in Rolla Vollstedt's Escort Radar Detector car. Though that speed would have put him in the middle of the eighth row, Vollstedt and Sneva got caught in what Rollstedt felt was a USAC/CART crossfire. According to Rolla the car had a small water leak and they put a catch can under the radiator. Steve Krisiloff objected to something about the car when it was on pit row ready for its qualifying run, but Tom Binford, the steward, let Sneva go out to qualify. After his run Sneva stopped at the head of the pit lane, his engine steaming, and a mechanic went to the car to check it. Jerry Karl protested that, suspiciously, Sneva qualified faster than he had been going in practice. The USAC officials could find nothing amiss when they inspected the car, but ruled that it was likely that something had been wedged in the popoff valve and the last Offy to take a starter's flag at Indy was disqualified. It was the first time in 46 years that an Offy did not race at the Speedway and the first year since 1929 that there was no four-cylinder car in the field.

In 1982, five Offys were entered at Indianapolis. John Martin spun in practice and Jan Sneva crashed. Rusty Schmidt did not complete his driver's test.

In 1983, only Vollstedt entered an Offy at the Speedway, and although Mark Alderson passed his rookie test in Vollstedt's #17 car and was running fast enough to make the race—over 190 miles per hour—rain cut short the final trials and Vollstedt did not get the car into the qualifying line in time. It was Rolla's last year at Indianapolis, and no one since has entered an Offy, a Drake, or a D-G-S in the world's greatest race.

Thus the mighty Offy passed into history and the Offy story ends; a $35,000 turbocharged, 1,200-horsepower Indianapolis powerplant, 57 years after its beginning in 1926 as a relatively cheap 125-horsepower racing engine for speedboats.

Epitaph for the Offenhauser

In 1971 Ethel Offenhauser died. Fred was left to care for his garden, play cards with his old racing friends, and contemplate the fortunes of the engine that he had nurtured and preserved. He never meddled in Meyer & Drake's business, but he did go down to the Drakes' new plant in Santa Ana to look over the new turbo Offy that still bore his name. On August 17, 1973, ten weeks after Rutherford set a new pole record at Indianapolis with a turbocharged Offenhauser engine, Fred died in his sleep at his home on 78th Street. The money he made in his shop in the Depression, during the war, and from selling the business to Meyer and Drake had supported him and Ethel for 27 years and his estate had grown to more than $500,000. He was buried at the Isle of Rest Mausoleum in Inglewood, California.

The players in our story have been many—builders, drivers, car owners, mechanics, machinists—from Harry Miller, the artist in steel and aluminum to Jerry Sneva, the last Offy driver to take a starter's flag at Indianapolis. Five men played large roles in this story. Harry Miller created the Miller engines out of his imagination. His were the sweeping ideas; the marvelous innovations sprang from his mind. His was the font of imagination, but in the end, uncontrolled and no longer disciplined, his visions trailed away and his greatness became futility.

Leo Goossen was the acolyte, the brilliant but unassuming draftsman and engineer who turned the Miller visions into blueprints from which mere men could construct the Miller engines. After Miller failed, Goossen waited patiently for fate to call upon him, drawing plans for two dozen engines to his patron's desires, engines sometimes as bizarre as Lance Reventlow's desmodromic Scarab, and some as strong and sound as Herb Porter's turbocharged Offy.

Fred Offenhauser was the practical man who kept Miller from soaring so high with his ideas that he crashed to earth. Fred was pragmatic enough to pick up ideas like the Duesenberg crank, the Hall cams, and the Ballot valve cups, and strong enough to persuade Miller of their value. He was tough enough to make what was left in the wreckage of Miller's business into a persistent, plain, engine that won races.

Dale Drake was a romantic who gave up flying when government bureaucrats began to judge his skills in the air. Because of his love of racing, Drake bought Offenhauser's business when Fred, ever-practical, was ready to leave it. Drake was the one who came to love the Offy the most, and 20 years later when it was as much his engine as Offenhauser's, to cast "Drake-Offy" into its cam covers. He was the man who pushed the engine to the heights at Indianapolis after it had been defeated by the multibillion dollar Ford Motor company and rescue it for a time from the dustbin of history.

Lou Meyer was a businessman who built engines because it was a good business. He continued in the 1930s to call them "Millers," after Offenhauser was making them and "ol' air compressors" when he himself turned them out. Meyer was never romantic about the Offy, and he never thought it necessary to put his name on them. When practical considerations suggested he sell to Ford, Lou did, saying it was time to move on. He was a driver, with a driver's unsentimentality about the equipment. His fame came as the winner of three races at Indianapolis more than as the builder of other men's engines.

Harry, Dale, Fred, and Leo had passed over. The Offy went in its turn, its time past. The old world had changed and a new world ruled the speedways.

John Drake still operates an engine shop in Mission Viejo, California, working on smaller-class sports car engines and producing a high-performance Chevy small-block water pump. He sold off the heavy machinery at the Daimler Avenue plant in Santa Ana and junked most of the tooling, made for obsolete equipment, not adaptable to modern computer control. For a time the shop produced parts for atomic weapons. Today he still has most of the patterns for midget Offys and makes a few of those parts.

The year 1983 was half a century after Harry Miller's bankruptcy and the 40th anniversary of his lonely death in Detroit. Dale Drake, Fred Offenhauser, and Leo Goossen carried the Miller and Offenhauser torch far longer than any other in the history of the internal combustion engine. The structure which Ernest Henry and *les Charlatans* had conceived and Miller, Offenhauser, and Goossen had so lovingly polished and perfected no longer ruled the race tracks of the nation and the world, but the design had begun to envelop a far wider universe as the great auto manufacturers adopted the elegant twin-cam architecture for light and efficient passenger car engines.

And still today on a few race tracks a vintage Miller or Offy ventures forth to growl into the lonely wind. It is much like the sound that old warriors say they hear on the gentle swales of Gettysburg or the Far Shore where the sea washes Omaha Beach. Somewhere Harry, Fred, and Leo are listening, listening for the rattle of a loose bearing or the click of a worn valve that will send them back to the old shop to once more smooth a line on a drawing or tighten a tolerance on the immortal Offy.

Bruce Johnston in his vintage Offy-equipped Garnant-Miller lines up for a run through the measured mile at El Mirage Dry Lake in 1985. El Mirage and Bonneville are the last places on earth where an Offy can be run flat-out for a competitive speed record.
Mark Dees/Author collection

Offy Today

By 1983 the Offys were defeated in professional racing. The fuel and boost restrictions at Indianapolis handicapped them far more than their V-8 competition. On the midget and sprint car tracks, the rules allowed engines adapted from stock blocks as much as 20 percent more displacement. The Offy may have been obsolete in some eyes, but if they had competed on an even basis they would certainly have lasted years longer.

So shed a tear for Harry, Fred, Leo, Lou and Dale. As with the iron men and wooden ships of centuries past, "The world shall not see their like again," (inscription on the clipper ship Cutty Sark, enshrined at Greenwich, England) nor hear the powerful old four-bangers growling down the dirt miles of Syracuse, Springfield, Langhorne, or Du Quoin.

But the Offys do still run on a score of tracks even as the end of the 20th century draws near, and they will undoubtedly run into the 21st. There are a dozen old-timer groups from coast to coast that still drive these marvelous cars. The Western Racing Association has a schedule that runs the cars from Phoenix, Arizona, to Calistoga, California. The IMCA Old Timers runs a few shows in Minnesota. The Antique Auto Racing Association displays the old sprinters and midgets (not all Offys of course) on half-mile fairground dirt tracks in Ohio. The Williams Grove Old Timers holds a show of old race cars on that famous track occasionally, and it has built a fine new racing museum and runs its own events on the rebuilt Latimore Valley, Pennsylvania, track four times a season.

Even the most famous drivers such as Mario Andretti, center, get a kick out of doing a few laps in a famous old car. Here, in 1990 at Nazareth, Pennsylvania, he prepares to drive Richard Maloumian's Gilmore Miller, which was raced to second place at Indianapolis in 1930 by Shorty Cantlon. *Author Collection*

The Atlantic Coast and the Bay State Old Timers run gatherings of the cars several times a summer on the paved midget tracks in New England. Bob Bahre and Vic Yerardi mount a classy show of vintage oval-track cars, motorcycles, and sports cars during a four-day event each summer at New Hampshire International Speedway. The two-day event for open-wheel cars on that fine paved mile is almost the last place in the world where Watson roadsters and other Indianapolis cars of similar vintage can strut their stuff.

Dave Uihlein, Chuck Davis, and the Miller Club have begun an annual gathering of pre-World War II championship cars, mostly Millers and Offys, on the repaved Milwaukee Mile where the older cars are displayed at speed and in all their glory.

In New Jersey, the National Old Timers have a racing museum at the Flemington Speedway and run monthly shows at that historic, though now-paved, track. Flemington's days are numbered but the museum will be moved and running of the old cars will continue at another New Jersey track. In Florida, the Daytona Antique Auto Racers run fall and winter shows at Zephyr Hills.

The Antique Automobile Club of America displays racing cars at its meets around the country, highlighted by the National Fall Meet at Hershey, Pennsylvania, each October. The old racing cars are run in the Hershey Stadium on Friday during the show.

Oval-track cars run occasionally with sports car vintage groups at places such as Philadelphia, Pittsburgh, Meadow Brook, Pocono, Willow Springs, Road America, Savannah, and many others. In the West, Steve and Debbie Earle's Monterey Historics at Laguna Seca is a prime event while in the East it is the Vintage Sports Car Club of America's Fall Festival at Lime Rock, Connecticut, that attracts a large collection of old race cars.

Vintage is not racing, strictly speaking, but the old Offenhausers can be run quickly enough to bring pangs of nostalgia to those who remember the growl of the Offy in years past. The sound and the smell and the dust and the feel is there. Quite a few of the drivers seen at vintage meets are retired professionals like Johnny Kay, Al Swenson, and Rodger Ward. Some of the drivers, though never professionals, get around the tracks pretty well. Author Mark Dees pounds the western pavements with a Dreyer big car carrying a mighty 318. Brian Johnson turns fast laps on the road course at Lime Rock, Connecticut, and drivers like Bill Cox and Marty Himes can bring back the feel of the 1940s at any vintage meet.

The Little Race Car that Could

I have run with the vintage groups since I found my 1948 Offenhauser-powered Kurtis midget in a barn in 1978. After three years of fitful restoration,

Rodger Ward, two-time Indianapolis winner, occasionally relives his glory days as here with the Ken Brenn #24 Kurtis Offy, (now red instead of its original blue) at Lime Rock, Connecticut, in 1989 at the reenactment of Ward's 1959 Formula Libre victory. *Author collection*

completed by Jim Barclay of Lebanon, New Jersey, my ex-Roy Hagedorn, ex-Tassi Vatis #9 has participated in more than 100 such gatherings from New Hampshire to Virginia; Bridgehampton, Long Island, to Dover, Ohio.

In the late 1940s and early 1950s, the Vatis #9 was driven to AAA feature victories by Ray Janelle, Tony Bonadies, and Johnny Kay. In ARDC, under Swede Anderson's wrenches, Bobby Boone had his best year in the car. We restored the car as it ran for Tassi in 1951–1956. When we took it to shows the inevitable question was: "How fast will it go?" The records showed that Rex Mays drove a similar Offenhauser-powered midget more than 147 miles per hour on the Bonneville Salt Flats on September 19, 1949. The question nagged: "How fast could *we* go?"

The late Roger Huntington, in a magazine article titled "The World's Fastest Midget Is Powered by an Offy!" described the effort we made at Bonneville to find out. Huntington's article continued: "Loaded with lead and powered by an ancient Offy, a legit antique is the fastest midget there is." The Vatis #9 is probably not faster than modern midgets powered by 250-horsepower Pontiac or Cosworth engines, but we went 156.905 miles per hour, broke Mays record at Bonneville, and as of early 1996 no midget has been timed faster on a one-mile straightaway.

The idea of making a run at Bonneville came up in 1985 when the #9 had won a National First Prize in the Antique Automobile Club of America's meet at Hershey, Pennsylvania. Later that year the car became eligible for the AACA's Grand National judging in Asheville, North Carolina. Someone suggested it would be interesting to win a show award as an antique and break a speed record the same year. We had visited vintage meets on the West Coast in 1984, and Mark Dees had told us the Utah Salt Flats Racing Association would welcome us at Bonneville. Mary West of USFRA confirmed that and provided the information we needed regarding safety rules and protocol. At home in the spring of 1986, we prepared the car for the Asheville show and built a roll bar for the salt. An expedition from Virginia to the western edge of Utah is not undertaken lightly, even though I knew the state well from 30 years of work as Washington correspondent for the state's largest afternoon newspaper, the Salt Lake City *Desert News*. We enlisted the help of Jud Holcombe and Paul Waterman from New England, and Mike Waldo from Park City, Utah.

The Mays record was set in the 2.0-liter international class for unblown engines (122.047 cubic inches), with N. J. Rounds' ex-Jack Balch Offy-powered Lujie Lesovsky chassis. In 1947, Danny Oakes had driven the Balch car 139.460 miles per hour at Bonneville with Riley carburetors and some streamlining including a fabric enclosure around the cockpit sides and a tall windshield. Oakes won the West Coast championship in 1948 and the Balch midget was a pretty hot car. In 1949, Mobil Oil sponsored a series of speed runs by Mays in the Novi Indianapolis car and at the same time Rounds took the midget back to the salt for another run with Hilborn fuel injection and a lower windshield offering less frontal area. Oakes had run some URA Blue Circuit races in 1949 and was under suspension by the AAA for unsanctioned activity, so Mays drove the midget.

Mays, though a national champion and an experienced Indianapolis driver, was never comfortable in a midget. According to hot-rodders who were at Bonneville in 1949, he got the car sideways and spun it at least once, but went on to set a new U.S. Class E record of 147.307 miles per hour.

Bonneville is a bizarre, dramatic place with violent, unpredictable weather. Twenty-five hundred miles from home our little expedition rolled up to the end of the Bonneville access road in July 1986 with several USFRA cars to find that a thunderstorm the night before had flooded the course. The salt is a level, impermeable layer from which rain must evaporate. It does not soak in or run off. The meet was canceled. We turned around and drove to Salt Lake City, stored the car and went home.

The next chance to run was at the Bonneville Nationals in August. As Huntington noted, "Going top-end racing at Bonneville these days is much more than a matter of strapping on your helmet and sticking your foot to the firewall." The Southern California Timing Association that runs Bonneville Nationals Incorporated (BNI) had a longer list of safety rules than USFRA. BNI was not going to allow us to run our roll bar. Jud Holcombe and I flew back to Utah in August and had a Salt Lake City dragster shop build, in one frantic night, an acceptable cage. It was safe, but it was ugly and it stuck up like a piece of scaffolding. It was definitely not aerodynamic. Huntington estimated it added 30 percent to the car's drag. Neither Oakes nor Mays had been required to use any kind of cage. Nevertheless, we trundled out to Wendover, passed tech and did our best.

We had had Gene Adams in Santa Ana, California, flow the Hilborn injectors, and we bought modern V-rated 184/60-13 sports car tires, but timing, gear ratios, tire pressure, and the like were educated guesses. In six runs our best time was 134.440 miles per hour. At the end we were spinning the wheels, throwing up a great spray of salt with 2.70:1 gears in the quick-change rear. The tachometer suggested we were turning the wheels at a 160 miles per hour rate but the timing clocks read 130. With 2.52 gears we could not get over 5,000 rpm, too little to make use of the engine's full power. We didn't have ratios in between those and we couldn't find any to borrow, but we thought we could go faster. When Speed Week ended we again stored the car in Utah and went home. A final USFRA meet in early October fizzled when an early snowstorm ended the salt racing season.

As our little team went home from Bonneville it was obvious that to get the full speed potential out of the little car would require a big improvement in traction and any possible reduction in wind drag that could be arranged. At 5,000 rpm we were making only about 110 horsepower on the last run. The potential peak power on methanol was likely more than 175 horsepower at 8,000 rpm. The problem was to gear the car correctly and get the power to the salt.

Jewel Barlow, an aerodynamics professor at the University of Maryland, offered us some advice on streamlining that we could accomplish without changing the whole character of the car—little fairings that were analogous to things Jack Balch had done in 1949. Ken Keir Race Cars in Maryland built us a roll cage that was strong but was also the minimum size and weight required by the rules. Huntington said that "just eyeballing it, it looked twice as clean aerodynamically." We made many small aerodynamic improvements: the grille was blocked off to eliminate unneeded air flow through the radiator, and a streamlined shield was made for the exhaust pipes where they exited the engine compartment on the right side. We tried a full windshield covering the front of the cage, but it proved (like that tried on the Balch car in 1947) to have too much drag and we went to a little 4x10-inch wedge of plastic on the cowl, just enough to throw the wind up over my helmet faceshield.

The most effective aerodynamic clean-up trick turned out to be replacing the 6-inch wide front tires with 2.50-17 Goodyears. These skinny tires were introduced in 1985 for fuel dragsters and funny cars. They have minimum frontal area, about one-third that of the 185/60-13's, and roughly the same as the 4.00x12 midget fronts of 1949 that are no longer made. Traction on the salt surface was a major problem, but there wasn't any rear tire that appeared to be substantially better than the 185/60s, when inflated to 25 psi or so.

Talking with old Bonneville hands like Bruce Johnston and Mark Dees convinced us that more ballast was going to be necessary in order to get downforce without aero drag. Just 70 pounds behind the seat had boosted our speed by some four miles per hour in 1986. After some textbook exploration, we put 200 pounds of lead over the rear axle for 1987 with provision for adding another 100 pounds as needed. Maximum potential gross weight of the original 850-pound car was 1,500 pounds with 60 percent of the weight on the rear wheels.

We didn't do much to the engine to increase power; in fact we reduced the displacement by 3 inches. Our engine was one Ken Hickey had built with a big block for Len Duncan to drive in eastern ARDC racing. It was 125 cubic inches, too big for the 2,000-cc class. We made a swap with Harold Seaman for a slightly smaller block, 121.5 cubic inches, which Ken installed over the winter of 1986–1987 to make us legal. Hickey, one of the most experienced of Offy mechanics, set up the engine for us with respect to spark timing and such. It would rev crisply to 8,000 rpm. My late wife, Joan, and our team of Holcombe, Waldo, Mike Katzmark, and Billy Watts set out for Bonneville in 1987 praying for good weather. We had exhaust gas temperature gauges and a Cygnus on-board computer loaned to us to record operating data on the runs and to help make adjustments.

The author's Tassi Vatis Offy being measured at Bonneville after its 1989 FIA record run. At left is FIA inspector Dave Petrali while Bruce Johnston confers on the special gauge needed to measure the cylinders' bore without dismantling the engine. The sponsors of the meet required the roll cage and other safety gear. *Author collection*

After clearing the new cage with the inspectors, everything worked. On the first run, with 2.84 gears, 185/60 tires all around, and 250 pounds of ballast, we clocked 140.230 miles per hour at 6,300 rpm. With 2.57 gears and wheel discs for more streamlining, we hit 145.71 miles per hour at 5,800 rpm. Fitting the narrow 2.50x17 front drag tires cleaned up the aerodynamics substantially. We added another 50 pounds of ballast and geared up slightly to 2.63. With that combination the speed jumped over 10 miles per hour to 156.280 at 7,900 rpm. That speed was obviously a new midget record, but we ran afoul of the BNI record structure. At the time there was no BNI class that we fit into. The nearest was for engines of up to 220 cubic inches and the record there was nearly 200 miles per hour. While we had exceeded the existing mark of the Balch car by more than 9 miles per hour in qualifying runs, BNI did not recognize that midget record and refused to allow us to make the two-way runs required to establish a new mark. We went home a little disappointed.

Actually, the Federation International De l'Automobile in Paris had reorganized the international record structure itself. The Mays record of 1949, being a national, but not international, mark had been dropped from the registry. The official International record then was 145.890 miles per hour, set in 1982 by John Bearce of Peoria, Illinois, in a 2,000-cc Mercury with Ford factory sponsorship.

The only way at the time to run for our record was another jaunt back to the Flats for the 1988 USFRA World of Speed meet. USFRA would allow us to run both ways for any record we wanted. We made no essential changes from the earlier set-up except for fine-tuning the engine, and we made a top one-way run of 159.775 miles per hour. Our best two-way average was just fractionally better than in 1987, at 156.902 miles per hour. We had hoped to crack the 160-mile-per-hour mark, but broke a rear axle spool. It was welded back together at a truck stop in Wendover, but then broke again, that time terminally, on an attempt to better 159. But we did finally have an official Bonneville record under our belts, and there was no question we had the fastest midget ever to run on the salt. That little 122-cube Offy had really kicked out the horses, and best of all, had held up to full-power, flat-out runs of more than five miles.

The team and I went back to Bonneville one last time in 1989. FIA inspector Dave Petrali was present and, with the engine a little off its best, we clocked a 153.198-mile-per-hour average, a speed that was properly documented, attested, and internationally recognized. The last tense moment came during measurement of the engine for the record. Since the Offy does not have a removable cylinder head the bore dimension was tricky to determine with the accuracy required. After considerable effort Bruce Johnston came up with a special gauge that fit down through the spark plug opening. Our engine measured precisely 121.50 cubic inches (1,991 cc).

Offenhauser Engineering Company–Meyer & Drake, Inc. Engine Production
Midget 97-inch Series 1934–1974

The Offenhauser shop records for a substantial number of the pre-World War II engines have been lost. Data for serial numbers 7-37, 86-100, and 102-231 have been reconstructed from Fred Offenhauser's scrapbook and other contemporary records. That information should be taken as approximate only.

S/N	Date	Purchaser	Cu.In.	Remarks
01	8/20/34	Earl B. Gilmore	96.9	First Mighty Midget
02	10/1/34	Barry Snyder	96.9	First ran Moto Speedway; won feature
03	11/05/34	Anne. S. Duffy	96.9	Art Boyce drove; sold to Don Lee then to Pat Warren
04	12/5/34	Fayte Brown	98.39	Sold to Joe Corrigan, 1939
05	12/15/34	Thorne Donnelly	98.3	Snyder drove at Chicago 2-5-35
06	9/1/35	Charlie Allen	94.8	
07	8/10/35	Jack Miller	98.96	Became Black Diamond Coal Spl
08	–/35	Frank Nickell	98.3	Emil Andres drove at Chicago
09	–/35	Willett Brown	98.3	
10	–/35	Willett Brown	98.3	
11	–/35	E.L. Cord	98.3	
12	–/35	Fred Friday	98.3	Owned by Householder, 1939; 102.244 ci
13	–/35	Stanley Dollar	90.88	supercharged; went in boat
14	–/36	Virginia Lyons	98.3	
15	–/36	Al Krause	96.9	
16	–/36	Willett Brown	98.3	
17	–/36	Mike Caruso	96.9	
18	–/36	Paul Russo	98.3	
19	–/36	Gerd Achelis	98.3	German aviator
20	–/36	Jess Fike	98.3	
21	–/37	Willie Utzman	98.3	
22	–/37	PeeWee Distarce	98.98	
23	–/37	San Hanks	98.3	
24	–/37	Judd Pickup	98.3	
25	–/37	George Capper	97.65	Ran in Chicago 1939
26	–/37	Fred Tomshe	98.2	
27	–/37	Mel Hansen	98.3	
28	–/37	Clyde Porter	98.3	
29	–/37	Pat Warren	98.96	
30	–/38	Pat Warren	98.96	
31	–/38	Swedberg	103.082	1939 displacement, Chicago
32	–/38	Arnold Krause	98.96	
33	–/38	R. Householder	99.08	
34	–/38	John Coutre	94.8	
35	–/38	Ed Van Nostrand	102.48	1939 displacement
36	–/38	Charlie Pritchard	102.10	Russo owned, 1939
37	–/38	Julius Buzzard	94.8	2-speed transmission, clutch, 2 carbs
38	–/38	Arthur Ulmer	94.8	Denver-Chicago Trucking Spl, 1939
39	?	Rudy Adams	?	
40	?	George Woelper	?	
41	?	Vince Dimatteo	98.3	Winfield cams (sold to John Balch 4/14/43)
42	?	Al Krause	94.8	
43	–/39	Mike Caruso	102.41	3 5/8 stroke; 12:1 com pression, dual intake
44	7/12/39	Mrs. Estelle Siech (Milwaukee)	98.96	15/16-in piston dome
45	?	Otto F. Ramer	98.96	
46	7/22/39	J.E. Jackson	98.96	1 updraft carb
47	?	Charlie Allen	98.96	Clutch
48	?	Tony Gulotta	?	2 carbs, Wico magneto
49	?	Wally Zale	?	2 updraft manifolds
50	?	Mark Light	?	2-speed transmission, 2 carbs
51	?	George A. Harvey	?	15/16 piston dome
52	?	Sherman F. Crise	?	2-speed transmission
53	?	Duke Nalon	98.3	13.5:1 compression
54	?	Frank Podrizini	94.88	15/16-in piston dome
55	?	Duane Carter	?	1 1/16-in piston dome
56	?	Jack Prickett	?	Wico magneto; 13 1/2:1 compression ratio
57	?	Ted Horn	94.88	10.7:1 compression ratio
58	?	Jack Prickett	?	
59	?	Unknown	?	
60	?	Tony Willman	94.88	#4 cams; 15/16-in piston dome
61	?	John Silcox (Ambassador Iron & Wire Company)	94.88	#4 cams, lightweight clutch, Wico Magneto
62	?	Freddie Mitchell	94.88	Clutch, quick-change assembly; #4 cams
63	?	Fred Friday	?	
64	?	Unknown	?	
65	?	Unknown	?	
66	?	Wilke	94.88	Marchese
67	?	Cecil A. Shaw	94.88	Dual Lenkert updraft carbs
68	?	Lloyd Axel	98.27	Burd piston rings
69	?	Mannix Automotive Service	94.88	#4 cams; 2-speed transmis-sion, 2 downdraft carbs
70	?	Wilke	94.88	(Marchese) #4 cams
71	5/1/40	Fred Tomshe	94.88	# 4 cams
72	?	Paul Swedberg	98.96	# 4 cams
73	?	Truesdell Oil Co.	94.88	# 4 cams; 2 downdraft carbs
74	?	Sport Briggs	94.88	2 Lenkert carbs
75	?	Fran Gardner	98.27	Multi-disc clutch; # 4 cams
76	?	Wilke	94.88	# 4 cams; large magneto
77	?	Wilke-Leader Card	114.18?	Special lightened, stroked crankshaft; #4 cams
78	?	Wilke	94.88	#4 cams
79	?	Wilke (Ed Mitchell)	103.13	2 Winfield carbs for alco-hol, # 4 cams. Went in Mitchell-Litke Fireball car
80	?	Allen Jackson	94.88	12 1/2:1 compression ratio
81	?	Wilke	94.88	#4 cams
82	?	Milt Eyerle	98.27	Tach drive
83	2/7/41	Fred Tomshe via Wilke	98.86	10 1/2:1 compression ratio
84	3/20/41	Wilke	94.88	#4 cams
85	3/26/41	Wilke	98.96	#4 cams; 10.5:1 compression ratio
86-100	?	Unknown		
101	7/17/41	Ted Halibrand	98.96	Last midget built before WW II
102-115	?	?	?	
116	-/-/46	Unknown	97	In Gib Lilly, later Bourgnon # 36 K-K midget
117-158?	?	?		
159	1/27/46	John Balch		Engine: $1,700.00; accessories $503.56 (may be out of sequence)
160-	?	?	Unknown	
?	-/-/46	Lou Fageol	90.8	Roots-blown, went in Twin-Coach Indy car
?	-/-/46	Lou Fageol	90.8	Roots-blown, for Twin-Coach Spl
? -171	3/8/47	Robert Wilke	98.26	re-sold to Matt Sandicie, Milwaukee
172-227	?	Unknown		
228	6/-/47	unknown	102.49	In Furci midget. Sold to Ken Hickey who put 120 block on it. Sold to G. White, 1983
232	6/13/47	Wilke	102.49	14:1 compression ratio; first engine with heavy timing gears

S/N	Date	Purchaser	Cu.In.	Remarks
233	6/16/47	Plaza	102.49	Bosch magneto
234	6/14/47	Schaeffer	98.27	new heavy timing gears
235	6/16/47	Floyd Trevis	102.49	
236	6/16/47	Bussard	102.49	#4 cams; 16:1 compression ratio
237	6/17/47	J. Whitehouse	102.49	
238	6/20/47	H. Meyers	98.27	
239	6/16/47?	H. Banks	?	
240	6/18/47	Bill Krech	102.49	
241	6/30/47	McBride	102.49	
242	7/7/47	Wilke	102.49	
243	7/8/47	Laird	98.96	
244	7/7/47	Leslie	98.27	
245	7/9/47	Dunning	98.27	
246	7/10/47	Bennett	98.27	
247	7/12/47	Tuffanelli	102.49	Bosch magneto
248	7/16/47	Lutes	102.49	
249	7/18/47	Wilke	102.49	Wico magneto
250	7/18/47	Koopman	102.49	
251	7/22/47	Daugherty	102.49	Bosch magneto
252	7/24/47	Fred Wick	98.96	
253	7/25/47	Morrison	102.49	
254	7/26/47	Wilke	102.49	
255	8/7/47	Harry McQuinn	102.49	
256	7/28/47	Walker	102.49	
257	8/6/47	Kurtis-Kraft	98.27	
258	8/8/47	Graves	98.96	
259	8/9/47	Wilke	98.27	
260	8/13/47	Casale	102.49	
261	8/14/47	Cleval	102.49	
?	8/20/47	TEST	102.49	
262	8/27/47	Bynum	102.49	
263	8/28/47	Wilke	102.49	
264	8/29/47	Wakefield	106.81	
265	8/29/47	Curtis	98.27	
266	9/4/47	Eddie Myer	102.49	
267	8/20/47	Test	102.49	
268	9/5/47	Frank DelRoy	102.49	Ken Hickey
269	9/5/47	Fresholtz	102.49	
270	9/8/47	Frank DelRoy	102.49	Johnny Ritter. Now owned by Ken Meyle
271	9/13/47	R.C. Wilke	102.49	
272	9/13/47	R.C. Wilke	102.49	
273	9/15/47	Wilke	98.27	
274	9/19/47	Hollywood Spring Co.	102.49	
275	9/1947	George Beavis	102.49	Sports car mounts
276	9/23/47	Wilke	102.49	
277	10/6/47	Chuck Greenlee	94.88	Special low block
278	10/6/47	Ed Haddad	102.49	
279	10/8/47	Wilke	102.49	
280	10/9/47	C.L. Smith	102.49	
281	10/14/47	Lemieux	102.49	Low block
282	10/7/47	Wilke	102.49	
283	10/15/47	Corrigan	102.49	Low block
284	10/16/47	L.J. Bruns	102.49	Low block
285	10/18/47	E. Allen	98.27	
286	10/20/47	A.J. Philipski	94.88	Special low block
287	10/21/47	Ted Halibrrand	102.49	
288	10/22/47	Frank Curtis	98.27	
289	10/24/47	Frank DelRoy	98.27	
290	10/28/47	Wilke	102.49	
291	10/29/47	Hall	102.49	
292	10/30/47	Frank DelRoy	102.49	(DeMarco)
293	10/31/47	Wilke	102.49	
294	11/3/47	Wilke	102.49	
295	11/5/47	DelRoy (Hickey)	102.49	Originally intended for Roscoe Hough
296	11/6/47	Wilke	102.49	
297	11/8/47	Wilke	102.49	
298	11/18/47	DelRoy	98.96	Dumraese
299	11/20/47	Frank Curtis	102.49	
300	11/21/47	Shanebrook	98.96	
301	11/25/47	MacLeod	102.49	
302	11/25/47	Ted Kessler	102.49	
303	11/19/47	Harry Meyers	102.49	
304	11/26/47	DelRoy	102.49	

S/N	Date	Purchaser	Cu.In.	Remarks
305	11/28/47	DelRoy	102.49	
306	12/2/47	John Snider	98.27	
307	12/5/47	Bynum	102.49	
308	12/11/47	Bynum	102.49	
309	12/19/47	Demmit	102.49	
310	12/18/47	B.A. Jacobson	102.49	
311	12/17/47	Johnny Pawl	102.49	
312	12/23/47	Wilke	102.49	
313	12/19/47	Wilke	102.49	
314	1/7/48	Dillon	102.49	
315	1/9/48	Paul Gibson	102.49	
316	1/13/48	Notthoff	102.49	
317	1/15/48	Stock	102.49	
318	1/21/48	Orendolf	98.27	
319	1/24/48	Wilke	102.49	
320	2/2/48	Randall	102.49	#5 cams
321	1/26/48	Wilke	102.49	
322	1/27/48	Stock	102.49	
323	2/6/48	Russell Lamarr	102.49	#5 cams
324	2/2/48	Householder	102.49	
325	1/28/48	Midwest	98.27	
326	2/4/48	DelRoy	98.27	Schaeffer Gear,#5 cams
327	2/27/48	Vultee	102.49	
328	2/12/48	Murphy Motors	102.49	
329	2/13/48	R.C. Wilke	102.49	
330	2/16/48	R.C. Wilke	102.49	
331	2/17/48	E. Brides	102.49	
332	2/18/48	DelRoy	102.49	N.Y. Show
333	2/26/48	Shaheen	98.27	
334	3/3/48	Shorty Burns	102.49	
335	3/4/48	Felix West	98.96	
336	3/5/48	Caccia	102.49	
337	3/5/48	Vern Orenduff	98.27	
338	3/6/48	Murphy Motors	102.49	
339	3/8/48	S.L. Anderson	102.49	#4 cams
340	3/10/48	MidWest	98.27	
341	3/8/48	Melvin Calvert	102.49	#5 cams
342	3/13/48	Wilke	102.49	
343	3/12/48	MidWest	98.27	#4 cams
344	3/17/48	Pollock (Shaeffer Gear)	102.49	#5 cams
345	3/22/48	Wilke	102.49	#5 cams
346	4/1/48	DelRoy	102.49	4/13/48, experimental
347	4/15/48	Cornachia	102.49	First midget w/insert rods
348	4/19/48	Henry Green	102.49	
349	4/20/48	Tadlock	102.49	
350	4/20/48	Spillar	98.27	#4 cams
351	4/20/48	DelRoy	102.49	#5 cams
352	4/21/48	Wilke	102.49	#4 cams
353	4/28/48	Fred Toth	102.49	
354	4/30/48	M.A. Walker	102.49	#5 cams
355	4/27/48	Loren Bennett	102.49	#5 cams
356	4/28/48	Spillar	98.27	
357	4/29/48	Greenman	102.49	
358	5/5/48	R.C. Wilke	102.49	Insert rods
359	5/5/48	DelRoy	98.27	
360	5/6/48	Lackinger	102.49	
361	5/7/48	McQuinn	102.49	
362	5/13/48	Paul Gibson	102.49	
363	5/13/48	Casale	102.49	
364	5/14/48	Gullota	102.49	
365	5/18/48	Templeton	102.49	
366	5/20/48	Wilke	102.49	Overhauled by Ken Hickey, 1995
367	5/25/48	Speed Parts	102.49	For Ken Hickey
368	6/2/48	Speed Parts	98.27	
369	6/3/48	MidWest	102.49	
370	6/7/48	John Ramp, Inc.	102.49	
371	6/9/48	R. C. Wilke	102.49	
372	6/15/48	Speed Parts	102.49	
373	6/16/48	MidWest	102.49	
374	6/22/48	R. C. Wilke	102.49	
375	6/23/48	Speed Parts	98.27	
376	7/2/48	Speed Parts	102.49	
377	7/12/48	Faas	102.49	

S/N	Date	Purchaser	Cu.In.	Remarks
378	7/2/48	MidWest	102.49	
379	7/8/48	Wilke	102.49	Owned by Wm St. George in 1996. In Bourgnon # 36 K-K midget
380	7/9/48	Hronek	102.49	
381	7/10/48	Wilke	102.49	
382	7/15/48	Speed Parts	98.27	
383	7/9/48	Hart Fullerton	102.49	
384	7/16/48	R. C. Wilke	102.49	
385	7/1648	R. C. Wilke	98.27	
386	8/3/48	Speed Parts	102.49	
387	8/3/48	Speed Parts	102.49	
388	8/5/48	F.C. Dunleavey	102.49	
389	8/5/48	Johnny Mantz	102.49	
390	8/9/48	A. Montgomery	102.49	
391	8/12/48	Wilke	102.49	
392	8/17/48	Speed Parts	102.49	
393	8/17/48	Perkins	102.49	#4 cams
394	8/23/48	Wilke	102.49	#4 cams
395	8/24/48	Speed Parts	102.49	
396	9/13/48	Speed Parts	102.49	Babbitt Rods
397	2/25/49	J. Pawl	102.49	
398	3/3/49	M.A. Walker	102.49	New crankshaft w/3-in diameter main journals introduced
399	12/48	Bennett	102.49	
400	4/23/49	Leslie	102.49	M-D went to 1/16-in larger diameter (13/16 in) wrist pins with this engine
401	3/49	Ramp	102.49	Maintained by Bob Higman
402	4/22/49	L. Fass	102.49	
403	4/23/49	J. Pawl	102.49	
404	4/26/49	J. Fuller	102.49	On-center connecting rod
405	4/26/49	J. Fuller	102.49	On-center connecting rod
406	4/29/49	Kurtis-Kraft	102.49	On-center connecting rods
407	5/13/49	Morosco	102.49	
408	5/12/49	R. Dunning	102.49	
409	5/19/49	J. Pawl	102.49	Offset rods, #4 cams
410	6/27/49	L.R. Fass	102.49	
411	6/21/49	J.N. Beck	102.49	3-in main journals
412	6/22/49	J. Fuller	102.49	3-in main journals with on-center rods
413	7/13/49	MidWest	102.49	J. Hunt magneto, 3" main journals
414	8/1/49	S. F. Carr	102.49	3-in main journals and larger than standard rod journals, #5 cams
415	8/16/49	Boswell	89.8	3-in main journals and larger than standard rod journals, Sports Offy
416	8/30/49	Test engine	106.81	Test engine with magnesium input manifold and supercharger with intercooler and large-journal crankshaft
417	4/12/50	Spare parts	102.49	#4 cams
418	4/26/50	Walter Johnson	102.49	Insert rods
419	9/14/50	DelRoy (for customer)	88.1	#5 cams, large-journal crankshaft with on-center rods, 91 Sports Offy, Babbitt mains, 2 SU carbs
420	?	Unknown		
421	8/27/51	George Tsurnos	98.27	#5 cams, Bendix magnetos
422	5/7/54?	Jack Hinkle	88.36	91 Sports Offy #4 cams, 2 sparkplugs per cylinder, large- journal crank, special 12 holddown stud block with matching crankcase
423	5/23/55	Allen Le May	88.36	Cadillac starter, 91 Sports Offy, 329 1/2 lb less transmission, #4 cams
424	5/10/56	Ray Tomaseski	102.49	Hilborn injectors, roadster chassis, Joe Hunt magnto
425	3/5/57	Harold Guidi	102.49	
426	7/26/57	Baker Engineering	102.49	
427	8/12/58	Kurtis, Ernie Alvarado	102.49	Roadster, reversed block, 15:1 compression #4 cams
428	7/13/59	Kurtis-Kraft	108.03	Roadster, reversed block
429	1/30/60	Yamaha	102.49	Set up for gasoline, Winfield input 133 cam, Winfield exhaust 131 cam
430	4/10/61	Walt Schwitzer	102.49	
431	11/19/62	Ken Hickey	105.94	#4 cams, Offy
432	10/5/64	Jack London	102.49	Winfield #133 intake cams, #4 exhaust cams
433	5/7/65	Caves Buick	102.49	
434	6/66	Gus Sohn (Linne)	109.59	Hilborn injectors, Winfield 132 intake cams; Winfield 130 exhaust cams
435	8/1/66	Art Shangian	102.49	Winfield 133 intake cams, Winfield 130 exhaust cams, Joe Hunt magnetos
436	10/5/67	Walter Schwitzer	106.64	Schneider cams, Hunt external coil magneto
437	?	Linne	105.94	
438	?	Gordon Reelie	102.49	Winfield #135 intake cam; Winfield 132 exhaust cam
439	7/1/68	J. Pawl (Ken Johnson)	102.49	Winfield #133 intake cam, Winfield # 131 exhaust cam
440	7/26/68	Cliff Correll	109.59	Schneider cams, injectors
441	12/11/68	Howard Linne	107.33	Winfield #133 intake cam, Winfield #131 exhaust cam
442	1/9/69	H. Linne	105.94	#133 24-62 intake cam, #131 62-18 exhaust cam
443	?/?/69	Glen Dennee	70.69	Roots-Supercharged Midget Offy; Winfield 144 intake cam, Winfield 138 exhaust cam
444	?/?/69	Bob Higman	63	Turbo-blown midget (1 of 2 built)
445	1/17/69	Jack Stroud	111.03	Winfield 143 intake cam, Winfield 138 exhaust cam, Chrysler valve springs
446	2-26-69	Mel Kenyon	107.33	Winfield 133 intake cam, Winfield 131 exhaust cam, 15:1 compression
447	6/17/69	Barry Handlin	111.03	Winfield 141 intake cam, Winfield 136 exhaust cam
448	8/15/69	H. Linne	111.03	Winfield 144 intake cam, Winfield 136 exhaust cam, Hilborn injectors
449	11/24/69	Howard Linne	111.03	Schneider intake cam, Schneider exhaust cam, Hilborn injectors
450	?	J. Pawl	105.25	Winfield 133 intake cam, Winfield 131 exhaust cam, Hilborn injectors
451	7/21/70	Dub Larson (Australia)	109.59	Winfield 133 intake cam, Winfield 131 exhaust cam, Hilborn injectors
452	10/15/74	Gene Hamilton (Bob Higman)		Only complete "120" midget sold. 124.96 On-center rods and crankcase, offset cylinders, 0.8125-in wrist pin diameter, Schneider intake cam, Schneider exhaust cam

Records of Known Serial Numbers of Midget Engines Serviced by Meyer & Drake, 1949-71

S/N	Date	Purchaser	Cu.In.	Remarks
307	4/29/49	?	102.49	Original owner:Bynum
308	4/29/49	?	102.49	Original owner:Bynum
107	3/30/53	E.Rogers	?	?
150	3/29/57	J.McDaniel	102.49	?
267	3/29/57	J.McDaniel	102.49	Originally built for shop test
406	4/8/65	H.Guttry	102.49	Original purchaser: Kurtis-Kraft
265	5/28/65	Bob Bahre	98.27	Original purchaser: Kurtis-Kraft
431	6/4/66	Bob Bahre	105.94	Original purchaser: Ken Hickey
445	7/27/71	Bob Olds	?	Original purchaser: Jack Stroud

Offenhauser Engineering Company/Meyer & Drake, Inc.
Engine Production 1947-1965 Big Engines: 220, 270, 255, 252

S/N	Date	Purchaser	Series	Cu. In.	Remarks
71	2/28/47	Henry Meyer	220	220.3	#4 cams
72	1/8/47	Dick Cott	270	270.2	
73	1/13/47	Jimmy Wilburn	270	292.1	IMCA
74	3/23/47	Greer	270	270.2	#4 cams
75	3/12/47	Marchese	255	270.2	#5 cams
76	2/19/47	Honore	270	218.2	#4 cams
77	2/11/47	N.J. Rounds	270	270.2	#5 cams
78	1/26/47	G. Pearson	220	220.3	
79	3/19/47	Don Lee, Inc.	270	270.2	#5 cams
80	3/20/47	Not Completed Parts went into S/N 178			
81	3/25/47	Salay	270	270.2	#5 cams
82	7/31/48	Lou Moore	270	270.2	#4 cams
83	4/28/47	Tuffanelli	270	270.2	#5 cams
84	9/9/48	Agajanian	220	220.3	#5 cams
85	5/7/48	Rex Mays	270	270.2	Winfield cams
86	1/13/49	Kurtis Kraft	270	270.2	#4 cams
87	6/18/48	Frankie DelRoy	220	220.3	#5 cams
88	6/28/48	R. Malamud	220	220.3	#4 cams
88(1)	10/15/48	Webb & Wales	220	220.3	#4 cams
89	1/16/49	Johnny Rae	270	270.2	#4 cams
90	11/12/48	Bill Corley	220	233.3	#4 cams
91	12/6/48	C. Mathews	220	220.3	#4 cams
92	1/28/49	Tuffaneli	270	270.2	#4 cams
93	2/8/49	Lou Rassey	270	270.2	#4 cams
94	2/24/49	E.M. Morris	270	270.2	#4 cams
95	4/1/49	Ernie Wolff	270	270.2	#4 cams
96	4/19/49	Joe Langley	220	240.1	#4 cams
97	6/2/49	F. Luptow	270	270.6	#4 cams
98	7/7/49	Pete Mocca	270	270.2	#5 cams
99	9/1/49	Tuffanelli	270	270.2	#4 cams
100	9/14/49	Buckner	220	233.3	#4 cams
101	12/14/49	Speed Parts	220	220.3	#4 cams
102	2/17/50	Granatelli	270	270.2	Winfield intake cam,#4 exhause cam
103	12/28/49	Kurtis-Kraft	270	270.2	
104	?	Unknown			
105B	3/23/50	I.R.C., Inc.	270	176.9	Supercharged Offy
106	3/14/50	Kurtis Kraft	270	270.2	Winfield carburetors
107B	4/12/50	Alden Sampson	220	176.9	#5 cam, supercharged
108	3/23/50	M.A. Walker	270	270.2	Winfield intake, #4 exhaust
109	4/5/50	MidWest Racing Equipment	270	270.2	#4 cams
110B	4/17/50	Murrell Belanger	220	176.9	#5 cams, supercharged
111B	4/21/50	Kurtis Kraft	220	176.9	#5 cams, supercharged
112	8/1/50	Russell Snowberger	270	270.2	1st Offy supplied fuel injection with Hilborn
113	?	Unknown			
114	8/18/50	Murrell Belanger	270	266.7	#4 cams
115	12/14/50	Hinkle Oil Co.	270	270.2	Winfield cams
116	2/22/51	Kurtis Kraft	270	270.6	Winfield cams, 1st Offy 270 with integral bellhousing, crankcase, and wider bulkheads and main bearing webs
117	3/1/51	Gene Cassaroll/ Kurtis Kraft	270	270.2	#4 cams
118	3/19/51	Brown Motor Co.	270	270.2	#4 cams, last hightower 270 Offy produced
119	3/5/51	Johnny McDaniels	270	270.2	#4 cams
120	3/12/51	Pete Wales	270	267.5	#4 cams
121	4/5/51	Pete Schmidt	270	262.8	#4 cams
122	3/23/51	MidWest Racng Inc. (Leitenberg)	270	270.2	#4 cams
123	4/9/51	Pete Salemi	270	270.2	#4 cams
124	5/15/51	Bob Scovell-Dregg-Myklebust	220	217.9	#4 cam intake, Clay Smith exhaust
125	4/16/51	Moeller	270	270.2	#4 cams
126	12/21/51	Dick Cott	255	262.8	#4 cams
127	12/27/51	Ted Nyquist	270	212.3	#4 cams
128	1/9/52	Ed Walsh	270	270.2	#4 cams

S/N	Date	Purchaser	Series	Cu. In.	Remarks
129	?	Duke Randall (Fannighetti)	220	217.9	#4 cams
130	1/23/52	Superior Oil Co.	270	270.6	#4 cams
131	2/18/52	Rotary Engineering-Roscoe Ford	270	270.6	#4 cams
132	2/18/52	Ben Paoli	270	262.8	
133	2/26/52	Allan Chapman	270	270.2	#4 cams
134	3/3/52	Bob Pankatz	270	262.8	
135	3/27/52	John McDowell (Kurtis Kraft)	270	270.6	#4 cams
136	4/2/52	Gene Casaroll	270	262.8	#4 cams
137	4/4/52	Jim Campbell	220	217.9	#4 cams
138	4/12/52	M.A. Walker	270	270.2	#4 cams
139	?	Pete Schmidt	270	262.8	#4 cams
140	4/28/52	McNamara Motor Express	220	217.9	#4 cams
141	5/6/52	Erickson (Clay Smith)	220	217.9	
142	7/3/52	Ken Hickey (Jake Vargo)	220	217.9	#4 cams (went in stretched midget)
143	7/17/52	Hart Fullerton	270	262.8	#4 cams
144	9/4/52	Emmett Malloy	270	262.8	#4 cams
145	1953?	J.C. Agajanian	270	262.8	
146	3/23/53	Ed Walsh	270	270.6	
147	1/30/53	Pete Schmidt	270	270.6	#4 cams
148	1/30/53	A.E. Dean (Ed Kuzma)	270	262.8	
149	2/25/53	W.M. Christensen	270	270.2	#4 cams
150	2/6/53	Auto Shipper, Inc.	270	270.6	
151	2/7/53	Lee Elkins (J. Pawl)	270	270.6	#4 cams
152	2/12/53	Sumar Enterprise	270	270.2	#4 cams
153	2/18/53	Travelers Trailor Co. (Ernie Ruiz)	270	270.6	
154	1/25/53	Ray Crawford	270	270.6	Winfield cams
155	3/13/53	Slick Airlines (Bill Holland)	270	270.6	Winfield cams
156	3/17/53	Andy Granatelli	270	270.6	Winfield cams
157	4/13/53	Joe Scapa for Merze Engineering	270	270.6	#4 cams
158	4/21/53	Kurtis Kraft (Belond)	270	270.2	#4 cam 36 degree layover
159	5/15/53	Jim Campbell	270	270.6	#4 cams
160	8/7/53	Tom Randall	270	270.6	#4 cams
161	9/15/53	Cincinnati Race Cars (Walter Moeller)	220	217.9	#4 cams
162	11/19/53	Ken Hickey (Sam Traylor)	220	217.9	#4 cams (Campbell drove)
163	11/19/53	Sumar Enterprises	270	217.9	#4 cams
164	1/12/54	Auto Shippers, Inc.	270	270.6	#4 cams
165	1/5/54	George Tilp (Adam Stamping & Mfg)	220	179.6	#4 cams, sports Offy
166	2/23/54	Bob Sweikert	220	217.9	#4 cams
167	3/27/54	Ken Hickey (Traylor)	220	217.9	#4 cams (spare engine)
XP40	5/7/54	Meyer & Drake	270	271.4	Aluminum webs & cup cam followers drilled for lightening, special cam housing cover for oiling to cams and cam followers
168	4/9/54	Roger Walcott (Herb Porter)	220	179.2	
169	7/15/54	Sumar Enterprises	270	270.6	
170	8/9/54	Briggs Cunningham	220	179.2	#4 cams, 180 Sports Offy
171	?	Ed Walsh	270	270.2	#4 cams
172	10/20/54	Lammers (H. Templeton, mechanic)	270	270.6	#4 cams
173	12/27/54	Rotary Engineering (Nichols)	270	270.2	#4 cams
174	12/30/54	Ken HIckey	270	270.6	#4 cams
175	1955?	Sumar Speed Equipment	270	270.6	
176	4/13/55	Briggs Cunningham	220	149.5	#4 cams, Sports Offy, magnesium crankcase side plates with breathers, special rear mount for Cadillac starter

S/N	Date	Purchaser	Series	Cu. In.	Remarks
177	?	Joe Baker (McKay)	270	270.2	#4 cams
178	3/22/55	George Weedman	270	270.2	#4 cams, parts from S/N 80used in this engine
179	?	Ernie Ruiz	220	217.9	#4 cams
180	11/30/56	Jones & Maley	270	251.5	1st. Offy 255 modified to meet new 1957 formula of 256 cu. in.
181	1/22/57	Ed Walsh	270	251.9	1st modified 255 to use new Winfield cams
182	1/31/57	Bonini (for Bignotti)	270	251.5	Winfield cams, 66, 65
183	1/30/57		270	251.5	Winfield cams, 67, 66
184	2/14/57	Ansted Rotary Engineering	270	251.5	Winfield 64, 66 cams
185	3/26/57	George Salih	270	251	Winfield 5 & 7 cams, 1st Offy Sidwinde3r for laydown installation
186	4/10/57	Frank Kurtis(Farina)	270	251.5	Winfield cams
187	1/28/58	Chuck Daigh (mechanic)	220	182.2	Engle cams, last 220-based Offy produced. (Scarab Formula 1 car)
188	4/21/58	Norm Demler	270	255.4	Winfield 65, 66 cams, Sidewinder Offy
189	5/1/58	Cars Inc. (Jones)	270	251.5	Winfield cams, Sidewinder Offy, ast 255 Series produced
190	1/10/59	R.C. Wilke	270	251.9	Winfield cams; Takio ChickieHirashima's first low-block 252 Offy
191	2/20/59	R.C. Wilke	270	251.9	Winfield 33, 31 cams, ordered with flat tappet cams and cups
192	2/25/59	Bignotti	270	251.9	Winfield cams, Sidewinder Offy
193	?	Unknown			
194	3/18/59	Dean Van Lines	270	251.5	Winfield 35, 31 cams, Sidewinder Offy with flat tappet cams and cups and new Hilborn curved injectors
195	4/3/59	Pete Schmidt	270	251.9	Winfield 35, 31 cams; Sidewinder Offy with flat tappet cams and cups
196	4/22/59	Jim Robbins	270	251.9	Winfield cams
197	4/22/59	Amos-Scawley	270	251.9	Winfield cams; built with flat tappet cams and cups
198	4/22/59	Bob Estes	270	251.9	Winfield cams; built with flat tappet cams and cups
199	1/1/60	Kenneth Rich	270	251.9	Winfield cams
200	2/26/60	George Salih	270	251.9	Winfield cams; Sidewinder Offy
201	3/10/60	Fred Gerhardt	270	251.9	Winfield cams, Sidewinder Offy
202	3/10/60	Forbes	270	251.9	Winfield cams
203	3/10/60	Pete Schmidt	270	251.9	Winfield 131, 133 cams
204	3/10/60	Jim Robbins	270	251.9	Winfield 131, 133 cams; Sidewinder Offy
205	4/1/60	Braund Plywood	270	251.9	Sidewinder Offy
206	4/8/60	Kelso Auto Dynamics (Lesovsky)	270	251.9	Winfield 131, 133 cams
207	4/8/60	Kelso Auto Dynamics (Lesovsky)	270	251.9	Winfield 131, 133 cams; Sidewinder Offy
208	2/1/61	Ken HIckey	270	251.9	Winfield cams
209	3/22/61	Hoover Motor Express (Quinn Epperly)	270	251.9	Winfield special cmas, 131, 132; Sidewinder Offy
210	3/15/61	Smokey Yunick	270	251.9	Winfield 133, 131 cams; flat tappet cams and cups built to run with reverse crankshaft rotation & first double row hold own stud cam housings
211	3/22/61	Baker Engineering	270	251.9	Winfield 133 and 131 cams
212	4/17/61	Ray Crawford	270	251.9	Winfield 131, 133 cams, built with special cam housings for externally plumbed high pressure cam oiling
213	1/17/62	W. P. Forbes	270	251.	
214	3/16/62	C. O. Prather	270	251.9	15:1 compression, Winfield 131, 133
215	8/31/62	Auto Lite	270	251.9	Winfield 133, 131 cams; Ford Motor Co. bought to scrutinize before designing their quad-cam V-8.
216	1/28/63	Johnny Pawl (Ernie Immerso) Wally Weir	270	251.9	15:1 compression
217	2/14/63	John Chalik	270	251.9	.476 lift, 14.5:1 compression
218	2/16/63	Van Liew	270	251.9	
219	3/18/63	Competition engineering (Wally Meskowski)	270	251.9	14.8:1 compression; Winfield 133, Engineering 131 cams; 1st late 252 lightweight Offy with magensium gear tower, am housings, side plates, front cover and cover adaptor, aluminum main bearing webs, oil pump, and larger capacity water pump
220	3/22/63	Herb Porter	270	251.9	late 252 lightweight Offy; bronze oil pump, set up for oil filter
221	3/28/63	George Bignotti	270	251.9	late 252 lightweight Offy; magnesium front yoke, etc. 452 lbs.
222	4/1/63	Leader Cars Inc. (A. J. Watson)	270	251.9	14.2:1 compression
223	2/14/64	A.J. Watson (Johnny White)	270	251.9	14.2:1 compression
224	3/28/64	Volstedt	270	251.9	14.2:1 compression, first Offy for use in a rear engine chassis
225	4/1/64	R. C. Wilke (Leader Cards, Inc.)	270	251.9	Winfield 130, 139 cams
226	4/10/64	British Motors	270	251.9	Winfield 139 (.476 lift), 131 (.456 lift); for a rear engine chassis
227	8/7/64	Vita-Fresh (Van Liew)	270	251.9	14.75:1 compression; for rear engine) chassis, lightweights engine, first with aluminum block
228	4/30/64	British Motors	270	251.9	13.5:1 compression; lightweight Offy with aluminum block set up for oil filter
229	3/29/65	Weinberger	270	251.9	14:1 compression; lightweight with aluminum block
230	4/9/65	British Motor Co.	270	251.9	
231	5/4/65	Halibrand Engineering	270	255.6	Winfield 141, 145 cams; first Post War over-square Offy
XO	7/8/65	Drake Engineering	270	250.5	Last naturally aspirated factory Offy, cast iron block 5/8" shorter than 252

Records of known serial numbers of big engines serviced by Meyer & Drake, 1950-1968

S/N	Date	Purchaser	Series	Cu. In.	Remarks
69	1950	?	?	?	?
70	4/6/51	Belanger	270	?	?
112	2/5/51	Snowberger	270	?	original owner: Snowberger
114	11/21/50	Belanger	270	?	original owner: Belanger
220	5/4/53	Walcott	270	262.85	original owner: Herb Porter
530	1/26/68	Gerhardt	159	?	?
219	3/6/70	Porter Competition Engineering (Meskowski)	270	?	original owern:
202	?	Porter	270	?	original owner: Forbes

Offenhauser Engine Record AAA & USAC Championship Racing 1935 - 1978

Most races except Indianapolis were 100 miles in length, run over oval or circular tracks of 1 mile in length. Pike's Peak was a hill climb of 12.7 miles and in later years road courses (RC) were added to the schedule. Two dirt Silver Crown races are included (1971, 1974)

Championship Race Results 1935–1978

Date	Track	Surface	Speed	Engine/Chassis	Driver
5/30/35	Indianapolis	brick	106.24	Offy/Wetteroth	Petillo, Kelly
7/4/35	St. Paul	dirt	77.26	Offy/Wetteroth	Petillo
8/24/35	Springfield	dirt	80.38	Miller/Duesenberg	Winn, Billy
9/2/35	Syracuse	dirt	83.54	Miller/Duesenberg	Winn
9/7/35	Altoona	dirt	86.54	Miller/Stevens	Meyer, Lou
10/1/35	Langhorne	dirt	91.89	Offy/Wetteroth	Petillo
5/30/36	Indianapolis	brick	109.06	Miller/Stevens	Meyer
6/20/36	Goshen	dirt	76.40	Sparks/Stevens/Sommers	Mays, Rex
9/15/36	Syracuse	dirt	82.37	Offy/Miller	Rose, Mauri
10/12/36	Roosevelt Raceway	paved	65.99	Alfa Romeo	Nuvaroli, Tazio
5/31/37	Indianapolis	brick	113.58	Offy/Stevens	Shaw, Wilbur
7/5/37	Roosevelt Raceway	paved	82.56	Auto Union	Rosemeyer, Bernd
9/12/37	Syracuse	dirt	87.49	Miller/Weil	Winn
5/30/38	Indianapolis	brick	117.20	Offy/Wetteroth	Roberts, Floyd
9/10/38	Syracuse	dirt	84.20	Offy/Lencki/Dreyer	Snyder, Jimmy
5/30/39	Indianapolis	brick	115.035	Maserati	Shaw
8/27/39	Milwaukee	dirt	83.651	Offy/Stevens	Stapp, Babe
9/2/39	Syracuse	dirt	74.899	Offy/Wetteroth	Rose
5/30/40	Indianapolis	brick	114.277	Maserati	Shaw
8/24/40	Springfield	dirt	87.45	Winfield/Stevens	Mays
9/20/40	Syracuse	dirt	85.254	Winfield/Stevens	Mays
5/30/41	Indianapolis	brick	115.117	Offy/Wetteroth	Davis, Floyd/Rose
8/24/41	Milwaukee	dirt	82.249	Winfield/Stevens	Mays
9/1/41	Syracuse	dirt	84.557	Winfield/Stevens	Mays
5/30/46	Indianapolis	brick	114.82	Sparks/Adams	Robson, George
6/30/46	Langhorne	dirt	85.14	Winfield/Stevens	Mays
9/2/46	Atlanta	dirt	---	Offy/Kurtis	Connor, George
9/15/46	Indianapolis	dirt	78.88	Winfield/Stevens	Mays
9/22/46	Milwaukee	dirt	84.81	Winfield/Stevens	Mays
10/6/46	Goshen	dirt	77.75	Offy/Wetteroth	Bettenhausen, Tony
5/30/47	Indianapolis	brick	116.33	Offy/Deidt	Rose
6/8/47	Milwaukee	dirt	82.28	Offy/Wetteroth	Holland, Bill
6/22/47	Langhorne	dirt	87.72	Offy/Wetteroth	Holland
7/4/47	Atlanta	dirt	75.21	Offy/Adams	Ader, Walt
7/13/47	Bainbridge	dirt	85.70	Offy/Horn	Horn, Ted
7/27/47	Milwaukee	dirt	85.96	Offy/Stevens/Lencki (Tucker Partner Spl)	Van Acker, Charles
8/17/47	Goshen	dirt	80.46	Offy/Stevens	Bettenhausen
8/24/47	Milwaukee	dirt	84.33	Offy/Horn	Horn
9/1/47	Pikes Peak	hill	44.94	Maserati	Unser, Louis
9/28/47	Springfield	dirt	92.51	Offy/Stevens	Bettenhausen
10/2/47	Dallas	dirt	86.00	Offy/Horn	Horn
4/25/48	Dallas	dirt	78.64	Offy/Horn	Horn
5/31/48	Indianapolis	brick	119.81	Offy/Deidt	Rose
6/6/48	Milwaukee	dirt	85.31	Offy/Kurtis	Andres, Emil
6/20/48	Langhorne	dirt	89.62	Offy/Kurtis	Brown, Walt
8/15/48	Milwaukee	dirt	85.32	Offy/Kurtis	Mantz, Johnny
8/21/48	Springfield	dirt	90.52	Offy/Horn	Horn
8/29/48	Milwaukee	dirt	86.73	Offy/Marchese	Fohr, Myron/ Bettenhausen
9/4/48	DuQuoin	dirt	88.38	Offy/Meyer	Wallard, Lee
9/6/48	Atlanta	dirt	79.27	Offy/Wetteroth	HansenMel
9/6/48	Pikes Peak	hill	47.07	Offy/Coniff	Rogers, Al
9/19/48	Springfield	dirt	88.69	Offy/Marchese	Fohr
10/10/48	DuQuoin	dirt	83.57	Offy/Kurtis	Parsons, Johnnie
4/29/49	Dallas	dirt	n/a	Offy/Kurtis	Parsons, Sr.
5/30/49	Indianapolia	brick	121.32	Offy/Deidt	Holland
6/5/49	Milwaukee	dirt	83.61	Offy/Marchese	Fohr
6/19/49	Trenton	dirt	75.77	Offy/Marchese	Fohr
8/20/49	Springfield	dirt	87.61	Offy/Lesovsky	Hansen
8/29/49	Milwaukee	dirt	85.81	Offy/Kurtis	Parsons, Johnnie
9/3/49	DuQuoin	dirt	90.06	Offy/Kurtis, Supercharged	Bettenhausen Sr.
9/5/49	Pike's Peak	hill	46.85	Offy/Coniff	Rogers, Al
9/10/49	Syracuse	dirt	85.00	Offy/Kurtis	Parsons, Johnnie
9/11/49	Detroit	dirt	81.26	Offy/Kurtis, Supercharged	Bettenhausen Sr.
9/25/49	Springfield	dirt	91.72	Offy/Kurtis	Parsons, Johnnie
10/16/49	Langhorne, Pa.	dirt	92.39	Offy/Kurtis	Parsons, Johnnie
10/30/49	Sarcamento	dirt	84.48	Offy/Kurtis	Agabashian, Fred
11/6/49	Del Mar, Calif.	dirt	85.35	Offy/Ewing	Davies,Jim
5/30/50	Indianapolis	brick	124.000	Offy/Kurtis	Parsons, Johnnie
6/11/50	Milwaukee	dirt	85.02	Offy/Wetteroth	Bettenhausen Sr.
6/25/50	Langhorne, Pa.	dirt	88.51	Offy/Kurtis	McGrath, Jack
8/19/50	Springfield, Ill.	dirt	91.26	Offy/Nichels	Russo, Paul
8/27/50	Milwaukee	dirt	90.61	Offy/Kurtis	Faulkner, Walt
9/4/50	Pike's Peak	hill	47.61	Offy/Coniff	Rogers
9/9/50	Syracuse	dirt	87.34	Offy/Kurtis	McGrath
9/10/50	Detroit	dirt	82.84	Offy/Moore	Banks, Henry
10/15/50	Sacramento	dirt	82.46	Offy/Kurtis	Dinsmore, Duke
11/12/50	Phoenix	dirt	78.01	Offy/Ewing	Davies, Jimmy
11/26/50	Bay Meadows, CA	dirt	86.16	Offy/Kurtis	Bettenhausen Sr.
12/10/50	Darlington, SC	paved	104.65	Offy/Nichels	Parsons, Johnnie
5/30/51	Indianapolis	brick	126.24	Offy/Kurtis	Wallard
6/10/51	Milwaukee	dirt	90.15	Offy/Kurtis	Bettenhausen, Sr.
6/24/51	Langhorne	dirt	92.36	Offy/Kurtis	Bettenhausen, Sr.
7/4/51	Darlington	paved	104.51	Offy/Kuzma	Faulkner, Walt
8/18/51	Springfield	dirt	90.05	Offy/Kurtis	Bettenhausen Sr.
8/26/51	Milwaukee	dirt	91.35	Offy/Kuzma	Faulkner
9/1/51	DuQuoin	dirt	88.31	Offy/Kurtis	Bettenhausen Sr
9/3/51	DuQuoin	dirt	86.56	Offy/Kurtis	Bettenhausen Sr.
9/5/51	Pike's Peak	hill	47.58	Offy/Coniff	Rogers
9/8/51	Syracuse	dirt	n/a	Offy/Kurtis	Bettenhausen, Sr.
9/9/51	Detroit	dirt	83.62	Offy/Fred Nichels/ Joe Silnes/Paul Russo	Russo, Paul
9/23/51	Denver	dirt	86.60	Offy/Kurtis	Bettenhausen Sr.
10/21/51	San Jose, Calif.	dirt	81.76	Offy/Kurtis	Bettenhausen Sr.
11/4/51	Phoenix	dirt	84.63	Offy/Kurtis	Parsons, Johnnie
11/11/51	Bay Meadows	dirt	87.70	Offy/Kurtis	Parsons, Johnnie
5/30/52	Indianapolis	brick	128.92	Offy/Kuzma	Ruttman, Troy
6/8/52	Milwaukee	dirt	91.35	Offy/Kurtis	Nazaruk, Mike
7/4/52	Raleigh	paved	89.10	Offy/Kuzma	Ruttman
8/16/52	Springfield	dirt	94.34	Offy/Nichels/Silnes/Russo	Schindler, Bill
8/24/52	Milwaukee	dirt	81.39	Offy/Kurtis	Stevenson, Chuck
8/30/52	Detroit	dirt	81.56	Offy/Kuzma	Vukovich, Bill Sr.
9/1/52	DuQuoin	dirt	88.40	Offy/Kurtis	Stevenson, Chuck
9/1/52	Pikes Peak	hill	47.87	Offy/Kurtis	Hammond, George
9/6/52	Syracuse	dirt	89.20	Offy/Kurtis	McGrath
9/28/52	Denver	dirt	88.04	Offy/Kurtis	Vukovich Sr.
11/2/52	San Jose	dirt	n/a	Offy/Kurtis/Schroeder Blakely # 15	Ball, Bobby
11/11/52	Phoenix	dirt	85.87	Offy/Kurtis	Parsons, Sr.
5/30/53	Indianapolis	paved	128.74	Offy/Kurtis	Vukovich Sr.
6/7 /53	Milwaukee	dirt	93.73	Offy/Kurtis	McGrath
6/21/53	Springfield	dirt	89.48	Offy/Kurtis	Ward, Rodger
7/4/53	Detroit	dirt	n/a	Offy/Kurtis	Ward
8/22/53	Springfield	dirt	90.80	Offy/Kurtis	Hanks, Sam
8/30/53	Milwaukee	dirt	88.94	Offy/Kuzma	Stevenson
9/7/53	DuQuoin	dirt	89.98	Offy/Kurtis	Hanks
9/7/53	Pike's Peak	hill	48.84	Offy/Kurtis	Unser. Louis
9/12/53	Syracuse	dirt	74.07	Offy/Kurtis (Belanger # 99)	Bettenhausen Sr.
9/26/53	Indy Fairgrounds	dirt	87.19		Offy/Kuzma Sweikert, Bob

Date	Track	Surface	Speed	Engine/Chassis	Driver
10/25/53	Sacramento	dirt	79.79	Offy/Kurtis	Bryan, Jim
11/11/53	Phoenix	dirt	83.86	Offy/Kurtis	Bettenhausen Sr.
5/31/54	Indianapolis	paved	130.84	Offy/Kurtis	Vukovich Sr.
6/6/54	Milwaukee	dirt	87.52	Offy/Kuzma	Stevenson
6/20/54	Langhorne	dirt	97.56	Offy/Kuzma	Bryan
7/5/54	Darlington	paved	123.01	Offy/Kuzma	Ayulo, Manuel
8/21/54	Springfield	dirt	92.57	Offy/Ewing	Davies
8/29/54	Milwaukee	paved	96.26	Offy/Kuzma	Ayulo
9/6/54	DuQuoin	dirt	n/a	Offy/Kurtis	Hanks
9/6/54	Pike's Peak	hill	50.83	Offy/Hunt # 27	Andrews, Keith
9/11/54	Syracuse	dirt	90.03	Offy/Kurtis	Sweikert
9/18/54	Indy Fairgrounds	dirt	84.65	Offy/Kuzma	Bryan
10/17/54	Sacramento	dirt	85.31	Offy/Kuzma	Bryan
11/7/54	Phoenix	dirt	84.40	Offy/Kuzma	Bryan
11/14/54	Las Vegas	dirt	84.82	Offy/Kuzma	Bryan
5/30/55	Indianapolis	paved	128.21	Offy/Kurtis	Sweikert
6/5/55	Milwaukee	dirt	98.80	Offy/Kuzma	Thomson, Johnny
6/26/55	Langhorne	dirt	95.73	Offy/Kuzma	Bryan
8/20/55	Springfield	dirt	90.52	Offy/Kuzma	Bryan
8/28/55	Milwaukee	paved	95.02	Offy/Kurtis Dunn # 89	Flaherty, Pat
9/5/55	DuQuoin	dirt	93.58	Offy/Kuzma	Bryan
9/6/55	Pike's Peak	hill	51.56	Lincoln	Finney, Bob
9/10/55	Syracuse	dirt	92.99	Offy/Watson	Sweikert, Bob
9/17/55	Indy Fairgrounds	dirt	83.98	Offy/Kuzma	Bryan
10/16/55	Sacramento	dirt	86.21	Offy/Kuzma	Bryan
11/6/55	Phoenix	dirt	N/A	Offy/Kuzma	Bryan
5/30/56	Indianapolis	paved	128.490	Offy/Watson	Flaherty, Pat
6/10/56	Milwaukee	paved	98.846	Offy/Watson	Flaherty
6/24/56	Langhorne	dirt	95.212	Offy/Kuzma	Amick, George
7/4/56	Darlington	paved	124.883	Offy/Templeton	O'Connor, Pat
7/14/56	Atlanta	dirt	n/a	Offy/Clemens-Scopa	Sachs, Eddie
8/18/56	Springfield	dirt	88.471	Offy/Kuzma	Bryan
8/26/56	Milwaukee	paved	92.736	Offy/Kuzma	Bryan
9/3/56	DuQuoin	dirt	91.706	Offy/Kuzma	Bryan
9/8/56	Syracuse	dirt	90.804	Offy/Kuzma	Bettenhausen Sr.
9/15/56	Indy Fairgrounds	dirt	80.727	Offy/Kuzma	Bryan
10/21/56	Sacramento	dirt	80.727	Offy/Watson	Jud Larson
11/12/56	Phoenix	dirt	91.826	Offy/Lesovsky	Amick
5/30/57	Indianapolis	paved	135.601	Offy/Epperly/Salih	Hanks
6/2/57	Langhorne	dirt	100.174	Offy/Kuzma	Thomson, Johnny
6/9/57	Milwaukee	paved	97.789	Offy/Lesovsky, Supercharged	Ward, Rodger
6/23/57	Detroit	dirt	86.90	Offy/Kuzma	Bryan
7/4/57	Atlanta	dirt	98.995	Offy/Lesovsky	George Amick
8/15/57	Springfield	dirt	96.015	Offy/Lesovsky	Ward
8/25/57	Milwaukee	paved	98.133	Offy/Epperly	Rathman, Jim
9/2/57	DuQuoin	dirt	90.948	Offy/Watson	Larson, Jud
9/7/57	Syracuse	dirt	94.294	Offy/DeBisschop-Watson	Elmer, George
9/14/57	Indy Fairgrounds	dirt	91.751	Offy/Watson	Larson
9/29/57	Trenton	paved	100.279	Offy/Kuzma	O'Connor, Pat
10/20/57	Sacramento	dirt	90.965	Offy/Lesovsky	Ward
11/11/57	Phoenix	dirt	86.001	Offy/Kuzma	Bryan
3/30/58	Trenton	paved	95.527	Offy/Kuzma	Sutton, Len
5/30/58	Indianapolis	paved	133.791	Offy/Epperly/Salih	Bryan
6/8/58	Milwaukee	paved	94.013	Offy/Kuzma	Bisch, Art
6/15/58	Langhorne	dirt	91.977	Offy/Kuzma	Sachs
7/4/58	Atlanta	dirt	87.146	Offy/Watson	Larson
8/16/58	Springfield	dirt	98.137	Offy/Kuzma	Thomson
8/24/58	Milwaukee	paved	97.864	Offy/Lesovsky	Ward
9/1/58	DuQuoin	dirt	94.734	Offy/Kuzma	Thomson
9/6/58	Syracuse	dirt	94.953	Offy/Kuzma	Thomson
9/13/58	Indy Fairgrounds	dirt	92.142	Offy/Kuzma	Sachs
9/28/58	Trenton	paved	99.368	Offy/Lesovsky	Ward
10/26/58	Sacramento	dirt	89.175	Offy/Kuzma	Thomson
11/11/58	Phoenix	dirt	92.738	Offy/Lesovsky	Larson
4/4/59	Daytona	paved	170.261	Offy/Watson	Rathmann, Jim
4/19/59	Trenton	paved	91.160	Offy/Kuzma	Bettenhausen Sr.
5/30/59	Indianapolis	paved	135.857	Offy/Watson	Ward
6/7/59	Milwaukee	paved	98.609	Offy/Lesovsky	Thomson
6/14/59	Langhorne	dirt	99.553	Offy/Kurtis	Johnson, Van
8/22/59	Springfield	dirt	95.186	Offy/Kuzma	Sutton
8/30/59	Milwaukee	paved	96.445	Offy/Watson	Ward
9/7/59	DuQuoin	dirt	93.267	Offy/Watson	Ward
9/12/59	Syracuse	dirt	94.122	Offy/Meskowski	Sachs
9/19/59	Indy Fairgrounds	dirt	91.032	Offy/Watson	Ward
9/27/59	Trenton	paved	97.398	Offy/Meskowski	Sachs
10/18/59	Phoenix	dirt	88.458	Offy/Kuzma	Bettenhausen Sr.
10/25/59	Sacramento	dirt	86.465	Offy/Kuzma	Hurtubise, Jim
4/10/60	Trenton	paved	95.486	Offy/Watson	Ward
5/30/60	Indianapolis	paved	138.767	Offy/Watson	Rathmann
6/5/60	Milwaukee	paved	99.465	Offy/Watson	Ward
6/19/60	Langhorne	dirt	100.786	Offy/Kuzma	Hurtubise
8/20/60	Springfield	dirt	90.600	Offy/Lesovsky	Packard,Jim
8/28/60	Milwaukee	paved	100.131	Offy/Watson	Sutton
9/5/60	DuQuoin	dirt	93.351	Offy/Meskowski	Foyt, A.J.
9/11/60	Syracuse	dirt	93.258	Offy/Meskowski	Grim, Bobby
9/17/60	Indy Fairgrounds	dirt	89.286	Offy/Meskowski	Foyt
9/25/60	Trenton	paved	99.223	Offy/Kuzma	Sachs
10/30/60	Sacramento	dirt	84.796	Offy/Meskowski	Foyt
11/20/60	Phoenix	dirt	89.079	Offy/Meskowski	Foyt
4/9/61	Trenton	paved	98.679	Offy/Kuzma	Sachs
5/30/61	Indianapolis	paved	139.130	Offy/Watson/Trevis	Foyt
6/4/61	Milwaukee	paved	103.860	Offy/Watson	Ward
6/18/61	Langhorne	dirt	99.601	Offy/Meskowski	Foyt
8/20/61	Milwaukee	paved	101.638	Offy/Watson	Ruby, Lloyd
8/21/61	Springfield	dirt	n/a	Offy/Kuzma	Hurtubise
9/4/61	DuQuoin	dirt	92.755	Offy/Meskowski	Foyt
9/9/61	Syracuse	dirt	95.090	Offy/Watson	Ward
9/16/61	Indy Fairgrounds	dirt	92.369	Offy/Meskowski	Foyt
9/24/61	Trenton	paved	101.013	Offy/Kuzma	Sachs
10/29/61	Sacramento	dirt	88.779	Offy/Watson	Ward
11/19/61	Phoenix	dirt	n/a	Offy/Kuzma	Jones, Parnelli
4/8/62	Trenton	paved	101.101	Offy/Meskowski	Foyt
5/30/62	Indianapolis	paved	140.293	Offy/Watson	Ward
6/10/62	Milwaukee	paved	100.700	Offy/Watson-Trevis	Foyt
7/1/62	Langhorne	dirt	93.186	Offy/Meskowski	Foyt
7/22/62	Trenton	paved	100.976	Offy/Watson	Ward
8/18/62	Springfield	dirt	92.625	Offy/Kuzma	Hurtubise
8/19/62	Milwaukee	paved	100.017	Offy/Watson	Ward
8/26/62	Langhorne	dirt	104.799	Offy/Watson	Branson, Don
9/8/62	Syracuse	dirt	95.751	Offy/Watson	Ward
9/15/62	Indy Fairgrounds	dirt	90.604	Offy/Kuzma	Jones Agajanian # 98
9/23/62	Trenton	paved	102.529	Offy/Watson	Branson
10/28/62	Sacramento	dirt	97.220	Offy/Meskowski	Foyt
11/18/62	Phoenix	dirt	92.124	Offy/Meskowski	Marshman, Bobby
4/21/63	Trenton	paved	102.491	Offy/Meskowski	Foyt
5/30/63	Indianapolis	paved	143.137	Offy/Watson	Jones
6/9/63	Milwaukee	paved	100.561	Offy/Watson	Ward
6/23/63	Langhorne	dirt	104.036	Offy/Meskowski	Foyt
7/28/63	Trenton	paved	100.403	Offy/Watson-Trevis	Foyt
8/17/63	Springfield	dirt	95.557	Offy/Watson	Ward
8/18/63	Milwaukee	paved	104.452	Ford/Lotus	Clark, Jim
9/6/63	DuQuoin	dirt	95.234	Offy\Meskowski	Foyt
9/14/63	Indy Fairgrounds	dirt	93.545	Offy/Watson	Ward
9/22/63	Trenton	paved	101.358	Offy/Watson-Trevis	Foyt
10/27/63	Sacramento	dirt	92.174	Offy/Watson	Ward
11/17/63	Phoenix	dirt	85.010	Offy/Watson	Ward
3/22/64	Phoenix	paved	107.536	Offy/Watson	Foyt
4/19/64	Trenton	paved	104.530	Offy/Watson	Foyt
5/30/64	Indianapolis	paved	147.350	Offy/Watson	Foyt
6/7/64	Milwaukee	paved	100.346	Offy/Watson	Foyt
6/21/64	Langhorne	dirt	102.552	Offy/Meskowski	Foyt
7/19/64	Trenton	paved	105.590	Offy/Watson	Foyt
8/22/64	Springfield	dirt	95.238	Offy/Meskowski	Foyt
8/23/64	Milwaukee	paved	104.751	Ford/Lotus	Jones
9/7/64	DuQuoin	dirt	97.800	Offy/Meskowski	Foyt
9/26/64	Indy Fairgrounds	dirt	89.056	Offy/Meskowski	Foyt
9/27/64	Trenton	paved	96.415	Ford/Lotus	Jones
10/25/64	Sacramento	dirt	91.451	Offy/Meskowski	Foyt
11/22/64	Phoenix	paved	107.736	Offy/Halibrand	Ruby, Lloyd
3/28/65	Phoenix	paved	106.456	Offy/Watson	Branson
4/25/65	Trenton	paved	96.184	Offy/Brabham	McElreath, Jim
5/31/65	Indianapolis	paved	150.686	Ford/Lotus	Clark
6/6/65	Milwaukee	paved	101.743	Ford/Lotus-Kuzma	Jones
6/20/65	Langhorne	paved	89.108	Offy/Brabham	McElreath
7/4/65	Pike's Peak	hill	57.74	Ford/Lotus-Eisert	Unser, Al, Sr.
7/18/65	Trenton	paved	98.522	Ford/Lotus-Bignotti	Foyt
7/25/65	Indianapolis	road	101.656	Ford/Brabham-Brawner	Andretti, M.

Date	Track	Surface	Speed	Engine/Chassis	Driver
8/1/65	Atlanta	paved	141.728	Ford/Watson	Rutherford, Johnny
8/8/65	Langhorne	paved	104.857	Offy/Brabham	McElreath
8/14/65	Milwaukee	paved	97.276	Ford/Halibrand	Leonard
8/21/65	Springfield	dirt	96.174	Offy/Meskowski	Foyt
8/22/65	Milwaukee	paved	100.474	Offy/Gerhardt	Johncock,Gordon
9/6/65	DuQuoin	dirt	88.792	Offy/Watson	Branson
9/18/65	Indy Fairgrounds	dirt	84.849	Offy/Meskowski	Foyt
9/26/65	Trenton	paved	99.953	Ford/Lotus-Bignotti	Foyt
10/24/65	Sacramento	dirt	86.710	Offy/Watson	Branson
11/21/65	Phoenix	paved	99.990	Ford/Lotus-Bignotti	Foyt
3/20/66	Phoenix	paved	98.828	Ford/Brabham	McElreath,Jim
4/24/66	Trenton	paved	99.904	Drake Offy/Lola	Ward, Rodger
5/30/66	Indianapolis	paved	144.317	Ford/Lola	Hill, Graham
6/5/66	Milwaukee	paved	96.515	Ford/Brabham-Brawner	Andretti, M.
6/12/66	Langhorne	paved	98.690	Ford/Brabham-Brawner	Andretti, M.
6/26/66	Atlanta	paved	139.319	Ford/Brabham-Brawner	Andretti, M.
7/4/66	Pike's Peak	hill	60.04	Chevrolet/Unser	Unser, Bobby
7/24/66	Indianapolis	road	95.373	Ford/Brabham-Brawner	Andretti, M.
8/7/66	Langhorne	paved	108.493	Ford/Eagle	McCluskey, Roger
8/20/66	Springfield	dirt	95.243	Offy/Watson	Branson, Don
8/27/66	Milwaukee	paved	104.061	Ford/Brabham-Brawner	Andretti, M.
9/5/66	DuQuoin	dirt	95.102	Offy/Meskowski	Tingelstadt, Bud
9/10/66	Indy Fairgrounds	dirt	96.582	Offy/Kuzma	Andretti, M.
9/25/66	Trenton	paved	105.127	Ford/Brabham-Brawner	Andretti, M.
10/23/66	Sacramento	dirt	88.568	Offy/Watson	Atkins, Dick
11/20/66	Phoenix	paved	104.697	Ford/Brabham-Brawner	Andretti, M.
4/9/67	Phoenix	paved	86.296	Drake-Offy/turbo Mongoose	Ruby, Lloyd
4/23/67	Trenton	paved	109.837	Ford/Brawner (Hawk)	Andretti, M.
5/31/67	Indianapolis	paved	151.207	Ford/Coyote	Foyt, A.J.
6/4/67	Milwaukee	paved	98.643	Ford/Gerhardt	Johncock,Gordon
6/18/67	Landhorne	paved	113.380	Ford/Lotus	Ruby, Lloyd
6/25/67	Pike's Peak	hill	58.35	Chevrolet	Vandervoort, Wes
7/1/67	Mosport (Canada)	road	102.77	Ford/Eagle	Unser, Bobby
7/23/67	Indianapolis	road	113.612	Ford/Brawner (Hawk)	Andretti, M.
7/30/67	Langhorne	paved	113.183	Ford/Brawner (Hawk)	Andretti, M.
8/6/67	St. Jovite, Canada (1st of 2 heats)	road	91.353	Ford/Brawner (Hawk)	Andretti, M.
8/6/67	St. Jovite [1]	road	96.88	Ford/Brawner (Hawk)	Andretti, M.
8/19/67	Springfield	dirt	86.323	Offy/Meskowski	Foyt, A.J.
8/20/67	Milwaukee	paved	103.386	Ford/Brawner (Hawk)	Andretti
9/4/67	DuQuoin	dirt	93.578	Offy/Meskowski	Foyt, A.J.
9/9/67	Indy Fairgrounds	dirt	95.567	Offy/Kuzma	Andretti, M.
9/24/67	Trenton	paved	92.223	Ford/Coyote	Foyt, A.J.
10/1/67	Sacramento	dirt	87.712	Offy/Meskowski	Foyt, A.J.
10/22/67	Hanford	paved	127.523	Ford/Gerhardt	Johncock,Gordon
11/19/67	Phoenix	paved	109.872	Ford/Brawner (Hawk)	Andretti, M.
11/26/67	Riverside	road	107.170	Ford-Weslake/Eagle	Gurney, Dan
3/17/68	Hanford	paved	121.511	Drake-Offy/Gerhardt	Johncock, Gordon
3/31/68	Las Vegas	road	113.269	Ford/Eagle	Unser, Bobby
4/7/68	Phoenix	paved	100.938	Drake-Offy/Eagle	Unser, Bobby
4/21/68	Trenton	paved	103.397	Drake-Offy/Eagle	Unser, Bobby
5/30/68	Indianapolis	paved	152.882	Drake-Offy/Eagle	Unser, Bobby
6/9/68	Milwaukee	paved	100.739	Drake-Offy/Mongoose	Ruby, Lloyd
6/15/68	Mosport (Canada)	road	105.727	Ford-Weslake/Eagle	Gurney, Dan
6/15/68	Mosport (Canada)	road	108.564	Ford-Weslake/Eagle	Gurney, Dan
6/23/68	Langhorne	paved	103.463	Drake-Offy/Gerhardt	Johncock,Gordon
6/30/68	Pike's Peak	hill	62.53	Chevrolet	Unser, Bobby
7/7/68	Castle Rock	road	83.168	Ford/Coyote	Foyt, A.J.
7/13/68	Nazareth	dirt	100.068	Offy/Ward	Unser, Al, Sr.
7/21/68	Indianapolis	road	96.80	Ford/Lola	Unser, Al, Sr.
7/21/68	Indianapolis	road	86.768	Ford/Lola	Unser, Al, Sr.
7/28/68	Langhorne	paved	107.650	Ford/Lola	Unser, Al, Sr.
7/28/68	Langhorne	paved	122.328	Ford/Lola	Unser, Al, Sr.
8/4/68	St. Jovite	road	96.49	Ford/Brawner (Hawk)	Andretti, M.
8/4/68	St. Jovite (Canada)	road	80.03	Ford/Brawner (Hawk)	Andretti, M.
8/17/68	Springfield	dirt	90.046	Offy/Meskowski	McCluskey, Roger
8/18/68	Milwaukee	paved	108.735	Drake-Offy/Mongoose	Ruby, Lloyd
9/2/68	DuQuoin	dirt	91.518	Offy/Kuzma	Andretti, M.
9/7/68	Indianapolis Fairgrounds	dirt	93.296	Offy/Meskowski	Foyt, A.J.
9/22/68	Trenton	paved	104.543	Drake-Offy/Brawner	Andretti, M.
9/29/68	Sacramento	dirt	87.118	Offy-Meskowski	Foyt, A.J.
10/13/68	Michigan	paved	161.812	Drake-Offy/Eagle	Bucknum, Ronnie
11/3/68	Hanford	paved	134.416	Ford/Coyote	Foyt, A.J.
11/17/68	Phoenix	paved	104.972	Drake-Offy/Gerhardt	Bettenhausen, Jr. Gary
12/1/68	Riverside	road	111.689	Ford-Weslake/Eagle	Gurney, Dan
3/30/69	Phoenix	paved	109.853	Chevrolet/Gilbert	Follmer, George
4/13/69	Hanford	paved	N/A	Ford/Brawner (Hawk)	Andretti, M.
5/30/69	Indianapolis	paved	156.867	Ford/Brawner (Hawk)	Andretti, M.
6/8/69	Milwaukee	paved	112.157	Drake-Offy/Gerhardt	Pollard, Art
6/15/69	Langhorne	paved	112.424	Drake-Offy/Eagle	Unser, Bobby
6/29/69	Pike's Peak	hill	58.52	Chevrolet/King	Andretti, M.
7/6/69	Castle Rock	road	84.337	Ford/Eagle	Johncock, Gordon
7/12/69	Nazareth	dirt	105.851	Offy/Kuzma	Andretti, M.
7/19/69	Trenton	paved	139.591	Ford/Brawner (Hawk)	Andretti, M.
7/27/69	Indianapolis	road	92.053	Ford/Gurney/Eagle	Gurney, Dan
7/27/69	Indianapolis	road	94.967	Repco/Brabham	Revson, Peter
8/17/69	Milwaukee	paved	106.758	Ford/Lola	Unser, Al, Sr.
8/19/69	Springfield	dirt	96.642	Offy/Kuzma	Andretti, M.
8/24/69	Dover	paved	124.978	Plymouth/Gerhardt	Pollard, Art
9/1/69	DuQuoin	dirt	94.724	Ford/King	Unser, Al, Sr.
9/6/69	Indy Fairgrounds	dirt	93.609	Ford/Meskowski	Foyt, A.J.
9/14/69	Brainerd	road	108.270	Ford/Eagle	Johncock, Gordon
9/14/69	Brainerd	road	112.641	Ford/Gurney/Eagle	Gurney, Dan
9/21/69	Trenton	paved	134.395	Ford/Brawner	Andretti, M.
9/28/69	Sacramento	dirt	93.526	Ford/King	Unser, Al, Sr.
10/19/69	Kent	road	85.559	Ford/Brawner (Hawk)	Andretti, M.
10/19/69	Kent	road	84.366	Ford/Lola	Unser, Al, Sr.
12/7/69	Riverside	road	105.797	Ford/Brawner (Hawk)	Andretti, M.
3/28/70	Phoenix	paved	N/A	Ford/Colt	Unser, Al, Sr.
4/4/70	Sears Point	road	86.179	Ford/Gurney/Eagle	Gurney, Dan
4/26/70	Trenton	paved	135.967	Drake-Offy/Mongoose	Ruby, Lloyd
5/30/70	Indianapolis	paved	155.749	Ford/Colt	Unser, Al, Sr.
6/7/70	Milwaukee	paved	108.299	Ford/Colt	Leonard, Joe
6/14/70	Langhorne	paved	106.302	Drake-Offy/Eagle	Unser, Bobby
6/28/70	Castle Rock	road	84.013	Ford/McNamara	Andretti, M.
7/4/70	Michigan	paved	140.625	Drake-Offy/Gerhardt	Bettenhausen, Jr. Gary
7/26/70	Indianapolis	road	92.799	Ford/Colt	Unser, Al, Sr.
8/22/70	Springfield	dirt	62.30	Ford/King	Unser, Al, Sr.
8/23/70	Milwaukee	paved	114.304	Ford/Colt	Unser, Al, Sr.
9/6/70	Ontario	paved	160.106	Ford/Coyote	McElreath, Jim
9/7/70	DuQuoin	dirt	98.155	Ford/King	Unser, Al, Sr.
9/12/70	Indy Fairgrounds	dirt	97.887	Ford/King	Unser, Al, Sr.
9/19/70	Sedalia	dirt	98.039	Ford/King	Unser, Al, Sr.
10/3/70	Trenton	paved	137.630	Ford/Colt	Unser, Al, Sr.
10/4/70	Sacramento	dirt	93.384	Ford/King	Unser, Al, Sr.
11/21/70	Phoenix	paved	116.807	Ford/Gurney/Eagle	Savage, Swede
2/28/71	Rafaela, Argentina	paved	166.909	Ford/Colt	Unser, Al, Sr.
2/28/71	Rafaela, Arentina	paved	148.816	Ford/Colt	Unser, Al, Sr.
3/27/71	Phoenix	paved	111.565	Ford/Colt	Unser, Al, Sr.
4/25/71	Trenton	paved	132.562	Ford/Eagle	Mosley, Mike
5/29/71	Indianapolis	paved	157.735	Ford/Colt	Unser, Al, Sr.
6/6/71	Milwaukee	paved	114.858	Ford/Colt	Unser, Al, Sr.
7/3/71	Pocono	paved	138.649	Drake-Offy/McLaren	Donohue, Mark
7/18/71	Michigan	paved	144.898	Drake-Offy/McLaren	Donohue, Mark
8/15/71	Milwaukee	paved	109.386	Drake-Offy/Eagle	Unser, Bobby
9/5/71	Ontario	paved	152.354	Ford/Colt	Leonard, Joe
9/6/71	DuQuoin	dirt (Silver Crown)	n/a	Offy/Watson	Snider, George
10/3/71	Trenton	paved	140.771	Drake-Offy/Eagle	Unser, Bobby
10/23/71	Phoenix	paved	110.333	Ford/Coyote	Foyt, A.J.
3/18/72	Phoenix	paved	102.805	Drake-Offy/Eagle	Unser, Bobby
4/23/72	Trenton	paved	146.211	Drake-Offy/McLaren	Bettenhausen, Jr.
5/27/72	Indianapolis	paved	162.962	Drake-Offy/McLaren	Donohue, Mark
6/4/72	Milwaukee	paved	109.131	Drake-Offy/Eagle	Unser, Bobby
7/16/72	Michigan	paved	140.685	Drake-Offy/Parnelli	Leonard, Joe
7/29/72	Pocono	paved	154.781	Drake-Offy/Parnelli	Leonard, Joe
8/13/72	Milwaukee	paved	111.652	Drake-Offy/Parnelli	Leonard, Joe
9/3/72	Ontario	paved	151.540	Drake-Offy/McLaren	McCluskey, Roger
9/24/72	Trenton	paved	143.236	Drake-Offy/Eagle	Unser, Bobby
11/4/72	Phoenix	paved	127.617	Drake-Offy/Eagle	Unser, Bobby
4/7/73	Texas	paved	153.224	Drake-Offy/Parnelli	Unser, Al, Sr.
4/15/73	Trenton	paved	138.355	Foyt/Coyote	Foyt, A.J.

Date	Track	Surface	Speed	Engine/Chassis	Driver
4/15/73	Trenton	paved	149.626	Drake-Offy/Parnelli	Andretti, M.
5/30/73	Indianapolis	paved	159.036	Drake-Offy/Eagle	Johncock
6/10/73	Milwaukee	paved	108.008	Drake-Offy/Eagle	Unser, Bobby
7/1/73	Pocono	paved	144.944	Foyt/Coyote	Foyt, A.J.
7/15/73	Michigan	paved	161.145	Drake-Offy/McLaren	McCluskey, Roger
8/12/73	Milwaukee	paved	108.320	Drake-Offy/Eagle	Dallenbach
8/26/73	Ontario	paved	179.910	Drake-Offy/Eagle	Dallenbach
8/26/73	Ontario	paved	164.161	Drake-Offy/McLaren	Rutherford
9/2/73	Ontario	paved	157.660	Drake-Offy/Eagle	Dallenbach
9/16/73	Michigan	paved	134.161	Drake-Offy/Eagle	Vukovich, Bill, Jr.
9/16/73	Michigan	paved	157.282	Drake-Offy/McLaren	Rutherford
9/23/73	Trenton	paved	135.625	Drake-Offy/Eagle	Johncock
10/6/73	Texas	paved	181.918	Drake-Offy/McLaren	Bettenhausen, Jr.
11/3/73	Phoenix	paved	115.016	Drake-Offy/Eagle	Johncock
3/3/74	Ontario	paved	176.873	Foyt/Coyote	Foyt, A.J.
3/3/74	Ontario	paved	172.673	Drake-Offy/McLaren	Rutherford
3/10/74	Ontario	paved	157.017	Drake-Offy/Eagle	Unser, Bobby
3/17/74	Phoenix	paved	116.663	Drake-Offy/Eagle	Mosley, Mike
4/7/74	Trenton	paved	125.615	Drake-Offy/Eagle	Unser, Bobby
5/26/74	Indianapolis	paved	158.589	Drake-Offy/McLaren	Rutherford
6/9/74	Milwaukee	paved	110.225	Drake-Offy/McLaren	Rutherford
6/30/74	Pocono	paved	156.701	Drake-Offy/McLaren	Rutherford
7/21/74	Michigan	paved	160.695	Drake-Offy/Eagle	Unser, Bobby
8/11/74	Milwaukee	paved	118.762	Drake-Offy/Eagle	Johncock
9/7/74	Indianapolis Fairgrounds (Silver Crown)	dirt	n/a (only turbo Offy ever to win a Sil ver Crown race)	Bignotti-Offy/King	Howerton, Jackie
9/15/74	Michigan	paved	142.141	Drake-Offy/Eagle	Unser, Al Sr.
9/22/74	Trenton	paved	135.372	Foyt/Coyote	Foyt. A.J.
9/22/74	Trenton	paved	155.799	Drake-Offy/Eagle	Unser, Bobby
11/2/74	Phoenix	paved	124.202	Drake-Offy/Eagle	Johncock
3/2/75	Ontario	paved	177.085	Foyt/Coyote	Foyt, A.J.
3/2/75	Ontario	paved	153.05	Drake-Offy/Eagle	Dallenbach
3/9/75	Ontario	paved	154.344	Foyt/Coyote	Foyt, A.J.
3/16/75	Phoenix	paved	110.971	Drake-Offy/McLaren	Rutherford
4/6/75	Trenton	paved	154.625	Foyt/Coyote	Foyt, A.J.
5/25/75	Indianapolis	paved	149.213	Drake-Offy/Eagle	Unser, Bobby
6/8/75	Milwaukee	paved	128.801	Foyt/Coyte	Foyt, A.J.
6/29/75	Pocono	paved	140.712	Foyt/Coyote	Foyt, A.J.
7/20/75	Michigan	paved	153.907	Foyt/Coyote	Foyt, A.J.
8/17/75	Milwaukee	paved	114.393	Drake-Offy/Eagle	Mosley, Mike
9/14/75	Michigan	paved	176.161	Drake-Offy/McLaren	Sneva, Tom
9/21/75	Trenton	paved	123.511	DGS-Offy/Wildcat	Johncock,
10/9/75	Phoenix	paved	111.055	Foyt/Coyote	Foyt, A.J.
3/14/76	Phoenix	paved	107.918	Drake-Offy/Eagle	Unser, Bobby
5/2/76	Trenton	paved	147.499	Drake-Offy/McLaren	Rutherford
5/30/76	Indianapolis	paved	148.725	Drake-Offy/McLaren	Rutherford
6/13/76	Milwaukee	paved	121.557	Drake-Offy/Eagle	Mosley, Mike
6/27/76	Pocono	paved	143.662	Cosworth/Parnelli	Unser, Al, Sr.
7/18/76	Michigan	paved	165.033	DGS-Offy/Wildcat	Johncock
8/1/76	Texas	paved	172.885	Foyt/Coyote	Foyt, A.J.
8/15/76	Trenton	paved	135.929	DGS-Offy/Wildcat	Johncock
8/22/76	Milwaukee	paved	121.907	Cosworth/Parnelli	Unser, Al, Sr.
9/5/76	Ontario	paved	143.246	Drake-Offy/Eagle	Unser, Bobby
9/18/76	Michigan	paved	164.068	Foyt/Coyote	Foyt, A.J.
10/31/76	Texas	paved	150.315	Drake-Offy/McLaren	Rutherford
11/7/76	Phoenix	paved	107.695	Cosworth/Parnelli	Unser, Al, Sr.
3/6/77	Ontario	paved	154.073	Foyt/Coyote	Foyt, A.J.
3/27/77	Phoenix	paved	111.395	Cosworth/McLaren	Rutherford
4/2/77	Texas	paved	157.711	Cosworth/McLaren	Sneva, Tom
5/1/77	Trenton	paved	151.288	DGS-Offy/Wildcat	Dallenbach
5/29/77	Indianapolis	paved	161.331	Foyt/Coyote	Foyt, A.J.
6/12/77	Milwaukee	paved	92.962	Cosworth/McLaren	Rutherford
6/26/77	Pocono	paved	152.931	Cosworth/McLaren	Sneva, Tom
7/3/77	Mosport	road	90.733	Foyt/Coyote	Foyt, A.J.
7/17/77	Michigan	paved	149.152	Cosworth/Parnelli	Ongais, Danny
7/31/77	Texas	paved	164.191	Cosworth/McLaren	Rutherford
8/21/77	Milwaukee	paved	103.798	Cosworth/McLaren	Rutherford
9/4/77	Ontario	paved	154.687	Cosworth/Parnelli	Unser, Al, Sr.
9/17/77	Michigan	paved	175.250	DGS-Offy/Wildcat	Johncock
10/29/77	Phoenix	paved	108.596	DGS-Offy/Wildcat	Johncock
3/18/78	Phoenix	paved	116.757	DGS-Offy/Wildcat	Johncock
3/26/78	Ontario	paved	162.810	Cosworth/Parnelli	Ongais, Danny
4/15/78	Texas	paved	173.594	Cosworth/Parnelli	Ongais, Danny
4/23/78	Trenton	paved	129.033	DGS-Offy/Wildcat	Johncock

[1] USAC road course meets consisted of two 100 to 150-mile heats, 1968-1975. At Ontario in 1973 and 1975 these events consisted of two 100-mile heats and a week later, a final 500-mile event.

Offenhauser Engine Specifications, 1926–1979

This data for all of the Miller and Offy fours plus the Hartz eight of 1932 is for standard engines. The horsepower, RPM, and bore and stroke information for the Offy engines is representative only. Different owners and mechanics used different engine dimensions, though at least at Indianapolis, displacement rules were enforced. Big "cheater" engines were often used at smaller tracks. Unless a driver ran away from everyone else, engines were seldom protested and measured. Actual power outputs varied widely dependant on state of tune, weather conditions, and numerous other factors.

Year	Engine[1]	Cyl	BorexStroke	Displ	CR	Valves/cyl	Main Bearings	Weight	RPM	HP	VIA
1926	Miller Marine	4	3.406x4.125	150.3	7:1	2	5	440	4300	115	86
1930	Miller Schofield	4	3.750x4.125	182.2	9.7:1	2	5	440	5000	115	86
1931	200	4	3.875x4.250	200.48	12:1	4	5	325	5000	190	72
1932	220	4	4.0625x4.250	220.36	12:1	4	5	325	5500	210	72
1932	Hartz	8	2.875x3.50	181.8	9:1	2[2]	5	320 (est)	7000	?	90
1933	255	4	4.250x4.50	255.38	12:1	4[3]	5	325	5200	250	72
1934	midget [4]	4	2.968x3.5	96.9	16:1[5]	2	3	237	7000[6]	90	90
1937	270	4	4.3125x4.625	269.55	15:1	4	5	500	5500	325	72
1937	318	4	4.5x5.0	318.08	15:1	4	5	540	5000	375 (est)	72
1949	176 (blown)	4	3.875x3.750	176.90	8:1	4	5	325	7200	460	72
1954	180 (blown)	4	3.967x3.625	179.6	8:1	4	5	325	6200	400 (est)	72
1958	255 (Low Tower)	4	4.28x4.38	251.89	15:1	4	5	452[7]	6600	325[8]	72
1966	168 (Roots)	4	4.125x3.125	167.05	8:1	4	5	380	8500	530	72
1966	168 (turbo)	4	4.125x3.175	167.05	8:1	4	5	360	8500	600	72
1969	159 (turbo)	4	4.030x3.125	159.520	8:1	4	5	360	9500	820	72
1975	DGS	4	4.281x2.750	158.25	8:1	4	5	370	9000	1000[9]	44
1974	Drake-Offy	4	4.281x2.750	158.25	8:1	4	5	370	10,000	1000+	38
1977	160-T (Drake)	V8					4	5			

[1] Engines made through mid-1933 were "Millers"; after 1933 they were made by Offenhauser, though until 1935 they were still sold as Miller engines. After 1946 they were made by Meyer & Drake until 1965 when they were made by Drake Engineeering & Sales Co.
[2] The Hartz and the midget engines were the only ones Offenhauser and Meyer & Drake produced as 8-valve engines in the *standard* form.
[3] Some 8-valve 220, 255, and 270 blocks were produced, for example engine s/n 76.
[4] In 1979, a few blocks were cast with bore and stroke of 3.00x2.50 displacing 70.69 ci for supercharged/turbocharged engines. Cases for the turbo midgets were "notchless," had on-center rod bearings, and were beefed up to handle the additional power.
[5] Compression ratio in the 1950s and later; some in the 1960s reportedly ran as high as 17:1.
[6] The normally-aspirated midget was making 175 hp @ 8000 rpm by 1965.
[7] The lightened version was eventually cut to 355 lb.
[8] Up to 420 hp was wrung from these engines when fully-tuned for qualifying.

Employees of Miller, Schofield, Harry A. Miller Inc., Offenhauser, Meyer & Drake 1913–1975

Regretably this list is incomplete; the only complete employee list known to exist is from Harry A. Miller Inc. bankruptcy, 1933. Other data is taken from the memory of employees, old photo identification, and other sources.

KEY:
(M) worked for Miller, before 1929
(S), worked for Schofield, circa 1930
(HAM) worked for Harry A. Miller Inc., 1931–33
(O) worked for Offenhauser, between 1933 and 1946
(D) worked for Meyer & Drake,Drake Engineering, between 1946 and 1979

Adamson, Frank M. (M) (O)
Anderson, John (S) (HAM) (M) (O)
Angel, J.C. (S)
Balmain, Andrew (M) (S)
Barnes, "Shorty" (M)
Barto, John (HAM)
Binyon, Bob (D)
Burback, Almon (HAM)
Caddy, "Doc" (M)
Calhoun, Leslie (M) (HAM)
Coryell, Harry (M) (HAM)
Derks, Ben (M) (HAM) (O)
Doig, Al (D)
Drake, Lem (D)
Drake, Dale (D)
Drake, John (D)
Eastman (M)
Edwards, John (M)
Fabian, Frank (S)
Flynn, Thomas (S)
French, Claude (HAM) (M) (O)
Fritz
"the Bolshevik" (M)
Gearhardt, George (S)
Gibson, Wm. (HAM)
Goossen, Leo (HAM) (O) (M)
Hamilton, W.P. (HAM) (M)
Harper (M)
Heckman "the hermit" (M)
Heinhold, Ted (HAM)
Hirashima, Takeo (D)
Jane (M)
Jenkins, Bill (M)
Kaufman, Fred (M) (HAM)
Kramer, Heinie (O) (M)
Kramer, Ed (HAM) (O) (M)
Kuhn, Herman (S) (HAM) (M)
Lavoie, Eddie (D)
Leonard (M)
Leugers (M)
Long, Al (D)
Lyster, L.A. (S)
Maher, Hank (D)
Marcenac, Jean (HAM)
Marshall, D.E. (S)
Mason, Malcolm (M) (HAM)
McNeil, J.A. (HAM) (M)
Metzler, Robert (S)
Meyer, Lou (D)
Miller, Ted (HAM) (M)
Moore, Art (M)
Offenhauser, Fred C. (O)
Offenhauser, Fred (M) (HAM) (M) (O)
Olepiewicz, Casper (M) (HAM)
Orsatti (draftsman)
Pearson, Ron (D)
Perkins, Ray(M)
Rogers, Ray (M)(HAM) (O)
Salih, George (D)
Sandau, Otto (M)(O) (D)
Shively, G.B. (S)
Smith, Frank (O)
Smith, Ray (HAM) (O)
Sobraske, Walt (M) (HAM) (O) (D)
Sobraske, Ed (M) (HAM) (O) (D)
Sommer, Phil (HAM)
Spengler (M)
Steele, Walter (HAM)
Stevenson, R.E. (S) (HAM)
Stone, Harry (HAM)
Tepe, Henriette (S)
Valli, Cesar (HAM)
Vogel, Herman (HAM)
Wade, E.J. (S)
Weil, Ernest (HAM) (O), (D)
Wenger (M)
Wigton, H.A. (S)

BIBLIOGRAPHY

AAA Yearbooks, 1946-1955.

Andretti, Mario. *What's it Like Out There?* Henry Regnery Company, Chicago, 1970.

Bagnall, Art. *Roy Richter.* Bagnall Publishing, Los Alamitos, 1990

Banning, Gene. *Speedway.* Spartus, Incline Village, 1983.

Batchelor, Dean. *The American Hot Rod.* Motorbooks International, Osceola, 1995.

Betts, Charles. *Auto Racing Winners.* Chas. L. Betts, Jr., Philadelphia, 1948.

Bloemker, Al. *500 Miles To Go.* Coward-McCann, New York, 1961.

Bochroch, Albert and Dean Batchelor. *Cunningham.* Motorbooks International, Osceola, 1993.

Bochroch, Albert. *American Auto Racing.* Penguin Books, New York, 1974.

Borgeson, Griffith. *Miller.* Motorbooks International, Osceola, 1993.

Borgeson, Griffith. *The Classic Twin-Cam Engine.* Dalton Watson Ltd, London, 1981.

Borgeson, Griffith. *Bugatti by Borgeson.* Osprey, London, 1981.

Borgeson, Griffith. *The Golden Age of the American Racing Car.* W. W. Norton, New York, 1966.

Brawner, Clint. *Indy 500 Mechanic.* Chilton, Radnor, 1975.

Brown, Allan. *The History of the American Speedway.* Slideways Publications, Marne, 1984.

Catlin, Russ. *The Life of Ted Horn.* Floyd Clymer, Los Angeles, 1949.

Clymer, Floyd. *Indianapolis Racing History.* Floyd Clymer, Los Angeles, 1945.

Clymer, Floyd. *Indianapolis Yearbooks.* Floyd Clymer, Los Angeles, 1946-64.

Crowell, Benedict. *America's Munitions. 1917–18.* Government Printing Office, Washington, D.C., 1919.

Cutter, Robert & Bob Fendall, *Encyclopedia of Auto Racing Greats.* Prentice-Hall, Englewood Cliffs, 1973.

De Paolo, Peter. *Wall Smacker.* Thompson Products, Cleveland, 1935.

Dees, Mark. *The Miller Dynasty.* Second edition. Hippodrome Publishing, Los Angeles, 1993.

Donohue, Mark. *The Unfair Advantage.* Dodd, Mead & Company, New York, 1975.

Dorson, Ron. *The Indy 500.* Bond/Parkhurst Books, Newport Beach, 1974.

Engle, Lyle. *A. J. Foyt.* Arco Publishing Company, New York, 1970.

Engle, Lyle. *Mario Andretti.* Arco Publishing Company, New York, 1970.

Ferguson, Andrew. *Team Lotus, The Indianapolis Years.* Patrick Stephens Ltd, Somerset, UK, 1994.

Fox, Jack. *The Mighty Midgets.* Hungness Publishing, Speedway, 1977.

Fox, Jack. *An Illustrated History of Sprint Car Racing.* Hungness Publishing, Speedway, 1984.

Fox, Jack. *The Indianapolis 500.* Hungness Publishing, Speedway, 1994.

Gabbard, Alex. *Fast Fords.* HP Books, Los Angeles, 1987.

Gates, Bob. *Herk Hurtubise.* Witness Productions, Marshall, Indiana, 1995.

Georgano, G. N. *The Encyclopedia of Motor Racing.* Viking Press, New York, 1971.

Girdler, Allan. *American Road Racing Specials.* Motorbooks International, Osceola, 1990.

Higdon, Hal. *Thirty Days in May.* Scholastic Book Services, New York, 1971.

Hitze, Edward. *Kurtis–Kraft Story.* Interstate Printers & Publishers, Danville, 1974.

Hungness, Carl. *GO—the Bettenhausen Story.* Hungness Publishing, Speedway, 1982.

Huntington, Roger. *Design and Development of the Indy Car.* HP Books, Tucson, 1981.

Karban, Roger and Virginia, Dowling, *Dirt.* Stellar Publications, Springfield, 1984.

Kleinfield, Sonny. *A Month at the Brickyard.* Holt, Rinehart & Winston, New York, 1977.

Kuns, Ray. *Automobile Racing.* Editions I-VI. Ray F. Kuns, Cincinnati, 1932.

Lacey, Robert. *Ford, the Men and the Machines.* Little, Brown & Company, New York, 1986.

Lerner, Preston. *Scarab.* Motorbooks International, Osceola, 1993.

Levine, Leo. *Ford, The Dust & The Glory.* Macmillan, New York, 1968.

LeVrier, Philip. *Texas Legacy.* Georgetown Lounge Productions, Siloam Springs, 1984.

Libby, Bill. *Foyt. Hawthorne Books*, New York, 1974.

Lucero, John. *Legion Ascot Speedway.* Orecul Publishing, Huntington Park, 1982.

Ludvigsen, Karl. *Gurney's Eagles.* Motorbooks International, Osceola, 1976.

Madigan, Tom. *Boss, The Bill Stroppe Story.* Darwin Publications, Burbank, 1984.

McCluggage, Denise. *By Brooks Too Broad for Leaping.* Fulcorte Press, Santa Fe, 1994.

Miller, Harry. *Catalogue.* Harry A. Miller Inc., Los Angeles, 1927.

Motter, Tom. *BCRA, The First Fifty Years.* Bay Cities Racing Association, Pleasant Hill, 1990.

Neely, William. *A. J. Foyt.* Times Books, New York, 1983.

Nolan, William. *Barney Oldfield.* G. P. Putnam's Sons, New York, 1961.

O'Brien, Lee. *Dirt Track Legends.* Graphic Publishing Co., Lake Mills, 1984.

O'Keefe, James and Joseph Freeman, *Encyclopedia of Auto Racing Winners.* In publication, Boston.

Peters, George and Henri Greuter. *Novi: The Legendary Indianapolis Race Car.* Bar-Jean Enterprises, Hazlewood, 1991.

Purdy, Ken. *All But My Life: Stirling Moss.* E P Dutton Company, New York 1963.

Redd, T. C. *When the Coliseum Roared.* DTS Publishing Company, Vista, 1983.

Rickenbacker, Edward. *Rickenbacker.* Prentice-Hall, Englewood Cliffs, 1967.

Robson, Graham. *Cosworth, the Search For Power.* Patrick Stephens Ltd, London, 1990.

Roe, Fred. *Duesenberg.* Dalton Watson, London, 1982.

Russell, Jim and Edward Watson, *Safe at Any Speed, the Biography of Joie Chitwood,* Witness Productions, Marshall, 1992.

Sawyer, John. *The Dusty Heroes.* Hungness Publishing, Speedway, 1978.

Scalzo, Joe. *Stand On The Gas.* Prentice-Hall, Englewood Cliffs, 1974.

Scalzo, Joe. *The Unbelievable Unsers.* Henry Regnery Company, Chicago, 1971.

Shaw, Wilbur. *Gentlemen Start Your Engines.* Coward, McCann & Gohegan, New York, 1955.

Smith, Carroll. *Prepare to Win.* Aero Publishers, Fallbrook, 1974.

Sorensen, Charles. *My Forty Years With Ford.* W. W. Norton, New York, 1956.

Stambler. *Racing The Sprint Cars.* G. P. Putnam's Sons, New York, 1979.

Taylor, Rich. *Indy, 75 years of Racing's Greatest Spectacle.* St. Martin's Press, New York, 1991.

USAC. *Official USAC Auto Racing Yearbook, 1972.* The Benjamin Company, New York, 1972.

Wagner, Fred. *Saga of The Roaring Road.* Clymer, Los Angeles, 1949.

Wallen, Richard. *Board Track Guts & Glory.* Dick Wallen, Escondido, 1990.

Walton, Kenneth E. *Offy, America's Greatest Racing Engine.* In preparation, Kansas City.

Watson, Ed and Dennis Newlyn, *Tattersall, The Legend.* Witness Productions, Marshall, 1991.

Wright, Crocky. *The Fabulous Nutley Velodrome.* Carl Hungness Publishing, Indianapolis, 1995.

Wright, Crocky. *Midget Auto Racing History.* Volumes. I-IV. Crocky Wright Enterprises, Speedway, 1980.

Yates, Brock. *Famous Indianapolis Cars & Drivers.* Harper & Brothers, New York, 1960.

FOOTNOTES

1 Borgeson, *The Classic Twin-Cam Engine*, p. 15.

2 The Liberty was not supercharged, but the Air Corps worked on supercharging to compensate for the loss of power in thin air at altitude.

3 Letter, Fred Offenhauser to Army Air Forces Material center, July 19, 1943.

4 Miller's "alloyanum" was made up of aluminum alloyed with iron, copper and traces of other elements. George Parker described the formula for the author:

.032% silicon	.185% magnesium
.308% iron	.001% chromium
3.650% copper	.057% titanium
.250% manganese	remainder aluminum (per Joe Raffin)

5 Letter, Leo Goossen to E. A. de Waters, August 23, 1918.

6 Report to Family Physician, November 12, 1918.

7 Borgeson, *The Classic Twin-Cam Engine*, p. 76.

8 Sobraske interview tape.

9 Letter, Rickenbacker to C. S. Fliedner, April 15, 1932.

10 Neal Gabler,*Winchell, Gossip, Power and the Culture of Celebrity*. Alfred A. Knopf, New York, p. 47.

11 *MOTOR TREND*, April 1975.

12 Although E.L. Cord bought the rights to the Miller front-drive in 1927, the first L29s rolled off the assembly lines in January 1929. The Cord used only the name of Miller's front-drive system, as it was difficult to shift and extremely fragile. C. W. Van Ranst adapted Leo Goossen's execution of the Miller idea into a transaxle practical for road use.

13 Federal Bankruptcy Court records.

14 Scully and his brother, Al, sent the car to Europe where Pete De Paolo drove it in Tripoli and at the Avus Speedway in Berlin, then, according to Mark Dees, brought it home and broke it up. The 308 V-8 engine went to Bunny Phillips who, in 1939, destroked it to 260 cubic inches, put it in a Bugatti Type 35 chassis, and ran it at Indy through 1946. Griffith Borgeson writes that the engine was destined for the Phillips Bugatti right from the 1933 sale.

15 Lucero, *Legion Ascot Speedway*, p.92.

16 Weirick went on to build cars that ran at Indianapolis nine times, two of which sat on the pole. *Poison Lil*, an Offenhauser-powered Weirick car, set a 21-second track record at Winchester and was the most famous "big car" of its time.

17 *Bergen Herald*, November 23, 1933.

18 Tape-recorded interview, 1974.

19 Letter, Offenhauser Engineering Company to Army Air Forces Materiel Center, Los Angeles, July 19, 1943.

20 The USAC statistical digest describes Floyd Roberts 1938 winning engine as an Offy. Jack Fox *Illustrated History of the Indianapolis 500* describes it as a Miller. Fred Offenhauser built the engine; Lou Moore may have entered it, a 270, as a Miller, though Miller built no 270s before his bankruptcy.

21 Lucero, *Legion Ascot Speedway*, p.63.

22 Lucero, *Legion Ascot Speedway*, p. 182.

23 Interview, Marvin Jenkins, July 5, 1995.

24 Interview by the author with Lencki 1992.

25 *New York Times* January 16, 1935.

26 *National Auto Racing News*, September 1939.

27 Personal conversation with Roy Hagedorn, 1979.

28 Roger Huntington, "The New Offy," *Speed Age Magazine*, March, 1950, p. 15.

29 Huntington, "The New Offy," p.15.

30 Frank Kurtis, "A Practical Approach to Torsion Bar Suspension," *Automotive Industries*, October 15, 1948, p.28.

31 Hitze, *The Kurtis-Kraft Story*.

32 Sampson moved to California and remained active in racing until 1951 when he died in an auto accident in New Mexico while enroute to Indianapolis. Lou Meyer happened along a few hours later and found the wreck, including the 270 Offy engine.

33 *Pacific Coast Speedway News*, June 19, 1946.

34 Resume of Mt. Equinox Hill Climb, May 21, 1950, Cornell Aeronautical Laboratory Inc., Buffalo, NY.

35 Another historian has attributed the Twin–Coach's construction to Floyd Trevis of Youngstown, Ohio.

36 Frankie Del Roy told people he "built" the car, a racing term that really meant "rebuilt." Frank Kurtis, who had actually assembled the car in his shop in early 1949, never forgave either Del Roy or the racing press, whom he blamed for stealing the credit he felt was due him.

37 In 1951 the author was occasionally go–fering for Bill Schindler, who lived nearby in Freeport, New

York. Bill, in the same #10 Chapman Offy he had driven at Indianapolis, took the early lead at Langhorne that June and it looked for a while as though he might win, but at lap 50 Bettenhausen in the #99 stood on the gas and sailed on by.

38 Vukovich said of the Keck car, "It looks like a roadster," and the name stuck.

39 The AAA's Kennerdell was unfazed. He told reporters, "I do not view the IMCA as a menace to properly organized and conducted auto contests."

40 Kelly Petillo drove a 318 at Indianapolis in 1937 but ran out of oil after 109 laps and finished 20th. The Tommy Lee 318 went into a sports chassis built by Frank Kurtis. The engine went into the collection of Willett Brown, Lee's partner.

41 The Hispano-Suiza was a 90-degree V-8. It was easy to unbolt the cylinders on one side and set the engine upright. Of course for more power one could use the entire V-8.

42 Gurney grew up on Long Island and attended races in 1948 and 1949 at Freeport Municipal Stadium where he became an avid fan of Ted Tappet (Phil Walters), driver at the time of a Kurtis Offy midget.

43 Leo Levine, *Ford, the Dust and the Glory*, p. 279.

44 Pop Green built a supercharged 91 cubic inch V-8 for Clarence W. Belt to drive at Indianapolis in 1928, but it dropped a valve on lap 32 and was credited with 27th place. George Riley built single-overhead-cam conversions for Ford V-8s just before World War II, but they were never fully developed for sprint car racing. Bill Spaulding had one in his 1932 Ford roadster and a few were used for 225-cubic-inch hydroplane racing.

45 Ford had had warning. During May practice, Gurney's soft Dunlops had chunked pieces of rubber, but Chapman shrugged off the incident, saying they would be fine for the race. TheFirestone-shod cars did so much better that the first 12 finishers all ran the distance on one set of tires.

46 The Robbins car went out on the 85th lap with a ruptured water manifold. In 1966, Foster hit the wall at the start, triggering an 11-car pileup.

47 Some influential owners, faced with having to field different chassis for pavement and dirt, lobbied to drop the dirt tracks from the championship schedule.

48 George Bignottti recalls that he did Foyt's engines himself at his shop at 1805 15th Street in Indianapolis. "We didn't have problems because our engines already had filters."

49 The Jones & Maley car never made the race after 1957. It spent many years as an advertising display atop a building in Indianapolis.

50 Gilmer was an old Philadelphia company that had been making power-transmission belts since the Model T days. The so-called "Gilmer" belt has teeth molded into it to give more positive drive, and when used as a timing belt, to maintain the relative positions of driving and driven pulleys without slippage.

51 The Besasie turbo gave a boost of 6 psi which improved a stock Chevrolet's horsepower by 34 percent.

52 Turbo lag is the time it takes for the compressor rotor to pick up speed and begin producing power after the driver nails the gas. With a "wet manifold," fuel that has condensed in the intake system will vaporize when the throttle is closed and engine vacuum increases. Rex Mays said that in 1940 and 1941 when he got to the end of the straight with the Winfield engine and backed off, it wanted to run faster. If the driving impeller is properly matched to the engine and the fuel flow is properly regulated, a turbo can produce more boost with less horsepower drain than either a Roots or a mechanically driven centrifugal blower.

53 Schwitzer had built the Roots superchargers for the Miller V–16 engines in Gar Wood's boat engines in 1931 and later for Gar Wood's Packard boat engines.

54 Hasse had been a carburetor engineer on the Novis.

55 A peculiarity existed in the sleeves: They were notched slightly to clear the valves. If a mechanic did not notice the small notches and orient them correctly, the valves would hit the top of the sleeves when the engine was started.

56 Gene White's crew tested both the Ford and the Offy on their dyno and found that the Offy was putting out 15 percent more torque than the Ford, though the higher-winding Ford produced more absolute horsepower at its rpm peak.

INDEX